THE NEW CHAIRMAN TAKES OVER IN THE BEST DEMOCRATIC TRADITION!

G.O.P NATIONAL CHAIRMANSHIP

REP MILLER

Gib Crockett
WASHINGTON STAR.

BILL MILLER:

Do You Know Me?

A Daughter Remembers

Libby Miller Fitzgerald

Best wishes — great to see you at reunion! — Love, Libby

Bill Miller: Do You Know Me?
A Daughter Remembers

Libby Miller Fitzgerald

Copyright 2004

ISBN 1890306738

Library of Congress Control Number: 2004113466

WARWICK HOUSE PUBLISHERS
720 Court Street
Lynchburg, VA 24504

To my dad, who would not have expected this book,
but would accept it with grace and love.

TABLE OF CONTENTS

Barry Goldwater

P.O. BOX 1601
SCOTTSDALE, ARIZONA 85252

May 20, 1996

Writing about my dear and valued friend, Bill Miller, is not easy. In fact, I would say from my standpoint it is almost impossible, but I'm going to do my best. When we talk about people who have gone, and try to do it in a nice way, we call it a eulogy, and that is what I am going to do, eulogize Bill Miller.

Even though I called him my friend for some thirty-five years, I think we need to recognize that talking about a man like Bill, who was born to serve, is a difficult task. Difficult, because he has done so very much that affects each of us in our daily lives. The only reason that we are here is to do unto others as you would have them do unto you. If we serve well, the dust that trails us as we walk down the path of life settles on all people and makes all people better. The question comes—did Bill serve well? Yes, he served well. He served with love and devotion to his wonderful family. He served with love and devotion to his country. He served with love and devotion to his state. I remember night after night, day after day, as he and I, during our political lives, sat and discussed current issues, talking about things in general, he would often talk about his love of Stephanie and his children.

One of the great things I liked about him is when he put his hand on the Bible to take his oath and would swear to defend the Constitution against all enemies foreign and domestic, he really meant it. Not all who said that oath fully meant it. That is one of our problems today. He not only meant it, he demonstrated it by serving his country in time of war. He demonstrated it by serving his country in times of peace, in the field we call politics. Because of these things and because of the way he was, he made every one of us better and he made this country a better place in which to live.

So I can say, with no prejudice and with a heart filled with promise and love, that the dust that followed Bill will settle on us and remind us of our responsibilities to our God, our family, and our country. Bill Miller was a man for whom I had deep affection and respect. He was a man other men like to be with—I think that is the best way to put it. I know he has made heaven and earth a better place to live.

PREFACE

"Do you know me?" asked the grinning, dapper, and vaguely familiar gentleman on the television screen in the opening line of the 1974 American Express commercial. "I ran for Vice President of the United States in 1964, so I shouldn't have trouble charging a meal, should I?" That erstwhile spokesman, Bill Miller, was the first politician to make one of those memorable and long-running ads, which depicted a once famous person who, for an intense period of time, was in the center of the public eye but later needed his American Express card for recognition. It was a subtle commentary on the fleeting nature of celebrity and political power.

Indeed, William E. (Bill) Miller, was one of the "small club" of those who had been chosen to run for the second highest office in the land as the Republican vice-presidential candidate in 1964. Not only that, but he had vigorously led the Republican Party as its national chairman during three of the most tumultuous years of its existence, was an influential member of the United States Congress for fourteen years, and had been an assistant prosecutor at the Nuremberg War Crimes Trials in 1945. And yet he could always joke in his self-deprecating style that his American Express commercial, ironically, had made him more famous than running for vice president ever had.

This is a memoir/biography of my father. I call it that because it is a blending of my memories and those of his friends and associates, as well as a researched, historical account of his considerable service to party and country. It is this blending, this piecing together of disparate memories and facts that, I believe, gives the story its truth, for none of us knew Dad in his entirety. This is the story of a uniquely bright, articulate, and politically savvy man who was warm and funny and beloved by all who knew him. It is also the story of how a father's choices impacted and molded his family, the footprints of his life on ours—in this case, the effect of political life, with its attendant privileges and emotional highs and lows, and the insights such a life gives into the political process and the virtues and foibles of its participants. His is a story that has not been told.

Fate and history placed my father at the nexus of a political movement and realignment that forever altered the Republican Party and the political discourse of this country. Former President Ronald Reagan acknowledged his debt to him when he wrote my mother at Dad's death in 1983: "In the 1964 campaign, Bill Miller gained the respect and gratitude of all Americans for his capable articulation of the principles of our party. All of us who have come after him are his beneficiaries."

But in reality, though he was Barry Goldwater's running mate in that seminal but decisive election loss to Lyndon Johnson, my father was not a founding member of what history now calls the "Goldwater revolution," which came to be seen, for some legitimate reasons, as exclusionary and mean-spirited. In many ways a man ahead of his time, the hallmarks of his service were political inclusiveness and a flexible conservatism that was compassionate long before that term was coined for George W. Bush in the 2000 election. Congressman Bill Brock of Tennessee, a bright young star in the Party in the early sixties, wrote me: "Bill Miller advocated the cause of Republicanism in a more humane way than that in evidence by some in our party today, and he did so with a wonderful, often dry, sense of humor."

Dad once said: "The Republican Party must forget anger in its ranks." His vision for his party, which contrasts so stunningly with the philosophy of the far right today, was of a "big tent" that *excluded* no one, that *included* anyone and everyone who subscribed to certain basic tenets of Republicanism. In the end, before returning to private life, he made one last move in his career-long effort to unify and broaden his party—a contribution that was as momentous as it is unknown.

Bill Miller grew up poor in a small, industrial Western New York town on the banks of the Erie Barge Canal, the grandson of Irish and German immigrants who built that once great waterway. His father was a janitor, his mother a milliner. A child of the Depression, he worked his way through Notre Dame—in those days, the destination that was every Catholic boy's dream—and then law school. He rose from a private in the United States Army to appointment as an assistant prosecutor for the Nuremberg War Crimes Trials after World War II, which left on him a lasting mark. As a young trial attorney who delighted in the adversarial jousting of the courtroom, he never planned a career in public life, yet was elected district attorney and then to Congress seven times by wide margins. Tapped at once to sit on the powerful Judiciary Committee, he sponsored and helped to shape, with his incisive and respected legal mind, the first civil rights bills since the Civil War.

As one of the most dynamic orators and skilled political organizers of his day, Dad was in 1960 and 1961 propelled by unanimous selection to the chairmanship of the two most fundamental operating elements of the Republican Party—the National Republican Congressional Campaign Committee and the Republican National Committee. He was expected to reinvigorate a party severely demoralized by Richard Nixon's narrow loss to John Kennedy in 1960 and to give its tired image a makeover—a younger, more relevant, and telegenic face. And he did. But more urgently, he was assigned the seemingly insurmountable task of uniting the liberals, moderates, and conservatives who were fighting for its very soul.

The intra-party warfare reached its dramatic climax at the 1964 Republican Convention at the Cow Palace in San Francisco. With the Party on the verge of tearing itself asunder over Barry Goldwater's inevitable nomination, there was really only one decision left to be made: a running mate. The bitterness of the primary battles had eliminated most of the possible contenders from the senator's consideration—men like Nelson Rockefeller, Bill Scranton, and George Romney. So the logical, if surprising, choice: the Catholic, moderate conservative congressman from electoral vote-rich New York State—Bill Miller, the unifier. And with one late morning call to our suite at the Hilton Hotel just off Union Square on the day he was to be nominated, the senator from Arizona catapulted my father and our family to a pinnacle we had never dreamed of reaching.

Though he was honored to be chosen as its standard-bearer by the Party he loved, it proved to be a difficult campaign for him personally—not run the way he would have liked it, always on the defensive, not being played to win. As I worked the campaign trail in 1964, on leave from my senior year of college, I experienced on his behalf the almost superhuman emotional, mental, and physical demands of a national campaign—the exhilaration and despair, the fervor and frenzy, the expectations and disappointments of the political arena.

Who was this man, whose name, like that of other defeated vice-presidential candidates, was destined to become an elusive answer on television quiz shows? In exploring the depth, complexities, and passions of my father's career and legacy, I found, not surprisingly, that I had understood only a small portion of what he was about—loving but preoccupied and distant, largely absent, and slightly intimidating, I admired him from afar. Men of his generation did not easily share their emotions, their thoughts, or their stories. And I, in earlier years, like most children, was not as curious as I should have been about the past of a parent I simply took for granted. Even if there had been the time or the inclination to question him back then, I am not certain I knew the right questions to ask. Only time, maturity, and greater awareness have revealed them to me, when, alas, he is no longer here to answer them.

What I know and understand now—after years of research and interviews and remembering of the jaunty man behind those thin dark ties with the ever-present Merit cigarette poised between his fingers, beyond his electrifying oration, his razor-sharp intellect, and his infectious and legendary sense of humor—is that this man combined an unusual blend of characteristics and was a politician in the best and noblest sense of that now demeaned word, indeed a statesman. A statesman with deeply held beliefs and values who played out with dignity, honesty, courage, and an amazing forthrightness his part on the national stage for a brief period of time, and who knew in the end, without the ego and attachment to power so endemic to many politicians, when it was time to go home.

When I asked Dad once why he never wrote his memoirs—he had, after all, lived and served during one of the most compelling and formative periods of our history, encompassing the Great Depression, World War II, the civil rights struggles of the '50s and '60s, the conservative revolution—with the humility that typified so many of what journalist Tom Brokaw has called "the greatest generation," his response was simply that it never occurred to him anyone would be interested in his life. If Bill Clinton believed, as he wrote in his biography, that "in politics, if you don't toot your own horn, it usually stays untooted," then Dad was of another school.

The question I asked myself many times was, "Can a daughter be at all objective when writing about her father?" I worried about that a lot. But then I would remember what political columnist David Broder said to me when I interviewed him at length in his *Washington Post* office about the years he covered my father on Capitol Hill: "Write the book you want to write. There will be someone who wants to read it and will be inspired." I have tried to go where the evidence took me in recounting and evaluating his career, to be as intellectually honest as possible. And I have tried to recognize when he might have done things differently or better, though that is, of course, a hindsight view, with information he did not have.

The fact is that I was told by so many, Republicans and Democrats alike, over the course of ten years of interviewing, that Dad's courage under fire, his fearlessness in standing up for what he believed, his dedication to principle, his patriotism, intellect, loyalty, and dignity were rare, and are in short supply in politics today. Also that his modus operandi and political philosophy, which was more about right and wrong than about right and left, have extraordinary and on-going relevance, as the public continues to lose respect for politicians and the GOP continues to become less of a "big umbrella" and more the exclusive home of the far right. His career-long struggle had been to counteract his party's twentieth century tendency to tear itself apart. And therein lies the possibility that Bill Miller might still be of interest, indeed an inspiration to those running the affairs of our country and the Republican Party, and to those contemplating a career in public life. It may be a truism to say that we can learn from the past, but sometimes old ideas do need to be revisited.

ACKNOWLEDGMENTS

As rich as has been the journey of writing this book for me personally, my only regret is that I did not do it sooner and finish it faster. By the time I started, we had already lost some of my father's closest associates and colleagues—people like Ab Hermann, Bill Warner, Gib Darrison, Lucian Warren, Paul Niven, and Chuck Von Fremd, to name just a very few of those whose memories would have been so precious. And along the way, many who did give generously of their time to be interviewed have since gone to their rest, unable to read the fruits of my long labor, the story of their friend, Bill Miller—Congressmen George Meader, Bob Wilson, and Peter Rodino, advance man Vern Holleman, and RNC Research Director Bill Prendergast were among them. I only hope they knew how eternally grateful I am for the Herculean efforts they made to dredge their memories for details of thirty and forty years ago.

My research took me to various presidential libraries (the Eisenhower, Kennedy, Johnson, Nixon, and Ford libraries), the Dirksen Center, the University of Notre Dame, the Dartmouth College library, the *Congressional Record* at the University of Virginia's Alderman Library, the Library of Congress video and audio archives, the National Archives' Nuremberg records, the Lockport Library, Lockport city and Niagara and Erie county clerks' offices, St. Mary's and St. Patrick's Catholic churches in Lockport, and assorted newspaper and magazine archives. I wish to thank the many dedicated archivists and employees at those hallowed places who helped me ferret out the information I needed. But the personnel in the Rare Book and Manuscript division of Kroch Library of Cornell University in Ithaca, New York, deserve a special thank you for the time they spent in making available to me on my several visits there the voluminous collection of the *Miller Congressional and National Committee Papers*—especially Herb Finch, who requested and acquired the papers in 1965, Phil McCray, and a student intern, Andrew Janis, who all tirelessly assisted me in research. I am further indebted to the staff at the Jones Memorial Library at home in Lynchburg, Virginia, for their kind willingness to receive and house some of those papers on loan so that I could do additional study without traveling to Cornell.

The late Senator Barry Goldwater is, of course, top on the list of those who were vital to this project. We sat for an exhaustive interview in his hotel suite in Washington several years ago, just the two of us, he now quite crippled, and the fondness with which he recalled memories of his long ago running mate was moving. He subsequently wrote a Foreword for this book, which I gratefully include. I am only sorry he did not live to see the finished product.

Also tops on my seemingly endless list of interviewees were Presidents Gerald Ford and George H.W. Bush, Senator Robert Dole, Congressmen Jack Kemp, Bob Michel, and James Rhodes, Governors William Scranton, Charles Percy and Robert Smylie, Congressman and Defense Secretary Melvin Laird, and Attorney General Richard Kleindienst—all contemporaries or friends of my father. There were other congressional colleagues as well—Steve Derounian of New York, Arch Moore of West Virginia, Bill Brock of Tennessee, Pat Hillings and James Corman of California, Bill Ayers of Ohio, Ed Derwinski of Illinois, Bill Avery of Kansas, Ed Foreman of Texas, Bill Cramer of Florida, Judiciary Counsel Dick Peet, Herb Maletz, and Cy Brickfield, and so many others—and all were most generous with their reflections. The admiration and respect with which, after all these decades, they still remembered Dad sustained me and continually reaffirmed my conviction that this book was worth writing.

The reporters who contributed were numerous—David Broder, Hugh Sidey, Roland Powell, Jack Germond, Hal Bruno, Jack Casserly, Chuck Quinn, Warren Weaver, Paul Budenhagen, Bob Curran, George Borrelli, Frank Fortune, to name but a few. To a man, Bill Miller was one of their favorites of all the public figures they covered during their long careers, mostly because he understood their needs and was always accessible, with amazing candor and honesty. He was also concise, every newsperson's dream, good for some meaty insider insights and quotable soundbites. He'd say: "Now you can't quote me on this, but here's what I think's going on."

But there are a special few without whom I could never have written this book. Bob Smalley, my father's campaign press secretary, and Ed McCabe, one of his chief advisors during the campaign of '64, have been my mentors from the day I began. Their wisdom and advice has guided me over these many years, and I appreciate their encouragement, their belief in me and my project, and their love for their "boss" more than they will ever know. The same goes for Jean Darrison, Naomi Glass, Jo Good, and Sylvia Hermann. I cannot count the times I called on them to ask for more names and addresses and to check details that only they, with their prodigious memories, could recall.

The list goes on and on—my debts are many: to George Christopher, mayor of San Francisco during the 1964 convention; to Congressman Peter King who took the time to give me a lengthy account of his visit with my father when he invited him to speak at Notre Dame Law School in 1968, and of the fabulous "three-hour graduate course in *real* politics"; to Bob Douglas and Joe Boyd, associates of Nelson Rockefeller's, who gave me such insight into Dad's relationship with the New York governor; to all the Notre Dame classmates from the Class of '35 whose memories of their years on campus with their friend Bill were astoundingly lucid and colorful; to Senator Warren Anderson, Bruce Sullivan, and the Honorable Larry Cook for their memories of Albany Law School days; to the folks who created Dad's American Express ad and regaled me with the tales of its making—Daisy Sinclair, Bill Taylor, and Mark Ross; to my cousins—Sister Mary Miller and her friend, Anna Mary Archie, who launched me on my genealogical search for Dad's roots, Jack and Bill Hinch, Dick Shults, and Mary Ruth Ricketts, all of whom filled in the blanks in his early years that I could not have known; to Dan and Catherine Parent, my godparents from CIC Army days in Richmond, who described in detail and with such fondness that special time they shared with my parents; to the men who shared the Nuremberg experience with my father and helped me reconstruct his days there—Roger Barrett, Whitney Harris, Ed Boedecker, and Drexel Sprecher; to my long ago, diligent Lynchburg College intern, Terry Snead; to all the former NRCC and RNC members and staff, like Paul Theis, Jack Mills, Flo Crichton, Pat Hitt, Polly Krakora; and the '64 campaign aides who recalled stories and relived for me those crazy days on the road—John Barnett, Dave Krogseng, Buddy Lewis, Bob Phillipson, Ginny Von Fremd, Lyle Mercer et al; to Ray Lee, especially, and to all the other Lockport/Buffalo/Niagara County pals of long ago who helped so much—the Garlocks,

Russell Rourke, Pete Corson, Jerald Wolfgang, Ben Hewitt, Clip Smith, Don Conlin, Don Charles, Norm Joslin, Neil Farmelo, Jack Gellman, Bob Barton, Bob Cleary, Fred Smith, Dutch Ulrich, and more. I am grateful beyond words for all of their contributions, large and small.

And then there were my "editors," those incredible friends—teachers, English professors, lawyers, history buffs all—who consented to read and comment, with honesty, on my manuscript, who found time in their busy lives, under tight time constraints, to plow through eleven chapters and make valuable suggestions for improvement. They went far beyond the call of friendship, and never will I be able to adequately thank them—Pat Doyle, Tink Neubert, Sandy Ainslie, Ken White, and John Halleron.

Still, after all is said and done, it is my family to whom I owe the greatest debt of gratitude—first and foremost, to my darling husband Paul, who read and reread and then read again chapter after chapter after chapter, my first-line editor with wise revisions and comments, more patient and supportive and tolerant than any husband should have to be for all the long hours I have had to spend on the computer and not with him. Without his constant encouragement, and sometimes forceful prodding, I would never have stuck with this until the end. My two daughters, Kelly and Cara, were my cheerleaders, always interested in my work and its progress, always buoying me and pushing me forward. I love them for that.

And my son Paul—it was he who helped me "find my voice," as they say in the literary world, who taught me how to tell a compelling story rather than an impersonal accumulation of facts. Accustomed to writing dispassionate stories as a journalist, it was a new style for me to learn, and he was a patient teacher. An extraordinarily talented writer himself, his "red ink," combined with his contagious conviction that I could indeed complete what I had begun, have been invaluable to me all along the way, and despite the fact that he was only thirteen when his grandfather died, he somehow possessed an uncanny insight into what he was about. My dear mother, brother Bill, and sisters Mary and Stephanie have all been faithful editors and unflagging supporters and suppliers of information. For all of this, and for all of them, "thank you" is hardly enough.

Last, but most importantly, I am forever indebted to my publisher, Warwick House, and to Joyce Maddox and Amy Moore who maintained the utmost composure and competence as I imposed upon them almost impossible deadlines for publication. From editing to layout to publicity and the myriad details in between, they were unfailingly patient, professional, and creative, and the product they fashioned from my years of labor is and always will be a source of great pride and satisfaction to me and many others.

CHAPTER ONE

THE NOMINATION

It was July 16, 1964, a cool, clear San Francisco summer Thursday evening just shy of seven o'clock. The cavernous, smoke-filled main hall of the sprawling sixty four-acre convention center compound that was known as the Cow Palace was packed to the rafters with more than 15,000 raucous, screaming GOP conventioneers and a legion of journalists. I, a college senior of twenty, and my seventeen-year-old sister Mary stood on either side of Mom and Dad atop a ten-foot-high podium platform waving in proud and joyous, if somewhat dazed, response to the frenzied, partisan multitudes arrayed below. Blinding lights illuminated us but turned the clamorous crowd to a blurry, undulating sea of red, white and blue outfits, hats, banners, placards, balloons and confetti. The pandemonium of cheers and chants was deafening. It was an unanticipated moment, the pinnacle of our family's political journey, a life-changing experience for all of us in some way.

It was exactly as H. L. Mencken had once described a political convention! … "then suddenly there comes a show so gaudy and hilarious, so melodramatic and obscene, so unimaginably exhilarating and preposterous that one lives a gorgeous year in an hour." Over the passage of years, such events can assume an almost dreamlike quality, may even seem as if they took place in another lifetime or had happened to someone else. And yet, feelings about the events can viscerally endure. It was a wondrous and intoxicating moment, one I wanted to freeze in time or at least never forget, a moment that made comprehensible an addiction to politics, and especially to political victory.

I wonder today why the breathtaking aura of that evening did not reduce me to a torrent of tears on the podium, for as all who know me can attest, I am prone to weepiness. The explanation is, I decided, that the necessity of self-composure had been so impressed upon me throughout our years in political life that I unconsciously reined in some part of my emotions. And as we stood there, I was keenly, if uncomfortably, aware that we were focused in the eye of ubiquitous cameras that were beaming us to television screens nationwide and indeed around the world—a realization guaranteed to render one inordinately self-conscious. Despite all preparation, I wasn't exactly certain about "the right thing" to do—we were moving into uncharted waters. These were the days when political children were seen and not heard on the podium, though I probably could have risen to the occasion if necessary. Thankfully however, I was not asked to introduce either my mother or my father.

The band played on and on—repeated renditions of Rodgers and Hammerstein's "My Boy Bill" from the musical *Carousel,* "On the Sidewalks of New York," the catchy old two-step that was sung in Al Smith's gubernatorial parade in 1918, and dearest to my father's heart, "The Notre Dame Victory March"—and our hearts swelled. Despite the vortex of heady events into which we were being suddenly and inexorably swept, I can still recall clearly the jumble of conflicting emotions that swirled within me as I stood there gently half-embraced by my father's arm.

There was tremendous pride in a man who had started life with so little and had been chosen from among so many for the honor of his party's vice-presidential nomination, and deep gratitude for the tangible affection and faith of so many devoted people. Mixed with that was bewilderment and growing apprehension about what lay ahead for us, about whether Dad, and we as a family, would meet the expectations of those who had placed their hopes in him. Those first moments of pure ecstasy almost, but not totally, eclipsed the humbling and daunting realization of what we were about to undertake.

Political conventions are quadrennial phenomena that belong in a class by themselves, akin perhaps only to religious revivals, to which they are often compared in the passion they inspire. To some, those who stay removed from politics, they seem silly and frivolous—meticulously orchestrated circuses that fool no one by their transparent attempt to appear spontaneous. But it is the passion, nevertheless, that is quite amazing—of people who care so much and are willing to undertake all the tedious work that makes our messy and contentious political system function, work that so many others are unwilling to do. And in this year of 1964, the emotionalism and devotion of these delegates to their hero,

Senator Barry Goldwater of Arizona—and by extension, to my father—as well as to their mission of wresting the Republican Party away from the "Northeastern liberal establishment" who had so long controlled it, almost defied description.

Dad was in many ways an unlikely man to be standing upon that platform that evening in San Francisco. He had never planned a career in politics. When he was young, public life, though rewarding, would have seemed insufficient for supporting a family. At that time, there were few perks in politics, such as large speaking fees, that could supplement the low salaries and yield the comfortable lifestyle for which he had hoped. A child of the Depression, raised in a modest home in a small industrial Erie Canal town in Western New York, he yearned for the financial security for himself and his family that he had never had.

His jovial father drank too much, worked as a janitor at the local Harrison Radiator plant, and didn't bring home much money. The mother he adored opened a hat shop, later adding women's apparel, in hopes of affording her only child the education he wouldn't otherwise have had. So with her help and the money saved from his thriving Christmas card and firecracker businesses, Dad made his way through the University of Notre Dame and Albany Law School and was destined, he thought, for a lucrative career in private law practice.

My father always loved the power and cadences of the spoken word. A precocious, quick-witted, and energetic little boy, he must have seemed a budding Clarence Darrow as he held forth on South Street in Lockport in front of his plain, clapboard house, decked out in vest, knickers, and tall socks, holding his buddies in rapt attention with his thoughts on the burning issues of their young lives.

Never shy, public speaking always seemed to come naturally to him—a gift of gab perhaps traceable to his mother's Irish heritage—and he honed his skill in theatrical productions and on debate teams throughout his school years. He sharpened his legal skills during World War II in the Judge Advocate General branch of the Army, and later as an assistant prosecutor at the Nuremberg War Crimes Trials. He had a passion for the courtroom and the work of a prosecuting attorney and he was good at it—he even won his wife in court when she was a witness for a case he was prosecuting for her mother. And that was where he planned to stay.

But fate had other plans. In the summer of 1950, the Republican congressman from his district unexpectedly announced his retirement after one term. Just as Dad was settling in as the Niagara County District Attorney, the local Republican Party urged him to run for the vacated seat. While he was reluctant, my mother—surprisingly, since she is hardly a power-behind-the-throne type—suggested that perhaps one or two terms in Congress would enhance his law practice and be a marvelous experience. "I was young and didn't realize the hardships," she reminisced later. So there Bill Miller stood on that podium, fourteen years and seven terms later, still not a wealthy man, contemplating the irony of reaching the peak of a mountain he had never intended to climb—"Steph gets the credit for this," he remarked with undisguised emotion.

He had gotten there in part by good fortune—a convergence of events that had put him in the right place at the right time—and partly because of his personality, his character, and his accomplishments. Dad was well known for his acute legal and political instincts and his fiercely competitive nature, complete with a tough exterior and occasionally rough language—thankfully used only in political backrooms—that left no doubt about his seriousness of purpose. Yet it was all softened by a warmth and a ready smile that, along with his honesty and candor, won him friends on both sides of the "aisle," as the political divide in Congress was called.

His innate self-assurance that seemed to inspire confidence in his ability might have seemed like cockiness to some. Yet crusty columnist Jimmy Breslin once remarked that "he shows almost none of the outsized ego that politicians seem to acquire the day they are elected."[1] Those eyes were dark and alert as he listened, reacting quickly to everything that was said. His infectious sense of humor was legendary. A first-rate joke and storyteller, he would chuckle mischievously in the telling, which invariably propelled his listeners into gales of laughter before he even reached the punch line.

The agility of his mind allowed him to grasp, process, and articulate large amounts of information quickly. Naomi Glass, one of his congressional secretaries, recalled many years later how, not an early riser, her boss would arrive at his Capitol Hill office in late morning and in a couple hours dispose of more correspondence and business matters than most men could do in a day. Being a private man, my father rarely hung around "the Hill" to socialize after work, preferring to come home and spend the little time he could with his family. So though his colleagues professed to admire and like him, few said they knew him well.

The press liked to caricature Dad's dapper physical appearance—he was small and wiry, often tanned, and impeccably well-groomed, suit never rumpled, four-pointed monogrammed handkerchief peeking from his breast pocket, white shirt stiffly starched, gold cufflinks pinching the snowy cuffs that emerged from his jacket sleeves, every strand of his shiny black hair pressed in place with Vitalis.

For cold weather he liked a Chesterfield coat with velvet collar, and his trademark became the jaunty black or pearl gray Homburg hat that he wore tilted at a rakish angle with brim rolled up. It all elicited from reporters comparisons to the slim, natty, colorful little Irishman, Jimmy Walker, Mayor of New York City in the roaring twenties. Once during a congressional campaign appearance at a Niagara Frontier industrial plant when an outspoken aide suggested he remove his hat because it was inappropriate to wear in this blue collar setting, he replied: "It's the hat I always wear; I like it, and I'm going to wear it throughout the campaign." And he did.

Despite limited means, my father was always somehow, even in college, described as a vision in sartorial splendor. Yet his taste was actually far from flashy—the dark suits were solid or pinstripe and the ties, about which we incessantly teased him, were unfashionably narrow and fairly unexciting. To the family's never ending consternation, there was usually a cigarette dangling between his fingers, later held in a holder as a concession to our pleas to cut down on his nicotine.

But it was his oratorical skills, more than anything else, that had won him acclaim in Washington and singled him out early from among the ranks of other young Republican congressmen. He had once facetiously speculated in a speech to Notre Dame alums that he had built up his powerful lungs by four years of cheering for hapless Irish football teams from high in the stands above the ten-yard line. His small physical stature was unquestionably enlarged by his voice, which was crisp, incisive, and authoritative, and it lent him a commanding presence. Growing up, I was always grateful that he rarely directed its full force at me, leaving to Mother the unpleasant job of disciplinarian.

Dad spoke with clarity and simplicity—his were not academic speeches, though they contained an impressive assemblage of facts that he somehow kept stored in his prodigious memory bank. Blunt and concise, you always knew where he stood. His ability to cut to the heart of a matter was almost surgical, his precision in finding the Achilles heel of an opponent unerring—a delight to most Republicans but the bane of Democrats. There were, in fact, times when even our family winced at the sharpness of his attacks, but it was his style.

The most oft-quoted reason Barry Goldwater chose my father as his running mate was that an exasperated Lyndon Johnson once quipped: "Bill Miller drives me nuts." Though obviously not the only reason for his selection, it is true that the combative New York Republican could verbally skewer Johnson like none other. On the president's "Great Society" program, his favorite line was: "Today, government has one hand in everybody's business and the other hand in everybody's pocket." He had previously worked over President Kennedy, calling him "The Foundering Father of the New Frontier" and the Bay of Pigs fiasco "a symbol of blundering unmatched in all our history."

In fact, Dad was not unlike his alma mater's pugnacious little leprechaun mascot who prances around the sidelines at football games taunting Irish opponents. He considered such criticism to be a part of his job as national chairman, the spokesman for the party out of power. But his relentless attacks inspired the Johnson team during the '64 campaign to assign a couple staff members the sole job of digging up personal dirt on the Republican VP candidate, just to neutralize him.

It was not as if we hadn't considered that he might be tapped for the vice-presidential nomination. Rumors to that effect were plentiful around San Francisco during the week prior to the opening of the convention on Monday, July 13. We had heard them even from the cocoon of our presidential penthouse suite—so lavish that it embarrassed my father—atop the new and, by the standards of the old venerable Nob Hill hotels, somewhat gaudy Hilton just off Union Square. Walter Cronkite was our only "neighbor," living in even greater splendor in palatial rooftop quarters. The Hilton, along with the St. Francis Hotel, acted as the co-nerve center of convention operations that, as chairman of the Republican National Committee, he was overseeing.

Though he had already been in residence at the hotel for a month, my mother, younger sister, Mary, and I had arrived in the city on Thursday, July 9 to join in the excitement of pre-convention activities. Mother and Mary had come from our summer cottage on Lake Ontario in western New York and I from my summer job as a guide at the New York World's Fair on Long Island. We had left behind at the cottage with our beloved housekeeper Luella, the "second family"—a much younger sister and brother, Stephanie, age three, and Billy, age five. Throughout the next few days, we were aware of steadily mounting, though unconfirmed, speculation that Bill Miller was Barry Goldwater's personal choice to be his running mate. We treated these reports as flattering but far-fetched, knowing full well that political speculation is often just that.

Immediately upon our arrival, callers and the press besieged Mother, to her dismay, with constant queries about what it would feel like to be the vice-presidential candidate's wife. Since she had not arranged for an assistant or a secretary and since Dad's schedule allowed us only brief and harried glimpses of him and no time for coaching, it was uncomfortably clear that we three women were on our own to cope with the hypothetical questions and incessantly ringing telephones. He appeared to have supreme, if unwarranted, confidence in our ability to craft our replies diplomatically so as not to embarrass him or ourselves, not to be misquoted, and not to convey either disinterest or excessive enthusiasm—a crash course, so to speak, in political soundbites.

What shopping and sightseeing we had hoped to do went by the wayside. The next four days whirled by in a kaleidoscope of gala occasions—there was precious little time for writing, but my diary briefly described a few: *Thursday night—dinner at Ernie's, met Walter Winchell, Alfred Hitchcock, Senator Javits, in bed at 2 a.m., 5 a.m. East Coast time, exhausted but too excited to sleep; Friday—lovely luncheon in the Roof Garden of the Fairmont Hotel, all candidates' wives present, Mother at the head table next to Peggy Goldwater, Mary and I seated with her daughters, Peggy and Joanne,*

*photographers everywhere. At night, limos take us to the Bohemian Club
for dinner hosted by Dad for all National Committee members; Saturday
evening—fun dinner with family and friends at the Bimbo Club 365,
wild floor show featured a girl dancing in a fish bowl; Sunday—Mass
at St. Boniface, priest practically endorsed the Democratic opponent of
California Republican senatorial candidate, George Murphy. Dad was
steaming! He isn't keen on priests telling people how to vote. Later, attended Oregon Governor Mark Hatfield's 42nd birthday celebration, Ike
and Mamie there; then on to the grand finale of pre-convention activities, the $500 a person (free for us) GOP Gala in the Civic Auditorium,
a dinner dance with a star-studded cast, all party notables present, TV
lights glaring, flashbulbs popping.*

Then the long-awaited moment at last arrived—amidst the
frenetic clattering of typewriters in the press galleries, the 28th
Republican Convention opened on Monday morning, July 13 at
10:35 a.m., with a resounding bang from Chairman Miller's sym-
bolically oversized wooden gavel. A small, slight man, 5'7" and
130 pounds ("in a very wet towel," as he used to say), the gavel
looked to be half his size and I was almost afraid he might topple
over as he forcefully wielded it.

By tradition, the national chairman opens the convention and
chairs the first session, which tends to organizational details, before handing the gavel over to the temporary and then finally to
the permanent chairman. I remember Dad being vexed when he
discovered that the arrangements chairman had failed to place a
box at the podium for him to stand on when he handed the gavel
to his tall, lanky friend, Senator Thruston Morton. The last minute
placement of a wooden Pepsi box sufficed to bring him nearly to
Morton's height. And through the sifting lens of hindsight I recall
a choir regaling the crowd with "Nobody Knows the Trouble I've
Seen," a prophetic selection considering the fate of the ticket that
finally emerged from this convention.

The evening session opened with a message from former
President Herbert Hoover, followed by Governor Mark Hatfield's
ringing keynote address excoriating "extremists" and provoking
boos from the delegates for his veiled reference to Goldwater's
supporters. Finally, in his last report as national chairman, my father delivered a rousing, prosecutorial speech searing the Johnson
administration for its ineptitude and ending with an urgent plea
for party unity: … *if we are to unite the nation to enact our foreign and*

domestic programs, we ourselves in this party must be united. Much has been said in the heat of this campaign for our nomination ... Once this debate ends, let it be finished.

Mother, Mary, and I sat rapt in our guest box just to the right of the podium, where we were to spend the better part of our next three days. Unintentional though it may have been, New York Governor Nelson Rockefeller's new wife Happy and Pennsylvania Governor William Scranton's family were seated in boxes directly across from us in the arena—both governors had opposed Goldwater's nomination until the bitter end and Scranton was still considered a possibility for second spot on the ticket. But what I remember most about that first convention evening was spotting the occasional "Miller for Vice President" placard with our dad's grinning mug bobbing among the delegates on the floor. We tingled with excitement and disbelief.

A highly organized effort on behalf of his nomination, without his explicit consent, was by now underway, with several headquarters in official operation. The press began reporting: "No name other than Representative Miller's is being heard in the corridors of San Francisco hotels or in the Cow Palace." Friends of ours from back east were calling excitedly to inquire about his chances. Still we brushed them off as flattering speculation.

I have often asked myself how our female trio could have been so, as the expression goes, "clueless" about the rapidly growing probability of Dad's nomination. I can only conclude that, as we were being ushered by staff members all week from event to event, we were insulated from conventioneers and those who knew the political gossip. When we were not attending some luncheon, reception, or dinner, we were in our suite preparing for the next one. Hairdos alone in those days were a major and time-consuming project—there were no quick blow-dry stylings. Your entire head had to be rolled in curlers, put in a bonnet to dry, then meticulously teased and sprayed until the desired helmet effect had been achieved. So it was no wonder that we had little time, except for a quick perusal of the *San Francisco Chronicle*, to stay abreast of fast-moving developments in convention affairs.

My father still had not spoken of the nomination with Barry directly, no official statements had been made, and he had much on his mind in the way of convention responsibilities before he could dwell on any such possibility. Since he and Mother, as well as Mary and I, were often going in different directions, we had little time to discuss and assess all the rumors or to benefit from his savvy advice about how to react to them. The best course for us, we decided, seemed just to contain our excitement and keep our feet planted firmly on the ground, although controlling our growing case of butterflies was becoming a Herculean task.

It wasn't until a little after noon on Wednesday, July 15, the day Goldwater was to be nominated, that he placed his call to our Hilton suite. The drama and tension of the vice-presidential selection had come down to the wire—how drastically different is the scenario today when that choice is made well before convention time and no suspense remains. Room service had just cleared our breakfast trays; we women were upstairs beginning our preparation for the Cow Palace session, which was to begin at 1:30 that afternoon.

Dad, his convention duties completed and at long last able to relax, sat alone outside on our terrace, cigarette in hand, lost in his own thoughts, basking in the warmth of the unusually fog-free San Francisco morning sun that shone brilliantly across the city's magnificent vistas. Looking back at that moment now through more mature and journalistically inclined eyes, I am amazed and chagrined that the multiple applications of Aqua Net on my completed coiffure somehow trumped sitting down with my father out on that patio to find out just what was going on behind those inscrutable eyes. If only I had been a smoker.

Richard Kleindienst, a Goldwater aide and later United States Attorney General, placed the call for Barry—after Barry's pithy declaration, "It's Miller"—and long-time friend and legislative assistant, Gib Darrison, was on our end to receive it. Since we suspected what the phone call might be, we all grabbed robes and flew down the circular staircase to the first floor. Dad came in from the patio and matter-of-factly took the receiver from Gib, betraying no particular emotion. On the other end of the line the Senator was brief and to the point—"Bill, you don't have to say yes or no right now. It could be a lonesome road but I would like to have somebody who'd go down the road with me. Will you do it?" Without hesitation, for by now he had anticipated the possibility of this moment, my father just as succinctly replied, "Yes, Barry. I'd be honored and delighted to walk with you." Barry said simply, "Thanks Bill," and hung up. Newspaper accounts called it "the shortest invitation in history."

As he replaced the phone on its ornate cradle and sat down on the couch, my father's face was placid, with that small, familiar, slightly mischievous smile turning up the corners of his mouth, his dark, alert eyes glinting. "Well, Barry asked me to run with him," he announced calmly to his expectant audience, looking pleased. Although he could not have been surprised, he seemed somewhat stunned, and quite moved. He was not an openly emotional person. Even within our family he was always low-key about these kinds of things—it came from a distaste for pomposity and a modesty and stoicism that was inherent to his nature and rooted in his humble beginnings. But now, at the twilight of his political career—he had already decided not to run for re-election to his House seat that year—he had been called one last time to serve the Party he loved, and just the smallest hint of pride crept into his demeanor.

Yet he understood why he had been chosen at this time and in this place; he had no lofty or false illusions about himself or his place in history. He had not sought fame and glory when he began his unplanned career in politics fourteen years earlier, had not sought to aggrandize himself along the way, and did not seek the burden of this last challenge. For if the polls were right, it would indeed be a difficult and uphill, and very likely an unwinnable battle against a formidable opponent. Still, he did feel like one lucky "son-of-a-gun"—a poor boy from a small town, privileged to be asked to join a man he admired personally to fight one last battle for many of the principles in which he believed so deeply. And, though he was weary and ready to return to private life, he could still relish a challenge. Relish, as he always had, the battle.

The female side of the family was somewhat less restrained. We were in a state of disbelief—something of this magnitude only happened to others. So accustomed to restraining our excitement and enthusiasm, so intent on being controlled, now the floodgates of our emotions released, and we hugged and screamed and cried—all the things we needed to do in the privacy of our room, before it was necessary to regain our composure to meet the waiting press.

We thankfully had some time to do that, for Barry, still feeling it presumptuous to announce his choice of a running mate before his nomination, was not due to release the decision until the next morning. We delayed our departure for the convention that day and spent the remainder of the afternoon sunning ourselves on our rooftop terrace and nervously planning our press comments, our outfits, and our hairdos. All of a sudden no dress I had brought was perfect enough, but shopping for another was out of the question.

That evening, the whole family, along with several good friends from home, spent an exhilarating few hours in our box at the Cow Palace watching Barry's inevitable but contentious nomination unfold, all the while girding ourselves for the day to come. Sharing our box was a lovely but relatively unknown former film star, Nancy Davis Reagan, whose husband was hoping to launch his career in national Republican politics that year. He got a lucky break that night when a last minute change in schedule allowed him to second Goldwater's nomination during prime time television coverage. His speech left a lasting impression.

With Goldwater's nomination made unanimous at the request of his erstwhile adversary, Governor Bill Scranton of Pennsylvania, the barely controllable convention recessed at 11: 10 p.m. Barry's daughters, Peggy and Joanne, decided to throw a party and invited me—Peggy and I were the same age and had represented our respective states in Washington's annual Cherry Blossom Festival just a year ago.

It was about 4:30 a.m. when I finally returned, bleary-eyed, to the Hilton and attempted to make my way quietly down our corridor, only to encounter, to our mutual astonishment, a small, sleepy man with a large television camera. When I asked why he was standing there at this ridiculous hour, he replied that he had been instructed to shoot film of anyone coming into or going out of our room at any time. I guessed he was expecting a stealthy Goldwater emissary to appear in the dead of night to pop the question to my father, who I could have told him would under no circumstances be awakened from his sleep. As he turned his camera my way and flicked on blinding lights, which at this hour I was certain did not flatter me, I beat a hasty retreat into our suite, not wishing to become a news item for the following day.

We woke early for the big day—not well rested but unable to sleep any longer. The news was now a poorly kept secret, as I discovered when I offered, in robe and curlers, to run next door to

Gib Darrison's room to borrow razor blades for Dad. Just outside our suite was crammed a bevy of television crews awaiting the official word on his candidacy. Devastated that my first exposure to the media as the vice-presidential nominee-to-be's daughter was so inelegant, I shrieked, slammed the door and told my father to forget it.

So after a rough shave with his dull blades, he rushed off to the Goldwater suite at the Mark Hopkins, spoke with the Senator briefly, then the two made their way to a previously arranged closed meeting of the state chairmen. As he was escorted through the kitchen into the guarded meeting room, word that he would get the number two spot had already been passed out. "Did you get the official word yet?" a reporter called out. "Not yet," he fibbed.

As he entered the room, the state chairmen, with whom he was immensely popular since as national chairman he had campaigned in all their states, burst into applause. Goldwater then introduced him as his running mate, and there were more cheers. Immediately afterwards, in a press conference across the street at the Fairmont Hotel, Senator William Knowland made the news public to the assembled news media. As Mother, Mary, and I stood by Dad's side, I realized this was the moment that would officially sweep our family from anonymity and thrust us with unsentimental abruptness into the harsh glare of the public eye. And our lives would be forever changed.

All four of us were then rushed back to the Hilton, where several impatient television crews had already set up to do "family features" on the Millers. Makeup people were ready to pounce. We spent several hours with the media, answering the questions we would answer so many times in the weeks and months ahead—how did we feel, what was Bill Miller like, what would be our role in the campaign, would we speak out on the issues (something the distaff side of political families did not do much of in those days), how would becoming public figures change our lives, what were our hobbies and interests, what were our fashion choices, did we do our own hair, and did we think we had a chance of winning the election in November? Ravenously hungry by this time, we finally ate the lunch that had been ordered up—it was already getting a bit nerve-racking to eat under the watchful eye of a note-taking press, looking up and smiling after every bite, hoping the stray piece of parsley hadn't stuck between our incisors.

Meanwhile, congratulatory phone calls, telegrams, and flowers began pouring in from friends and well-wishers all over the country—even from some of Mary's and my long lost boyfriends. I remember one of Dad's favorites was from Fathers Hesburgh and Joyce of Notre Dame: "We take immense pride at Notre Dame in your selection as the vice-presidential candidate for the Republican Party."

Learning to be quick-change artists, we donned our convention outfits. Within two hours, we had all assembled in our suite for the ceremonial trip to the Cow Palace. The group included several aides and my family's dearest friends from Lockport and Washington who had all flown in to share this triumph with us.

As we made our way down the hallway, the enormous wheeled tripod of an enthusiastic cameraman caught Jean Darrison by the leg and sent her sprawling—so much for the dignity of an auspicious moment. We proceeded to the sleek cavalcade of black limousines, bedecked with small American flags, that was awaiting us outside, flanked by police and security cars. They were private security—Pinkertons, in blue uniforms—for despite President Kennedy's assassination less than a year ago, it wasn't until 1968, after his brother Robert's assassination, that Congress mandated Secret Service protection for all presidential and vice-presidential candidates.

Outside my tinted window, evening was settling over downtown San Francisco as it receded in the distance—that crazy, hard-partying jewel of a city that novelist Frank Norris called "the city that never sleeps." As we whirred by, curious passersby gawked or waved or shouted congratulations; all the sights and sounds of what I thought was the most romantic city in the world drenched my senses in a kind of blurred collage. I wanted to savor, to etch every detail of the ride in my memory, but it was all so frenetic.

As our drivers wended their way out of the city and through San Mateo County toward the waiting convention hall—losing their way three times in the six and a half mile trip—the nominating and seconding speeches for Dad crackled on the car radio—*Gordon Allott, senator from the great state of Colorado: I am here to nominate the great congressman from the state of New York, the hard-driving chairman of the Republican National Committee, the Honorable William E. Miller! ... traveled the length and breadth of this country ... the intelligence, the will to win ... —To second, The Honorable Steve Derounian, congressman from the state of New York: ... an illustrious alumnus of Notre Dame, a strong, articulate gentleman who inspires confidence, who is a battler ... —The Honorable John Volpe, governor of Massachusetts: ... moral integrity and ability ... tireless energy ... —The Honorable Bruce Alger, congressman from Texas: ... he has brains and courage ... and have you seen Miller's girls, Stephanie, Mary Karen, and Elizabeth Anne? ... —The Honorable Ed Foreman, congressman from Texas: ... adds spark and spirit and drive ... courage of his convictions ... America needs Bill Miller!*—Cheers and applause—*Order please!*—Then the Roll Call of the States: *Alabama proudly casts 20 votes for Bill Miller! —The Virgin Islands, three votes! —Bill Miller is the unanimous nominee of this convention for vice president of the United States!*—More wild cheers and applause. In the pulsating, ongoing litany of adulation for my father, only the repetition of his name registered in my ears, so surreal was the moment.

In an attempt to break the tension of our seemingly endless ride, someone in the car launched into a story about how the Cow Palace acquired its odd name. It was constructed under President Franklin Roosevelt's Works Progress Administration in the late 1930s and early 1940s and was initially, and still sporadically, used as an indoor fairground for livestock shows. A reporter from the East Coast is purported to have come out to California during its construction, seen the fairgrounds, observed the surrounding urban squalor, and commented: "You've got people living in the streets and you're building a palace for cows." And tonight—well tonight, I mused, it would be a palace of jubilant GOP "elephants."

When our entourage at last pulled into the gates and up to the rear entrance of the Palace, pandemonium engulfed us. We were bustled through a long tunnel, met at the end by our escort committee composed of Congressman Ed Derwinski and assorted delegates, including Dad's boyhood friend Ray Lee. While waiting breathlessly in Permanent Chairman Thruston Morton's trailer office, we could hear Charles Percy, candidate for governor of Illinois, introduce the nominee: *... judicious political leader with a powerful grasp of national and international issues ... chosen above all for one overriding reason —he is fully qualified to be president of the*

United States ... a fighting candidate, a winning candidate, a dedicated Republican, a distinguished American, the next vice president of the United States—the Honorable William E. Miller! As the escort committee led, security guards ushered us forcefully through the noisy throng of delegates into the hall and up onto the speakers' platform, that now familiar "Notre Dame Victory March" playing us in.

The demonstration was lusty and long, nearly fifteen minutes, delegates singing, cheering, and marching, through the haze of cigarette smoke their lips and lungs forming not words but merely noise. Hundreds of "Miller for VEEP" posters imprinted with my father's oversize head burst from all parts of the hall, bobbing furiously—we smiled and waved and smiled some more. Little did I know then that my facial muscles would ache with that smile for the next three months. It is no wonder that politicians often seem plastic and fake—conjuring up sincerity day in and day out would prove to be the toughest challenge of the campaign ahead.

As the convention orchestra completed its final rendition of "The Victory March," the raucous crowd subsided, took their seats and fell to silence. Mother, Mary, and I demurely retreated to our seats behind Dad. His dapper, dark blue suit and ramrod posture made his slim frame seem larger than it was. His voice was confident and resonant as always, his speech brief but heartfelt—there had been only a day to prepare it. He was solemn, and weary I thought—it had been a long, pressure-filled week. He stumbled once—called Barry "the Senator from Indiana"—he never did that. But my heart swelled with pride.

There are at this moment no words to convey my feeling, he began. Then the newly minted nominee went on to proclaim his love for his country and his party and to praise the courage and integrity of his running mate. There was an absence of partisanship tonight in this well-known party "sharpshooter," and subtle praise for supporters of civil rights legislation—*crusaders for justice, crusaders for equality of opportunity for every person on the face of this earth.* He continued: ... *my family and I here pledge ourselves to you that we shall devote our hearts and our hands, our energies and our abilities, our spirit and our enthusiasm in this greatest challenge of my life.* And then the expected close: ... *now I humbly accept the great honor you have here bestowed upon me—your nomination for the vice-presidency of the United States.*

Bedlam again—the bands and the crowd, to steal a line from that famous song we had heard so often, truly shook down "the thunder from the skies." Mom came up from behind and tapped my father on the shoulder so he would move over and make room for her—political wives knew to do that. As he wrapped his arm around her, I thought how beautiful and poised and radiant she was—people always remarked that she looked barely older than her daughters. Convention Chairman Thruston Morton tapped the candidate again so he would make room for a little girl to hand Mother a bouquet of red roses. Then Dad turned to Mary and me, beckoning us to join them. And "My Boy Bill" played on.

It occurred to me in all this mayhem how curious is the phenomenon of celebrity in America, the insatiable eagerness to project upon ordinary people who are total strangers—but who happen to be rock stars or athletes or, in this case, politicians—emotions and expectations that may or may not be deserved. But in these maiden moments of our celebrity voyage, I, the idealistic college senior of the sixties, vowed to treat these expectations most seriously.

Next came Richard Nixon's moment in the limelight. Defeated for the presidency in 1960 and for the California governorship in 1962, he now appeared to be a man in the twilight of his political life, in search of a niche. Tonight it would be the wise and tempered veteran political warrior pleading for party unity. He strode onto the platform, flanked by the young and fresh-faced John Ehrlichman and Bob Haldeman, planted a kiss on Mother, delivered a well-received speech, then introduced the Party's new standard-bearer.

The long-awaited moment had finally arrived—the crescendo of a four-day symphony of frenzy. The Goldwaters emerged from the entrance tunnel, eight strong, marching into the hall and up onto the platform to "The Battle Hymn of the Republic." With the dais now filled to capacity, there were abundant kisses, hugs, and handshakes. The children—Barry Jr. and Mike, Joanne and Peggy and their spouses, Mary and I—milled around our waving parents, our families now united for better or for worse.

Hundreds of red, white, and blue balloons burst from the vaulted ceiling above, descending upon the celebrating delegates and us. Despite a large number of them landing on cigarettes and exploding like a giant corn popper, a three-foot-deep bank soon piled at the foot of the podium, threatening to engulf us. The prolonged demonstration was at last quieted by the candidate's first words—I remember thinking how natural, how personable, how sincere and handsome he was. Barry's last words precipitated a final outpouring of emotion—which gave the deceiving impression of perfect unity in the hall.

In looking back, I am struck by the delicious irony of that moment in time, that at the very juncture when my father was closing out his years in public life, we were thrust back up to such a dizzying height. He had announced early in 1964 that he was retiring. Though this was not the first time for such an announcement—he had made it periodically since he first came to Congress in 1950—this time he meant it. An anecdote underscores one of the reasons for his decision.

Since being elected chairman of the Republican Congressional Campaign Committee in 1960 and subsequently assuming the national chairmanship of the Party in 1961, he had traveled almost constantly. He had crisscrossed the country from north to south, east to west, building grassroots organizations, raising money and recruiting candidates. After one such exhausting seventeen-day trek, he returned home to Mother and his very young son and daughter—at the time, ages three and just newborn. With him was Ab Hermann, his executive director from the National Committee. As Dad, bone-tired, trudged slowly into the house, he was greeted noisily by his brood, and a wan smile brightened his weary face. Mother offered baby Stephanie for a kiss and then whispered to Billy, who was attached to her skirt, "Hug your Daddy, Billy." My brother hesitated, seemed confused, then lunged forward and threw his arms around Ab. They all dissolved in laughter, but it reminded the chairman all too painfully that he was becoming a stranger to his children.

So why did he accept the vice-presidential nomination just as he was about to end his political career and admittedly yearned to become a private citizen again? The answer is a simple one, a human one I suppose—he felt he had nothing to lose. He could help the Party he loved, and at the same time leave, he hoped, a proud legacy for his hometown and his family.

And there was one more thing. The word I have heard most frequently from his friends and associates to describe him, in countless letters and conversations, is "patriotic"—it comes up again and again. As one of "the greatest generation" that journalist Tom Brokaw immortalized in his books, service to country was embedded in his psyche. Herb Crispell of the *Buffalo Evening News* captured Dad well when he wrote in 1964: "Bill Miller is many things to many people. Above all else, to those who know him well, the Republican candidate for vice president is a truly dedicated, patriotic American. He's the type of guy who gets a lump in his throat when Old Glory is unfurled in a rippling breeze."

Herb quoted him as saying: "What happens to me isn't important. What happens to my country is important." Those words may sound corny, but the decision to run in '64 was that simple for my father. Though he was deeply concerned about the rifts in his party, especially since he had spent the last four years trying to heal them, he believed in the positive and indispensable mission of the Republican Party at this juncture in the history of our nation, and he was proud and thrilled to be able to be a part of it one more time.

And as for our family, it became readily apparent that we had embarked upon a challenging and unfamiliar, yet thrilling, adventure that would take us we weren't sure where. There was great hope. Although the polls were direly predicting catastrophic defeat in November, all things seem possible at convention time. Even Dad, the political realist but never a pessimist, believed that if he and Barry fought a good fight, they had an outside chance to win—or at least that's what he told us. Veteran politicians are, after all, sustained by their knowledge that seemingly lost battles can often be turned into victories by all manner of events.

For the first time in his career, this might not be one he would win, but as a fierce competitor he would give it all he had. "Let me tell you, in the strictest confidence, I don't like to lose," he once told the Notre Dame football team. "I didn't like to lose my seat in the stands any more than any of you like to lose on the field. And I've carried that spirit with me into politics. I hate to be a good loser. I don't intend to laugh off defeat by saying, 'Oh well, there's another Tuesday,' any more than you accept defeat by saying, 'Oh well, there's another Saturday.' "

Shortly after my father's nomination, a reporter asked me if I thought that his experience as a congressman was adequate preparation for the presidency. The newspaper account of the incident goes like this: "The question was obviously loaded, but Libby gazed blindly at the questioner and replied: 'Abraham Lincoln served only one term in the House of Representatives before he went to the White House.' That was the end of the questioning and indicates the self-assurance and confidence that Mr. Miller—and his family—carry into the campaign."[2] How I managed to have this pithy historical fact at the tip of my tongue at precisely that moment is still a mystery to me today. And I surely do not recall feeling any measure of the self-assurance that it inadvertently conveyed.

We heard from the home front via the media. A bevy of news people had descended upon our summer cottage, besieging my toddler siblings with questions about their reaction to their daddy's triumph. Billy responded simply, "I dunno. You have to ask him. He done it," followed by the puzzled query, "why does everybody wanna talk to me?" Stephie looked, from a picture we spotted in a San Francisco paper, somewhat like "a CARE package," as Dad put it, as if her seriously knotted naturally curly locks had not been combed since Mother had left her. When reporters showed her a picture of her parents and older siblings, she remarked thoughtfully, "Oh yes, I 'member them." It was time to go home.

CHAPTER TWO

SMALL TOWN BOY

MILLER / HINCH FAMILY TREE

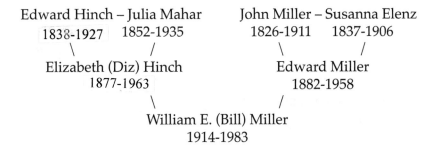

Edward Hinch – Julia Mahar
1838-1927   1852-1935
\   /
Elizabeth (Diz) Hinch
1877-1963

John Miller – Susanna Elenz
1826-1911   1837-1906
\   /
Edward Miller
1882-1958

\   /
William E. (Bill) Miller
1914-1983

The immigrants who melded to form the heart and soul of my father were all converging on Lockport, New York, at about the same time—the late 1840s. I confess I had never thought much about the serendipitous events of those days that brought together such courageous and disparate people from all over Europe seeking a better life in a new world, people whose genes would become forever mine. Nor did Dad regale me in my childhood with tales of the heroic struggles his family endured to make their place here, to make his place possible. He was a practical man who did not dwell on the past but lived in the present. And so my search for the roots from which he and I sprung began with only a few spare and unconnected details gleaned from the sepia memories of aging relatives. It led me to all the usual genealogical haunts, and finally pushed me across the broad Atlantic to Europe.

The Millers were fleeing the German Confederation, a loose and hapless union of thirty-nine independent states, lands taken from a vanquished Napoleon and divided between Austria and Prussia by the Congress of Vienna in 1815. These two superpowers continually vied for political control of the union, while the masses of poor peasants inhabiting them rapidly despaired of hope that the power-hungry feudal princes or kings, to whom they were forced to pay homage, would bring the changes needed to better their lives. They chafed under severe feudal restrictions, lack of religious freedom, and lack of freedom of press and assembly.

In 1848, the growing political and social unrest within the German Confederation exploded. After four years of severe crop failures, slowed business activity, spreading famine and unemployment, the clamor for reform had gathered irreversible momentum. News of revolution in France in March 1848 was all that was needed to set off revolts and demonstrations in cities and towns all over this tinderbox: the powerless lower classes, uneasy about the loss of their traditional way of life, had finally been driven to open rebellion.

All the existing state governments collapsed. A new Parliament was elected, controlled by liberals who were determined to forge a united Germany out of the erstwhile confederation of states, but the provisional government they set up was never able to impose its will on the feudal princes, who in short order reasserted their authority. After a year of haggling and disagreement among liberals and conservatives about what to do with the new government, the hopes of the spring of '48 were dashed, the status quo prevailed, and the German Confederation of 1815 was reestablished. So much for the revolution whose dream was to spawn a great German federal state based on the popular will and human rights.

Amidst such bleak prospects, it is no wonder then that my dad's grandfather, Jean Muller, soon to become John Miller, at age twenty-three an experienced tailor, decided to hop a ship to America in May of 1849. Life in his mostly Catholic hometown of Wormeldange, on the sunny, fertile bank of the Moselle River in the little Duchy of Luxembourg, had been idyllic before the turmoil of the German Confederation had engulfed it. Now, concerned about his future, he cast his imagination toward the more secure and prosperous life he might find in America, where he would be able to practice his trade in peace and dignity. Still, I would imagine he felt no small amount of trepidation as he set out alone from his parents' home, a German-speaking young man with no idea of what lay ahead.

Jean, an industrious and responsible boy, had been learning to fashion fine men's clothing since the age of seventeen, working first for his parents, then a Mr. Hansen in Ettelbruck, and finally Nicholas Schultz of Mersch—towns just down the road from his, nestled amid ancient castles and churches in the rolling countryside of the Moselle valley. When he was "sworn by the Town of Wormeldange to go to America on May 13, 1849," Jean was described as having "blonde hair, blonde eyebrows, gray eyes, covered forehead, ordinary nose, ordinary mouth, round chin, and long face." My father, of jet-black hair and brows, deep brown eyes, uncovered forehead and very long nose, was to inherit little of his paternal grandfather's visage.

In 1847, two years before Jean would embark upon his voyage across the Atlantic, a little fair-haired ten-year-old named Susanna Elenz had departed her German homeland with her parents, arriving in Buffalo, New York, on the blustery shores of Lake Erie. When Jean disembarked nearby in Lockport in 1849 at the age of twenty-three, it would still be ten more years before fate would bring the two together and unite them in marriage to forge a life and a family in their adopted home—and eventually produce my dad's father Edward.

Meanwhile, across the sea in Ireland, social upheaval of another kind was setting the stage for a simultaneous transatlantic exodus from the shores of Europe, which would bring my father's maternal ancestors to America. They were part of the great wave of Irish immigrants who descended upon this country in the nineteenth century, fanned out in all directions, and in their inimitable fashion, changed the fabric of life wherever they settled.

In the wake of the infamous potato famine (1846-1850) that claimed the lives of over a million Irish men, women, and children and drove one million more from their native land, a poor farmer named Patrick Hinch, from County Wicklow outside Dublin, packed up his wife Margaret and four small children and boarded a ship in 1848 bound for New York Harbor. The eldest of the Hinch children was a sturdy nine-year-old lad named Edward, my dad's grandfather-to-be. Patrick and Anna Mahar, in similarly dire straits, departed Ireland in 1847, and on American soil five years later, in 1852, they gave birth to a little girl called Julia. Eighteen years later, she would become Edward Hinch's bride and my father's grandmother, as they bore among their children Dad's mother Elizabeth.

By the time they emigrated, both Edward and Julia's parents were already middle-aged with sizable families. No doubt, like most of the Irish, they had endured years of hunger and lived a life largely on credit and charity, due to frequent crop failures even before the previously unknown blight of 1845 hit their crops. As is widely known now, the "famine" that spread across Ireland in that year was not the result of a complete lack of potatoes, the staple in the Irish diet; rather, it was due in part to the enforced British exportation of what healthy crop remained after a severe blight had blackened and rotted much of the potato crop. The Irish peasants were reduced to a starving mass bound for the soup lines, which the British belatedly instituted in 1848.

In addition, Catholics in Ireland had long suffered discrimination at the hands of the English since the despised union between the two countries had been pressed upon their island and its inhabitants in 1801. So with no laws to protect them from the religious and ethnic prejudices of their repressive British occupiers, it is quite understandable—amidst all else—that the Hinches and Mahars finally decided to abandon their tenuous existences and native soil to start over in a strange and distant, but promise-filled land.

It is, perhaps, only amazing that they waited as long as they did to leave. No doubt they struggled to raise enough cash for the long trip. But beyond that, anyone who has beheld the picturesque, mysterious beauty of the crystalline lakes and the rocky, flowering, undulating hills of the Irish countryside can well understand the mythic magnetism of the place and how wrenching it must have been, on some deep level, to leave this home behind.

When this assortment of my father's forebears arrived in New York Harbor in the late 1840s, after what was surely not a pleasant voyage on barely sea-worthy ships, they can only have been overwhelmed. They were all rural people from modest towns, hamlets even, and New York City, by any measuring stick, was a riot of noise, confusion, and bustle. Perhaps they had heard from relatives or friends who had come before them that job opportunities and a more pastoral life were possible upstate.

In any event, without wasting much time, they would have boarded packet boats—four-decked steamers, once drawn by teams of galloping horses—that took them up the fabled, pristine Hudson River of Washington Irving. At Albany, they turned west and slightly north on the Erie Barge Canal, which would take them to the western most reaches of the state. Though safer and more comfortable than traveling over primitive roads in wobbly stage-wagons minus shock absorbers, this was hardly an easy or inexpensive trip—over 500 miles, traveled at a mile and a half an hour, a cent and a half a mile. No doubt only the eager anticipation of a new life could have sustained them through this tedious last leg of their journey.

Why, of all places they might have gone, did these German and Irish immigrants to the "land of opportunity" choose Lockport, New York? Lockport, and the entire western New York area, has fallen upon hard economic times in recent decades, beginning even when my father was still in Congress in the early 1960s. So it does indeed require some historic perspective to recall what the area was like back in the late 1840s, when job opportunities were plentiful.

The Erie Barge Canal was the key to Lockport's attraction, indeed to its very existence. This amazing new passageway that connected the Atlantic Ocean to the Great Lakes system, this engineering marvel, was somewhat like today's interstate highway system—the "superhighway" of that day. The first important national waterway built in the United States, it provided a route over which horse-towed barges could haul goods and raw materials from East to West and vice versa. Naturally, the towns that grew up along its original 363-mile course prospered.

As soon as the exact route of the canal had been laid out, the location of the five locks determined, and authorization for construction given by the New York State legislature, speculators began buying up all the uninhabited forestland in Niagara County surrounding the route. In 1821, the selected contractors advertised for 1,200 laborers for the section of the route that passed through Niagara County, to which an excess of sturdy, if weary, Irish men, fresh off the boat and ready to work, responded. And the digging began.

As they dug—slashing through a sixty-foot escarpment of solid rock for three years—there began a steady flow of merchants, lawyers, doctors, and craftsmen to meet the needs of this army of workmen. Thus was the village of Lockport born—a cluster of log cabins built around the great locks of the canal. It was an exhilarating time.

When the canal, derisively coined "Clinton's Ditch" by those who opposed it—it was New York Governor DeWitt Clinton's idea—officially opened on October 26, 1825, there were glorious celebrations. Many feared, however, that with completion of the canal, its attendant labor force might move on and Lockport might become a ghost town. But happily, only a few hundred Irish canal workers departed the burgeoning village that October, and Lockport continued to grow.

By the mid 1830s, traffic on the canal had increased to such an extent that its depth and width were entirely inadequate, so the legislature authorized its enlargement. After much controversy and many delays, the additional work was finally completed in 1860. The waterway was enlarged once again in the early 1900s, but the Erie Canal never again regained the importance and vitality it possessed in its early days. The development of railroads after the Civil War cut deeply into its use, as did the trucking industry later in the twentieth century. While Lockport's founders dreamed of it becoming a major industrial center, instead, greater industry eventually centered at nearby Niagara Falls because of its cheap hydroelectric power, and at Buffalo, twenty miles to the southeast on Lake Erie, which became the state's second largest city.

But by 1845, when my Irish and German ancestors were about to hit town, Lockport was thriving, its first big industries—lumbering, quarrying, and flour making—all made possible by power from the surplus water of the canal's spillway. Vast quantities of oak, stone, and flour were being shipped to the eastern parts of the state as far as the Atlantic seaboard. Trees were falling at a furious rate, buildings and businesses sprouting everywhere—saw mills, foundries, grist mills, gun factories, cabinet shops, groceries, clothing, book, drug, and dry good stores. The unpaved streets were muddy and rutted, lit by night with gas lamps, hopelessly clogged by day with farmers' rigs, horse drawn hacks and a few fancy coaches belonging to the town's budding aristocracy.

Frances Trollope, an Englishwoman who wrote a travel book detailing her cross-country journey through the states, sneered at "what the Americans call improvement" upon beholding the aforementioned chaos. She did not endear herself to Lockportians by describing their young city thus: "It looks as if the demon of machinery, having invaded the peaceful realms of nature, had fixed on Lockport as the battleground on which they should strive for mastery.... Nature is fairly routed, and driven from the field, and the rattling, crackling, hissing, splitting demon has taken possession of Lockport for ever."[sic]

When Jean Muller arrived in this thriving, chaotic town, he fortuitously found work as a tailor almost at once, as well as a room at the inn of a William Watson and later in the home of Mr. Thompson and his wife, Mary. Jean seemed eager to engage in the duties of citizenship in his adopted home, a privilege denied him in his homeland, for he was naturalized, as "John Miller," at the earliest possible moment, five years after his arrival on American shores. Yet he appeared somewhat conflicted about his new identity when he signed those papers, with a somewhat shaky hand, here as "Muller" and there as "Miller." Though he did officially become John Miller at that moment, it is intriguing that when he died, "Muller" was etched on John's imposing tombstone in St. Mary's Cemetery.

It is not known exactly how John met his wife, Susanna Elenz of Buffalo—perhaps through a tightly knit network of German friends in the area. Family lore has it that he frequently walked the twenty miles from Lockport to Buffalo to visit her. While a fellow today might consider that excellent training for a marathon, I suspect John did it not for fitness but out of necessity—there were as yet no trains running that route and renting a horse-drawn carriage might not have fit the budget of a struggling tailor.

In any case, Susanna, duly impressed with her energetic suitor's devotion and strong constitution, married him in 1857. The Millers settled in and became a vital part of a group of German immigrants who, in 1859, founded St. Mary's Catholic Church. First situated in an old frame building once used by Episcopalians, they eventually built their own Gothic revival red brick church, now faced with yellow brick, in 1885 beside the Erie Canal. By the late 1860s, the couple had established what was to be, until 1996, the Miller ancestral home at 366 High Street. John, in possession of an emerging business acumen, also bought up a large tract of land that stretched all the way down that block, which later, when cut into individual lots, netted him a small fortune.

Yet life was not easy in those days, not even for a successful tailor. John and Susanna started their family of twelve a year after their marriage, and they hatched a new addition roughly every two years until their last, my dad's father Edward, was born in 1882. It is difficult today to fathom the magnitude of the tragedy that befell them in 1865, when their first three children—ages four, six, and seven—all died of an epidemic, possibly typhoid fever, within days of each other. When two-week old twin boys Henry and Joseph died in 1881, the Miller's German stoicism, which was later to mark my father, must have been tested to the breaking point. A daughter Louisa, who had been ostracized from the family for marrying a Protestant, died in her thirties, leaving only five of the twelve Miller progeny to survive their parents, and only three of those lived to a ripe old age.

The Millers were hard working, church-going, solid citizens. Those qualities, along with the honesty, thoroughness and practical bent that characterized most of the early Germans who emigrated here, made their absorption into American life relatively easy. John and Susanna and their family loved the outdoors, and they lived a simple, family oriented life. Patriarch John, when not tailoring, was an avid gardener. In his later years, he grew an impressive array of vegetables, flowers, and fruit trees; he kept a root cellar and reared chickens in a backyard coop—all of which he shared generously with relatives and friends. An orphanage in the next block on High Street provided playmates for my grandfather Edward and his siblings. Trips to St. Mary's cemetery were a family tradition. Since they owned neither horse nor carriage, the journey consisted of an all day walk and a picnic. Flowers were brought to be carefully laid at the modestly inscribed and sadly plentiful family gravestones that always seemed on the verge of outnumbering the living.

John was to work steadily at his trade, eventually building a thriving business of his own, not retiring until well into his seventies—his parents back in Wormeldange surely must have been proud. All his surviving children finished school and went to work at age seventeen, but John appears to have passed his skills as a custom tailor to just one. There was a tinsmith, a machinist, and assorted clerks among them, but only a daughter, Louisa, was to carry on her father's trade.

When mother Susanna died in 1906 at age sixty-nine, no doubt physically and emotionally spent after twelve pregnancies and half as many funerals, son William and his family moved in with John at the house on High Street. And there the aging patriarch remained until, as the *Lockport Union Sun and Journal* recorded on February 13, 1911, "an old and respected resident of this city, aged 85 years, has died." Born in 1914, my father was never to know his German grandparents.

By the mid-1850s, Lockport was heavily Irish, in some wards as much as 35 percent so. About 60 percent of all the regular Army soldiers stationed at Fort Niagara at that time were born in Ireland. Johnny Cleary, a sweet-voiced singer, and Chauncey Olcott, the famed Irish balladeer and composer of "My Wild Irish Rose" and "When Irish Eyes are Smiling," both hailed from the area. Two decades later, the Hodge Opera House, Lockport's grand multi-purpose center of culture and commerce on the corner of Main and Market, became the scene of many a contest among locally renowned Irish boxers with names like Duffy, Mulligan, McDonough, and Murphy. One such occasion in 1910—when a bloodied Donovan accused McCann of having "a pound of lead" in his glove—produced an unruly mob that forced police to close down the house for the night, no surprise for an Irish get-together.

And among those colorful Irishmen were my father's maternal grandparents-to-be. By 1855, his maternal grandfather, Edward Hinch, had acquired three more siblings, and the family of nine was snuggly settled into what the census takers called a "shanty"—they described all Irish residences that way for some reason. A "shanty" was a wooden lean-to propped against a larger structure, and most of the "shanties" in Lockport were situated in the north end near the Canal where most of the Irish lived and worked. Whether or not the census people knew the word itself came down from the Gaelic *sean tig*, meaning old house, who can know. Yet its deliberate and repeated usage seems appropriate, considering the appearance of the residences and the nationality of the occupants in question.

A year or so later, at age seventeen, like most boys at that time, Edward, the oldest of the Hinch brood, went off to work. He was a "laborer," according to the census, probably on the small farm his father had managed to acquire just outside town, but possibly on the enlargement of the Erie Barge Canal. The center of Hinch family life soon became St. Patrick's Catholic Church, located on Church Street right in the midst of the canalside Irish quarter. St. John's parish, once the only Catholic church for all of Lockport, had recently abandoned that building for larger, fancier quarters eastward across the canal on donated land. But Father O'Farrell and his band of humble Irish working folk decided to stay put, and they renovated and reopened the old sanctuary in 1864 under the name of their patron saint.

The Mahar family, who would give young Edward his bride several years later, had found their way to the same Irish community in Lockport as the Hinches. They settled on Prospect Street, surrounded by a bevy of other Mahars who had all come from Ireland to work on the canal, and it was there that little Julia, my father's grandmother-to-be, was born to Patrick and Anna in 1852.

Julia grew to be a tall, slender, kind girl. Edward knew her from the neighborhood and St. Patrick's Church, where both their families worshipped. They fell in love and tied the knot in 1870, he at the ripe old age of thirty-one and she a mere eighteen. Together they produced a family of eight, four boys and four girls, the second oldest of which was the delicate Elizabeth, my father's mother.

Edward was an enterprising sort, determined to improve upon his father's lot in life as a laborer. Around 1881 he started E. Hinch and Son, Hard and Soft Coal and Wood Company, a thriving concern well into the twentieth century until coal finally declined in favor as a source of heat. He and his eldest son, George, who helped run the company, became so prosperous that they began buying up real estate for the family all over the area—the 1887 county directory records that Edward owned forty acres. Among his holdings were a farm and apple orchard near Lake Ontario in Olcott, the family's first home, and the subsequent long-time family residence at 99 Church Street in Lockport, diagonally across from St. Patrick's where Edward rarely missed daily Mass.

I am uncertain how the Irish Elizabeth Hinch, "Diz" as Edward and Julia's second daughter was called, eventually met her German beau, Edward Miller—John and Susanna's youngest son. But by the time they were married in 1909, the various nationality groups, once each huddled with "their own" for security, were beginning to mix and mingle with each other. St. Patrick's and St. Mary's, the couple's respective Catholic churches, were not far apart and perhaps they held joint functions.

As prolific as the Miller and Hinch patriarchs were, their progeny were considerably less so. Edward and Elizabeth's only child, my father, was born in 1914—an occasion of some joy since it had come late in their lives—in a simple rented apartment. He was named after an Uncle William on both sides of the family, both of whom, inauspiciously for Dad's future, died quite young, one during the World War I influenza epidemic and the other of a hand infection from cutting down a tree in his backyard. No penicillin in those days. A boarder lived with the Millers at the time, a Mr. Lynch who was a worker on the Erie Canal, and he reportedly held my father in his arms upon his arrival home from the hospital and declared authoritatively, and presciently, to the new mother, "He's got the head of a statesman."

It was once written of my father, "In twentieth-century America few candidates for either of the nation's two highest offices have risen from such humble beginnings."[1] While that may have been a bit of an exaggeration, it is likely that without the generosity of Elizabeth's older sister Margaret, who gave the Millers a modest, two-story frame house on South Street in a respectable Irish Catholic middle class neighborhood shortly after Dad's birth, the family might never have owned their own home. Still they never owned a car and they walked everywhere—to shops, to St. Patrick's parochial school, to church for Mass on Sundays, to the high school.

Dad's father, nicknamed "Dutch," could be charming and jovial, a lighthearted man and practical joker, but for whatever reason he had a rather checkered work career. He was at various times a salesman in a grocery, a telegraph operator, a clerk in a gentlemen's furnishings store, an employee of the city Water Department, a bridge painter, and a deputy sheriff with jail duty. He even started a laundry business in Niagara Falls with his wife's brother Ed, but both men had an affinity for the bottle and the enterprise failed within two years. Grandpa ended his working years as a janitor at the Harrison Radiator plant of General Motors, the largest employer in Lockport.

There is no knowing of course how close the Millers were in the beginning—children never asked about such things in those days—but my father remembered their relationship as distant, each going his and her own way. Soon, Dutch began drinking too much, hanging out often at a fraternal club on Main Street called Eagles, which was similar to but lower in status than the Elks Club. Dad remembered all too well being embarrassed to bring friends home, never certain of his father's condition.

Even I recall visits to my grandparents' home at 36 South Street as a little girl when Grandpa, affectionate but loud, would perch me on his lap and I'd wince at the feel of his rough whiskers and the smell of beer on his breath. Yet Mary and I would squeal with delight when he would lead us, somewhat conspiratorially, down the creaky old stairs to his cold, dark, dirt-floored cellar room where he stored brown felt bags of long-collected silver dollars, and bestow upon each of us one or more of the large shiny coins. But my father was never close to his father. He rarely spoke of him, and I never probed the reasons. I suspect Grandpa was an alcoholic in a day when no one understood alcoholism, when it was not considered a disease, just a moral weakness.

On the other hand, Dad simply adored his mother. He called her a "saint," perhaps partly because she so loved him and partly because he perceived, even at a young age, that she had to endure a loveless marriage. Diz was everyone's favorite among the eight Hinch children. I remember her only as a gentle, elderly woman, very slight, with thin lips and a neat, gray pageboy hairdo covered with a net and sometimes a nice hat. I remember she spoke softly but laughed readily in a dainty sort of way. But my father used to tell me what a kind-hearted, highly intelligent, energetic, and disciplined woman she always was in her younger years. Once a rural elementary school teacher, his mother was a serene and modest lady of great strength and resources who never complained. She rarely raised her voice, as she persistently pushed Dad along and encouraged him to study. She would do just about anything for the son and only child upon whom she doted.

By 1923, two years after the laundry business had folded and her son was barely ten, Diz Miller understood that her husband would never provide the opportunities and the education she desperately wanted for little Bill. So despite the almost nonexistence of female entrepreneurs in those days, Grandma, in partnership with her younger sister Anna and with the financial help of her father and brother in the coal business, opened a millinery shop on Locust Street just off Main—the Lockport Millineria. Hats were, of course, de rigueur in those days. The spunky pair soon added women's dresses and accessories to their inventory and quickly gained a reputation for carrying top quality and quite fashionable merchandise, catering to the carriage trade of the city. It is remarkable how vividly and fondly Lockport residents still remember that shop today.

Dad's mother worked tirelessly in the store for some thirty years as the family's main breadwinner, until it burned down in April 1950. She did well but was also extremely frugal. He suspected in those years that she often went nights without eating in order to save money to educate and clothe him. It was not until many years later he learned that was indeed the case.

Though it would seem that his early years might have been lonely—no siblings, his mother tending her shop daily, his father rarely home—his friends and family remember him as a happy child, "full of joy, his mouth always wide open in a big smile," recalls cousin Jack Hinch. Luckily, there was a plentiful stock of colorful Hinch relatives around to keep him company and cast a watchful eye—three loving aunts, four attentive uncles, and assorted cousins. And a few Miller aunts, uncles, and cousins to boot.

Yet of necessity, Dad became self-sufficient early in life—Cousin Jack remembers that he did pretty much what he wanted to do. Whether it was putting golf balls into tin cans sunk into his backyard (a precursor to his fair to middling adult golf game) or collecting discarded tin foil wrappers in his little cart, he was always surrounded by a pack of friends of whom he was the undisputed leader. He was apparently an irrepressible character—precocious, mischievous and fun loving. "Your dad was always bouncing with energy and full of ideas," laughed Jack. "Quick-witted and scrappy," he added. I cannot count the number of times those exact words were used to describe my father throughout his life.

And did he love to talk—his Grandma Julia called him "mouth almighty." By age three, he was occasionally seen on the phone ordering groceries for his mother. There is a priceless picture of him, with bowl-like haircut, standing in his backyard next to a little girl—both about five years old—apparently in the midst of an animated diatribe and pointing his tiny finger in her face as if to make an emphatic point. A high school teacher once recalled how extraordinary was his vocabulary, how words "just used to pour out of him," a garulousness surely traceable to his Irish heritage. Several of his Hinch uncles were charmers who reputedly could talk almost anyone into almost anything.

And so, too, did Dad seem to have a way of endearing himself to the local denizens, including the mothers of his chums who affectionately called him "Little Billy Miller" and were always inviting him to stay for dinner. Many years later, as a practicing attorney, he reportedly did legal work for those mothers free of charge, as well as for the sons he played with. He apparently charmed his teachers in much the same way, which no doubt enabled him to get away with all sorts of antics that other children could not.

A Hinch family get-together was held many Sundays and all holidays. The dinners were held at Grandpa Edward and Grandma Julia's home on Church Street or at Dutch and Diz's house on South Street—long elaborate meals with all the aunts, uncles, spouses, and cousins, numbering at least twenty people, followed by five or more tables of contract bridge. My father had no idea how to play the game in the beginning, but with his quick mind and his mother's expert tutelage, he was a fast learner.

Prophetically for the future, "Little Billy Miller" made the headlines of the *Lockport Union Sun and Journal* as far back as 1926: "South Street Boy Corresponds with Local Congressman." The article went on to relate that the eleven-year-old seventh grader at St. Patrick's School was "taking a keen interest in citizenship early in life."

The class assignment was to write an essay on the All-American Ship Canal project being promoted by the Honorable S. Wallace Dempsey—it would link Lake Ontario with Lake Erie for ocean-going vessels without using Canada's Welland Canal. Dad's composition won and was sent to the congressman as a letter: "I can't talk for the grown up citizens yet, but I assure you we young Americans want it as you have outlined it," and he ended, "When I grow up I want to be as helpful as you are." I suppose if it were possible to pinpoint where an entire career in public service begins, a letter such as this would be as good a guess as any.

Lockport was by now a reasonably prosperous town of about 25,000, referred to almost reverently as "the city" by those who lived in the neat but modest farmhouses of the surrounding countryside. It was thoroughly American, a prototypical small town with its attendant socio-economic groupings. The canal had long since neatly divided it approximately in two—south of that deep gorge were the elegant mansions and walled estates that dated to the mid-nineteenth century; north of it, sloping steeply downhill, was Lowertown—working-class, industrial, largely black.

Standing on the canal's precipitous banks, looking down on the furiously swirling dark waters being continuously raised and lowered by the five heavy locks, the massive gates laboriously groaning open to release patiently waiting barges, was doubtless a thrilling and awesome sight for young boys. Otherwise, the waterway had little effect on the local economy anymore, and the tranquil city that surrounded it was a far cry from the chaotic days of the rough and tough workmen who built it. All in all, life in Lockport was unremarkable, uncomplicated, far from the seat of power and events of great significance—as Joyce Carol Oates, the well-known author who hails from the area, once noted.

Summer trips with Cousin Jack down one of those country roads of aging but verdant farms to Olcott Beach on Lake Ontario to visit Grandma and Grandpa Hinch's cottage were a special treat, and among the happiest and most memorable days of my father's young life. The boys knew Grandpa Edward with his full head of smooth white hair only as old and remote—he was by then well into his eighties—but Grandma Julia, fourteen years his junior, was lively and fun.

Dad loved the brilliant, perfectly clear days when the sun's rays danced on the calm, sapphire-blue lake like thousands of glittering, floating jewels, the water so pristine back then you could see every smooth pebble that covered the squishy bottom. Small power boats sliced jauntily through its glassy surface; mammoth freighters hauling important cargo to important places loomed miniaturized on the distant horizon, the mysterious and enchanting world of Toronto—which on a very clear day you could actually see—just beyond.

There were the famed Niagara County orchards—peach, cherry, and apple—that bordered the lake in all directions, where the boys could run and pick and eat to their heart's content, or until their stomachs ached. And all the honky-tonk stuff kids loved before there was Disney World and gigantic, heart-stopping roller coasters—rides like the carousel, Ferris wheel and bumper cars, and tossing pennies into jars for cheap stuffed animals that usually split their seams before you got them home.

He carried that child-like love of Olcott into his adult years when we lived in Washington and owned a summer cottage there. And he passed it on to us. The few weeks that he was sometimes able to spend with us in the waning days of summers after Congress at last adjourned were the most peaceful of his pressure-filled life. He had never learned to swim, in fact feared the water a little, as had his mother. Yet he loved the lake. One of the most enduring memories I have of my father from those days is his slim, jaunty outline leaning on the wire fence that separated our backyard from the steep bank that fell to the retaining wall below, looking contentedly out over the water, cigarette in hand, deep in his own thoughts, perhaps of days gone by.

School came easily enough to Dad, as one of his old English teachers explained: "He was a scrappy son-of-a-gun. He was no scholar, but he had a tremendous memory and was marvelous in rebuttal. When he started talking, nothing could stop him, and if he believed in something, heaven and hell couldn't change him."

Though neighbors remember him as a studious boy, sometimes helping other neighborhood boys with their homework, he seems also to have had a knack for not letting his work interfere with his fun. By the time he arrived at Lockport High, his life was so filled with social events and assorted extracurricular activities that it is a wonder he ever had time to study. There were the Hi-Y Club dances and dinners, interclass sports, class plays, and debate team, for which he won numerous awards. The most notable production of his early thespian career was the senior play, in which his performance as the aspiring office boy "Beansy" Blake was rated "unusually pleasant and amusing," and which thereafter affixed him with the nickname of his character.

Always slight and not very sturdy physically, in fact sickly at times, my father's athletic prowess was limited to his church's basketball team and baseball, at which he was actually fairly good as a young boy—and he knew by heart the names and records of every professional baseball player on every team. His cousins remember him, nevertheless, as a ferocious competitor, determined to win at everything, even if he didn't play it. Cousin Dick Shults remembers when Dad wanted to play him in tennis. Dick at the time was the city high school champion and cousin Bill played little tennis. But he borrowed a racket and proceeded to return every ball Dick hit him until he won two sets by exhausting both of them. Whether it was ping-pong, pool, gin rummy, bridge or any game at all, he was tenacious, and usually the winner.

Girls had by now become a major part of his life—Jack Hinch recalls that he and my father grew apart when Dad suddenly became far more "socially advanced" than his cousin. His classmates remember that he was immensely popular with the girls and the boys, very friendly and extroverted, always ready to have some fun, and always so funny. That's what they all remember the most—his incomparable sense of humor, his ability to see the funny side of almost anything.

Whether it was bumming a ride with the boys from the corner of Market and Main—decked in navy surplus bell-bottom trousers with red bandanas hanging from the hip pockets—to Olcott for the Boeckmann's Sunday Special (chicken and biscuits for thiry-five cents) or for the summer dances at the Olcott Beach Hotel (ten cents a dance, three for twenty-five cents) to which they finagled free tickets by bribing the ticket taker with a bottle of booze, hanging out at one of their two favorite ice cream parlors to meet their heartthrob of the week, or hunting for secret sources of home brew (beer) or hard cider (Shep, the old janitor at the Palace Billiard Room, could get it for them for fifty cents a gallon)—Billy Miller was a boy always on the go. He ended his high school career with a speech as Salutatorian for the 1931 Class Day, which was reportedly a foreshadowing of the orator he was to become.

Throughout his formative years, Dad, though fun loving, was ambitious and serious minded when he needed to be. He seemed to know instinctively that in addition to his mother's hard work it would be necessary for him to help earn whatever privileges he hoped to have. And so he became an entrepreneur at an early age.

Every July he would build a fireworks stand on the sidewalk in front of his mother's store, clearing what was an astronomical sum in that day—$100 or more. He ran a thriving annual Christmas card business and he always had jobs of one sort or another—at Hosking's Ice Cream Confectionery on Main Street or at Harrison's Radiator Company running the heater pack line. With the proceeds from all this and the help of his Aunt Anna, Uncle George, and widowed Aunt Margaret, who unbeknownst to anyone had stashed away money for her favorite nephew, Dad was able to pursue the dream of every Catholic boy in those days—attending the University of Notre Dame. Glued to the radio for their weekly football games, boys like him felt an almost mystical kinship with the school, and the issue of finances out of the way, all that remained for the fulfillment of his dream was the application process

Getting into Notre Dame was a far simpler proposition in 1931 than it is today—"just the facts ma'am": your name, address, birth date, high school grades, two letters of recommendation, and a one-line answer to the question, "What is your reason for choosing the University of Notre Dame?" My father wrote, in typical straightforward fashion, "because of religious affiliation and scholastic standing." There were no interminable lists of enriching extracurricular activities, no excruciatingly creative parent-written essays required. Having secured the recommendation of his favorite teacher, Maria Snyder, whose constant refrain in her rigorous English classes was "where is your purpose sentence?" and the kind words of his principal, Edmond Evans, he thought he was all set. But there was a hitch.

August arrived and he had not yet received his letter of acceptance. It was the only place to which he had applied and, never short on self-confidence, he assumed there would be no problem. So he wrote the Registrar a letter, brief and to the point. I must quote it in full because it is so typical of his life-long habit of knowing exactly what he wanted, going after it with tenacity, and going to the top to get it.

Dear Sir,

I sent in my application for admission to your University last April. I received acknowledgement of my money order for $25 and was informed that you wouldnotify me later concern-

ing my acceptance. To date I have not received any statement from you.

Two weeks later, through my instigation, another Lockport boy, Wm Spalding, sent in his application, and two weeks ago received notice of acceptance.

Being practically certain that I have the required units, and fearing there may be some oversight, or that a statement from you might not have reached me, and as I am very anxious to go to Notre Dame, I am taking the liberty of writing you again.

Very Truly Yours,
Wm. E. Miller

Suffice it to say, three weeks later Dad was boarding a train for South Bend.

It is difficult to imagine what a seventeen-year-old boy, who had never been farther than twenty miles from his small town, would have felt as he rolled, alone, for the better part of a day and night through the belching industrial cities along Lake Erie and the endless, flat and empty farmland of the Midwest toward a new home some 550 miles away. As fearless and self-assured as Bill Miller seemed even then, I suspect he had a few butterflies. But I never actually asked him about all that.

When he arrived on campus on what might have been a typically sweltering South Bend September day in his usual dapper but somewhat rumpled-from-traveling cord suit and vest, suitcase and old beat-up portable record player in hand, he would have gone straight to Main Building to check on his dorm assignment and found that he'd gotten his second choice, Dillon Hall. And he would have met, to his relief, a talkative group of boys, mostly warm and friendly and accepting of each other, no matter the diverse backgrounds from which they had come.

Though he doubtless failed to appreciate it at the time, the vast campus he was seeing for the first time in 1931 was nearing the end of a breathless two decades of expansion. Despite the cataclysmic events that had swept the world during that period—the bloody Great War, the Depression, the rise of Fascism—Notre Dame had prospered and grown. No fewer than twenty-nine buildings had been built or renovated since 1910, including nine residence halls, the South Dining Hall replete with handsome dark wooden chairs and tables, and the famous football stadium, which at the time was rarely filled. Even Sacred

Heart Basilica with its awesome gothic spires was undergoing a tasteful renovation.

Making a significant contribution to this rapid growth was one of the greatest football dynasties of all time—Knute Rockne, George Gipp, and the Four Horsemen. They had stormed the Northeast and taken an increasingly impressive football program to national fame by winning an unofficial national championship in 1924, spawning a new enthusiasm for collegiate football. The campus paper noted: "Rockne's success enabled poor Catholic boys of all descents to have a shot at an education." So as you can imagine, when my father arrived, the campus and the football world were still reeling from Rockne's tragic death in a plane crash earlier that year, in March.

However, former Notre Dame professor Tom Stritch reminds us in his memoir that "long before football was invented, Notre Dame caught the imagination of American Catholics."[2] Poor Irish immigrants and their American descendants in particular have always claimed the school as theirs, and they became its heart and soul. What Father Sorin had hoped for when he "carved it out of the Indiana wilderness in 1842"[3] was an institution that would not only develop moral character but also be a leader in Catholic intellectual excellence. Father John O'Hara furthered that goal during his presidency by hiring world-renowned scholars fleeing Europe and Hitler in the 1920s and 30s, thereby increasing the graduate school presence at the University.

By 1931, the Depression had somewhat shrunk the student body and with the array of new dorms, it was now possible for everyone to live on campus. That was not quite mandatory but strongly encouraged, since it enabled the Prefect of Discipline to more closely monitor the boys' activities. With money tight for most of them anyway, it was the cheapest place to live. So Dad's only fling with off-campus living, now so common, was the two months he and the other Dillon Hall assignees had to wait while their dorm, still under construction when they arrived as freshmen, was completed.

One of the first year required courses was mysteriously called "Bionomy." Not surprisingly, the first question asked in the class was inevitably: "Why is this class called Bionomy?" The response of Professor Bocskei: "Because we are going to teach biology the first half of the semester and botany the second half." The biology portion turned out to be a modified sex education class and the students apparently exhibited such intense interest that there never was a botany lecture. Attendance was a perfect 100 percent, Bionomy classmate Al Lawton recalls. It may be worth noting that my father scored a mere seventy in this course—a D, as it were. I'm not sure of the implications of that, except that it may somehow account for the notable lack of sexual scandal in his future political and personal life.

The rules and regulations of the 1930s, designed, as they were, to mold moral character, might strike one as harsh and restrictive by today's *Ally McBeal* co-ed bathroom standards. The boys griped about lights out at 11 p.m., no girls or liquor in the dorms and the other myriad seemingly Draconian laws. Yet there was no shortage of clever ways found to circumvent or ignore them, and it is doubtful the un-permissive mandates stifled any fun at all. One classmate recalls the time when Father Marr found Dad and a friend carrying a rather heavy carton into the front door of Walsh dorm, in preparation for a large gathering in their room. When the priest asked, "What's that, boys?" my father brashly and ingenuously answered, "Liquor and beer, Father." Marr laughed heartily and continued walking on down the steps, leaving the two young men to ponder whether he didn't believe them or just gave them a pass. They suspected it was the latter.

Bill Miller's first foray into political organization came near the end of his freshman year, and it was ill-fated—his buddy Louis Hruby recalls that their group of "freshies" wised up quickly about the seriousness of campus politics. A group of them had put up a slate of candidates for sophomore class officers, with Dad as campaign manager. Exerting minimal effort, they went down to a crushing defeat.

So in the room above the arch of Lyons Hall at the beginning of sophomore year, the group planted the seeds early to elect the president of their junior class. Their candidate would be his roommate and dear friend from the campus Buffalo Club, Tom LaLonde, and my father, now a seasoned campaign manager, was to have a second chance at exercising his political skills. The result this time, after a hard-fought campaign, was resounding success, to be repeated again the following year when he got Tom elected president of the Student Activities Council. Once when the candidate made a suggestion to his manager about campaign strategy, Dad's reply, after listening quietly, was: "Tom, you go ahead saying 'hello' to all the boys and remembering their names, which you're really good at, but you leave the thinking to me."

Of course, there was a payoff to the successful manager both times. Tom rewarded him the first time with the Junior Prom chairmanship. The chairman's date, Pat McArdle from St. Mary's College across the street, rated an oversized picture on the "Society" page of the South Bend paper as the prom queen, and the campus paper ran a picture of the honored couple captioned: "Chairman Bill Miller looks out of the corner of his eye (at Pat)." Louis Hruby, who wrote the copy, recalls that he had to restrain himself from saying what he really wanted to say about that "look," or risk being censored by the Faculty Board of Publications. From all reports, the class judged the prom, held at the elegant Palais Royale with the popular Ted Weems band, a huge success.

"Blue Circle reorganized with William Miller as Chairman," announced *The Notre Dame Scholastic* in September of 1934. That was the second "carrot" from President Tom LaLonde to his savvy campaign chairman for a job well done. Membership in the Circle, a subsidiary of the Student Activities Council, was cut from thirty-five to eighteen that year and "great care was exercised in the selection of members, inasmuch as the purpose of the organization is honorary as well as utilitarian," reported the campus paper.

In the past, the Circle had been almost a group of glorified cheerleaders whose main job was to rally enthusiasm among the students for the football team, but now it was supposedly taking on new and more dignified dimensions. Its members were to mediate between students and the University Disciplinary Board in suspension cases, usher at concerts, plan the programs for pep meetings, hire prestigious speakers for the student body, and generally act as the guardians of sacred Notre Dame traditions—which occasionally meant dunking boys who defied them in one of the two on-campus lakes. Bolstering the Notre Dame spirit would prove to be a particularly challenging task this year, since the football team had compiled an abysmal record the year before—"the giant is sleeping," the *Scholastic* had somberly observed.

Once again, Dad's college buddies attested to the fact that he made better marks in his studies with less apparent effort than anyone they knew. Even a friend from home recalls that when he once paid an unexpected visit to Notre Dame the day before a huge exam, my father sat on his bed for a few minutes perusing the text book from Mr. Plunkett's Latin course, slammed it shut, went out for the rest of the night and proceeded to ace the exam. He would rarely eschew a night at Paddy's with beers, Limburger cheese sandwiches and good visits with "the Boys" for a night of hard work in the library. Though not considered an intellectual, his mind was called "sharp as a tack." In sophomore year, the game of contract bridge hit campus and he, along with his good friend, the young economics professor Lee Flatley, spent considerable hours in a tower room of Sorin Hall teaching the perils of over-bidding to assorted buddies and other professors. All those Hinch family bridge games had finally paid off.

"The Dap," short for dapper, was a nickname given to Dad early in his college career, and it stuck with him. "Bill was always meticulously attired. Indeed, if there had been any sort of award for appearance, Bill would have been an easy winner. I'll always remember him in his trim clothes and tab collared shirts," recalls his friend Al Lawton. That impression was reinforced by a "Man About Campus" article in the school paper which marveled at how "Dapper" could maintain the crease in his pants over a whole weekend and "show up at nine o'clock Monday morning with a press that you could sharpen a pencil on. He has a penchant for stiff collars and wears them as though he actually likes them."[4]

It has always been a bit of a mystery to me how he managed this legendary sartorial splendor—these were after all hard times and he had limited funds. His dorm rooms were sparsely furnished—a spindly table tied with a two-inch rope in rickety fashion to the radiator, and a dresser, affectionately called his "Louis XIV piece," with drawers that didn't work but faces that pulled off so socks, shirts and underwear could be stuffed in from the front. But with the money he earned and what his relatives occasionally sent, I suspect it was a priority for my proud father to dress well in order not to be labeled a poor boy.

The truth is that his salesmanship talent is what saved him. He and Tom LaLonde secured from the Balfour Company the class ring and pin concession, which proved to yield them a fairly lucrative commission. The entrepreneurial pair also clinched the campus Christmas card concession. And finally, Dad's past success in the fireworks business prompted him to launch a similar venture on campus with another friend. That alone, he reported to his cousin Dick Shults, confidentially and with great pride, netted him $4,000 after four years, an impressive sum by any measuring stick.

This student-cum-salesman routine was doubtless time-consuming, but it was the middle of the Depression and boys had to scramble to find spending money for their perks—dance tickets, beers, occasional tickets on the South Shore Line for trips to Chicago. Tuition, room and board was just under $500 freshman year, which, while akin to pocket change by today's tuition standards, was hard to come by in the 1930s.

My father considered debating one of the most formative of his college activities, despite recalling his team, though strong, as somewhat less illustrious than the school's famed football team. Eugene Blish, an erstwhile teammate, gave me a most insightful and prescient description of my father from those days:

> Bill had a strong, manly attitude and expression, a memorable voice and diction and forceful command of the language, whether he was describing last week's football game or the New Deal policies of FDR. Bill was youthful, confident and self-reliant, far more mature for his age than the rest of us. No doubt about it, Bill was blessed with strong convictions. In a very persuasive way, he would let you know exactly what he thought was best for the world, for the United States of America, for Upstate New York, for Notre Dame, for Alumni Hall, and for Bill Miller.

Coach Bill Coyne demanded that his boys train themselves to take both the affirmative and negative of a debate topic. The universal collegiate debate subject one year was the world-wide acquittance of all World War I debts, and Dad explained one day at practice how hard it would be for him to argue the side of that issue in which he did not believe. "On the other hand," Blish added, "when Bill would speak for a cause he sincerely believed was right, he was a fearless, overpowering, intimidating public speaker. That's when we all wanted to be teamed up with Bill Miller."

Gene Blish, obviously reveling in the opportunity to recall his old friend and teammate of so long ago, continued to offer me his memories of my father:

Bill walked around the campus like he was suspended at a level about three inches above the rest of us—just high enough to be above the black cinder pathways, the temporary wooden boardwalks in front of Dillon and Alumni Halls, or the gummy Indiana mud that surrounded us in all directions on rainy days. But all that aloofness was okay; we all understood that wild, unpredictable, fun-loving Bill Miller. He was the outstanding leader among our classmates—an accomplished, decent and most respected individual.

A 1934 campus newspaper feature article took liberties with an Oliver Goldsmith poem to pithily sum my father up:

In arguing, too, the Dapper owned his skill
For, even tho' vanquished, he could argue still;
While words of learned length and thundering sound
Amaz'd the gazing rustics rang'd around;
And still they gaz'd, and still the wonder grew,
That one small man could know all he knew.

So with his Bachelor of Arts diploma in hand, a pre-law major in economics and minor in public speaking, an academic record that was not brilliant but respectable, a batch of good buddies from cities far-flung from Lockport, and some new-found political savvy, a small town boy walked proudly across that improvised stage in the old Field House in June of 1935. His parents were there, finally able to see where his mother's sacrifice had enabled their son to spend four important years of his life.

He was ready to move on, enthusiastic about a future he knew was far more promising than any that could have been forecast for him twenty-one years ago. He remarked in a speech many years later:

It is not until one has been out of school for several years that he fully understands in how many ways his University has placed its stamp upon him. Notre Dame, dedicated to the development of the whole man, makes its imprint on mind and will, soul and body of its graduates. We alumni don't all leave here with the poetic genius of a Father O'Donnell, the deep human sympathy

of a Cardinal O'Hara, the intellectual brilliance of a Yves Simon,
or the athletic achievements of a Knute Rockne, but something
of what these men — and many others — have imparted to Notre
Dame is likely to rub off on us.

My father remained for the rest of his life deeply proud of
Notre Dame, of its values and academic excellence and what it
stood for, and proud and grateful that he had been lucky enough
to be a part of it. Mother told me that Dad once confessed to her
that he had cried when he arrived at Notre Dame, for homesick-
ness, and that he cried four years later when he left. Now granted,
I never saw my father cry. But given the deeply rooted attachment
he had to the school for the world it had opened to him, his tears
are surely plausible.

CHAPTER THREE

THE ROAD TO NUREMBERG

With his assertive personality, strong convictions, and persuasive powers—honed from the time he had riveted that little girl in his backyard with a vociferous lecture to the hard sell he used to get his college buddy elected to two major campus offices—the courtroom was inevitably where my father was headed. None of his family had been in law or politics—in fact, most hadn't even been to college. Yet he remembers that somehow the lawyer bug bit him early: "I wrote an essay in the seventh or eighth grade—my teacher showed it to me years later—where I said I wanted to be a trial lawyer. I'd always planned to go to law school; I just knew I would."

Albany Law School of Union University was where he chose to go. It would have been closer and cheaper to attend the University of Buffalo Law School, but I suspect his burgeoning interest in politics inclined him toward the state capital. Albany was only about a four-hour train ride from Lockport, but with the remainder of his earnings accrued as an undergraduate, he had managed to buy himself a used gray Plymouth convertible for the trip back and forth. It was his first in a long line of convertibles.

He rented a room in a local home, like all the other law students. In those lean times, boarding students from local colleges and universities was a way Albany residents brought in a little extra income. Once again, Dad's mother and generous aunts chipped in to help with the annual tuition of about $300. He also landed himself a paying job in the state legislature throughout the school year. It was perhaps a twist of fate that when he was searching for jobs around the capital, there happened to be an opening on the Republican side, for which he was hired. His political affiliation had not yet been set in stone—none of his classmates seem to remember if he was a Republican or a Democrat—but both his parents had been long-time Democrats and his father had been active at one time in Democratic ward politics. It is probable then that his exposure in Albany nurtured an interest in politics and cemented an emerging inclination toward Republican thinking.

Albany was the oldest independent law school in the state of New York and one of the oldest in the country, a midsize private institution located in a massive granite Tudor-Gothic style building a mile or two from the capital district. It claimed the distinction of having the highest number of graduates to pass the New York bar exam on the first try. Because of its proximity to state government, state officials, policy makers, and prestigious jurists visited frequently to speak, and a great many of the graduates went on to prominent elective or appointive government offices.

The class of '38 started out with ninety-six students and ended up with forty-eight at graduation. The familiar refrains of former classmates from high school and college echoed in memories of my father elicited from his law school colleagues—his fastidious attire, facility with words, ability to get by with a minimum of effort, working hard and playing hard. "Talking came easily to Bill Miller," one friend remembered. "His razor sharp mind could absorb material so quickly that he didn't need to spend a great deal of time on his studies, much to the chagrin of his more compulsive friends and his professors. Somehow he always landed on his feet, never without an answer to a question."

He often spent the evening before an exam with Joe Stephen, the class whiz, in the Fountain Grill on New Scotland Road across from the Law School, grilling him for all the necessary information in lieu of opening his own books. Ed Shea chuckled as he reminisced about how his loquacious friend would frequently borrow his class notes and then get a better grade than Ed did. And he can still remember the hoodwinked professor muttering, "If you all studied as hard as Bill Miller, you'd get someplace too."

Warren Anderson, who later became the long-time Republican Leader of the New York State Senate, recalled being on the freshman jury when Bill Miller prosecuted a case in the Moot Court Trial that traditionally capped the final semester of law school. He remembers well how Dad's innate feeling for the law and his speaking skills blended to win him the coveted prize for excellence in trial work. "That was better than being first in the class," Anderson added. "After that, everyone knew Bill was going somewhere."

During summers between law school years, he worked at a law firm in Buffalo. After securing his law degree in the summer of 1938 and passing the bar exam in October of that year, he joined a much older, well-established attorney, Montford C. Holley, in general practice in Lockport. Times were tough then, just coming out of the Depression, and young lawyers had a hard time drumming up business. Guaranteed salaries were almost non-existent. You got paid a little whenever the lawyer for whom you worked got a good fee, for all the running around you did for him—ten to fifteen dollars a week was a good start. But with only half his graduating class even able to find paying jobs that year, this newly minted attorney figured ten bucks and the experience were more than enough to get him out of the starting gate. And being the scrambler he was, he managed, despite the hurdles, to build his practice rapidly and to become a full partner in Holley and Miller by 1940.

Upon returning home to Lockport two years earlier, my father had gotten involved politically with the Young Republicans—all his new friends and associates were in that party. The Niagara County area was becoming overwhelmingly Republican, and so that was where he found his philosophical home. The local speaker's bureau for the Wendell Willkie-for-President campaign in 1940 offered him his first opportunity to flex the political muscle that he hadn't used since Notre Dame, so he signed up for speech making on behalf of the man he earnestly hoped would oust the already two-term President Franklin Roosevelt. Dad was becoming increasingly opposed to the rampant expansion of government programs that the popular president had fathered.

Later that same year, he was selected by federal judges to serve as one of two U.S. Commissioners for the western district of New York, a post he would later describe as "a glorified justice of the peace." Still, there was an element of visibility and profile in this succession of appointments and opportunities, and together with the community connections he was making as a member of the Junior Chamber of Commerce, the Rotarians, and the Elks—among others—he was gradually transforming himself into a well-known and fairly prosperous trial attorney.

It was at this point that my father met the first challenge in his life that he had to work really hard to win. He was three years out of law school and trying a messy case on behalf of a local restaurateur, whose eldest daughter's former boyfriend was attempting to extract money from her—a sturdy and comely woman still in possession of a mild Slavic accent inherited from her parents who had emigrated from Poland. Mary Wagner was her name and the principal witness in the case was her younger daughter, Stephanie. Only recently out of high school and nine years her interrogator's junior, Stephanie Wagner was reportedly "a stunning beauty who captivated him at once. Miller recalled that she was a good witness, though it would be assumed his assessment was more than a professional one."[1]

When the case was eventually won, Dad decided to deliver the good news in person instead of by phone, willingly making the twenty-mile trek out to Olcott where the Wagners owned a summer cottage on Lake Ontario. As the story goes, he pulled up to the house in his spiffy convertible, pompadour neatly Vitalised in place, and found young Stephanie alone. It was three hours later before he recalled the message he had originally come to deliver. And three dates later, on her birthday in January 1942, he proposed—"while I was still calling him 'Mr. Miller'!" exclaimed Mother, still somewhat unbelieving, in relating the story to a reporter twenty-one years later of how she was swept off her feet. That is, the gregarious attorney didn't so much *ask* her to marry him as *told* her they were going to be married. As they were strolling into dinner at a yacht club, he informed her, "I'm a man of decision, and I'm going to marry you."

But Mom didn't exactly have marriage on her mind at her young age, though she was admittedly fascinated with her suitor's "keen mind, suave manner, and quick wit." So they were unengaged, engaged, and unengaged several times. As always, Dad knew exactly what he wanted, and he would persist until he got it. His tenacity, his certainty, the confidence he exuded as an established twenty-seven year old lawyer quite simply overwhelmed and intimidated the young and inexperienced eighteen-year-old, and it took her a while to get used to him.

She herself was considered a pretty good catch, truth be told. With brains and beauty she had graduated near the top of her class at Lockport High, and she still had girlhood dreams—of going to college, of being a professional dancer or a fashion model. But her divorced mother, who had raised her alone, insisted she stay at home to work in the family restaurant. Mom was still adjusting to that disappointment—one she never fully got over—when "Mouth Almighty" himself, all grown-up, barnstormed onto the scene.

As luck would have it, in June of 1942, his amorous efforts were put on hold upon receipt of greetings from his local draft board. Pearl Harbor, December 7, 1941, and the United States' inevitable entry into the World War had necessitated a drastic increase in the armed forces. So my father, despite the fact that he was now twenty-eight years old and classified 2-A—engaged in an occupation considered essential to the national or community interest—was unceremoniously sent off to Fort Meade, Maryland, a "buck private" in the 76th Division of the 385th Infantry.

Whereupon his fiancée, the ring now back on her finger, dispatched an irate Letter-to-the-Editor of Lockport's daily paper, decrying the fact that a lawyer's talents should be put to such poor use—"putting a square peg in a round hole," as she aptly called it. Probably *not* because of that letter, but happily for Dad, and no doubt for the Army, his career in the infantry was brief. In basic training, he had taken apart a machine gun as ordered and was unable to reassemble it, such was his abysmal lack of mechanical aptitude. He always said he wasn't sure they *ever* got it reassembled.

So in short order, the Army found a more cerebral spot for the young lawyer-turned-private—assignment to the newly formed Counter Intelligence Corps, the "Spy Catchers of the U.S. Army"[2] or "America's Secret Army,"[3] as it has been called in historical retrospectives. The forerunner of the CIA, the wartime CIC operated both overseas and domestically, and it was primarily charged with identifying German, Japanese, and Russian spy networks. The CIC was formed in 1942 in response to a growing need for counterintelligence, which at the time was in the rudimentary stage of becoming an acknowledged, organized component of our national defense. In addition to vital overseas work, it was felt there was a need to ferret out covert enemy activity within the U.S., particularly so that the Russians could not utilize their military alliance with this country as a means of infiltrating and launching a substantial Communist movement within our borders.

There were four weeks of Agent Basic Investigators' training in Baltimore and later another month in Chicago, learning to become "miniature FBI agents," as one alum described it to me. The new initiates were trained in surveillance and interrogation techniques, taught how to defuse bombs and use small firearms, and instructed in the making of plaster casts for footprints and fingerprints. Karate and judo practice were part of the soldiers' weekly regimen, but marching in civilian clothes through Grant Park in downtown Chicago was probably the most curious part of their routine. Finally, after these four rigorous weeks, came my father's assignment to the less-than-glamorous sleuthing post of Richmond, Virginia. He and his fellow agent assignees joked frequently about all the menacing spies whom they would soon expose lurking in and around this genteel southern city.

Taking advantage of a weekend attached to a three-day pass in February of 1943, Special Agent Miller rushed home to Lockport to tie the knot with his patiently waiting fiancée—as the times dictated, large events were telescoped into small, hurried ones. They were to have been married in the campus chapel at Notre Dame, but like so many a wartime plan, that one was scrapped. So after a Friday ceremony in St. Patrick's Church, where Dad's Irish kinfolk had first begun worshiping almost a century before, it was off to New York City for a brief honeymoon. The trip to Hawaii that he had used to lure Mom into marriage also had to be postponed. Then it was back on the job in Richmond—only this time with a woman on his arm who would remain by his side for the next forty years. The new marriage got off to an inauspicious start when the apartment lease he had signed fell through and the only thing the young couple could find was a musty, Civil War vintage walkup with rickety, creaking steps.

The next two years were filled with some bizarre assignments, a little intrigue, and a great deal of investigative work. It was all classified and confidential. The agents did not wear uniforms but civilian clothes, allowing my father to remain the meticulous dresser that he was—Homburg hat, well-tailored suits, smart elevator shoes to add an inch or two to his small frame. They packed 38 revolvers but rarely used them. Mother remembers that their neighbors didn't even know her husband was in the Army—he could never talk about his work and they always wondered what he did.

His primary assignment was to thwart espionage within the ranks of the Army by completing background checks of high-ranking officers and enlisted men being considered for highly sensitive positions. For a little variety, Agent Miller investigated the possible sabotage of an airplane that crashed on the outskirts of Richmond, interrogated injured paratroopers at McGuire General Hospital to obtain intelligence regarding their landing in Normandy in June of '44, stood guard on the hillside near a wrecked train carrying hundreds of German POWs captured in the North African campaign to a prison camp in the mountains of Virginia, checked for sabotage in factories manufacturing military equipment, and drove all over the state in his 1940 black Buick to interview potential witnesses in espionage cases.

Amidst all this cloak and dagger work, there was, to be sure, a mild-mannered quality to the time spent in Richmond, considering the state of the world beyond: occasional golf outings at the Country Club of Virginia, after which all involved would retire to the clubhouse for some moderately high stakes bridge games that Dad always considered a sure way to enhance his fairly meager income; melancholy evenings spent with army friends on the lawn in front of the Miller's tiny red brick house on North Ashlawn Drive, nursing scotch and sodas, all the fellows yearning to return to their lives and doing some hopeful post-war planning. For my parents that included adding more to their brood of one—I had brought a touch of sunshine into their uncertain lives, born on a shivering January day in 1944. So cold was it that the pipes froze in our little bungalow while Mother and baby lay in the hospital, and after five days we returned to a heatless home.

But future plans would of course have to be delayed as the war persisted, and after two years of CIC work my father was growing increasingly frustrated that he could not contribute more to the Army in the area in which he had the most knowledge—the law. So in January of 1945, without initially realizing what a long shot it would be, he made application to Judge Advocate General's School, otherwise known as JAG.

The spots in each forty-person JAG class were fiercely coveted by lawyers throughout the Army. Despite his having all the necessary qualifications on paper and a commendable Army record, Dad would need a highly influential sponsor to separate himself from the crowd of applicants. With his talent for making the right connections, he had no doubt befriended JAG officers and other Army brass whom he encountered on visits to CIC headquarters in Washington over the last two years. Whatever it required, I am certain he went after it with a vengeance, and, not surprisingly, he was successful in securing an assignment.

In early February 1945, he departed with great anticipation for Ann Arbor, Michigan, to the temporary wartime JAG school set up at the University of Michigan Law School. Mother and I, now a year old, followed close behind by train, with assorted infant equipment in tow.

The school had officially begun in February 1942 in Washington, D.C., moving seven months later to Michigan. As World War II continued, the Army realized the need for providing its lawyers with more specialized legal education to help them handle the increased volume and complexity of their responsibilities in the administration of military justice, which the war's end would surely bring.

JAG school was rigorous, intensive work, mastering the intricacies and new developments in domestic and international military law; the professors, experts assembled largely from Michigan Law School, were top notch. A primary factor motivating absolute dedication to the learning at hand was the fear of flunking out and being sent to the front. A recent ruling from the Draft Board had announced that even young fathers were not exempt. The course lasted seventeen weeks, with half the class graduated as 2nd lieutenants and half as 1st lieutenants. On May 18, after three years in the Army, Private Miller officially and with great relief became 1st Lieutenant Miller.

First lieutenants were all sent to the new War Crimes Division of the Judge Advocate General's office in Washington. It was a plum assignment since it was at first assumed that the entire division would be going to Japan or Germany after the war to investigate war crimes. Dad's job was to research and write answers to legal questions from his superiors about war crimes on the front, though neither he nor many others at the time had even begun to comprehend the enormity of Nazi atrocities.

In addition, he made a couple of trips a month to Staten Island to interview returned prisoners of war about their treatment by the Germans. Mother and I, in the meantime, were ensconced in a rental home in Maryland, Mom doing her part for the war effort by growing a "victory garden." Despite her lack of experience in the horticulture department, we soon had corn, tomatoes, and string beans coming out of our ears, and I was still too young to help eat them.

With the dropping of atomic bombs on Hiroshima and Nagasaki in early August of '45, it became apparent that victory over the Japanese was imminent and that the nightmare of war, after six bloody years for the Europeans and four for the U.S., would finally draw to a close. The previous May 8 had already marked the defeat of the Axis powers in Europe. Churchill, Stalin, and Roosevelt had agreed at Yalta that there should be some sort of an international trial of the Nazi war criminals, though Churchill's private offhand desire had been to just summarily shoot them all.[4] Now with FDR gone, President Truman summoned Supreme Court Justice Robert Jackson to head the prosecution team for the United States.

Jackson was at first overwhelmed by the enormity of the task, for he had only a few months to organize and prepare for the most momentous and complex trial that would ever be held. "There were no precedents, no existing body of law, not even a court."[5] The half-hearted attempt to hold war crimes trials after World War I had ended in a fiasco. So he was ponderous and selective in choosing the 150 lawyers who would accompany him to Nuremberg, and he relied on a few people, like General "Wild Bill" Donovan of the Office of Strategic Services (OSS), to collect names for him. There were several Attorney and Solicitor Generals invited, all of whom brought along a cadre of associates and colleagues that collectively formed a "who's who" of the nation's legal establishment.

Since the JAG War Crimes Division did not move in its entirety to Nuremberg as had been expected, I cannot know for certain how my father made the list. It is likely because of someone he knew in JAG school, perhaps a professor who knew Jackson and recommended him. The JAG alums were a relatively small, elite and close-knit group who all looked out for one another. In addition, his almost three months in the War Department had been spent in the International Law section, which gave him a leg up on the assignment.

But as a Nuremberg colleague of his explained to me,

Connections were important but it had more to do with competence. At the top level, there were all sorts of people who were there because they were big shots. Some wanted to run for office, like Tom Dodd [future U.S. Senator from Connecticut and father of current Senator Chris Dodd]. But the lower echelons of people, many of whom went on to great heights, were highly skilled lawyers who were often more competent than the top people. Top people were glamour, lower people were hard working and picked for their ability rather than their prestige.

There was also the fact that Dad, like Jackson, was an upstate New Yorker of humble birth who had attended Albany Law School and was something of a small town "country lawyer."

Needless to say, he was extremely honored to be selected for such a challenging and trailblazing assignment. Like all the other young, idealistic lawyers about to embark on this journey, he had no idea what lay ahead, and probably only a vague sense of the history that he would be part of and would help to make. So at the end of August 1945, having no idea how long he would be gone, my father sent his teary young bride and year-old daughter back to Olcott to live with Grandma in a small cottage aptly named "We Three." Jackson had decreed that families were not invited. He shipped out to London for a few days of evidence gathering before heading on to the site of the trials, Nuremberg, Germany, arriving on September 1.

Journalist Tom Brokaw, in his book *The Greatest Generation*, makes particular note of the reticence of the World War II generation to share their experiences with their families.[6] They were called to serve and they did, and their extraordinary acts of duty and patriotism profoundly and forever changed the world, as well as our lives and theirs. Yet they found it difficult to share that time and place with those who were not there. And so it was with my father and his experience at Nuremberg. His time spent there and what he encountered became, I think, just another layer of his life that our family, regrettably, never thought to peel back and probe. So it is only from those who were with him and from the speeches he gave upon his return home that I have been able to piece together the story of that extraordinary four months of his life.

What he saw when he arrived in Nuremberg, the old walled city of toy makers, was a sight for which he was totally unprepared. Much of what was once a medieval town of great natural beauty—across the Rhine, over forests and mountains, just a little more than 200 miles from grandfather John Miller's hometown of Wormeldange—was now a pile of ruble. The panorama of destruction extended as far as one could see, every inch of undulating wreckage covered with white dust. Allied saturation bombing and artillery shelling had left upright only roofless shells of buildings and slices of walls, much like the eerie pieces of the World Trade Towers facades in lower Manhattan that were left standing after the stricken buildings collapsed on September 11, 2001. Only dim lights flickering from cellars in the debris revealed that people still inhabited them. The remnants of former roads were lined with banks of garbage; silence and death enveloped the devastation.[7]

Dad's destination was the Grand Hotel, headquarters of the trial staff. Though partially bombed, it was habitable and the U.S. Army, with the help of German prisoners, was feverishly cleaning and patching the establishment in preparation for the flood of international jurists who were daily descending upon the city. To reach the upper floors, "guests" had to walk up three flights and then across suspended planks to their rooms in the only section of the building that was still intact—the main corridor was gone.

There was, in the early days, no hot water for showers, and sleeping late was impossible due to the racket of repair crews in full swing by 7 a.m. just outside the bedroom windows. In an effort to make life in these shabby surroundings a bit more amenable, a special dining room was set up for staff, where dinners were incongruously served by German waiters in formal tailcoats. The U.S. Army, which ran everything in Nuremberg at this point, also set up an officers' nightclub to keep the troops happy, with free nightly floorshows, thirty-cent drinks and dancing to a G.I. orchestra.

After settling himself in his sparse hotel room, a new arrival like First Lieutenant Miller was taken on a tour of the Palace of Justice, or Courthouse as it came to be called by the occupying Americans, soon-to-be scene of the historic trials. It was a ten-minute bumpy ride down the road toward the town of Furth, dodging assorted military vehicles and dilapidated German cars. Its massive and elaborate Wilhelmine style façade, though slightly battered, was miraculously intact; inside, around the main courtroom, spread the maze of offices, still filled with occasional remnants of German administrations, which housed the

legions of laboring document analysts, translators, and interroga-
tors. The whole building was damp and dreary, and until they got
the heat working, cold. Behind the Palace of Justice lay the tightly
guarded jail with its twenty-two nefarious prisoners, the most
senior surviving Nazi leaders, and the gymnasium that would
house the gallows on which they would die if convicted.[8]

It appeared that the Grand Hotel would be home for a while,
since the billeting officer was temporarily on leave in Paris. But
happily for Dad, Major Frank Wallis, his superior and a fiery, aggressive Boston lawyer, arrived from London and put on a push
to find more suitable housing. Without much further delay, on the
evening of September 22, the Major, my father, and seven other
American officers moved into what had been some unknown
German's spacious private home—at 22 LindenStrasse, in a
genteel area untouched by the war, called Dombach, just beyond
Furth. It was an ideal location, ten minutes from the Courthouse
and twenty minutes from the hotel, diagonally across the street
from Justice Jackson's more luxurious quarters and, more importantly, directly across from the officers' mess which had been set
up on that street.

The house was a large brick dwelling with tile roof, surrounded by sprawling well-planted grounds and complete with
two hausfraus to clean and do laundry. Most fortunately, since
cold weather was imminent, it boasted a central heating system,
a rarity in Europe at the time. When the men arrived, they found
fresh cut roses filling every room and Mrs. Brown, their kindly
caretaker, to greet them. The first evening in their new quarters
was a convivial one, spent in unpacking and getting settled and
the drinking of more than a little cognac.[9]

Life in Nuremberg settled into a routine. The Army sent a
vehicle to pick the lawyers up at their billets and take them to the
Palace of Justice at about 9 a.m. They worked all morning and,
until mid-October when a cafeteria opened in the Courthouse,
grabbed a half-hour lunch at the Grand Hotel, then worked until
a group retired to the hotel for dinner. Evenings were filled with
planning sessions and seminars on Nazism and various aspects
of international law, socializing in the officers' club, or, as the
workload increased, working until 10 or 11 o'clock at night.

If one was lucky enough to get back to the billet early, there
were always bull sessions over drinks with the guys, or writing,

reading, listening to the radio, and in Dad's case, often playing cards. All personnel were allowed one day off a week, on Sunday. But as the deadline for trial briefs neared and the work pace took on a more feverish tone, the chief of the Documentation Division, Robert Storey, warned in a staff memo that the workweek's outlined procedures might be rendered completely obsolete.[10]

However, the Sunday routine did remain fairly sacred throughout, in the interests of sanity and balance: rugged volleyball games in the backyard of Justice Jackson's estate from 10 to 12 in the morning, followed by lunch at the Grand Hotel and a trip to Soldiers Field for a rousing football game between Army divisions. The games were quite a sight to see, with all the usual festive trappings of stateside gridiron contests, plus 20,000 attendees standing in salute when the National Anthem was played.

The frustrations were many in the early days of working on the trial. In short, it was pure chaos—trying to assign duties and define the lines of authority and responsibilities for staff members in uncharted waters, battle the potent egos of so many able and prominent men who were thrown together and fighting over turf, and control the rivalries and jealousies between divisions. Keeping up with the deluge of captured documents that were pouring into Nuremberg from London, Frankfurt, and all over Europe, with a severe shortage of translators, was an additional headache. Though it is possible no administrator, no matter how skilled, could have done better in the circumstances, it was generally felt that Robert Jackson "had neither talent nor inclination to wrestle with these problems."[11] Though a gracious gentleman, an accomplished prosecutor, and an eloquent and passionate orator, even he once allowed as how he was simply "no administrator."

The disorganization and lack of coordination and direction from the top grew worse by the day as Jackson continued to duck issues and failed to intervene in conflicts or make final decisions on anything for fear of offending people. "If a law office operated the way this outfit has, it would be out of business in no time," griped the gruff Frank Wallis in his diary.[12] Discouragement with the case was widespread and many feared the entire undertaking might come completely undone.

Dad started out in the Projects Branch of the Documentation Division, working on Committees II and III, studying war crimes and crimes against humanity. When the London evidence collection was brought over and merged with the Nuremberg collection in mid-September, he was called to Central Document Files to help integrate the two sets, index them, and set up a combined procedure for handling them.

It wasn't until well into October that the final organization plan for trial preparation was approved and implemented. The delay was due to the fact that the plan had to conform to the indictment to be handed down to the Nazi defendants, which did not take place until October 19. There had been, predictably, extended legal haggling among the four prosecuting powers—the U.S., England, France, and Russia—over the precise wording of the indictment and which parts of it would be assigned to which country. To Justice Jackson's satisfaction, the United States was given Count One and part of Count Four, and so was able to open and set the tone of the trial and control the majority of the case.

My father was assigned to work on the briefs for Count One, under Colonel Andy Wheeler and Major Frank Wallis—"The Common Plan or Conspiracy." That count concerned the Nazi conspiracy to acquire control of Germany and the means used to acquire that control, specifically, the suppression, persecution, and elimination of political opponents and all minorities. The opening of the trial was set for November 20, and the deadline for producing briefs was November 10.

Now the heat was on. The immensity of the job was frightening, especially as much of the work that should have been done over the summer still remained to be done.

The staff worked almost non-stop and late into the night for the next month. "We are all walking around in a legal fog—working our heads off. The Courthouse is as busy at 10 p.m. as it is at 10 a.m. Tempers are getting short, people are irritable, we are at last getting ready for trial and we are all getting dead tired,"[13] records Frank Wallis, Dad's housemate and case leader.

My father's job was basically to build the case for his section of the indictment—to outline the proof necessary for the case, to examine, analyze, and correlate the staggering number of documents collected on the issues of his case and evaluate their sufficiency to prove those issues, and to find additional evidence where necessary. With the shortage of translators, it was always difficult to obtain documents in a timely fashion. Another challenge he faced was in correlating evidence from the Documentation and the Interrogation Divisions—some of the evidence needed for his case would come from captured and translated Nazi documents and some would come from interrogations of the prisoners being held behind the Courthouse.

There was, however, a distinct separation, even animosity between the Documentation and the Interrogation Divisions. Colonel John Harlan Amen, a tough former New York State Attorney General with a prodigious ego who was extremely jealous of his turf, headed Interrogation, and he zealously guarded his prisoners from questioning by anyone outside his division. And yet in the numerous speeches Dad gave about his Nuremberg experience after he returned home, he recounts personally interrogating Hermann Goring and other prisoners to ascertain the authenticity of certain documents to be submitted as direct evidence in the trial.

In fact, his boss, Frank Wallis, himself quite an operator and a man with some clout in the hierarchy, knew how to work around Amen's obstinacy and often found ways for his men to interrogate prisoners if they deemed it necessary. So it is likely that he was responsible for setting up the Goring interview for my father and securing an interpreter for him, which was necessary even though the Nazi general knew considerable English, often correcting the interpreter's mistakes and laughing at humorous remarks before they were translated.

Hermann Goring, once corpulent but now reduced in size by prison fare, was the undisputed number-two Nazi after Hitler, the closest to the Fuhrer in his thoughts and actions. It was he who had been largely responsible for creating the Gestapo and the concentration camps. He was arrogant, supremely poised and confident, and totally unrepentant for the horendous crimes of which he was accused. His casual candor in confirming his responsibility for them later in court, as if it was petty theft, revealed a complete lack of shame or regret.

He was also cunning, extremely lucid, knowledgeable, well prepared, articulate, and, at times, sarcastic in his defense. Robert Jackson, the star of our prosecution team, would meet his match in Goring during cross-examination in the trial and be disastrously bested by him. In the end, this clever and manipulative man would even deny his jailers the satisfaction of executing him by taking his own life with a cyanide pill practically under their eyes. Just being in his presence, with his intimidating, unnerving stare, his feigned pleasant demeanor and calmness in the face of his dire predicament, was disconcerting and somehow menacing, and it left my usually confident father shaken.

Saturday, November 10 arrived and the weary band of lawyers limped to the finish line, filing their briefs and meeting their deadline at the appointed hour of 5:45 p.m. "But this case will go down in my mind as the outstanding example of how not to prepare a case—the lack of leadership, direction, and coordination has been outstanding," vented Frank Wallis in his diary.[14]

The boys held a much-needed celebration that night, but Dad, rarely one to miss a party, never made it. He had landed in the hospital suffering from total exhaustion. His cousin, Dick Shults, stationed elsewhere in Germany, happened to arrive that weekend to visit him and was surprised to find him missing from the house. From his hospital bed, he related to Dick the haunting story of interrogating Hermann Goring.

The next ten days until the opening of the trial were spent further refining the cases to be presented. A wire service article which appeared in the Lockport paper reported that during that last week, "Lieutenant Miller, by a personally conducted interrogation of Wilhelm Frick, former Nazi Minister of the Interior and one of the principle defendants, secured from him a sworn statement in which he implicated himself and many other defendants in wholesale murders during the early years of the Nazi rise to power."

One evening, after dinner in the mess across from the billet, my father and a few of the fellows sat around the house and talked, drank scotch, listened to music, played a bit of craps and poker. It was a clear, crisp night with a full moon and before turning in they all stood on the porch, feeling homesick and longing to be with the ones they loved. Though they and many others were skeptical at that point that all would be ready by November 20, the trial of the International Military Tribunal did indeed open as scheduled with great pomp and ceremony.

Though he never recorded his emotions on that day as he sat at the counsel table for the United States prosecuting attorneys, Dad was deeply awed by the import of the historic moment he was witnessing. "It was beyond anything that word or pen could describe," he would later say. The defendants, seated grim-faced in two rows before a dark paneled wall, were evil incarnate, but in their plain, rumpled, regalia-stripped military uniforms, they looked so ordinary, so pitiful, so incapable of conceiving and wreaking such monstrous destruction and misery upon the world. Opposite them sat the four men who would decide their fate—the judges from the United States, Great Britain, France, and Russia.

On the third day of the trial, Major Frank Wallis presented the first phase of the American case, the one my father had helped to prepare, the "Common Plan and Conspiracy." It described all that had happened in Germany during the pre-war era—seizure of control by the Nazis and the consolidation of that control by terror, the ruthless purge of the opposition, the destruction of organized labor, the persecution of the churches, the persecutions of the Jews, the militarization of the youth and of the country—all in preparation for a gigantic war of aggression aimed at the domination of Europe and the world. Wallis used 438 documents for his case, winnowed down from the thousands Dad and his team had processed.

To celebrate the successful presentation of their case, Wallis and Andy Wheeler, the Section 1 chiefs, threw their staff a huge party that night at their quarters. And what a party it was—tail-coated waiters from the hotel, the mess sergeant, formerly of the Stork Club in New York, serving up five hundred canapés, two cases of liquor consumed, singing and piano playing, "just a hell of a jolly drunk," Wallis records.

As the trial continued into early December, it became apparent that it would drag on for a very long time, well into the following year. In fact it would not end until October 1, 1946, with nineteen defendants convicted—twelve condemned to death by hanging, seven to prison terms—and three acquitted. Twelve more trials of 190 lesser defendants would occupy the next three years. The language problem throughout was monumental and tedious, as every word of the proceedings was translated into French, German, Russian, and English. There were also the diplomatic problems—forcing lawyers and judges from four disparate systems of jurisprudence to somehow reach agreement on the myriad of issues and technicalities that arose daily.

My father attended the court sessions most days, riveted by the reactions of the defendants to their own words in incriminating documents they never knew the prosecution possessed, and to the sickening concentration camp films shown in court. But, except for loose ends, his work was done. The bickering and in-fighting was growing worse and living conditions less pleasant, and the prospect of spending Christmas in Nuremberg was not a happy one—even with the little silver-tinseled Christmas trees the maids had placed in each room of their house. The court, over Justice Jackson's protest, declared a two-week holiday recess, which precipitated a flood of requests to be relieved of duty to return home, Dad's among them.

After more than three years in the service, he, like so many others, was eager to get back to his wife and family, to restart his life. He had acquired the requisite points for discharge and if you had a good enough reason, Jackson would let you go. Affidavits from home arrived to provide the reason: "his mother and young family needed him." So with a morass of bureaucratic red tape thus avoided, Lieutenant Miller was happily set to depart for home on December 12, alongside his colleague and friend, Frank Wallis.

There was, of course, one last party in the old billet. The nine men, strangers who had been thrown together to share so many long and pressured hours and untold amounts of cognac and talk, spent their last Saturday night as a group reminiscing and looking forward. They opened Christmas boxes sent from home and sang songs with lyrics they had composed about the trial and various members of the staff—"all verses ending with the lines 'Bring on the tickets, we are heading for the U.S.A.!'—which line was lustily sung."[15] Captain Whitney Harris composed a poem of farewell "To Frank and Bill," with an imagined last will they might leave to the house and the staff:

> To bewildered Storey we leave the glory
> To ambitious Amen the degree of layman
> To wandering Dodd the help of God
> To bumptious Gill daily volleyball drill
> To the boys at our billet our liquor we will it
> And to dear Mrs. Brown what we cannot down
> To Jackson, we laugh, a brand new staff
> And to all the rest—the very best.
> For these fine bequests we both of you thank
> Good old Bill and dear old Frank.

Dad played his last volleyball game in Justice Jackson's backyard the next morning, despite the 16-degree temperature. Then there were packing and release papers to tend to and a final sumptuous dinner at the Grand Hotel with the full staff. On a cold snowy Wednesday morning, bright and early, he and Frank bade a fond but relieved farewell to the house and boarded their ride to Frankfurt. Whitney Harris told me years later that he regretted seeing his young colleague go—"He was one of the most likeable members of our staff, kind and amiable, and dedicated to his work."

The ride over the snow-covered mountains to Frankfurt was at once magnificent and perilous, inching their way at ten miles an hour past an unsettling number of wrecked vehicles. Once safely in Frankfurt, the pair picked up their orders, which called for ship priority to the U.S. from Le Havre on the coast of France, then boarded the night train to Paris.

A chance meeting on the train with an acquaintance from Lockport, Lt. Frank Wendyes, who was stationed outside Paris in a lovely Versailles chateau, gave a boost to their next day. They were the grateful recipients of a welcome shower and shave at Wendyes' quarters and a car and driver for a day of sightseeing to Montmartre, the Left Bank, and the Champs Elysees.

The next day, a jeep and a farm boy from Nebraska named Butch arrived at the chateau to drive the two homeward bound soldiers to Le Havre, a seaside town northwest of Paris, whole sections of which had been obliterated by German bombs and artillery during the invasion of Normandy. After discovering they were listed on the USS *Lincoln Victory*, all that remained was to wait. But the long hoped for prospect of being back on American soil and reunited with their families by Christmas was not looking good.

Sunday, December 16, arrived and Dad and Frank had reason to believe it would be their last day at Camp Home Run, the "dismal hole," as Frank described it, which was the Army's temporary holding base in Le Havre. They sat around and read and griped and speculated on whether or not they would make it home for Christmas. When the sun came out they took a walk down to the beach—the devastation of the German fortifications there was stunning. Finally, at 11:30 that night, a huge tractor truck picked up the soldiers—luggage, blankets and all—and delivered them to the docks. As they rumbled through the wreckage of this sad city, they hoped never again to see such destruction and misery.

Their less-than-luxurious quarters were in the aft hold of the *Lincoln Victory*, thirty-nine officers in one room. But as "it is clean and as we are heading home, nothing matters,"[16] wrote Frank. The men finally fell asleep about 2 a.m. and when they awoke four hours later to a brilliant sunrise, they discovered to their chagrin that they were still dockside. Shortly thereafter, two tugs appeared to pull their ship out to sea, and they were on their way to Boston harbor. After a thoroughly wretched ten-day passage in rough waters, they arrived home on December 27. It would not be a Christmas to remember.

Frank Wallis and my father—colleagues, housemates, shipmates—parted ways on the blustery docks, one having reached his final destination but the other with one leg of his journey yet to go. When at last Dad reached Lockport, there was so much to make up—a Christmas to belatedly celebrate, a law practice to restart, a house to be found for his now reunited family, little time for sentimentality as my mother remembers, despite their four-month separation. After a hectic ten-day leave—he was not officially separated from the Army until mid February—the soldier attorney was off again to Washington, where he met with the English and American appointees leaving for Tokyo to prosecute Japanese war criminals, to give them the benefit of his experiences at Nuremberg.

Nuremberg had been the single most important and formative event in my father's life to this point, after Notre Dame. It left him with a burning desire to uphold personal freedoms, for it would be a vivid and enduring reminder that they must never be violated for any cause. It shaped his convictions on many legislative issues with which he would become involved in future years, but mostly it instilled in him an appreciation of the potential dangers of overly intrusive government. "Nuremberg was a seminal, pinnacle experience for all of us; nothing afterward has quite reached this," he once admitted.

The trial was called at the time "an ambitious attempt to forward human justice, an imaginative but risky innovation in international law."[17] Dad and the other participants hoped, even assumed, that what they had created would have some kind of permanence, would stand, despite its flaws, as a precedent with which the world could pursue justice and maintain sanity in the future.

But that was not to be. While the trial succeeded in documenting Nazi Germany's atrocities in excruciating detail for all time and beyond question, it has not deterred aggression nor crimes against humanity, and the precedent it set in international law of punishing those responsible for war crimes has not been consistently followed. In the intervening 50 plus years, until the late 1990s, there have been 24 wars between nations, costing six and a half million lives, and 93 civil wars and wars of independence taking another 15 and a half million lives. There were Cambodia, Uganda, El Salvador, Nicaragua, Yugoslavia—and not once, until 1993, was the conscience of the world so outraged as to mobilize the punishment of the ruthless perpetrators.

When I was invited to the 50th Reunion of the Nuremberg participants in Washington, D.C. in 1996, as a relative of a participant, that was the regret I heard the most. Young men and women when they went to Germany in 1945, these old legal warriors were now well into their eighties and this reunion would no doubt be their last. They were anxious to share their thoughts, afraid their memories and insights would die with them.

They were at least somewhat cheered when almost fifty years later "the ghost of Nuremberg began to stir"[18] at long last, as author Joseph Persico optimistically put it in his 1994 book on the trials. In 1993, the United Nations Security Council had voted unanimously to create an international war-crimes tribunal to prosecute atrocities perpetrated in Rwanda and the former Yugoslavia. While the drama of Nuremberg was absent from those trials, as well as the focus of the world, there was at least the hope that with the legal precedent set in the Palace of Justice five decades earlier, "law that supercedes nations and justice that penetrates frontiers may yet be achieved."[19]

Sad though it is, however, my father and so many of the Nuremberg alums did not live to see this glimmer of hope for the fruits of their work. And what they did not and could not have anticipated in 1945 is how much more troubling and difficult the concept of justice that crosses international borders has become in the 21st century than it was even in their day.

CHAPTER FOUR

CONGRESS—FIERCE FIGHT OVER THE NIAGARA

My father returned to Lockport in 1946 a war hero of sorts, a local celebrity. His experience in Nuremberg was beyond what most in that small, quiet town in western New York could even imagine. They were hungry for a first-hand account of all they had been reading about in their papers for the past six months. So invitations to speak at meetings, luncheons, and dinners of various civic groups began pouring into his office. By 1948, the erstwhile assistant prosecutor estimated he had given 200 speeches on the war crimes trials to a wide area of the state and parts of Canada. He would describe the purpose and significance of the Nuremberg trials and address some of the controversies that continued to swirl about them.

The legacy of Nuremberg has always been a mixed one. There were those critics, fifty years ago and still today, who question the validity of the court—what legal authority did other nationalities have to pass judgment on Germans for the crimes they initially committed in Germany against Germans? And, as regards crimes they committed during war against other peoples, were only the Germans guilty? What about their allies, the Italians, or the crimes of the Russians, or for that matter, America dropping the atom bomb on Hiroshima and Nagasaki? Did it all just amount to victors' vengeance upon the vanquished, or was it a fair trial?

If my father had any doubts about the fairness of the Nuremberg trials, he did not voice them in public. Privately, Mother remembers that in fact he did have some faint nagging legal doubts, but overall he felt that, considering the complexity of the undertaking, they were brilliantly executed and fairly and humanely judged. And that it was vital they be held, for as Nuremberg author Joe Persico put it: "Could the Allies merely walk away from murder so vast and so calculated?"[1] Political commentator George Will once wrote that the tribunal "served the unique imperative of civilizing postwar vengeance." Dad, too, believed there was a thirst in the world at that time for all that evil to be overcome by good—for justice, however flawed.

The most recurrent and enduring charge was that the trial was "ex post facto justice"—that it tried acts which were not defined as crimes until after the fact. Counts One and Two of four counts against the German defendants concerned their actions in initiating aggressive war, or "crimes against peace" as they were called, when, at the time, critics alleged, there was no international law making aggressive war a crime. The trial was setting, they claimed, a dangerous new precedent.

But my father maintained in his speeches that the International Military Tribunal (IMT) was on firm ground on this issue, inasmuch as Germany was the first signatory of the Kellogg-Briand international pact of 1928 outlawing war as a method of settling disputes. The twenty-two Nazis on trial in Nuremberg, who planned and launched a war in Europe in 1939, were indeed the first violators of that pact and were guilty of an illegal act. He added that since international law had been essentially archaic up to the Second World War, one of the purposes of the IMT was to set precedents that would clarify and strengthen that law for the future.

In reply to criticism that the trial took too long, that it could have been done with more simplicity, with just enough evidence to convict, Dad would point out that the prosecutors were not only trying twenty-two Germans in Nuremberg. They were also creating history, collating and preserving thousands of documents of evidence for the world record, "all of it authentic and irrefutable, of unbelievable cruelty and sadism." The value for peace, he said, was that with all the evidence of guilt which the trial supplied daily to German newspapers and which could be used to teach German school children about the Nazis, another generation could not arise that doubted their nation's culpability in launching World War II and murdering millions of helpless peoples.

Of course, at the time he was speaking on Nuremberg, it was too early for a definitive verdict on the trials, and he knew that. He knew that only the perspective of time could reveal their enduring significance, and even more than a half century later, that verdict is still out. But what he firmly believed and spoke about in his time was that as a nation we must be ever vigilant not to repeat Germany's mistakes, as unlikely as that might seem.

He urged constant awareness of the buildup of hatred between groups and races, and he would warn of that danger often throughout his political career.

"Disinterest is the real danger," my father also warned, "and the lack in our country of the interest that is required of everyone in a democracy should be of concern to all." I remember him repeating the old adage years later, in urging civic involvement upon his children or his various audiences: "If you're not part of the solution, you're part of the problem." Hitler could only happen, he believed, because the masses relinquished involvement, reason, and control—a good lesson to remember today when often little more than half our eligible voters cast ballots in local and national elections.

As time wore on, interest in Nuremberg waned as people, including Dad, got on with the business of life. He resumed his partnership with Montford Holley and returned to the general practice of law, with new contacts and sources of business garnered from his speech making. Upon the unanimous recommendation of county Republican organizations, Governor Tom Dewey appointed him an assistant district attorney, which, happily, provided additional income and visibility for his interrupted but burgeoning legal career.

He continued in that position until January 1, 1948, when the governor appointed him district attorney for Niagara County to fill an unexpired term. His appointment was ratified in the regular election the following November by a majority of over 13,000 votes. It was the same election in which Dewey was the surprised loser to Harry Truman in his race for the presidency and Democrats swept to a landslide victory across the country.

The DA job was part-time but busy. And Dad had become a father again—I had a new baby sister named Mary Karen. Mr. Holley was now quite elderly so his young partner formed his own practice with another lawyer friend, Hank DeLange. Hank described his partner of those many decades ago as a sharp trial lawyer with a marvelous voice and a quick grasp of a situation, in continual demand as a speaker and master of ceremonies—"He could speak so well extemporaneously, and he always had a feel for what people wanted to know and hear." Soon, the two took in a third partner, Fred Smith, and Fred recalled how much Dad taught him about practicing law in those days. He'd say,

"Freddie, you can make money practicing law, not necessarily because you have a great knowledge of the law—you can look that up in a book—but it's knowing how to handle people, the juries and courts, your clients."

Newspaper coverage of my father's years in the district attorney's office tells of a fearless and energetic crusader for law and order and for the cleanup of local government corruption in a no nonsense style. He was successful in convicting the chairman and another member of the Niagara Falls Zoning Board of accepting bribes, and he launched a zealous crackdown on illegal gambling in his district. In a day when we're surrounded by legalized gambling in Nevada and New Jersey and elsewhere, not to mention the plethora of state lotteries, this priority seems almost quaint. But law-abiding citizens in those days were incensed at these supposed dens of iniquity in their midst.

There was one particularly large and opulent gambling emporium, The Four Corners Club, operating clandestinely on two floors over a restaurant in North Tonawanda. Law enforcement officials had been trying for nearly two years to close it down. They had pulled six raids, but each time the operators had been tipped off in advance and the raiders found no incriminating evidence. Finally, "they fell prey to the top-secret machinations of Mr. Miller,"[2] as well as the sheriff and chief of police.

After six weeks of careful planning and the hiring of two special investigators to infiltrate the operation, the trio personally led two wagons full of deputies armed with tear gas, axes, and sledgehammers on a spectacular surprise raid worthy of a season-finale of *Law and Order*. The day ended with 300 arrests, twenty-four indictments, more material and paraphernalia than they could process, and a once prosperous establishment in shambles. That event precipitated a chain reaction of other private gambling clubs closing themselves down for fear of a similar fate. Mother recalls that throughout Dad's gambling cleanup campaign, there were threats on his life and ours, as well as bribes proffered to lay off the lawbreakers. My sister and I were too young to be aware, but it was a tense and frightening time.

But the real crisis point of my father's term as a young district attorney, covered prominently even by Washington, D.C. newspapers, was unquestionably the riot he quelled during an eighteen-week CIO labor strike at the Bell Aircraft Corporation near Lockport in late summer of 1949, for that action was to have continued repercussions on his future political career. It presented a conundrum that he was to face many times—the intersection between the need for law and order and the occasional necessity for drastic action to further legitimate demands. He was a sympathetic, caring man, but at the same time, he believed fiercely that change should come peacefully and within the boundaries of the law that he was sworn to uphold. The two sides of his nature often battled for dominance.

Bell Aircraft held lucrative government contracts for defense work. The CIO United Auto Workers Local 501 that struck the plant in June 1949 demanded a ten-cents hourly pay boost and a pension plan. The company apparently was unwilling to enter into collective bargaining to settle the strike, and, as it dragged on, more and more engineers, technical people and office workers, whose unions were not on strike, made the decision to cross picket lines and return to their jobs.

These non-strikers were frequently harassed, but on the morning of September 7, they were met at the main gate of the plant by a "goon mob," as the local papers described it, armed with guns, clubs, stones, ammonia, and an array of other terror-wreaking tools. They assaulted, kicked, punched, and cursed the workers, pelted the mounted sheriff's deputies with stones, stopped worker-loaded buses, broke their windows, and beat the hysterical passengers. People bound for work by car were forced out of their cars, chased, and beaten with clubs, sometimes right in their own yards and in front of their families. Scores were injured and hospitalized. District Attorney Miller issued an urgent call to Governor Dewey for state police assistance for the overwhelmed local forces, as the violence continued into a second day.

It was at this pivotal point in the ever deteriorating strike that my father made his dramatic visit to the Bell plant by helicopter, where he interviewed the injured in the infirmary to get their affidavits for use in prosecutions. He also spoke passionately to the several hundred employees inside who had managed to safely break through the dangerous melee and get to work, assuring them that they had every right under a court order to cross the picket line and that they would have police protection to do so. But he also cautioned them that they did not have the right to retaliate.

Dewey chartered a plane to fly the union chief, the sheriff, and the DA to Albany for a peacemaking conference. The union leader refused to go unless "Miller withdraws the trumped-up warrants for the arrest of our leaders," to which Dad, conspicuously short on patience for lawbreakers, offered the emphatic rejoinder: "There is no possibility whatsoever of the warrants being withdrawn. I don't give a damn if he ever goes to see the governor. I'm surprised he is not in jail himself. I'm almost certain there is a warrant out for him too."

After two days, union leaders called off the riot. The situation remained tense but peaceful, and the strike was finally settled several weeks later. After a month-long trial that my father repeatedly emphasized was not an anti-labor union trial, five of the twenty-three men originally accused were convicted. Among them were the top two local union officials, which proved, the DA pointed out, that the violence was planned and executed at the highest levels. Of the other three convicted, one was a local Bell plant striker and the other two were imported from elsewhere, as riot specialists, it was implied.

Dad, of course, thereafter became the target of union charges that he was "pro-capital and pro-management," a charge that deeply pained him, since he had come from a family of laborers. He emphatically maintained that a non-striker's right to work and a striker's right to strike peacefully were equally important. He often bemoaned the fact, increasingly a part of public life, that "you're called pro-management if you're interested in maintenance of justice and preservation of law and order." The validity of the union's demands was not for him to judge, though he might have been sympathetic to them. His job was to prosecute those who broke the law to pursue them.

Despite the union leadership that was henceforth to work actively against him throughout his career, many of the rank and file of labor were loyal supporters, grateful for the strong stand he had taken on their behalf. Local papers praised the young DA for his courage and efficiency, for thinking more of the duties and obligations of his office than the votes he might lose by his drastic action. They noted that the thorough evidence he amassed in his cases often forced guilty pleas that eliminated lengthy trials and saved taxpayers money.

Contrary to the impression created during this period by my high-energy father that he was extremely ambitious and might be aiming for higher office, he had no such plans. A local reporter remembers he later recounted his public life "as if every event were no more than an interruption in his law practice. 'I never went into the state retirement system—much to my (later) chagrin—because I never expected to stay in public life.' Indeed, he says he even considered his district attorneyship as temporary until he built up his private legal practice." [3]

The event that changed the course of Bill Miller's life was another man's decision—in 1950, incumbent Republican Congressman Bill Pfeiffer of the 42nd District, which included Lockport, Niagara Falls, and parts of Buffalo, decided not to seek reelection. After more than three active years in the Niagara County DA's office, Dad was the obvious Republican candidate to replace him. In fact, there was little discussion of anyone else. When approached by Pfeiffer and the county organizations, however, he shocked the upstate political world by announcing that he was not interested in the office—"in the best interests of my family." The reality was that he now had two children, his law practice was flourishing, and he was not eager to take on the added expense of maintaining two homes, one in Washington and one in New York, should he win.

Several weeks later, he turned political prognostication on its ear by announcing he was available, explaining: "I have been prevailed upon by my many friends and associates in private and public life to reconsider my decision." Among the voices prevailing most strongly upon him was his wife's—Mother offered that it was a great honor to be asked to run and that one term in Congress would be a good experience and might enhance his law practice. Bill Pfeiffer also convinced him that Congress was a part-time job. In truth, the idea of public service was becoming more appealing to my father after his years in the Army and the DA's office, though it was always at war with his fear, typical of many a Depression child, of the associated financial struggle.

His one stipulation if he were to run for the Party's nomination for the congressional seat was that he must receive the endorsement of Republican organizations in both Niagara and Erie Counties, the two counties that comprised his district. This was forthcoming without a hitch. He then ran in the primary as the endorsed candidate against two independents and defeated them decisively by 12,000 votes. His Democrat-Liberal opponent in the November election would be an attractive teacher from Tonawanda, Mary Louise Nice.

With the beginning of the campaign, the repercussions from the Bell strike began, and they continued to dog him throughout the race: "CIO plans all-out drive in 42nd congressional district for Miss Nice," read the headlines. The local CIO-PAC even planned to mobilize the state organization to work against the man who had incurred their wrath by prosecuting their members for rioting. Dad repeatedly refuted the charge that he was anti-labor, and his consolation was that over 2,000 CIO members had signed his petition, proof that it was mostly the leaders and not the rank and file of labor who opposed him. The local papers, which endorsed him unanimously, concluded that the attacks and misrepresentations of CIO leaders were turning out to be an asset for the Republican candidate.

It was no surprise then when Miller won the election handily by nearly 23,000 votes or 60 percent of the total ballots cast, with a whopping 77 percent voter turnout, exceeding even the hopes of his staunchest supporters. All told, he had spent approximately $1,500 on a campaign that was considerably less complicated than modern day endeavors—little television, a few newspaper and radio ads, some small fundraising dinners, but mostly up close and personal encounters with citizens in bingo halls and fire stations, at card parties, rallies, cookouts, civic clubs, and ethnic gatherings. District committeemen went door-to-door distributing campaign literature.

In the end, my father was helped by the fact that nearly the entire Republican slate in the state won; it was a mid-term election during Harry Truman's presidency and there was widespread dissatisfaction with Democratic economic policies and Truman's handling of the Korean War. But local party leaders interpreted their new political star's convincing victory as the voters' repudiation of the labor leaders who had actively campaigned against him.

So, life in Washington began. It would last far longer than my parents at that time imagined, and end far differently. They made the initial decision not to move the family to Washington during the time Congress was in session. Since we now owned a home in Lockport, and I was firmly ensconced in first grade, the neophyte congressman decided he would just return to Lockport whenever breaks in his schedule allowed.

When he flew to Washington the day after Christmas in 1950, his first order of business was to find himself bachelor accommodations. It was not easy—housing in the nation's capital was at a premium, and not very affordable for someone of his limited means. There were members of Congress with personal resources who were settled in lovely Georgetown townhouses, but this was not an option for my father.

He did find his congressional digs spacious, by the standards of those days—three rooms instead of two to house his lean staff of three on the top floor of the Old House Office Building, now known as the Cannon building. He had the foresight of Gib Darrison, the experienced legislative assistant whom he had inherited from his predecessor and who already knew the ropes in the office assignment game, to thank for that coup. Gib would remain a loyal friend and aide to Dad for his entire career.

Home after his first few days as the freshman congressman from the 42nd district of New York in January of 1951, he summed up the experience as having both bright and difficult sides. He had been sworn in with the other 434 members of this large and raucous body "as if they were a group of draftees being drafted into the army."[4] It would be interesting and exciting for certain, but, for starters, his spiffy 1949 green convertible, parked only a block away from the House Office Building on Capitol Hill, had already been stolen.

The second complication was in gaining admittance to the House chambers to hear President Truman deliver his State of the Union address. "I was a little late in getting to the House and went to the door of the Democratic side of the chamber. The doorkeeper didn't know me and told me I couldn't enter," the newly-sworn legislator reported. He didn't bother identifying himself, but finally found his way to the Republican side and was welcomed in. Always able to laugh at himself, he seemed to get a big kick out of his first faux pas.

In a few months time, my father decided he would indeed move the family to Washington. This was not a part-time job and he abhorred living alone in a hotel room, eating out, and traveling back and forth, all of which he had to pay for out of pocket. There was, however, a frightening delay in the moving plans when Mother had a serious automobile accident in Lockport and landed in the hospital with a fractured skull. As soon as she recovered and sold the house, home for the four of us became a small, red brick, rented bungalow in Alexandria, Virginia.

Mom and Dad enjoyed the novelty and excitement of Capital life for the first term. The pace was hectic, what with entertaining a constant stream of visitors from home, the requisite volunteer work, and endless social events that impinged on family life. There were more invitations to teas, luncheons, bridge parties, garden parties, embassy receptions, White House functions, and other assorted congressional affairs than could ever be accepted. Mother, at the tender age of twenty-six, found herself totally overwhelmed, as the youngest member ever of the 82nd Congress Club, composed of wives of congressmen who began serving in 1950. Before she figured out how to say "no," she was elected its second president and found herself hosting the likes of President and Mrs. Truman, Mamie Eisenhower, Pat Nixon, Queen Elizabeth of England, and Queen Julianna of The Netherlands. It was a long way from Lockport High School.

My father came to Congress with high expectations placed upon him by his district. They expected from him the same courage he had shown when he opposed a powerful labor union he believed was wrong. Coming with high popularity from a politically stable district, it was thought he could become a "career congressman" who would someday head a powerful committee if he desired, though that was far from his intentions.

It was also noted that he came to the nation's capital with an understanding of the Communist threat—the major preoccupation of the era—that exceeded a mere book and newspaper knowledge. Dad often related how he had tried to work with the Russians during the Nuremberg War Crimes Trial, but soon realized that they had no intention of being a real ally of ours. He believed they had first started working against us with a vast espionage system many years earlier. And he understood that the basis of our strategy in dealing with Communists must be firmness, for if you give them a little, they will take a lot.

While he disclaimed the McCarthy hearings for their excesses and the manner in which the ruthless and over-zealous congressman from Wisconsin conducted them, he did believe there was a need to investigate subversive influences both in and out of government. Though I personally wish he had denounced McCarthy more strenuously, it is difficult for us to comprehend today the hysteria over Communism so prevalent at that time, an hysteria exacerbated by the Russians' testing of an atomic bomb and the start of the Korean War in 1950.

Above all, the constituents of the 42nd District thought it unlikely that the time-honored tradition in Congress of freshmen being seen and not heard would prevent their feisty new congressman from letting his colleagues know what was on his mind and theirs—and they were right. He wasn't in his seat but a few weeks when he introduced a bill that would launch the fiercest and most protracted fight of his congressional career, spanning his first seven years in Washington.

The fight was to keep the development of a vast new hydroelectric power project at Niagara Falls (it would be the largest such facility in the Western world) out of the hands of the government and to get it built by private enterprise. An accelerated atomic energy program in support of new defense plans after Korea had necessitated the production of significant new quantities of electricity.

The crux of the problem confronting the government and the American public was where to get the additional power and who should bear the costs of building the new facilities. Though there had been a trend toward public power development in the late 1940s, many legislators, with their heads now bumping against the debt ceiling, were beginning to oppose new plant construction at public expense, believing that the tax-paying, private electric industry could and should meet the growing peacetime need. The Niagara power issue would become part of the classic private vs. government-financed power debate that had ensued since the late 1800s, involving other projects in other places, but rarely with such bitterness and tenacity.

This legislative battle would pit my father against the most potent politicians in New York State—Governors Tom Dewey and Averill Harriman, Senators Herbert Lehman and Jacob Javits, Congressman Franklin Roosevelt Jr. (derisively nicknamed "Junior" for his ambitious and publicity-seeking efforts to fill his late father's shoes), and above all, Robert Moses, New York

City Parks Commissioner and legendary czar of public works in the state for over four decades, a fearless, intimidating man who rarely lost a political battle. All these men had the ability and the wherewithall to make his political career a short one. Common wisdom said: "Don't fight Bob Moses, you can't win," for he could and did ruin, politically and personally, people who opposed him. So powerful was Moses in the state that Dad must have seemed like an annoying flea on his back that wouldn't go away.

But none of the above fazed my father. He believed passionately in private enterprise, that it was a vital part of the foundation upon which our country was built and has remained strong, and that it was part of the platform he ran on when he was elected decisively in 1950. In addition, private power was clearly the mandate of his largely conservative constituents—every time he polled them on the Niagara power issue, 90 percent favored private over state or federal development.

By 1952, his congressional office had accumulated eight bound volumes of letters, proclamations, and resolutions from individuals, cities, towns, counties, and villages, from farmers and industrialists, and from every civic organization imaginable throughout his district and the state in support of his private Niagara power bill. Three-quarters of the state's newspapers and almost the entire New York congressional delegation was behind him. Even his erstwhile adversaries, the labor unions—thirty of them, including the New York State Federation of Labor—endorsed further development of Niagara Falls power by private industry. "You can strike, bargain, and negotiate with industry," they admitted; "you can't do that with the government." But all that support notwithstanding, Bob Moses and the powers-that-be insisted that either the state or the federal government must own and run the project.

The saga of the Niagara power fight began in 1950 with the Niagara Redevelopment Treaty between the United States and Canada. The magnificent, scenic spectacle that is Niagara Falls straddles the international border between the two North American cousins. As the second largest waterfall on the globe next to Victoria Falls in southern Africa, it attracts some twelve million tourists to view its awesome beauty each year. One fifth of all the fresh water in the world lies in the four upper

Great Lakes—Michigan, Huron, Superior, and Erie—and their vast runoff empties into the thirty-six- mile long Niagara River, eventually cascading with a deafening roar over the vertical cliffs of dolostone and shale that form the falls. This large dependable flow also gives the site the greatest concentration of natural hydroelectric power potential in the United States.

Preserving that beauty had always been a common interest of the U.S. and Canada. Numerous informal agreements over the years had stipulated how much water each country could safely divert from the Falls for other purposes, without impairing this great wonder of the world. The 1950 treaty formally fixed certain minimum flows of water, which varied with the season of the year and time of day, and authorized the diversion for power purposes of all water in excess of those minimums equally to the United States and Canada. There was, at the time, a vital need for additional power on the Niagara Frontier, one of the oldest industrial areas in the nation, to feed industries essential to the national defense. The hitch was that when our Senate ratified the treaty, it specified that Congress, rather than the Federal Power Commission, must authorize any further development project on the American side.

Seven more years would pass before that authorization would occur, so convoluted were the politics involved in the issue and the gridlock that resulted. In the meantime, Canada hopped right on their end of a redevelopment project, starting construction in 1951 and completing it in 1954. While our Congress remained interminably embroiled in controversy about who would construct our part, Canada was able to use the millions of tons of water flowing over the Falls daily that belonged to the U.S., thus benefiting their economy at the expense of ours. My father, more than once, called this "an American tragedy." But I'm getting ahead of myself.

When Dad submitted his bill to the Congress in March of 1951, with full constituent support behind him, he was confident of success for several reasons. First and foremost, government in this country had rarely undertaken a project whose sole purpose was the production and sale of hydroelectric power, with no dam involved. Government had only been involved in producing such power when it was the by-product of multi-purpose public works projects, such as dams for navigation, flood control, reclamation, or irrigation (like the massive TVA development in the Tennessee Valley), or when the size and complexity of the project was beyond the means of local or private enterprise. In those cases, even my father would support public development.

Secondly, Niagara Mohawk Corporation and its predecessor, the largest of the five-company consortium of private utilities that proposed to develop the new Niagara power, were the only entities that had ever built and operated hydroelectric facilities on the American side of the Niagara River, and they had been doing so, with a license from the Federal Power Commission, for over fifty years. This new project would only be an extension of their facilities that were already in place.

Time and experience had taught these private utilities how to solve the considerable engineering problems of producing this power, such as controlling the enormous ice jams that often impeded the flow of water in the river in winter. They owned the land and rights of way required for the additional development, had drawn plans for the project as far back as 1920 in anticipation of the growing need for electric power in the area, which plans were now updated and still technically and economically sound, and they were prepared to start construction at once, without the further studies that the state or federal government would be required to do. Dad quipped that "the Army Corps of Engineers probably didn't even know where the Niagara River was," and that "the State Power Authority had never even owned or operated a power plant."

There was one last important factor that he felt was on his side—cost. The projected price tag was 400 million dollars. Niagara Mohawk and the four other private power companies, which together had been providing 90 percent of New York State's power for many years, were able and ready to finance the new hydropower project in its entirety, without the use of public funds. My father's point was that since taxpayers were already staggering under a heavy load of taxes for defense and economic and military assistance to other nations, why should their money be spent on something private industry could pay for? Seemed simple, but it wasn't.

There were two competing plans offered for consideration to the Congress—the Roosevelt/Lehman bill for Federal construction of the Niagara project and the Dewey/Moses plan for construction and ownership by the New York State Power Authority. The proponents of both bills professed outrage at what they called a "power grab" by greedy private power companies to take ownership of "the people's water" for their own profit. They claimed that in the end, absent the profit motive, state or federal government could provide cheaper power for consumers.

My father's reply to these charges was that all of America's resources belong to the people—coal, gas, timber, oil—but that if we allow the government into the mining of coal, the pumping of oil, the cutting of timber and all industries related to our resources, we will have complete socialism: "If you let government get into everything that belongs to or serves the people, you destroy competition and end up with a socialist economy, which we as a nation long ago rejected."

He insisted that the American approach had always been to let private enterprise develop these resources, subject to regulation by a public service commission that would set rates and limit profits, so as to prevent price gouging and monopolies. He loved to quote Governor Dewey himself on the subject who, upon returning from a trip to the Far East in 1951, had this to say: "Only in America, where the power industry has largely remained free of government ownership, is there still an almost adequate supply of power ... it was driven home again and again that competitive private enterprise is the only system which can meet the needs of a modern society." The reason for the Republican governor's change of heart on this issue when it came to Niagara power development can only be surmised, but it could have been related to the iron hold the indomitable Robert Moses exerted over most elected officials in the state.

Though it might seem that a tax-paying private industry would have to charge more for power than a tax-exempt government subsidized enterprise, Dad contended that the typical inefficiency of a government operation negates that difference: in a private operation, there is "no payroll padding, no lugheads who don't know the business because they are good ward healers." But more importantly, money would have to be found somewhere to compensate for loss of the substantial taxes that the private power industry paid, once government puts them out of business. The five private utilities in New York were paying $170 million dollars in taxes in 1952; after redevelopment, they would pay an additional $23 million. For the city of Niagara Falls, that meant one-third of their entire revenue. Local taxes would inevitably have to be raised to pay for the shortfall.

Well, despite the prestigious competition, my father's bill finally made it through the House of Representatives in 1953 with votes to spare, 262 to 120. All but one of the Republican members of the New York delegation, Jacob Javits, voted for it, and 32 of 41 members of the entire delegation voted in favor. This was no small accomplishment for a freshman congressman. His elation, however, was to be short-lived.

When the legislation moved on to the Senate Public Works Committee late in the session, an irate Governor Dewey requested an urgent appearance before its members for the purpose of squelching the measure's momentum and pleading for a state power bill. And that succeeded in blocking any further Senate action on the Miller bill until the next session began in January of 1954. How ironic it was that the very man who had launched Dad's political career by appointing him assistant district attorney of Niagara County in 1946 was now to be his nemesis.

But before the next session opened, a political bombshell landed in Western New York: "Congressman Miller, who has single-handedly been leading the crusade for private power development of the Niagara, will not run for reelection to his seat again in 1954," headlined the local newspapers. The announcement—"As a husband and father of two small children I could best serve my family from both a financial and paternal point of view by retirement from the burden and rigors of public life"—came as a complete surprise to his friends and supporters and all Republicans in the district, who were convinced he would become a fixture in Congress. Even his mother and his Lockport law partner professed to know nothing of his decision.

An additional reason for my father's retirement that surfaced was that he was "sick and tired of hearing Congress complain about being hamstrung by pressure groups." He claimed his patience was exhausted with congressmen who tell him they won't work for a particular piece of legislation because labor or farmers or some other organization doesn't like it. "You seldom hear anyone say, 'I'll vote for this because it's good for America,' " he declared. He made those remarks in a speech to the Buffalo Rotary Club, in a moment of pique, and though he later denied that they constituted his real reason for deciding to end his brief political career, I suspect there was some truth to them.

Everyone in Washington recognized, of course, that lobbyists were a "necessary evil," but that reality didn't keep politicians from President Truman on down from frequently lashing out at the influence peddlers. In 1946, Congress passed the Federal Regulation of Lobbying Act, which attempted to put pressure groups in a goldfish bowl. They were supposed to tell all—how much they receive and from whom, and how much they give and to whom. But the law was so vaguely written and unenforceable (the Justice Department had tried without success to penalize violators) that it came to be regarded as a joke, and each year fewer lobbyists took the trouble to register.

"The only way to avoid legislation by pressure groups is to have 100 percent participation of all Americans in voting," Dad claimed. He was deeply concerned that only half of all eligible citizens bothered to register or vote and that, absent a clear mandate from the people, well-heeled pressure groups often get away with "legislative murder." Does this complaint sound vaguely familiar today?

He was an efficient, get-it-done person. His experience as a trial attorney had been that if you do your legwork thoroughly and present a solid, irrefutable case, you usually win the day. What he was learning now in Congress, after three years of frustrating work on the power bill and other legislation, was that the right thing, the best thing, does not always win, due to the pressures of interest groups. One of his biggest disappointments had been that he couldn't even get the Eisenhower administration, which was on record as pro-private enterprise and against "creeping socialism," to abandon its neutralist stance and muster the courage to come out strongly in support of his private power bill. There was too much fear of losing the political support of Republican powerhouses in New York like Dewey, Javits, and Moses, all of whom supported state control of the Niagara power redevelopment project.

But the primary reason for my father's early decision to bow out of politics was, as he said, personal—the family. The demands of the long hours, weeks, and months spent on congressional work were keeping him from spending much time with us. There were always at least two or three meetings or social events a week to attend at night, and Mary and I were usually in bed before he returned home. And the truth was, there wasn't anything more important to him in his life than his family—not even Niagara power.

At the beginning of the hot Washington summers, the four of us would pack half our belongings, it seemed, into boxes to ship to our summer cottage in Olcott on Lake Ontario, stuff ourselves and two black cocker spaniels into our Oldsmobile and Chevrolet and set out, caravan style, on the thirteen-hour carsick ride north for a three months stay. Congressmen were required to maintain a legal residence in their district, and though ours was small and unpretentious, the anticipation of returning to that idyllic spot each year was thrilling for all of us.

The sad fact was, however, that sessions of Congress stretched later and later into the summer as the years went on, sometimes until late August or early September, so by the time Dad got back up to Olcott to join us for the things he loved most—steak cookouts with sweet local corn and tomatoes, family croquet and badminton matches, boat rides on the lake—we were about to return to Washington to begin the new school year. Then he had to spend the better part of the next two to three months back in the district, either campaigning for reelection or tending to constituent concerns—he felt he owed that to the people who supported him. This topsy-turvy life was unquestionably not family-friendly.

The bottom line was that he simply did not feel he could *afford* to stay in Congress any longer—the financial sacrifice was too great, as it was for many others who were not born wealthy. Maintaining two homes on a salary of $15,000 a year was a strain. By the time he paid for the high cost of living in the Washington area, our private school bills, and his taxes and campaign expenses, there was little left over. He also averaged at least twenty-four air trips back home for political obligations and public appearances during the eight to nine months when Congress was in session. "How many trips did the government pay for?" a reporter once asked him. "Only one a year," answered Dad a little sadly.

Despite all those understandable reasons for retirement, a move began in mid-1954 among Republicans in the district to draft him, or at least pressure him to reconsider. Area newspapers editorialized about what a loss he would be, not only to the area but also to the Congress and the nation, and that he was "destined for higher things if he could afford the sacrifice of a public career."

They praised him extravagantly for "his independent voice that has been heard and respected in Washington," "his courage in resisting pressure groups and taking a stand even when it was not popular," "his effective championing of private enterprise," and "his accessibility and attentiveness to his constituents' concerns and problems, regardless of political affiliation." The *Niagara Falls Gazette* gushed: "He is one of the ablest representatives this district has ever sent to Washington." The press also mentioned the unfortunate truth that "if he leaves the fight now, private development of Niagara Falls will have lost its most effective champion." Letters from friends and supporters began deluging my father's office.

The sincerity of this outpouring weakened his resolve. After some deep thought and counseling with Mother and with local party leaders, especially William Lee, a former state senator who had persuaded him to start his political career in the first place, he changed his mind—much to the relief of Republicans who had no idea how they would replace him on the ticket, and to the chagrin of Democrats who were salivating over his seat. In announcing his intention to run for reelection in 1954, Dad admitted: "I would be less than human if I did not say that this response has been one of the most gratifying and heartwarming occurrences of my life."

I think the primary factor that in the end influenced him to run again was the realization that he could not leave the Niagara fight until it was finished, that he had a moral obligation to shepherd a private enterprise bill through the Senate and, on behalf of his constituents who were so heavily counting on him, to make certain there was no federal or state control of Niagara resources. He had thought the battle might be over by the end of his current term, but, thanks to Governor Dewey's eleventh hour move and the lack of political courage characteristic of an election year, it was now likely his bill might get bogged down in the Senate and be carried over into the next congress. Besides, it would give Dewey, Moses, and company way too much satisfaction to leave the Niagara power field wide open for them to triumph.

Despite the reapportionment of his district to his slight disadvantage, my father was reelected by an even greater margin—33,000 votes—than in his previous elections. Since Niagara power was the single most controversial and debated issue in the campaign and since he defeated a candidate who championed a combined federal-state approach, he interpreted his victory as a resounding mandate to press on with his crusade for private power.

But his running feud with Moses, Dewey, Roosevelt, and Lehman continued unabated, and nothing could dislodge the Miller/Capehart bill from the Senate Public Works Committee in 1954. Dad still contended, to no avail, that his opponents' plans were against the overwhelming wishes of the people of his district and the state, that there was near unanimity among the states' newspapers and chambers of commerce on a preference for private development of Niagara Falls power, and that the Niagara area could be economically destroyed by the loss of millions of dollars in taxes if the private utilities were put out of business.

As predicted, his bill died in committee that year. It was a major disappointment, and would have been even more so had he known that was the end of the only Republican-controlled Congress he would ever see. The process would have to start all over again in the 84th Congress beginning in January of 1955. This Niagara power battle was already one of the most protracted and fiercely fought legislative battles in congressional history. And Robert Moses was just getting warmed up.

The newly appointed chairman of the New York State Power Authority, now emboldened to throw his weight around even more, threatened to "fight in every court in the nation if necessary" to prevent private development of Niagara River power. The resultant court fights could delay our use of the American waters for ten more years, he warned. "Rule or ruin" appears to be Moses' motto, alleged one editorial—"if he can't have his way, we won't get anything." Lucian Warren of the *Buffalo Courier Express* noted ruefully, "Before this issue is settled, the torrents of words on the subject may well exceed those of the spill over the Niagara."[5]

So new bills were introduced and my father trudged on, repeating his impassioned testimony before the House and Senate

Public Works Committees, and pleading with his colleagues not to pass a public power bill that would send the bulk of Niagara power out of state. But hearings continued until adjournment once again put off a decision until the following year. It was now 1956, the second session of the 84th Congress, and power experts were saying the cost of the six-year delay in development of Niagara power on the American side of the river was incalculable.

Then disaster struck. On June 7, 1956, at 4:30 in the afternoon, before hundreds of horrified onlookers, three earth-jarring rockslides sent two-thirds of the huge Schoellkopf power plant tumbling into the foaming Niagara River gorge half a mile below Niagara Falls. The largest hydroelectric station in the sprawling Niagara Mohawk power system lay in ruins. And after six long years of exhausting legislative battling, the hopes of Congressman Miller and all the private power advocates in the state went down river with it. Just completing eighth grade, I do not recall the ca-tastrophe even registering on my teenage radar screen, but it was a surreal and crushing event for Dad.

There was now a power emergency on the Niagara-Erie Frontier. Niagara Mohawk was forced to buy power from Canada at exceedingly high rates to supply the many vital electrochemi-cal and metallurgical defense industries it served. The power was so expensive that these consumer industries would soon have to severely curtail their operations or relocate, costing tens of thou-sands of jobs. The area was in danger of becoming a ghost town, and the need for prompt action was urgent.

Despite the emergency situation, the power issue remained stalemated for the remainder of the 84th Congress, with neither private nor public power advocates yet willing to compro-mise. There were "some rough tactics on the part of the public power crowd to eke out an 18-16 vote in the House Public Works Committees in favor of the Lehman-Buckley Public Power Bill,"[6] which the Senate had passed earlier that year. But the bill was subsequently blocked from reaching the House floor for debate by the Rules Committee—the conservative congressmen who sat on that committee would sooner sell their grandmothers into slavery than vote for public power.

By the time the 85th Congress opened in January of 1957, my father knew, with the instincts of a realistic politician, that he now had to compromise more drastically than he had ever imagined.

It was possible to rebuild the Schoellkopf plant and proceed with private power development of the rushing waters of the Niagara, but the new Congress was once again Democratically controlled, so there was no hope of getting a private bill through the liberal Senate, and less hope of getting a public bill passed by the more conservative House. That meant continuing deadlock, which would not serve his district well.

Additional pressure for an immediate settlement had also developed: a rancorous and lengthy civil rights debate was looming, and if passage of a Niagara bill did not happen quickly and smoothly, it could well get shunted aside again. Time was of the essence. The statement Dad issued through the media to his constituents explaining his new course of action was tinged with sadness and regret.

His first priority now was a workable bi-partisan compromise solution of the Niagara redevelopment problem. He was determined this time to secure the consensus of all his erstwhile opponents before he even introduced a bill. So he got New York's Senators Ives and Javits to join him in sponsoring the bill, lined up Governor Averell Harriman to urge the state's Democratic congressmen to vote for it, and at long last won the public endorsement of the Eisenhower administration. Robert Moses was still deviously trying to circumvent the Congress and get a quick license for his Power Authority, but when it was denied, he, too, came on board.

The compromise deal would authorize the State Power Authority to build and operate the new generating facility, but require them to give the private utilities, who would surrender their water rights to the state, a role in the distribution and sale of the power from the Niagara project. Most importantly, it would establish a system of payments by the tax-exempt Authority to the Niagara area in lieu of taxes.

The settlement was disappointing and disheartening for my father, but he believed it was the best he could get. He opened his oft-repeated testimony before the Public Works Committee, for the seventh straight year, with the weary words: "I sincerely hope that throughout your career in public office you will never have to fight so bitterly and so long as I have to protect the best interests and earnest desires of your constituents."

Then began the intensive legwork. It was no mean feat to sell the new formula to some very balky conservative Republicans, to convince them that a public power project on the Niagara, even though working in partnership with private enterprise, was the correct solution. He spent endless hours in Capitol Hill's cloak-rooms healing the breech between Republicans and Democrats on the issue and quietly cajoling diehard private power enthusiasts, with whom he had been formerly allied, into forsaking their traditional dislike of any form of public power to save the critical industrial complex of Western New York. He remarked, upon emerging from a meeting of conferees from both sides, that his group "was just as happy as if they were attending a funeral."

The interminable saga of the Niagara power battle at last came mercifully to an end. The House passed my father's joint compromise bill in August of 1957 by a decisive 313 to 75 votes, and soon after the Senate followed suit, perilously close to ad-journment. He and Senator Robert Kerr, Democrat of Oklahoma, were given primary credit for pulling together the impressive bipartisan coalition.

The victory was bittersweet. The fight at Niagara had been called the supreme test in the U.S. between two ideas of govern-ment—and Dad's idea had not prevailed. But at least it meant the earthmovers and steam shovels might move into action at Niagara Falls by the coming fall to start the now $600,000,000 power project, and the suffering economy of his district might be rescued. The liberal big guns in the state had had their way, at the expense of the people's wishes, and the hope of Niagara area residents now was that they would not pay too big a price for "getting the job done" on a compromise basis.

Local newspapers thanked Bill Miller for all the years "of vig-orous and courageous, albeit frustrating, efforts to have Niagara's power redeveloped in the traditional American way, by private enterprise," and they professed to understand, though regret, his final decision to compromise. I expect my father felt the pen Ike sent over to him after signing the bill into law on August 21, 1957, was small compensation for the lack of support the president had given a loyal Republican for seven long years.

So what happened in Niagara Falls after the legendary power battle of 1951-57 ended? In 1958, the New York State Power Authority launched what had by then grown to a $720 million project. It was completed in 1961, by which time Niagara Mohawk had ceased power production at the oldest privately developed major hydroelectric site in the country, driven out of business by a competitor who paid no taxes. The end of private power removed in excess of $41 million of assessed valuation from the city, school, and county tax rolls. To help ease the burden on local taxpayers, the state legislature directed the Power Authority to pay the city and the school district a paltry $3.7 million over a four-year period. Despite these payments, a sizable increase in local tax rates became necessary.

Robert Moses had trod through New York State like a colossus, claiming that public authorities were efficient and cost the taxpayers nothing. The press and the public believed him for forty years—he was a legend, a feared and fearless defier of politicians. But Robert Caro, a Moses biographer, concludes that public authorities were inefficient, indeed very wasteful, and they caused a tax loss that drained cities. And he asserts that Moses, the appointed public works "czar," neither questioned by or responsible to the public, ran roughshod over democratic processes, never compromising, or taking community considerations into account in his decisions.[7]

Moses had insisted early in the battle between public and private interests in the Niagara project that tax assessment losses would more than be made up by new industry, as well as by expansion of the existing industrial complex, all of which would be spawned by the increased power supply. But no new industry arrived. And the expansion of existing industry was undercut by the costly modernization programs needed to convert their equipment to meet the state's requirements. Industrial employment in Niagara Falls dropped from 29,000 in 1956 to 19,000 by 1961.

The State Power Authority's Niagara project license expires in 2007, and a relicensing process is currently underway. There is a board, numerous committees, a website—all studying the allegedly negative effects on the area of the compromise legislative decision forty-five years ago to put the further development of power at Niagara into public rather than private hands. That's the problem, the locals now say—there was no study done in the beginning on what the long-term local impact of public power might be. Robert Moses was not interested in that.

So much of what Dad predicted came true: the tax base was lost so taxes went up, industry cut back or left, unemployment rose, property values declined. It was a veritable ripple effect. And, moreover, by the time the public Niagara hydroelectric project served the whole state and areas outside the state, Niagara Falls never got the cheap power it was promised. As early as 1962, only a year after the new facility opened, *Buffalo Evening News* reporter Jerry Allen saw what was happening. He wrote my father for material to develop a story about power rates at Niagara Falls being higher than ever.

So what did the city get in return for losing a major portion of its tax base? That's what school boards and local governments are now asking. The general consensus four decades later: not enough to compensate for all they lost. So, this time around, the locals intend to extract as much as they can from the Authority in return for backing their license renewal. There is mention often that if Bill Miller had gotten the private power development he and so many others who really cared about the area had wanted, things might be different on the Niagara Frontier today.

After rolling up his biggest personal majority to date in the election of 1956, when he was finally, he hoped, on the threshold of wrapping up the power fight, Dad appeared so secure in his seat that he might keep it indefinitely if he chose. But with one of the major jobs he had come to Washington to accomplish completed in 1957, he once again began to contemplate private law practice and a quieter life back home.

Before he had announced anything officially, one local paper got wind of his quandary: "A popular legislator is home from Washington to wide, public acclaim for a spectacular achievement and disquieting, personal thoughts on his political future." As he mulled the same financial and family factors that had nearly prompted him not to run for reelection four years earlier, political prognosticators predicted: "It is extremely doubtful that anyone will be able to change his mind this time."

"Where do I go from here?" he mused in one interview. "I am forty-three years old now and have been in Congress eight years. I think I've reached the point where I either have to hope to become a permanent congressman or do something else. In later years, there may be no choice." He also had another concern.

Amid all the adulation for his accomplishments, he understood that his long battle over Niagara power and the eventual compromise he won was politically expensive in his home state. "Remember a man named Tom Dewey?" smiled Dad. And he recalled 1953 when he had clashed with the powerful three-term former governor on the power bill. "Mr. Dewey doesn't forget," he said wistfully, "and he is still a big political force in this state." But then, "there is more to life than politics," he added.

He was haunted by the risk of waiting too long to leave: of being away from the practice of law for so long that he lost touch, of going out a loser rather than a winner. But the upside, which became clearer to him as he discussed it all with Mother, was that his influence and effectiveness in Washington was growing. Building seniority in the nation's capital is a slow and tedious process, and he was finally enjoying, he admitted, the recognition and respect of his peers for his speaking and legal skills and for his independence of judgment.

More and more frequently the Republican Party was coming to him with special assignments, and the Campaign and Speakers Committees of the Republican National Committee and Congressional Campaign Committee were enlisting him to speak all over the country on behalf of Republican candidates. After making one national telecast, he received a tongue-in-cheek telegram from some old Notre Dame buddies, designed to ensure that he not become too inflated with his increasing importance:

It is the wish of these citizens of the great Midwest that the government shall follow policies as set forth by you today. We pray that all members of the Class of Thirty-Five will be alive to back you when your name is put forth for higher office, not withstanding the fact that few of the class thought you would ever graduate, much less reach the high pinnacle in government you now are inhabiting.

Also enticing was the fact that if Congressman Ken Keating, who was running for one of New York's Senate seats, was elected, he would vacate his spot on the House Judiciary Committee and Dad would move up to second ranking Republican member. Judiciary was the work he loved the most and where he spent the greatest amount of his time. The higher you ranked, the more influence you had on legislation. Keating once wrote him that his "sound judgment, judicious approach and conscientious study of the issues have contributed greatly ... You have had an important voice in the formulation of much significant legislation. You have been an effective force in preventing much unwise legislation."[8]

After considering all this and heeding the usual pressure from the local GOP high command, my father ran again in 1958 and handily defeated his opponent, a man whom he had beaten once before. Finding anyone willing to run against him was an increasingly difficult task for the Democrats. With his 35,000 vote plurality, he had also bucked the national trend, for it was otherwise a disastrous year for Republicans across the country. Amidst charges that the Eisenhower administration had let the nation's defense systems slide, many less fortunate candidates were plowed under by a Democratic landslide.

As he turned his eyes back to Washington, D.C., Dad realized he had much work left to do there. A century's worth of turmoil was coming to a head on the threshold of the nation's capital, as issues of civil rights for black Americans could no longer be ignored.

CHAPTER FIVE

CONGRESS—A ROLE IN THE FIRST CIVIL RIGHTS DEBATE

Just as the seemingly interminable fight over Niagara power was nearing a welcome end, Civil Rights surged front and center on the congressional stage. It would be the major issue to concern my father, indeed all the legislators, for the next several years, and he would play a significant role on the Judiciary Committee in shaping the first bills to emerge from Congress since the Civil War, arguably the most important legislation of that or any decade. "The political giants of the 1950s and 1960s ... wrote the social, environmental, and civil rights policies that to this day shape political debate in America," wrote newspaper columnist Joel Connelly.[1]

Dad had been appointed to the House Judiciary Committee only a few months after he began his first term in 1951. It was the lawyers' committee, one of the most important committees of the Congress. At that time, about 70 percent of the most substantive legislation that moved through the House came from Judiciary. It was a plum assignment for a freshman, and both parties picked their members carefully. Democrat Emanuel Celler of Brooklyn ruled Judiciary with an iron fist.

Most of the work of congressional committees is done in subcommittees, which are assigned the various bills that come to the main committee. It is there that key battles are fought over crafting legislation that will ultimately reach the House or Senate floor. Subcommittee #5, Anti-Trust and Monopoly, was the busiest and most prestigious of House Judiciary's five subcommittees, assigned highly controversial legislation such as civil rights. It was Manny Celler's baby; he chaired it and he picked its members.

Like my father, Manny was tough and bright, and he knew how to play a hard political game. They both possessed an acerbic wit and an acute grasp of the law. Manny liked the young Bill Miller for that, so he eventually selected him as one of three Republicans for his Anti-Trust subcommittee. But his new recruit was blunt, outspoken, and never reticent about taking a stand, and he and the fiery, liberal, partisan chairman, who dominated the committee and ran a tight ship, often locked horns on the legal technicalities of bills. When Dad bested Manny on a point of law, the chairman was not pleased. Yet he would often seek my father's legal advice. In the end, they shared a mutual respect and an unusual friendship, and even on occasion co-sponsored bills.

Dad grew into a difficult position on the committee. In 1958, Bill McCullough of Ohio became the ranking Republican member of Judiciary, just ahead of him. He was an old school gentleman: reserved, a bit stubborn, well motivated, but not a forceful leader of the minority. Congressman George Meader of Michigan, who ranked just below my father, was much the same. Celler cultivated McCullough assiduously, always including and elevating him, so as to neutralize the ranking Republican and make him less inclined to oppose the chairman. This irritated Dad, forcing him to be the tough Republican on the committee, the one to voice dissent when the minority disagreed with Manny's approach.

A letter from the chairman of the Federal Communications Commission in 1957 pointed up another of my father's tasks: "I wish to thank you for your vigorous and courageous statement … in answer to Chairman Celler's outburst at the Federal Communications Bar Association luncheon. Would that more Republicans had the courage to refute broad generalizations and groundless charges with the simple facts as you did," he wrote Congressman Miller. I have no idea what Mr. Celler's inflammatory comments were, but he was known for being occasionally intemperate in his impatience to get things done. Apparently Dad was sometimes required to use his diplomatic skills to smooth feathers the irascible chairman had ruffled.

Otherwise, his role on Judiciary came to consist more of clarifying and refining legal points than of crafting legislation. He would press witnesses about inconsistencies or obfuscation in their testimony, without insulting them or hitting below the belt—there was no grandstanding for the television cameras as often occurs today. He listened well. When he spoke, he was persuasive and articulate, with the tenacious investigative skills of a probing prosecutor, and his legal opinions were highly respected by fellow committee members. "When he fired away in his inimitable manner," recalled Dick Peet, former Republican Counsel for the Judiciary Committee, "everyone, Republicans and Democrats alike, would sit up and listen."

The 1957 Civil Rights Act was a landmark law, the first to address inequality between the races since Reconstruction. Though it has been eclipsed in historical memory by the far stronger Acts that followed it in 1964 and 1965, it made those laws possible. Though it was considerably watered down by the time it reached President Eisenhower's desk, the very fact that a civil rights bill could finally pass both the House and the Senate, despite the virulent and decades-long opposition of Southern Democrats, was in itself a momentous milestone. "The Civil Rights Act of 1957 was hope [for African Americans]," asserts author Robert Caro.[2] Indeed, it breached southerners' resistance and began the erosion of legalized separation of the races in America. My father played an important role on the Judiciary Committee as one of the architects of this groundbreaking bill.

"When a Civil Rights bill is passed, a Republican president will do it," predicted Oscar DePriest in 1940, the first African American elected to Congress since Reconstruction. Republicans did, after all, consider themselves the heirs of the Great Emancipator, Abraham Lincoln. And their record since then had been admirable. The Thirteenth Amendment to the Constitution outlawing slavery, the Fourteenth prohibiting states from abridging rights of citizens, and the Fifteenth prohibiting states from denying the right to vote because of race were all passed by Republican-dominated Congresses, with the approval of Republican presidents. The first Civil Rights Acts (from 1866 to 1871) were all passed by Republican Congresses and signed by Republican presidents.

In 1877, a Democratic-dominated Congress attempted to repeal these civil rights laws, but President Hayes, a Republican, vetoed the effort. Then, in 1894, thirty-nine provisions of the Civil Rights Acts were repealed under Democratic President Cleveland and a strongly Democratic Congress. Nothing happened in the field of civil rights for black Americans after that, until 1957. Republicans made many attempts in the intervening years to pass legislation, but their efforts went down to defeat by Democratic filibusters. It always seemed ironic to Dad, in light of that record, that in the mid-twentieth century the Democrats claimed to be the great champions of civil rights, a claim that went largely unchallenged.

Now by the 1950s, some Republicans had turned more conservative with regard to the powers they were willing to grant the federal government. It was a reaction to the vast expansion of that power during the New Deal years. Yet they were still not as divided on the civil rights issue as were their colleagues across the "aisle," as the passageway separating the two parties' seats in the houses of Congress was called. Though liberal Democrats were eager for civil rights legislation, they understood that the bitter and divisive battle it would undoubtedly launch within the ranks of their party would be politically far too expensive. Harry Truman had learned that lesson when he proposed comprehensive civil rights legislation in 1948. It predictably failed to pass the Senate, where powerful southern segregationist senators, all Democrats, had a stranglehold on the crucial Judiciary and Rules Committees.

Oscar DePriest's prediction notwithstanding, when Dwight Eisenhower, the first Republican president in thirty years, was elected in 1952, the issue of civil rights for black Americans did not appear to be at the top of his agenda. The Cold War and the nation's defenses seemed far more pressing, and he felt that progress, albeit slow, was already being made in the field of civil rights by quiet, administrative actions. Eisenhower was once heard to say, "I don't believe you can change the hearts of men with law.... If you try to go too fast in this delicate field that involves the emotions of so many millions of Americans, you're making a mistake." But as fate would have it, if he were not to lead the country in this, he was forced by fast-moving events to respond, as the long-festering civil rights movement came into its own on his watch and inexorably gained momentum.

The mileposts of the movement whirred by in a kaleidoscope of anger, bloodshed, and fear—*Brown vs. Board of Education*, Rosa Parks and the Montgomery, Alabama bus boycott, Emmett Till's brutal murder, U.S. Army troops in Little Rock, a defiant Governor Orville Faubus, frightened black children huddled at the doors of all-white schools, lunch counter sit-ins, Martin Luther King's peaceful marches. Now there was no going back, or even standing still. It became a battle of wills: the more southerners resisted the new court rulings, the harder black people, and those who had come to their aid, pushed for their long-overdue rights.

There was no question that Congress had to act. But in what fashion? With what haste and severity? That was the critical dilemma. The Thirteenth, Fourteenth, and Fifteenth Amendments to the Constitution, as well as numerous laws and statutes on the books since the late 1800s, had already established the equality of races before the law and the right to vote and use public accommodations free of harassment. Yet quite obviously those statutes had not been enforced.

What's more, individual states retained the right to make their own voting rules, so in spite of federal laws, states found ingenious ways to circumvent and undermine them. In the South, intimidation, official apathy, and obstacles such as poll taxes and literacy tests meant that few African Americans registered to vote. In the North, segregated schooling was *de facto* law due to the segregated neighborhoods and school districts that resulted from the "white flight" to the suburbs following *Brown vs. Board of Education.*

In spring of 1956, Attorney General Herbert Brownell, with Eisenhower's tacit support, finally took the bull by the horns and sent down to the House Judiciary Committee some guidelines for writing civil rights legislation. Then the battle lines formed. There were essentially three camps: northern liberals who wanted to force upon southerners wide ranging legislation that would right a myriad of wrongs all at once; conservatives from the South and elsewhere who felt that any interference by the Congress in state laws such as voting rights was unconstitutional and totally unacceptable; and those in the middle who were genuinely supportive of civil rights for African Americans, but wary about the violations of the constitutional rights of others that hasty passing of the necessary legislation might produce.

My father fell into the third camp. The bills he initially co-sponsored and introduced on behalf of the administration were essentially the same as Judiciary Chairman Celler's bills, if somewhat less inclusive. They called for a new division and an additional assistant attorney general within the Justice Department to monitor civil rights abuses; and they established a Bipartisan Commission on Civil Rights to investigate allegations of abuse, appraise the effectiveness of existing civil rights laws, and submit a periodic report to the president on its findings and recommendations. Hearings on the various bills dragged on for months before the Anti-Trust subcommittee, the full Judiciary Committee, and finally on the House floor. Emotions rose to the boiling point about the particulars of the bills, and whether there should be any bill at all.

The procession of southern witnesses before the committee—assorted governors, attorneys general, and congressmen—unwittingly began to educate Dad and the other legislators on the dimensions of the civil rights abuses they had been tolerating in their states for decades. In Mississippi, Governor Coleman offered the fact that, out of nearly a million black residents of his state, only 8,000 voted, and he seemed to think there was nothing unusual about that statistic. When my father pressed him as to how he could explain the discrepancy, he surmised that it was because they hadn't paid their poll tax. When he was probed about what sort of questions prospective voters were asked when they applied to register to vote, the governor characterized them as "routine vital statistics." The actual questionnaire was revealed to contain the following: write and copy a section of the Mississippi Constitution selected by the Registrar, write a reasonable interpretation of that section, and write a statement setting forth your understanding of the duties of citizenship under a constitutional form of government.

Dad was shocked at what he was hearing in committee sessions day after day, almost disbelieving. At one point he requested that Chairman Celler call witnesses before their committee who had personally experienced the discrimination that was being described. The allegations of abuse made by organizations representing the victims, such as the NAACP, were so egregious that he somehow wanted to make certain they were real. Southern officials had continually denied these inequalities with such eloquence, vehemence, and sincerity.

In reading the transcripts of these committee hearings, the evolution of my father's thinking on the problem emerges. It was complex and multi-layered, not as easy to resolve as it was for those on both extremes of the issue. The more he heard, the more he understood the compelling need for change. Yet he was torn between two deep convictions: as a humane man, he knew it was time, once and for all, to ensure equal treatment of all Americans, regardless of the color of their skin; but it was also necessary to safeguard the states' rights and limited government he believed was so vital to our system, and certain individual rights that can too easily be trampled in the rush to right old wrongs. This belief in the sacredness of the Constitution and the sovereignty of states' rights was not for him a cloak for racism, as it was for many legislators from the eleven states of the Old Confederacy. It was a sincere and honest conviction.

Despite his growing awareness of the grievous injustices being suffered by black Americans, Dad felt the Congress faced at this juncture a potentially dangerous situation with regard to individual rights. The 1957 Civil Rights bill, as originally proposed, would allow unsubstantiated allegations of civil rights abuse to be brought before the Civil Rights Commission; those accused would have no right to a trial by a jury of their peers. This, he feared, was a slippery slope. The racists who would deny black citizens their constitutional rights were unappealing, even despicable; but if they were charged with a civil rights violation, their legal constitutional rights must be safeguarded as vigilantly as anyone else's. That is the American way, he said, just as we must protect the right of free speech for proponents of all sorts of popular and unpopular political and social views.

There was one more factor at play in my father's thinking. As a realistic politician, he understood all too well the necessity for the art of compromise. He saw that no civil rights bill would ever survive the pothole-laden path through Congress without an attempt to make it somewhat palatable to the southern bloc. As weak as the resultant bill might be, he finally determined it would be better than no bill at all.

He was admittedly frustrated by the seeming inability or unwillingness of southerners to grasp the urgent and obvious need to change their ways. They could not understand the gap between their professed reverence for the Constitution and their failure to honor it for all Americans, and would not respond to legitimate black demands for equality. Yet he was also somewhat sympathetic to their horror at the prospect of hordes of Washington bureaucrats descending upon their towns and cities, restraining orders in hand, harassing and looking over the shoulders of their registrars, councilmen, mayors, and police force. As a proponent of small federal government himself, he understood to some extent their passionate determination to hold on to the rights they believed the forefathers had intended for the states. Even though that determination was now frequently a cloak for the perpetuation of segregation, it was deeply embedded in their history.

The particulars of election laws had always been a prerogative of the states to set and regulate—with all due respect to the framers of the Constitution, perhaps not such a good idea in retrospect, considering the discriminatory laws that existed uninhibited for so long in the South. The Constitution does, however, give the U.S. Congress the authority to change state regulations; the need to do that was becoming increasingly obvious and imperative in the 1950s, even to constitutional conservatives like my father.

He pressed the southern witnesses before his committee on what they found most objectionable about the administration's civil rights proposals, attempting to discern if there was anything at all they could accept. But it soon became abundantly clear that they were opposed to any and all bills. So he then set about trying to correct the legal flaws and pitfalls he himself began to see in the bills.

Despite vigorous debate in subcommittee in 1956, he was not able to obtain the perfecting changes he had hoped for in the legislation that he, Senator Ken Keating, and others had fashioned on behalf of the administration from Attorney General Brownell's guidelines. Nevertheless, he voted the bill, as it was, out to the full Judiciary Committee. When the full committee finally sent it to the House floor, the bitter debate that ensued there still did not result in the amendments he had championed. Chief among them was an amendment that would provide for a jury trial for anyone called before the Civil Rights Commission and accused of abusing the civil rights of another. Dad considered the jury system the central and inviolable feature of American justice.

So at this point, he made a move that stunned some of his Republican colleagues and bill co-sponsors and angered the administration, which he had largely supported. It was one of his independent, I-don't-care-how-many-votes-it loses-me stances, based on what he believed was the right thing to do at the moment. It was considered devious by some, courageous by others.

He rose on the House floor on July 19, 1956, to move a parliamentary procedure that would kill the administration bill he had co-sponsored. He opened his statement with these words:

As one who all my life has believed and even now believes fundamentally in the proposition of civil rights; as one who sponsored this legislation; as one who voted for it in the subcommittee and in the full committee, but as one who after further deliberation and after listening to the debate, and one who is a lawyer, I must in good conscience state that I make this motion in utter sincerity because I am profoundly convinced that this legislation in its present form will destroy more civil liberties and civil rights than it will ever protect.

My father rarely spoke on the House floor, and when he did, he was known to have a solid legal perspective that was generally respected on both sides of the aisle. Minority Leader Joe Martin was, therefore, alarmed. He rose after the speech, red-faced and barely controlled, to "regret the statement of my good friend from New York" and to warn his Republican flock that "if they follow the southern democracy in the defeat of this bill, they will seriously regret it."[3] Dad's motion was defeated, and the bill went on to be passed by the House, without his vote. There was no chance of it going on to the Senate that year, as everyone knew, for it was late in the session and southerners on the Senate Judiciary Committee, chaired by staunch Mississippi segregationist James Eastland, would be certain to keep it bottled up until adjournment. Which they did.

My father's stance had been a tough personal and political one for him to take, and though it may have seemed precipitous, he had made it after long agonizing and soul-searching. He went against the wishes of his president and many of his constituents and colleagues, as well as his own real desire to see a civil rights bill succeed. It was also a decision that would come back to haunt him. That one vote was held against him many years later when he ran for vice president, in an attempt to portray him as a racist.

I have often wondered why he risked so much on a stand that was politically incorrect and unpopular and that made him appear to be siding with the allegedly racist southern bloc. He had stated that he voted against the measure "not because of any 'unholy alliance' with the South, but because of my profound devotion to the constitutional system of government which I have taken an oath to protect and preserve." He obviously understood the political risks, but, as a colleague from California explained many years later, "He wanted to bestow equal rights in a fair and equitable manner."

Immediately, Drew Pearson, the widely-read, unabashedly liberal and muckraking columnist of those days, charged that Dad was just "scratching someone's back in return for a favor that someone will do for him." Specifically, Pearson alleged that if Miller would try to block civil rights, two southerners on the Rules Committee, Colmer of Mississippi and Smith of Virginia, would agree to block the Lehman Niagara Falls public power bill. The power bill that my father so disliked had already been passed by the Senate. The only thing that could thwart its passage that year in the House was a blockade in the Rules Committee, of which Colmer and Smith were key members.

While congressmen do indeed make occasional tradeoffs or "deals" on behalf of their pet bills, those two congressmen had voted consistently against public power throughout their careers; they were known to be solidly behind private development of Niagara Falls power. So there was hardly a need to make a "deal" for their votes to kill public power.

Dad, plain and simple, was a strict constructionist of the Constitution and the judicial system, some might say too strict. And he was determined not to preside over the erosion of the constitutional rights accorded to states and individuals that he prized so deeply:

> In the emotion and hysteria surrounding this legislation, it must be remembered that in this country, thank God, we still have a government of laws and not of men... This legislation, in the hands of the wrong type of commissioners or law-enforcement officers, could be a vehicle for the persecution of any or of all of us, unless the bill includes proper constitutional safeguards. If the day ever comes when it is felt expediency is more important than constitutional law, we will come very close to the total destruction of the principles that have made our country the greatest and strongest in all the world... If we disregard our Constitution and our laws in an effort to help [black people] now, someone else at another time may also disregard the Constitution and laws of the land to destroy them.

Immediately upon the opening of the 85th Congress in 1957, civil rights legislation was again on the agenda. Hearings resumed in Judiciary Subcommittee #5 on bills similar to those submitted by my father and his cosponsors and passed by the House at the end of its session the previous year. Now he set about anew to get what he couldn't get the year before—amendments to the bills that he felt were necessary to make them constitutionally sound.

His first objection was that the Civil Rights Commission created by the legislation would have the authority to subpoena anyone in this country to any place within the country, no matter how far distant from their home, and hold them interminably at their own expense. The subcommittee voted unanimously to amend the bill to provide that a witness could only be subpoenaed to a place within the judicial district in which he resides and that he must be paid a witness fee and a mileage allowance.

Dad further charged that under the present bill, a person could be subpoenaed for interrogation on loose, unsubstantiated allegations. The subcommittee, again by unanimous action, amended the bill to provide that all allegations against someone must be sworn to in writing.

His third objection was that the current bill permitted the utilization of an unlimited number of volunteers to work for the Commission on Civil Rights who would be paid a per diem allowance. His concern was two-fold: first, such a situation would not allow Congress to retain sufficient jurisdiction over the operation of the Commission; second, considering the highly emotional issues the Commission would be investigating, there was a strong likelihood that all sorts of organizations and zealots, biased on one side or the other of the issues, would deluge it with volunteers. The Judiciary Committee unanimously accepted my father's amendment restricting the number of volunteers to fifteen, with no more than eight from any one organization.

His fourth charge was that this civil rights bill now being considered authorized the attorney general to institute legal action in the name of an individual against another individual, without having the permission of the person in whose name the action was to be taken. It was thought, rightfully, that black victims of voting discrimination might be too intimidated or too poor to undertake legal action themselves to remedy their situation. Yet this provision raised to southerners the specter of an all-powerful attorney general unmercifully harassing them. So the committee, though not on Dad's motion, acquiesced to their fears, voting to allow the attorney general to institute action for the protection of civil rights in the name of the United States, rather than as an attorney for one individual.

But unquestionably, the most contentious element of the civil rights debate in 1957 was the amendment once again proposed by my father, and subsequently by several liberal Democrats as well. It would require a jury trial for defendants accused by the Justice Department of criminal contempt for disobeying a judge's order in civil rights cases—e.g. a white official who defied a court order allowing black citizens to register to vote. He reasoned the amendment was necessary since normally those accused of criminal contempt of court when the United States is a party to the action are entitled only to a trial by a judge. Dad believed a jury trial was a sacred right, especially when the punishment could be jail or a substantial fine, as it is for criminal contempt.

The problem was, of course, that juries in the South were all white in those days, since only registered voters were eligible, and blacks were not registered. Therefore, it was unlikely that such a jury would convict white defendants accused of civil rights violations. At least that was the underlying and often unspoken belief of civil rights supporters. While the justice system in the South was undeniably far from impartial, my father feared that elimination of jury trials in this field could set a precedent for future Congresses applying similar legislation for different reasons to different groups. He called this attempt to bypass the jury system "destroying the constitutional rights of all in order to preserve the civil rights of some."

Interestingly, he has been somewhat vindicated in this belief by a later Supreme Court decision. In a 7-2 ruling in June of 2002 that juries, not judges, must make the final decision as to whether a convicted killer gets the death penalty, Judge Ruth Bader Ginsburg penned the opinion of the majority, an unlikely alliance of conservative and liberal-leaning justices. Rejecting arguments that judges can be more evenhanded and less emotional than juries, she wrote: "The Sixth Amendment jury trial right ... does not turn on the relative rationality, fairness or efficiency of potential fact-finders." Likewise, Dad used to say that suspending jury trials for white men tried by white juries for violating black civil rights could lead to the belief that Irishmen were not capable of convicting an Irishman, that Italians would not convict an

Italian, or that laboring men and women were unlikely to convict a laborer.

His Trial by Jury Amendment lost in the full Judiciary Committee by a close vote of 15-17, but the issue was far from dead. When the bill was reported out to the full House for debate in June of '57, the controversy raged again. Opponents of the amendment railed that allowing a jury trial in civil rights cases would cause delay in prosecuting those cases and nullify the government's ability to protect, promptly and effectively, every American's right to vote.

My father dismissed delay as an argument against the amendment, for he claimed he had seen cases "where judges take four times longer to make up their minds than does a jury in reaching a verdict. But even if delay were a valid argument, it would be a mighty foreign argument to our system of government." And then he reminded his fellow legislators that the cumbersome nature of our system of checks and balances, as compared to the streamlined nature of totalitarian governments, was the price we had to pay to preserve our freedoms.

The people supporting the jury trial amendment were, of course, doing so for a variety of reasons. The entire southern bloc of congressmen was vigorously pushing it as a way to mitigate the federal government's efforts to punish local voting rights abuses; people like Dad wanted it for legal and moral reasons, so integral to the American concept of freedom was the right of the accused to a trial by a jury of their peers. And he differed with the southerners on one important point. They insisted on a jury trial for all contempt cases, criminal and civil, which would have seriously thwarted the government's enforcement efforts. He wanted them only for criminal contempt, which is punishable by a substantial fine or a prison sentence and when therefore a defendant's freedom is at stake. There was a significant difference.

Would my father's amendment "eviscerate" the civil rights bill as some of his colleagues claimed? He admitted that he frankly didn't know, that there were no precedents to study, and that this was one of the matters the new Civil Rights Commission would be expected to investigate. "If at the conclusion of their study they report that this jury trial amendment effectively sabotages the efforts of the Federal government to guarantee voting rights," he said, "even I, at that time, might be willing to subscribe to such a drastic measure as the elimination of jury trials, like I have always been willing to yield certain inalienable rights in time of war or national emergency."

In supporting the Trial by Jury Amendment, Dad had once again parted ways with the Republican administration and with some of his Republican colleagues in the House—President Eisenhower and Attorney General Brownell were vigorously fighting the amendment. Though he was the leader of a group of northern Republicans in favor of the jury trial guarantee, he vociferously denied that he was "in league" with southern Democrats seeking to kill civil rights legislation. He noted that he had voted against amendment after amendment proposed by southerners in the Judiciary Committee, all of which were designed to weaken the bill.

One of the more astounding pieces of biased reporting I have ever encountered occurred about this time. My father for the most part appeared to be thick-skinned about such things, but in reality he was enormously sensitive and often deeply wounded by allegations in the press that his motives were less than honest. Yet he rarely replied to media criticism—I remember this one incident.

For whatever reason, he had become one of Drew Pearson's favorite victims. A Pearson commentary in the *Washington Post* in March 1957 alleged that "Representative Miller, congressional friend of the power utilities, was still helping his southern friends when he introduced his hamstringing civil rights amendment." The columnist did not attempt to explain what the "hamstringing amendment" was or the reasons for its proposal. So the article drew a detailed response from Bill Miller in a press release five legal pages long, a refutation point by point of all the allegations made.

It started by pointing out that, apparently unbeknownst to Pearson, because of the Schoellkopf power plant disaster of the year before and the critical power situation on the Niagara frontier, Dad was no longer promoting his private enterprise bill. He had introduced a compromise measure: "With very slight differences, there was no longer any conflict existing concerning the Niagara power project that has to be resolved by the House of Representatives." And there was no need, therefore, to make so-called "deals" with southern congressmen to get his power bill passed, he added. In a letter to my father shortly after the release of his statement, a fellow New York congressman, who shared his disdain for the muckraker, wrote: "In your usual lawyer-like way, you have put Mr. Pearson in the ash can. Let him stay there."

To add insult to injury, on May 29, 1957, just two months after Pearson had written the scathing article about Congressman Miller for proposing his "hamstringing [jury trial] amendment," he wrote admiringly: "Congressman James Roosevelt of California, a staunch backer of civil rights, has written a letter to Attorney General Brownell, which indicates he may accept the southern view regarding trial by jury." Indeed, Roosevelt was one of many civil rights advocates who were becoming increasingly skeptical that the traditional right of trial by jury should be weakened. In Pearson's view, such a stance was apparently acceptable, even praiseworthy, for a liberal Democrat, but not for a conservative Republican.

Dad put up a full fight for his limited jury trial clause on the floor of the House, but, despite the increased support, it was defeated. When the Eisenhower Civil Rights bill finally came up for a vote in the House in mid-summer, he cast his vote in favor. Ninety per cent of Republicans did the same, while only 52 percent of Democrats voted "yea." Even though he would have liked the bill better with the amendment, he felt that, with the changes he had engineered in committee from the previous year, it was acceptable. In the end, his constitutional doubts were trumped by a true empathy for the plight of black Americans, which prompted many of his contemporaries who recalled memories of him for this book many years later to call him "a compassionate and flexible conservative."

When the House bill reached the Senate, political machinations reached a fever pitch. Majority Leader Lyndon Johnson assured his southern colleagues that he would reinstate the amendment requiring jury trials for *all* contempt cases, civil as well as criminal. That was the price to be paid to prevent a filibuster and secure their support. Though initially Republicans and liberal Democrats were adamant about not supporting such an amendment, Johnson proceeded to make it clear that he would not allow a bill to pass without it. Succumbing to political realities, the Senate passed the Civil Rights bill, with a full jury trial amendment, by a vote of 72 to 18. Despite their unhappiness, not one Republican voted "nay."

Republicans, from Eisenhower and Brownell on down, were furious when Johnson virtually demanded the House accept the Senate version without a conference—the device used to reconcile differences between two versions of a bill. The president remained adamant against the Senate bill and encouraged House Republican Leader Joe Martin to hold out for the stronger measure the House had passed. Despite enormous pressure on House Republicans, my father included, to fall in line behind the Senate bill, they stood united against a full jury trial amendment and ended up with trial by jury only in criminal contempt cases, which is what Dad had wanted in the first place.

There were many who felt that the 1957 Civil Rights bill, after all those hours and weeks and months of impassioned debate, ended up a tepid, token bill. But had it been much stronger, it might not have passed at all. Though the original legislation had addressed a broad range of civil rights for black Americans, the end result simply gave the attorney general new powers to enforce only one right: their right to vote. But it broke the ice. As Lyndon Johnson would say in his trademark earthy fashion, to justify the gutted bill: "Once you break the virginity, it'll be easier next time."[4]

The battle for more rights would be waged again in 1960 and 1964, with my father continuing to play a role. The '57 bill had combined a grudging realization that African Americans had for too long been treated as secondary citizens, with a recognition that new laws in this field had to be gradual enough to win the cooperation of those who must change their way of life in order to live under them. The more antagonism and strife created, the more protracted would be the period of accommodation.

As could have been predicted, the 1957 Civil Rights Bill proved to be minimally effective. During the next two years, black voter registration increased imperceptibly. With individual states still in possession of the legal right to establish their own voting rules, people of color were routinely denied permission to register, made to wait long hours for an application, or found their applications inexplicably lost or discarded. Not only that, but there had been a violent outbreak of bombings against black churches and schools in the South, as well as interference with federal suits and investigations.

Republicans and liberal Democrats had been most disturbed about what Johnson and the southern Democrats had negotiated out of the recent bill in order to get it passed, namely Part III, which would have enforced equal opportunity in voting, schools, jobs, housing, transportation, and all public facilities. So now the administration and the president, not renowned for their passion about civil rights, but with due credit for groundbreaking legislation, were resolved to try again.

While little legislation is free of politics, civil rights proposals in those days were enmeshed in arguably the most complex web of political aspirations, frustrations, and backroom maneuvering ever witnessed since the birth of our democracy. First and foremost, it was becoming clear that the black vote could become a crucial factor in elections henceforth, and both parties were vying for that vote. Powerful and entrenched southern Democratic committee chairmen, in league with some conservative Republicans, had always been the nemesis of civil rights bills. But now Republicans of all shades were committed to civil rights legislation, and liberal Democrats feared their party stood to lose that coveted bloc of black voters. And continuing unrest was making it clear that black citizens and their leaders were highly dissatisfied with the progress being made on their behalf.

Of utmost importance in this morass of political intrigue was that the "cog" in the machine of future progress was flagging. Lyndon Baines Johnson, who had grudgingly engineered passage of the 1957 Civil Rights bill, was growing noticeably less enthusiastic about the subject. However, as his biographer, Robert Caro, suggests, "His interest in the 1960 Democratic presidential nomination made it impossible for him to avoid the civil rights issue."[5] While Johnson needed liberal support to secure the nomination, what he needed above all was southern support. The master of getting-something-for-everybody-in-a-contentious-situation had, however, pushed the southern senators and their revered dean, Richard Russell of Georgia, about as far as they would go.

When the Eisenhower administration introduced in late 1958 and again in early 1959 a civil rights bill that would have restored much of what had been eliminated from the '57 bill, the measures made it through House Judiciary, with both Manny Celler and my father fighting hard, though for slightly different versions. In the end, they stalled again in the Rules Committee, led by the uncompromising Howard Smith of Virginia.

When a bill, after some procedural maneuvering had extricated it from Rules, finally did pass the House and reach the Senate, southerners staged a filibuster—the filibuster Johnson had talked them out of in 1957. This time he opposed any attempt at cloture to shut it down. The civil rights legislation that eventually passed into law in 1960, after two months of windy speeches and copious bargaining and horse-trading between congressional leadership and the administration, had been "weakened to the point of meaninglessness."[6] It was not a proud day for either political party.

Some would argue that failure to pass more meaningful laws in the 1950s reflected Eisenhower's reticence to put his full moral weight behind his proposals. On the other hand, after years of federal apathy, something was finally being done. The only direction in which the federal government could go from 1960 on was forward, toward civil rights advancement. As the tortured congressional effort to eradicate black civil rights abuses came to fruition in the Civil Rights Bill of 1964, my father and his party would face still further challenges.

It is easy now, with the perspective of forty-five years, to see the need to force change on the South, although there is some truth to the idea that you cannot change the hearts of men with laws. The new laws did not change the hearts of all southerners or anyone else who wished to deny African Americans their rights as equal citizens, but they did force compliance that in time evolved into acceptance. The Supreme Court decision on school integration and the first civil rights legislation of the '50s forced wrenching changes on southerners and others. But it was plain that the pace they themselves would have chosen for change was unacceptable in light of the desperation being felt in black communities.

Unfortunately, in the emotions of the times, those who had any reservations about particular provisions of the civil rights bills were often characterized as racists and opponents of equal rights, people like my father who were most anxious for civil rights progress but wanted it done soundly. There are many things we do not know from where we stand at a certain point in history, but which we see clearly and know with certainty later. The extent of the atrocities being inflicted upon black people, the complicity of political power in the South, and the degree to which the system was stacked against blacks has only been revealed fully with time.

Though at times I have wished Dad had been less concerned about the technicalities of law and more impetuous about righting the wrongs being suffered by African Americans, I have come to a certain appreciation for a voice of reason and moderation such as his in times of crisis. Such voices are being heard again, urging that our government be more accountable for its actions with regard to constitutional rights as it responds to the threat of terrorism in the twenty-first century following the devastation of 9/11. It is interesting that the voices forty plus years ago were Republican; today they are largely Democratic.

There are some parallels between the civil rights crisis America faced in the 1950s and the threat of terrorism it faces in the early twenty-first century. Back then there was an urgency to fix intolerable conditions for our fellow citizens of color, whereas now there is fear, and a compelling need to protect our homeland against unimaginable horrors. Both emergencies have tempted us to abridge the rights and liberties of the "accused" or the suspect—southern racists then, those of Middle Eastern descent now—and to take action that is alien to our tradition and our system. But we justify these actions because of the overriding necessity of the times. My father was wary then, and he would be wary now.

Though the century-old denial of equal rights to black Americans was rapidly becoming a national crisis in the mid-1950s, he stressed that while Congress must find an immediate way to remedy that situation, they must also think of the long term. They must preserve, protect, and work within the rules that our forefathers forged that define us as a free and civilized nation. He warned then and would warn today, I suspect, of the perils inherent in rushed and emotional legislation to solve urgent, controversial, complex problems, simply in the interest of appearing to be doing something decisive.

CHAPTER SIX

CONGRESS—THE TUMULTUOUS '50s ROLL ON

There were, of course, many other issues and experiences for my father over these tumultuous years of the 1950s. I singled out public vs. private power and civil rights because they were two important legislative battles that were bitterly entangled in ideology and in the politics of the day, and because they have had lasting interest and relevance. The baseball antitrust exemption would be another such issue.

If you have ever complained about the high cost of taking the whole family to a professional baseball game, which at one time was an inexpensive treat, or bemoaned the trading of one of your favorite hometown players to another team, or mourned the loss of your entire team to another city, you might be surprised to learn that the cause of all these distressing occurrences goes back a long way. And it was something Dad and others tried, to no avail, to prevent.

It all began in 1922 with the *Federal Baseball* case, in which the Supreme Court held unanimously that organized professional baseball did not involve interstate commerce and, therefore, was not subject to federal antitrust laws. Baseball was called "unique" and not a business—an assertion that even back then seemed difficult to justify. Yet, except for minor objections, there was no public outcry or demand for Congress to get involved in the matter. In fact, there was basically a thirty-year period of governmental non-intervention in any professional team sports. Congress was content to be a sports facilitator rather than a sports regulator and to let professional sports regulatory bodies do the job of monitoring and correcting problems.

In 1953, the Supreme Court reconsidered and reaffirmed the *Federal Baseball* doctrine in *Toolson v. New York Yankees,* pointing out that Congress could have brought baseball under the antitrust laws during the past three decades had it seen fit to do so, but it did not. Subsequently, other professional sports began petitioning the court regularly to extend to them the same protective umbrella that baseball enjoyed.

It steadfastly refused to do so, and in 1957 did just the opposite by ruling in *Radovich v. National Football League*[1] that professional football was indeed subject to antitrust laws even though professional baseball was not. In an odd corollary, the justices admitted that their decision might be considered "illogical," but that any problems resulting from it should be solved by legislation rather than court decision. That ruling was a fairly explicit way of telling Congress that the proverbial ball was now in their court.

The legislators had three options: completely exempt all professional team sports from the antitrust laws, put baseball under the antitrust laws along with all the other sports, or, the middle-of-the-road approach—make certain aspects of all professional team sports subject to the antitrust laws and other aspects exempt. Variations on the third option appeared to be the most feasible choice.

In anticipation of legislation, my father issued a call for a thorough congressional investigation of professional sports, particularly football. A rabid sports fan, he had long been concerned about some of management's actions, as well as what he called "the confusing and almost ludicrous situation confronting professional football and baseball as a result of the recent Supreme Court decision," which he feared threatened their existence. While he noted that he and the American people certainly favored less rather than more government control in the field of sports, he warned that if owners did not keep their houses clean and voluntarily regulate themselves, the government would surely do it for them.

His concern was mainly aroused by the abortive efforts of football players to obtain recognition and bargaining rights for a players' association. They had tried unsuccessfully for years to extract certain rights and benefits from the owners' association—things like a guaranteed yearly contract with a guaranteed minimum yearly salary for the players, protection from wage loss due to injury, pay for training periods and preseason exhibition games.

Soon after the hearings of the Judiciary Antitrust and Monopoly Subcommittee got underway in the summer of '57, football Commissioner Bert Bell quite suddenly announced that he would formally recognize the Football Players Association. The players were deeply grateful to Dad and to Manny Celler for their comments during the hearings, clearly indicating their distaste for the owners' refusal to grant the players the common American right of collective bargaining, which comments they felt undoubtedly prompted the owners to reverse their stand.

Later that year, my father offered a bill for Judiciary Committee consideration that would have removed baseball's antitrust exemption. Time ran out in the session before it could reach the House floor. The following year, his thinking having evolved after countless hours of testimony, he joined with another Republican and two Democrats on the committee to introduce bipartisan legislation that would put all professional sports on the same footing. They would all be subject to antitrust laws but exempt from those laws when it came to what teams called their "sports practices." That would include such things as playing rules, organization of leagues and associations, territorial agreements, and employment of players. By separating the sports from the commercial aspects, the congressmen hoped to protect teams from expensive and potentially ruinous litigation in areas that were vital to their health and prosperity.

The bipartisan bill passed the House overwhelmingly, but adjournment prevented consideration by the Senate. When the 86th Congress opened in January of 1959, the persistent congressmen tried again. This time Dad and his co-sponsors addressed a new concern—radio and television broadcasts of major league baseball games, which were threatening minor leagues with extinction.

Because these broadcasts were exempt from antitrust laws, minor leagues were unable to protect their home gates by prohibiting the broadcasts from coming into their cities during their home games. So the new bill, while nearly identical to the previous year's measure, would have one important addition: instead of completely exempting the regulation of radio and television sports broadcasts from antitrust laws, it would limit the exemption to telecasts originating within seventy-five miles of minor league home communities on days of their home games. Both Ford Frick, commissioner of baseball, and Bert Bell, commissioner of football, heartily endorsed the plan. The National Association of Broadcasters, quite understandably, bitterly opposed it. They warned that it would allow a total blackout of major sports tele-casts for a large part of the viewing public.

Neither this sports antitrust bill nor any other ever became law during the decade of the 1950s, since no consensus could be reached on how to fashion it. Some limited aspects of the baseball antitrust exemption still stand forty years later, thanks to intense lobbying against changing the status quo (baseball spent 1.2 mil-lion dollars on this issue in 2001), lack of public pressure, and congressional reluctance to touch what is still to some degree a "sacred cow," despite the fact that baseball may no longer be, as it was called for so long, "America's favorite pastime."

As the baseball industry continued to grow dramatically after 1960, its conflicts drew more public and congressional attention. Its ability and/or willingness to regulate its own affairs repeat-edly came into question, so the antitrust exemption was gradu-ally whittled away. In 1973, a bill prohibited television blackouts of home games that are sold out seventy-two hours in advance. The granting of free agency in 1975 to Dave McNally and Andy Messersmith effectively ended the most hated portion of the exemption—the reserve clause, which had bound a player to a team until the owner traded or fired him. The Curt Flood Act of 1998 revoked baseball's antitrust exemption in the area of labor relations.

There is some difference of opinion as to whether the an-tiquated antitrust exemption was ever the cause of baseball's problems. Some would argue that without the exemption and therefore being subject to antitrust laws football teams have managed to work together far more harmoniously in matters that contribute to the common good of their sport, like the draft and revenue sharing, than baseball ever has. One thing can probably be said with certainty, however, and that is that baseball is most definitely as much a business as any other professional sport—as my practical father once, long ago, pressed his colleagues to recognize.

Would anything have been different if forty years ago he and his colleagues had been able to end the confusion and put all pro-fessional sports on the same basis—as exempt or not exempt from antitrust laws? Who can say? It was one of his many frustrations with the system that he could not do that.

The term "private enterprise" was not just a Republican cliché for my father. His belief that the federal government should do only what individuals and localities cannot or will not do for themselves was a passionate one. Political foes in the Niagara power fight liked to tag him a "big business congressman," because of his support for the private power industry. But rather than being a champion of big business, he was actually a stickler for safeguarding the rights of small businessmen and individuals, his meticulous legal mind always attuned to how those rights can so easily be trampled in large and complex bills. His mother had, after all, owned a small business, not to mention his own entrepreneurial ventures in high school and college.

In February 1959, the Supreme Court announced a decision that could have a significant and adverse effect on small businesses engaged in interstate commerce. That decision produced an avalanche of mail to congressional offices. Existing law had always been understood to preclude multiple state taxation. Now the new court ruling opened up the possibility for states to tax companies that did nothing more than solicit orders either by a salesman within their state or through the mail. Though large corporations could afford the attorneys and accountants necessary to keep books for the payment of some thirty-four different state taxes, this was a heavy burden for most small businesses to bear. The chaos and confusion that ensued about the whole issue was making it impossible for them to operate.

Dad was at once appointed to a special Judiciary subcommittee to investigate this complex problem. Upon his motions, the subcommittee, and subsequently the full Judiciary Committee, unanimously reported out stopgap remedial legislation to give temporary relief to small businesses. With him as Republican floor manager, the bill passed the House, went on to pass the Senate, and was finally resolved in a House/Senate Conference Committee under his leadership.

There were also frequent efforts to portray Bill Miller's belief in private enterprise as somehow antilabor. Indeed, since his run-in with labor leaders in the violent Bell plant strike almost a decade earlier, unions had not traditionally been his friends. Yet they should have been. On the Judiciary Committee he fought a persistent and no-holds barred battle against big business for almost four years as the House sponsor of the Federal Construction

Bill, which would establish fair bidding procedures in government construction contracts. Every labor union concerned was on his side.

He often invited labor groups to his office to listen to their problems, and at one such conclave several unions were explaining to him their stand on a meatpacking controversy. The participants were so astonished by his sympathy toward their cause that they momentarily forgot themselves and exclaimed that they might actually endorse him in his next election. While he consistently supported labor's right to peacefully bargain collectively, he, like so many Americans, was fed up with the corruption and ruthlessness of certain labor leaders. He voted for every bill that would curb their power, and particularly their ability to restrain trade and force "closed shop," or union membership, on all workers.

Federal aid to education was always a troublesome issue for Dad. He had frequently voted in favor of bills that appropriated relatively modest funds to specific needs, such as scholarships in the engineering and scientific fields. When faced with far-reaching legislation that proposed large-scale funding for school construction and teachers' salaries, he kept an open mind on the subject for some time but finally voted against such bills. He feared that such unprecedented federal involvement in local schools would bring with it more federal control than he believed wise. The second reason for his opposition was more complicated.

He argued that since New York State at that time paid nearly 20 percent of the total federal tax bill, New Yorkers would in effect end up contributing heavily to the construction of schools and payment of teachers' salaries in other states. He had worked tirelessly over the years to secure federal contracts for the Niagara Frontier in order to alleviate the double digit unemployment rate that pained him so deeply and personally. Too often he found that his home state's industries were just not competitive with industries elsewhere, largely due to the tax cost of doing business in New York. "After paying a state income tax, state and county taxes on real estate, a school tax on real estate, and often a sales tax, why," he asked, "should New Yorkers pay for states like Mississippi or Alabama that choose not to have income or school taxes, but who lure industries out of New York to their areas because of the absence of those taxes?"

Medical care for the aged was another difficult issue for my father. Growing demand for such care was becoming a pressing and controversial item by mid-century. He had a permanently hospitalized mother in her eighties whom he supported, so he knew well the financial strain of medical expenses for the elderly. Medicare was not yet born and early proposals to attach such care to Social Security, like the Forand bill, were meeting with widespread fear that they would produce "socialized medicine." Legislative offices, including his, were virtually flooded with opposition mail on the subject, and Forand went down to defeat.

He wanted some legislation in this area, but he pointed out that since a great many elderly were not covered by Social Security, they would not benefit from medical care attached to it. He also claimed that adding a Medicare-type program to Social Security could raise payroll taxes, particularly for workers in the lower income brackets, to the point of being an unbearable burden.

Dad preferred a system of voluntary health insurance coverage, with some federal grants for the indigent aged such as the Kerr-Mills Bill offered, and he and his cohorts prevailed when the bill passed and was signed into law in 1960. Subsequently, that plan proved inadequate in its coverage, so he and thirty others co-sponsored the Bow Amendment to supplement it with more extensive voluntary insurance, again backed by some federal assistance. He wrote a letter to House Republicans urging their support, but to no avail. The Republican plan was replaced in 1965 by the Medicare program, as part of Social Security, that Lyndon Johnson had made a cornerstone of his "Great Society."

Remember that All-American Ship Canal that my father had written his congressman about as a boy of eleven? Well last but not least of my father's legislative accomplishments during his first ten years in Congress was a bill appropriating $100,000 for an engineering survey for that long-ago proposed waterway around Niagara Falls on the U.S. side of the international boundary. It would by-pass Canada's congested Welland Canal and link Lakes Erie and Ontario for ocean-going ships. Congressman S. Wallace Dempsey would surely be smiling down on his now grown-up constituent for continuing the fight for the languishing project that he had begun some thirty years earlier.

Dad always said he wasn't one of those "junketing congress-men"—the only time he went overseas after the war was in 1959 to visit The Hague as a Judiciary Committee member studying the World Court in connection with the "Connally Amendment." But he was appointed over the years to an assortment of special committees that utilized his skills as a prosecutor and the investigative expertise he had gained at Nuremberg. Some jobs were more memorable than others, but at the time they did concern burning issues.

Like the impeachment of plucky Supreme Court Justice William O. Douglas, who in 1953 precipitously granted a one-day stay of execution to Julius and Ethel Rosenberg just as they were about to meet the electric chair. They were the couple who had been convicted of giving our atomic secrets to the Russians, and after two years, all their appeals and clemency petitions had been rejected. Just the day before the execution date, two young lawyers had grabbed Justice Douglas outside the high court as he was packing to go home for summer recess, presented him with some legal technicalities that they claimed invalidated the Rosenberg's death sentence, and begged him to issue a stay.

He did so, to Attorney General Herbert Brownell's great displeasure, but it was put aside the following day by an unprecedented reconvening of the whole court. A congressional committee was promptly organized to study grounds for impeachment, to which my father was one of five House members appointed. While there were actually no legal grounds for Douglas' impeachment, congressional leaders felt legislation might be needed to prohibit a single justice from ordering stays of this kind in the future.

One Judiciary Committee assignment that my father found particularly rewarding was the probing of Japanese American evacuation claims. It was a chance to make amends for this blot on our history of inhumanity and prejudice, when the national hysteria and insecurity that followed Pearl Harbor had rendered every Japanese American in this country suspect as a traitor. He and five other members of the Subcommittee on Claims were appointed to hold a week of public hearings in San Francisco and Los Angeles in 1954 on a bill to amend the well-intentioned but inadequate Japanese American Evacuation Claims Act of 1948.

That Act had awarded over $23 million to some of the more than 120,000 loyal citizens, accused of no crime, who had lost most of what they owned when forced by President Roosevelt's Executive Order #9066 to evacuate their homes on the Pacific Coast in the winter of 1942. That amount turned out to be less than ten cents for every dollar they had lost. When the detainees were finally allowed to return in 1945 from the remote, dusty, barbed wire-surrounded internment camps in Oklahoma, Arkansas, Utah, and Idaho, euphemistically called "relocation centers," they had little to return to—their land and businesses had mostly been expropriated or vandalized.

By 1954, twelve years after the evacuation began, there were still over 3,000 remaining claims to be settled, totaling in excess of $62 million, so cumbersome and costly was the adjudication process. It was necessary to find a way to expedite those long overdue claims to keep them from dragging on interminably, both to relieve the human suffering our government had so unjustly inflicted, but also to promote better relations with a now peaceful Japan.

After listening to the heartrending stories of over 150 witnesses, the committee made sixteen specific recommendations for a far broader, more generous and flexible bill than the one already proposed. They received moving letters of thanks from witnesses who were deeply impressed by the sympathy and knowledge with which the committee members heard their problems.

However, politics, complaints from the Justice Department, and adjournment all conspired to delay passage and signing of a final claims settlement bill until June of 1956. There were those in Congress and the attorney general's office who were reticent to reopen the whole issue, or who believed that our government was justified in ordering the wartime evacuation as a precautionary move. After several amendments in both House and Senate, the final bill was not all my father and his fellow subcommittee members had wanted, but it was all that could pass Congress and get the job done in a timely fashion.

What the amended bill left unaddressed, since it was far too controversial at the time, was the issue of an apology to the Japanese for the unprecedented suspension of their constitutional rights. The Japanese American Citizens League spearheaded a movement to put that on the national agenda beginning in the 1970s.

Their effort resulted in President Ford formally rescinding Executive Order 9066 and President Carter creating a commission, which concluded that the Japanese World War II detention was not warranted by military conditions but was the result of "race prejudice, war hysteria, and a failure of political leadership." In 1989, President George Bush signed a law that guaranteed a fund for additional reparation payments to the internment survivors or their descendants. Almost a half-century after evacuation began, and thirty-five years after my father's efforts, the process of compensating for real property loss had finally evolved into redress for loss of freedom and an acknowledgment of the injustice of the Japanese internment.

Of all Dad's experiences in his first ten years in Congress, the one that left perhaps the most indelible mark upon him, and that he mysteriously never spoke of, was his viewing of an atomic bomb test. In 1954, a handful of congressmen were selected to travel to the remote Frenchmen Flats in Nevada as observers of a bomb blast that would be far stronger than the one that had obliterated Hiroshima.

They were first shown the simulated military battleground that had been created in a reservoir where the bomb would be detonated, complete with seven-foot thick barricades, hospital units, trenches and sandbags, and live pigs dressed in the camouflage clothing of soldiers. The congressmen were then sanitized, outfitted in rubber suits and goggles, and situated on a knoll about seven miles from the test site.

They heard the countdown, shielded their eyes—despite thick goggles they were told not to look—and though they had been forewarned, it felt like a huge oven door had opened upon them. A furious wind wrenched trees this way and that and blew pebbles into the men's faces, leaving small bloodstains. When they returned to the bombsite to witness the results of the test's immediate impact, they were awed and speechless—a condition in which politicians do not often find themselves.

The seven-foot barricades had been shattered, the hospitals destroyed, the grass scorched, and worst of all, the pigs seared. Animal rights groups would have something to say about that today. All the way home, the legislators could talk about nothing but the horrors of the bomb and how dire was the need to avoid its use, to curb the madness that was such an integral and terrifying component of the cold war.

As he was closing out his first decade in Washington, my father took on a time-consuming new assignment. He was one of five (out of forty-five) New York congressmen appointed by Governor Nelson Rockefeller to a newly formed bipartisan New York State Steering Committee investigating ways to alleviate the state's serious unemployment problem, which were most severe in his own area. The state's economy was being gradually strangled by a plethora of taxes that were reducing the competitiveness of its industry, a situation that definitely alarmed him. While he respected Rockefeller's efforts to raise taxes in order to balance the budget and support the many social services people were demanding, he was afraid the state's social programs were simply ballooning out of control.

In light of this unfortunate situation, the committee's difficult job was to promote the Empire State's economic interest by somehow luring more government contracts, even as it was losing them to lower-tax, cheaper labor states in the South and West. They recommended the improvement of transportation facilities and harbors and tried to generally find ways to make New York a more attractive place to do business. The ability of the group to offer thorough data and constructive suggestions to potential customers, as well as to bring pressure to bear on them, was considerable. They did win some significant battles for the state's economy. If they detected unfairness in dealing with New York State industry, the offenders would, without doubt, hear strenuously from the legislators.

The most accurate description of Bill Miller thus far in his career would be "maverick," though others have tried to pigeonhole him as a down-the-line conservative. He was in some ways a harbinger of conservative-leaning politicians like John McCain— more centrist and tolerant than many of his more doctrinaire colleagues. Anything but predictable, there was an independent streak that ran strong in him. He didn't seem to unduly concern himself with how popular his stand on any given issue might be; no doubt that was because he was never wedded to a permanent political career. His letters to constituents were polite but frank when he disagreed with them on an issue or rejected their request that he support a bill they favored.

My father's independence in voting was underscored by a tabulation in the *Congressional Quarterly* which showed that while Congress backed President Eisenhower on 76 percent of roll call votes in the 1958 session, his support stood at 44 percent. The local press, always supportive of their congressman to the point of being almost totally uncritical, praised him repeatedly for his courage in standing by his convictions on controversial issues, for being "truly a representative and not a rubber stamp."

Dad once said: "I think the government should be liberal when it comes to human beings while conservative with the taxpayers' money." His votes over the years suggest that he was sensitive to the needs of the less fortunate, within budgetary constraints, perhaps because he himself had come from such need. He supported raising the minimum wage and making it more inclusive, increasing Social Security benefits and expanding its coverage, extending unemployment insurance benefits to those who lost jobs, and liberalizing immigration quotas to admit persecuted peoples and reunite families. His empathy for immigrant groups and their challenges was especially deep-seated, and he worked closely over the years with the multitude of nationalities that populated his district. He even once co-sponsored with fellow New York Congresswoman Katherine St. George an equal rights amendment for women, not exactly a priority of the standard conservative agenda.

Though my father's support of President Eisenhower on domestic issues throughout Ike's eight-year tenure was unpredictable, it was strong in the field of foreign affairs. He was, like the soldier turned president, a firm internationalist, a believer in engagement in the world—probably a legacy of his days in Nuremberg. There he had seen and heard firsthand the dire results of isolationism, of not getting involved early in world events that threaten to extinguish human life and freedom. And he was of the opinion that if the isolationist tendency of the Senate, the prime arbiter of our foreign policy, had not been so unyielding in the years following the First World War, perhaps there might not have been another great war, or a Nuremberg.

Dad strongly endorsed Eisenhower's military interventions in hotspots around the globe to protect peace and freedom. In fact, he advocated fighting the Communist menace on three fronts—military, political, and economic: giving uncommitted countries abundant military equipment to protect themselves against Soviet encroachment, educating them about the perils of Communism and the advantages of democracy, and offering them limited funds to build their infrastructure and relieve poverty.

If anything, Congressman Miller was even more aggressive in foreign policy than his president. He pushed for strengthening of the World Court in The Hague by removing restrictions that we had once placed on its rulings, and he suggested summit meetings with Soviet leaders before Eisenhower or Secretary of State John Foster Dulles had stated their positions on the idea. He opined, "As long as we're talking, we're not shooting"— he was not alone in thinking that if another war should ever start, it was probable there would not be enough people left in the world to rebuild it.

My father once wrote a stinging reply to a constituent who had written complaining that he had deserted the conservative cause by voting for foreign aid: "In Asia today, there are a billion people who have two things in common: all of them are hungry and none of them are white. They would like to have bread with freedom and dignity, but bread they must have, and if they don't get it from the free world, they will take it from the Communists, and a billion people would go behind the Iron Curtain."

When he first went to Washington in 1951, Dad launched a project that he repeated annually throughout his tenure and which several other members of Congress subsequently adopted. It was an extensive questionnaire on all the legislative issues that might come before each session of Congress and it was sent to all the newspapers in his district to publish. They dutifully executed this civic responsibility, publishing the results of the poll as well. "In voting on questions which come before the Congress, I must make my own independent judgment as to what policies are best for the nation. However, I need also to weigh the views of those whom I was elected to represent," he wrote in prefacing his questions.

There were anywhere from fifteen to thirty extremely detailed questions that would require considerable interest in and knowledge of current events to answer. People were to cut out the questionnaire, check their preferences among the multiple choice answers and send it to my father's office. It was usually returned by at least 25,000 people, who seemed delighted to be asked for their views and often expounded at great length on extra sheets of paper. If there was a theme, it was that the respondents were mostly salt-of-the-earth, blue-collar people who were frightened of socialism and government interference in their lives. They were sick and tired of their hard-earned money being taxed and "given away" in foreign aid and expensive government programs.

Dad also tried other ways of staying in touch with his district. The most popular was his fifteen-minute weekly radio "Report from Congress," which he recorded, starting in 1951, in the Old House Office Building studio to air on Saturdays and Sundays on several local Western New York stations. As time-consuming as the project was, it was deemed worthwhile since the audience was strong and the response lively. At about the same time, he began filming a fifteen-minute television program to beam back to his constituents, alternating weeks with Senator Ken Keating.

A periodic newsletter was abandoned early on, after receiving forthright comments such as "I couldn't care less" and "don't waste the government's money sending this to me anymore." As far as constituents staying in touch with him, he loved and welcomed the many thoughtful, personal letters expressing opinions on legislation, and all of them were answered personally by him. He thought less of printed cards and form letters, but he always encouraged the public to make itself known on issues loudly and clearly in any way it could.

The last maverick move my father made in closing out his first decade in Congress was surely not designed to win him friends in high places in New York State. It was 1959, President Eisenhower was nearing the end of his eight-year tenure and Vice President Richard Nixon was the obvious successor to his mantle. But Nixon had not yet made his intentions known, incredible as that might seem today when candidates sometimes throw their hats in the ring a full two to three years in advance of a presidential election.

Nixon's only real competitor for the top spot on the 1960 Republican ticket would be the highly acclaimed new governor of New York, Nelson Rockefeller. Despite the fact that Rockefeller had only been elected to his first public office a year earlier, he was young, gregarious, dashing, and wealthy, a scion of a renowned family that, like the Kennedys, was the closest thing this country had to royalty. The governor had made it known, unofficially, that he was interested in the job. And it was understood that Dad and the rest of the Republicans in the New York State congressional delegation, indeed all loyal Republicans in the state, would fall in behind their governor if he decided to go for it.

Then Bill Miller, with his trademark feisty independence, dropped a bombshell on the Party. In June of '59, at the height of the Rockefeller "boom," he became the first national public figure and the first New Yorker to announce his support of Richard Nixon for president. The reasons for this seemingly brazen move that put his political neck on the line were simple to him at the time: it was "Nixon's turn," and he had earned it—by experience, training, and performance. He had been given far weightier responsibilities and inclusion in affairs of state as vice president than Harry Truman had ever been given by FDR, and he had proven his abilities, especially in dealing with foreign leaders.

Dad actually liked Rockefeller personally far better than Nixon, and as the years went on he would like the latter less and less, but there was no doubt in his mind that Dick Nixon was the strongest candidate the Republican Party could present to the nation at this time. While he admired Rockefeller's obvious appeal and considered him a future presidential candidate whom he could enthusiastically endorse, he felt he was too new to the scene, had not yet built his base of support or proved his mettle.

Although my father made it clear that he was speaking as an individual and a congressman and not for the state party in his pronouncement, he was bucking his county and state Republican chairmen, beholden to their governor for their patronage, and they were not happy with him. Nevertheless, he quietly set out to build support for the vice president among New York's Republican congressmen and to garner delegates for him to the convention the following summer.

I can remember, as a fifteen–year-old, the excitement of an elegant buffet supper my parents held for Pat and Dick Nixon about this time at our new home in Bethesda. Invitees were the House Republican leadership and the entire New York State congressional delegation, including Senators Ken Keating and Jacob Javits. In preparation, cleaners polished every doorknob and candlestick in sight, bustling caterers arranged impossibly sumptuous platters of food, gigantic floral arrangements arrived, and sober, dark-suited Secret Service agents prowled the grounds selecting their stations—all this mayhem supervised by my worried and harassed mother. Having the vice president of the United States to your home was not a small or routine undertaking, even for a veteran congressional wife.

By the time the appointed hour arrived, however, she was appropriately composed, my sister Mary and I were suitably outfitted in our teenage best from Woodward and Lothrop to mingle with the distinguished guests, and our quiet, dead-end street was flooded with a seemingly endless cavalcade of sleek, black government limousines. The neighbors were by then all hanging out their windows to observe the extraordinary spectacle.

In meetings with Nixon after his early endorsement, Dad urged the VP to declare sooner rather than later his intention to run for president, attempting to nudge him to a decision. He then tossed his spurned governor a small bouquet by declaring that an ideal ticket would in fact be Nixon for president and Rockefeller for vice president. In the end, despite angering a few of his fellow Republicans, he was lauded by the hometown papers for sticking his neck out "when most politicians were hedging until they could find out how the wind was blowing."

All in all, the decade of the fifties had been a good run for my father, despite the fact that he had been in the minority for all but the first two years of Eisenhower's presidency, from 1952 to 1954. As a talented and persuasive man, he was continually frustrated that in the minority you could not get your own legislation passed. You could not initiate it and if you did, it would come out with the majority party's label on it. In a chamber as large as the House, it took many years and much patience in those days to acquire any significant influence, such as the chairmanship of a committee.

Yet he had surely become an expert in government, and his work had brought him widespread contacts that could be beneficial for his law practice whenever he chose to return to it. The range of experiences and issues with which he had dealt was beyond anything he had ever anticipated in his life. He had not sought public office but had accepted it, and he would admit that he was the richer for it. His one sadness was that his beloved mother, who in large measure had made all this possible by her hard work long ago, who had taken such a keen interest in every step of his career, could no longer savor his successes. The haze of failed memory had once and for all robbed her of the recognition of where and what he was.

The downside of life in Congress, in addition to the financial strain, was still the lack of time for the family. There was also the fact that Mom and Dad had never become enamored with or entirely comfortable in the Washington social scene. In the beginning, when they were wide-eyed with the newness of it and learning the ropes of the city's intricate protocol, it all seemed so impressive.

Eventually, the superficiality of the life style and the realization that they were primarily liked and invited because of the power my father possessed in the political structure became somewhat unpleasant and disconcerting. Mother used to say they knew how important they were by where they sat at a dinner party in relation to the host and hostess, how far "below the salt" they sat, as the expression went. In Washington social circles, such things were noticed. But all those aggravations notwithstanding, Washington had by now become home.

For my part, I had virtually grown up there, occasionally romping the majestic, bust-lined, cavernous halls of the Capitol with my father or hopping one of the electric carts for the speedy underground ride from the House floor to his office. I loved when he took me with him on a school holiday. I would sit at his imposing desk or wander the echoing white marble corridors outside his door, peeking into other congressional offices where I always elicited bright hellos. Always dressed in my Sunday best for those days, I could hear my shiny, black patent leather shoes click and tap, or slide, on the slippery, polished floors. I could stand on a chair and help the secretaries, Naomi and Jean, take copies of a speech or a bill off the clunky ditto machine, being most careful not to smear the messy blue ink from my fingers onto my fancy dress.

A reporter once noticed me sitting with my dad on opening day of a new congressional session, squeezed with him into his big leather front row seat on the House floor and calmly reading one of my favorite childhood books, *Little Women* by Louisa

May Alcott, during the historic proceedings. To my dismay and delight, that event rated a small tidbit in the hometown newspapers, where I was always called Elizabeth Anne, at my mother's insistence I supposed. Then there was the day he took my sister and me to the House floor to hear a bill debated. Little did we know it would be a contentious foreign aid measure, and that "the argument," as we called it, would last until 4:30 in the morning. Unable to stay awake in the gallery, we were roused repeatedly by the guard, who informed us that we were breaking the rules.

There were all sorts of exciting and privileged activities for congressional children, though it never occurred to me then how special they were. It was not privilege that flowed from money but from the proximity to power, that perpetual password in the nation's capital. I, of course, took it all for granted, as we do most things that are integral parts of our lives.

There were teas at the White House with First Ladies and their children—I especially remember the Nixon and Johnson trios, never imagining that I would meet the latter as adversaries on the campaign trail many years later. There were special seats for inaugurations and the parades and glittering balls that followed, official limousines, VIP tours, once of the United Nations with Ambassador Henry Cabot Lodge and once at West Point with two dashing cadets who were my father's appointees from the district. There was the chance to be the New York State princess in the annual Cherry Blossom Festival at the Tidal Basin—the princesses not chosen for their beauty but for their father's position, and thankfully not required to sing or wear a bathing suit. My two long-suffering Naval Academy escorts were tugged and pulled around for an entire week of balls, cocktail parties, and other gala events. I remember missing my chance for ten all-expenses-paid days in Japan when the spin of the gigantic wheel that picked the queen landed a millimeter from New York State. All these strands woven together formed the fabric of life in my father's orbit.

He was not around much while I was growing up. I don't remember being resentful of that: somehow I guess I intuitively understood that the absence of political fathers went with the territory, and I sensed how much he wished he could be there. He often came home late, after Mary and I had eaten and were buried in our homework—long sessions of Congress, a dinner, or a speaking engagement detained him. On the rare occasions when he was home, Mom shielded him from our pestering questions to give him a respite from politics, though I hungered to hear it all.

I can remember him sitting alone in his oversized red leather chair in our small den for long hours at night, unwinding, filling his ashtray with cigarettes, nursing a beer or two, reading, or sometimes just looking into space. I wanted so much to know what he was thinking, but I never could decide exactly what to ask—his quick mind with its vast store of knowledge seemed intimidating to me as a young girl. Truth be told, I was always a little afraid of asking a stupid question.

Mother had made a decision early in their political life—that all congressional wives must make at some point—about how deeply to get involved in the glamorous social whirl of the capital. Some feel they owe it to their husbands to do it all, both on their own and at their husband's side—Lady Bird Johnson admitted to that choice; others decide that being home with their children, giving them some stability in that potentially tumultuous life, is their more pressing duty.

Mom chose the latter. It was not an easy decision. The pull was strong to accept every enticing invitation that arrived, and staying home alone with the children when your husband was gone night after night had its frustrations. Though she did a certain amount of socializing, and I remember the lonely feeling on the occasional day when she wasn't there after school, I remember more often finding her immersed in sewing beads and sequins on assorted felt articles she volunteered to make each year for the handmade craft booth at our school Christmas bazaar.

One thing I did miss was when Dad couldn't make Father/Daughter Field Day at Stone Ridge, my Sacred Heart grammar and high school. It was such a big event in my life, a whole day of games and fun with my father, and it always felt like he was the only one not there, though I am quite certain that was not the case. I did feel very special and proud though when he was invited to school to debate my friend Cokie Roberts' father, Democratic Louisiana congressman Hale Boggs, on some controversial issue of the day for the entire student body. The agility of his mind, the incisiveness of his speech, and his sharp wit used to thrill me—I especially loved it when he made all the girls laugh. In an attempt at emulation, I tried debating, with far less success than my father. I used to remember the following day all the things I should have said to nail my opponent. My recollection is that Cokie made mincemeat of me on the debating team.

Another special event of those young years was tagging along with Dad when he gave visiting school classes from his district a personally conducted tour of the Capitol. Today there would be a member of a congressman's twenty-person staff with the sole job of giving such tours, but in those simpler days of three-person staffs, the "head honcho" often gave them. Or at least Congressman Miller did, and he gave his groups the first-rate tour.

After a special luncheon in Speaker Sam Rayburn's private dining room, he would lead the awed assemblage to the floor of the House of Representatives, where he mustered as simple an explanation of the labyrinthine parliamentary procedures of that body as was possible. I was always so impressed with his ability to do that. The tour also included a visit to Speaker Rayburn's office, Vice President Nixon's office, the Senate Chambers, and the Supreme Court Building. The finale was, of course, the beaming group picture with the congressman on the Capitol steps. There is an amazing number of those aging photos resting in my father's files.

The only traumatic recollection I have of those early years in Washington came in March of 1954, when I was just ten. A band of Puerto Rican nationalists, demanding statehood for their island, sprayed bullets wildly across the House floor from the visitors' gallery, seriously wounding five congressmen. There was almost full attendance on the floor as members, "sitting ducks," poured in to cast their vote on a Mexican migrant labor bill. It was actually a miracle that there were not countless fatalities.

It happened at 2:45 in the afternoon, as I was just about finishing my school day. I remember being stricken when I heard the news. As it turned out, Dad was on his way to the House floor to vote when the shooting began, delayed a few fortuitous minutes by a meeting with a labor union group in his office. Just before he arrived, two bullets had splintered the back of the seat he habitually occupied, the second seat to the right of the House Majority Leader. Only that small delay had kept him from being, perhaps fatally, among the victims. He was shaken for many weeks, as was our whole family, by what might have been.

So almost before we knew it, we had been in Washington for nearly ten years. And we had a new family member—brother Bill Jr. was born in 1959, my parents deciding that they were much too young to only have two such "grown-up" daughters as Mary and me. So excited was Dad about his son that he whispered repeatedly to Mother, as she groggily emerged from anesthesia—"Mom, it's a boy, it's a boy!" The *Lockport Union Sun and Journal* snapped the first mug shot of the tiny, wailing heir to the Miller name just as he emerged from the delivery room, and they crowed over their coup. "President Eisenhower said he wanted youth in the Republican Party, so we gave it to him," quipped the proud father to waiting reporters.

In his political life, Bill Miller had managed to stay a bit above the fray of local politics in his district. All sides somehow seemed indebted to him for the many favors he had done for them and for his district over the years, and, to be honest, because he kept winning. His constituents were also devoted to him, for even as his time and responsibilities in Washington increased, he was always available by phone, and he was known for never forgetting even their smallest personal requests.

Yet at the end of 1959, with another election looming, as it annoyingly does for congressmen every two years, the speculation that always clung to him began again about whether "the reluctant candidate" would be a candidate. It was well known that in 1958 he had run for reelection only at the urgent request of the GOP high command. But this time he ended the talk early with his announcement that he would indeed seek a sixth term, which was political bad news for Niagara / Erie County Democrats who were once again faced with finding an opponent. The decision seemed easier for my father this time—I think perhaps because he had gotten wind of a move afoot to draft him for a party job that would be a quantum leap for his political career, and would significantly alter the course of his life and ours.

CHAPTER SEVEN

FIRST LEADERSHIP ROLE

The next four years were to offer my father, quite unexpectedly, the opportunity to dramatically and permanently change the focus and effectiveness of two of the fundamental operating elements of the Republican Party: the National Republican Congressional Campaign Committee and the Republican National Committee. When Congressman Richard Simpson, a tough conservative from Pennsylvania, died in early January 1960, he left vacant an important political job that was not well known off Capitol Hill. Yet when Dad was recruited to fill the spot, it would launch his swift rise up the ladder of national recognition and influence within the GOP.

The chairmanship of the National Republican Congressional Campaign Committee, or NRCC, carried with it the major biennial responsibility of getting as many Republicans elected to the House of Representatives as possible. That was no small feat, since with the exception of the 80th and 83rd Congresses, the Party had been in the minority since 1932. A modest but significant success in that daunting job catapulted my father just a year later, in 1961, to the national chairmanship of the GOP.

Congressmen John Rhodes of Arizona and Bob Wilson of California both take credit for landing him the NRCC job. Both were active members of the Committee and believed in its importance. They were eager to see it reinvigorated from the somewhat moribund state into which it had fallen since Dick Simpson, who had minimal political savvy and interest, had taken over in 1955. Rhodes was looking for someone from the East who was not identified as a rigid ideologue. At that time, there was a preponderance of Midwest men in top posts of the party high command—from Indiana, Wisconsin, and Iowa—and he felt there ought to be more balance at the leadership level.

Though Dad was not a member of the Campaign Committee, the Arizonan had put his name at the head of a personal list of eight possible chairmen, asserting that "all of us have had a lot of admiration for Bill Miller for a long time." He had apparently been impressed by what he called my father's "sometimes rugged but always courteous individualism and independence, his frank and friendly temperament, his boundless energy, and his articulate and fiery speeches on the House floor that demonstrated his ability to handle himself in the rough and tumble of debate." So he floated his New York colleague's name in an NRCC meeting, just to get some reaction. The response was positive.

In the meantime, Congressman Wilson, admittedly more interested in the logistics of campaigning than in legislating, would actually have liked the job for himself. But a fellow Californian, Richard Nixon, strongly prevailed upon the genial congressman to defer to Miller instead. In fact, he commissioned Bob to approach Dad about taking the job. With his presidential nomination almost a certainty later that year, the vice president was loath to get personally involved in any party machinations. My father listened with interest but was forced to admit that he knew little of the workings of the committee that he was being recruited to chair.

Momentum for him gathered quickly, however. His tentative response to increasing press assertions, such as "The Lockport Republican, with his ability and his geography, appears to have the inside track to be elected chairman of the powerful Republican Congressional Campaign Committee," was that he would not actively seek support for the post. But if elected, he could not refuse the opportunity to serve his party. Though he was certainly flattered by the attention and the faith of his colleagues who asked that he consider the job, this would be a new direction for him. It would undoubtedly be a time-consuming diversion from the legislative and legal focus of his congressional duties for the past ten years.

There was another reason for his reticence to jump at seeking the new post: he had no desire to be part of a divisive intra-party battle over the chairmanship. As it happened, the only other contender for it was none other than Bill McCulloch of Ohio. As No.1 and No. 2 Republicans in seniority on the House Judiciary Committee, he and Dad had been good friends and co-workers on legislation for many years. McCulloch was currently vice-chairman of the NRCC, and the man the late Chairman Simpson had designated as acting chairman during his illness.

Most committee members, however, seemed to feel the Ohioan lacked the fiery partisanship that was needed at this juncture, as they were gearing up once again to launch their elusive quest for control of Congress in 1960. But despite limited support, McCulloch insisted on staying in the race. My father, meanwhile, was being assured of firm support for his candidacy by state after state. So he decided that while he too would remain in contention, he would not personally engage in any campaigning that might destroy party unity or embarrass his friend.

There was still another bit of political intrigue going on behind the scenes that did threaten this unity. A cabal of about twenty young Republican "Turks," Bill Miller among them, had only recently succeeded in ousting former Speaker of the House, Congressman Joe Martin of Massachusetts, from his job as House Minority Leader. They had felt his competence was slipping and that he lacked aggressiveness, and they wanted to replace him with the younger, more vigorous Charles Halleck of Indiana.

Hoping they could accomplish the coup peacefully by offering Martin the chairmanship of the Republican Policy Committee instead, the group was chagrined when the old warrior went down fighting and threatening reprisals in a bitter contest. One of his last hurrahs, he hoped, would be to get his friend Bill McCulloch the NRCC post. He wanted that victory even more when he discovered his newly anointed nemesis, Halleck, was actively marshalling votes for Miller. "Anything Charlie Halleck wants in this session, I'm against," fumed the spurned leader.

At the last minute, when it became apparent that my father would win by a margin of at least two to one, McCulloch pulled out of the race, piqued that the mantle he thought Simpson had passed to him was being unceremoniously snatched away. Dad was elected chairman by acclamation on January 21, 1960.

The first move he made was to retain his erstwhile opponent as legal counsel for the NRCC, an attempt to assuage the Ohioan's hurt feelings and heal the old wounds of the Halleck-Martin scrap, which, to his regret, the recent contest had laid bare. Always one to conciliate party differences rather than to create them, he recognized the importance of mollifying the Old Guard, who felt they were gradually being eased out of party councils, and bringing them on board for the fight ahead. It was all the more important that he do so since his selection was seen as swinging party leadership even further in the direction of youth and "moderate" Republicanism.

Then he hit the ground running, optimistically, perhaps somewhat overoptimistically, predicting that the GOP would secure a majority in the House of Representatives in the upcoming November election. They would need to win an additional 67 seats to accomplish that ambitious goal. More specifically, they had to retain all 151 seats they then held, win back the 44 seats they had lost in the disastrous 1958 election, and take at least another 23 seats to gain control. Dad's friend and fellow congressman, Mel Laird, remembers him in his new role as a sort of "bantam rooster," bouncing around with more energy than any other congressman he knew as he attempted to keep many balls in the air at one time.

My father's claim that he welcomed his new job as both "an opportunity and a challenge" was surely an understatement, for he knew that he had his work cut out for him in a decidedly uphill battle. Success could skyrocket his stock in the Party; failure would do just the opposite. Despite any private uncertainties he may have had about the outcome and its possible repercussions for his own future, he approached it all with his exterior trademark air of supreme confidence and determination. "Politically I know I'm supposed to say we can do it," he once quipped, "but I really mean it."

The National Republican Congressional Campaign Committee was nearly 100 years old by the time he took the helm. Its birth during the tumultuous congressional election year of 1866 was part of a Radical Republican effort to get more of their kind elected to Congress. The Radicals were in a titanic struggle with President Andrew Johnson over how to conduct Reconstruction of the South following the devastation of the Civil War. The former wished to harshly punish the South; the latter wanted a more conciliatory approach. Henceforth, in less contentious times, the committee has simply been about finding and helping to elect, in a professional and organized manner, attractive Republican candidates, of any stripe, to the House of Representatives.

The NRCC is composed of one congressman from each state that has some GOP representation in the House. That being an unwieldy group, the day-to-day affairs are run by an unsalaried chairman, along with his paid executive director and a staff, in

Dad's day, of thirty. The chairman automatically becomes part of a triumvirate, which, along with the chairman of the Republican National Committee (RNC) and the chairman of the Republican Senatorial Campaign Committee, manages the electoral fortunes of the Party. The position carries significant authority and influence, particularly in an election year, but even more in a presidential election year. The quality of congressional races in those years could have a powerful impact on straight ticket voting for president, which was considerably more prevalent years ago than it is today.

When he came on board in 1960, my father found a dispirited and floundering committee in dire financial and psychological straits. Since the highpoint in 1952 of winning both the presidency and control of the House, the Republican Party had been battered by significant congressional losses in three consecutive elections—1954, 1956, and 1958. In fact, in 1958, shortages of campaign funds due to poor planning by the RNC and the NRCC, a mild economic recession that Republicans were blamed for, and general apathy all contributed to a whopping loss of forty-eight seats. GOP strength in the 435-member House dropped to an embattled 153 legislators. The campaign organization that had steadily grown in strength and professionalism since 1946, with a year-round permanent staff now firmly established, was forced to lay off some valuable members.

Now in 1960, the committee was gearing for what most observers considered to be one of the most important congressional battles in the Party's history, to try to end the long stretch of minority status that many Republicans had almost come to accept. "Miller, who had developed a congressional reputation as a scrapper, carried this vigor into his new job and boosted morale of committee staffers as the 1960 campaign neared," recorded the official 100-Year History of the NRCC published in 1966.

He did seem to enter this somber scene like something of a whirling dervish. Suddenly, the committee and its chairman that had heretofore been little heard from was all over the papers—photos of Dad, cigarette in hand, in Chesterfield coat and jaunty Homburg tilted slightly at an angle, walking briskly back and forth from his congressional office in the Cannon Building to NRCC headquarters in the Congressional Hotel, shots of the chairman on the phone, always on the phone, with that big black receiver cocked to his ear, eyes twinkling, half-smile sneaking across his face as if he knew something no one else did.

Colorful, fighting press releases began emanating weekly, sometimes daily, from this prolific new party spokesman, pronouncements critiquing every word and movement of candidate and then President John F. Kennedy. They were bitingly partisan, of course, sometimes too much so for my taste, with clever phrases produced by a committee speechwriter and designed to be catchy enough to win media attention. That was always a challenge for the party out of power. Congressman Barney Frank of Massachusetts once commented that "nonpartisanship and partisanship are equally important aspects of democracy. What we 'partisan bicker' about are some of the most important questions a society can debate."[1] That is undoubtedly true, but it is one of the least appealing aspects of a job that was guaranteed to make my father a lightning rod and a thorn in the opposition's side.

Straightforward and decisive about what needed to be done, he took immediate charge of the committee—reshuffling and beefing up the staff with hardened veterans, putting the best people he had, many of them canny former newsmen, in charge of the campaign, public relations, advertising, and field divisions. The output of campaign materials for the use of incumbent Congressmen and new candidates was stepped up. And "a mighty effort was launched in some sixty to seventy key Democrat-held districts, once held by Republicans, which had been designated as prime targets for GOP candidates."[2]

Bob Wilson recalled that Dad was particularly good at raising money, the most urgent need in those lean times. In fact, he put the committee on an entirely new and stronger financial footing, an effort that Wilson, when he succeeded him as chairman, continued and improved. Bob admitted that my father's secret to success was his big smile, his winning personality, and his encouraging prognosis for the Party.

Dad used to call money the "mother's milk" of campaigning. Although it cost only about $60,000 to $70,000 to run for Congress in the early sixties, a seemingly paltry sum, the chairman had little "milk" to distribute to his recruits when he entered his new job—about $500,000. Spread over some seventy races, that allowed for a meager $7,000 per race. The Republican National Committee could only afford to funnel him 25c on every dollar they collected, but barely half of that had been forthcoming. The NRCC traditionally only roused itself to collect a little money of its own just before elections. John Rhodes recalled that the most he ever got from the committee was $500. Chairman Simpson would get on a train and travel around the country with a little black bag to parcel out what few funds he had.

My father's complaint had always been that in recent elections Republicans lacked good, forceful, articulate candidates, as well as an effective grassroots organization of precinct workers. He aimed to do something about both. He personally took on the job of actively recruiting, screening, and developing attractive—preferably young—men and women with some government or business experience who could win. He and his crack field men proceeded to scour the country. That kind of thorough search had never been done before.

A supremely practical political operative, he demanded a pragmatic evaluation of every congressional district, based on detailed surveys. He became almost as good as his savvy right-hand man, Bill Warner, at analyzing their weaknesses and retaining in his memory the contours and complexion of each one. One of his major concerns was that the Party was sitting out far too many races around the country—in almost a third of the 435 House seats, no Republican was contesting the Democrat. His theory was that if the Republican Party were ever to grow, if it were ever to be anything but the minority party, it must become a presence in areas where it had previously been unsuccessful or nonexistent.

It was obvious to him that the GOP must definitely begin to field candidates in big cities and the South, both of which had been virtually ceded to the Democrats. He understood that there were some seats that were unwinnable, and he was not about to spin his wheels on those. But Jack Mills, his astute campaign director, remembers that if Republicans ever came close to control of Congress, his boss would "go after the Lord himself."

The reality was that though finances were improving—a budget of $2,000,000 had been approved by the finance committee—there was still no endless supply of money. So it was important, Dad felt, to concentrate funds in districts where they had the greatest opportunity to win. For instance, the Republicans had lost forty-five seats in 1958 by a total of only 200,000 votes. He reasoned that they could win them back by getting to the polls at least some of the 8,000,000 Republicans who voted for President Eisenhower in 1956 but didn't bother to vote at all two years later. Funds would definitely be targeted to those seats. No longer was the disorganized "shotgun approach" to be used, when only candidates who had the most pull or made the most noise got financial support from the NRCC.

Another innovation of Chairman Miller's, still in use today, was the concept of campaign schools for Republican hopefuls. There had been little in the way of guidance or training in the techniques and strategies of political campaigning for those aspiring to run for Congress. So in August 1960, he opened a two-day "school" in Washington for over 150 congressional hopefuls from some thirty-five states, as far away as California and Alaska. The chairman pronounced that he was pleased with the high turnout.

A morning meeting with the president in the White House was first on the agenda. That was followed by work sessions crammed with information on foreign relations, defense, economic problems, space and scientific progress, labor and social legislation, agriculture, the national political campaign, and the individual House races. This heady experience was concluded by a luncheon with Vice President Richard Nixon, who pointed out to the group, now on mental overload, his determination to carry into office with him in the fall a Republican-controlled House.

The "students" were dispatched back to their home states, imbued with new vigor and enthusiasm, and with comprehensive campaign kits chock full of information and suggestions in hand. One interesting footnote here—a young injured war veteran from Kansas, later to run for president of the United States, was among this novice group. Senator Bob Dole reminisced later about how crucial my father's influence was on his political life, and he remained grateful for the kindness and interest his senior colleague had shown him in his early days in Washington.

So that his newly elected freshmen congressmen would not rest on their laurels, the chairman then set up an orientation school for them upon their arrival in Washington, also a first for the NRCC. He reasoned that once they got elected, there was no legitimate excuse, save personal or political ineptitude or adversity, for not getting reelected, *if* they handled their first two years well—those were the most vulnerable years.

Along with teaching the newcomers how to run their offices effectively, Dad believed it was also important to give them some fundamental rules about how to communicate with their constituents, to project themselves and tell the story of their service. His aim was to make good congressmen better. Accordingly, the radio-television-film office of the campaign committee was made available to freshmen legislators, with coaching, to make tapes for shipping back to their districts. They were encouraged to use it often.

Jack Mills has vivid memories of my father during his busy year at the NRCC. They worked closely together, often on the road, and on those trips at the end of a grueling day of speeches, meetings, and interviews, they would stay up late with a few beers, telling war stories and jokes and unwinding. He remembers in particular what an extraordinarily funny man his boss was, with a knack for regaling an audience of one or many: "Your dad would habitually begin his speeches with a humorous story or remark, usually apropos of the place or situation he was visiting and related with his mischievous, wry smile, always tickling his listeners without offending them." Yet ironically, Jack thought, "Bill would caution the young recruits he brought to Washington for his candidate schools about trying to be funny, about how telling jokes on the podium can backfire." He considered it too risky an occupational peril for novice politicians, whose every lapse of discretion at once becomes juicy fodder for the media.

Bill Miller was, according to Jack's account, among the best speakers and debaters he had ever encountered. He also knew how to handle the media with an unusual skill that seemed to come naturally to him. "He could answer a question on *Meet the Press* or *Face the Nation* for five minutes and not say a damn thing if it was a question he didn't want to answer. But he did it so eloquently and diplomatically that the interviewer thought he'd gotten a great answer!" recalled Jack, laughing heartily. "The thing was," Dad's colleague went on, "Bill could just crush an adversary with his grasp of the facts, but he never came across as mean-spirited, like Jesse Helms or Al D'Amato would." Such praise was no doubt merited, but I always told the chairman, expert that I thought I was, that he should smile and look more directly into the camera in his television appearances.

The fact was that my father was good to the media, and they appreciated that. For the most part, he liked and trusted them, and the feeling was mutual. About once a month, he would invite six or seven press people whom he particularly trusted, like Dave Broder of the *Evening Star* and later the *Washington Post*, to the committee for an informal, off-the-record chat. No question was ever barred. No query ever went unanswered. He was known for giving reporters stories with a "hook,' or newsworthy item, and he would slip them all sorts of juicy insights and canny observations about people and events that make grown newsmen salivate but that they agreed to use only for "background." None of them ever betrayed his confidence, even though some of the information would have doubtless made sensational copy. An observer once marveled that Dad was willing to take that risk.

Broder recalled him as one of the most accessible politicians he ever covered. Honest and direct, he understood journalists' deadlines and always returned their phone calls. Invited often to speak before the National Press Club—universally agreed to be the toughest audience a politician can face—I was told he would give such utterly frank and informative replies to questions that it might have been more politic to duck that his visits often produced comments to the effect that he should be considered as a potential candidate for president.

But the most admirable quality my father's campaign director remembers about him is that he absolutely forbade the use of "dirty tricks" to win a campaign. "Too many people in politics are willing to substitute them for doing the hard precinct work that it takes to win the honest way," said Jack. Dad would say over and over, when his staff came to him with sordid personal material they had dug up on various Democratic opponents, "That's bunk. Forget it. We're not going to use it."

Jack Mills remembers one incident in particular. There was a liberal incumbent Minnesota Democrat that they badly wanted to defeat, who was known to have a drinking problem. A zealous NRCC researcher uncovered the fact that the Congressman, a former judge, had accumulated several drunk driving arrests on his record, including a recent one. The staffer was pushing to give this information to the man's Republican opponent as ammunition for his campaign.

Several top aides were in favor of it, but the chairman immediately quashed the whole idea. "I know the guy, and I know his wife. They're nice people and they have wonderful children. We're not going to get into that," he barked abruptly. As a postscript, the Republican candidate in the race eventually got the information from another source and used it; it backfired, and he lost the election. The irony is that the media often liked to characterize Bill Miller as a "gut fighter," but those who knew him best knew him to be just the opposite.

On Monday, July 25, 1960, almost exactly six months after Dad had begun leading the NRCC, a reasonably united Republican Convention was set to open in Chicago. It would give the answering call to the Democrats who had just nominated their unlikely combo of Senators John Kennedy and Lyndon Johnson in Los Angeles. The only surprise would be whom Richard Nixon would choose as his running mate. When newsmen queried my father about that, he still threw out the possibility of his pet ticket of Nixon/Rockefeller. But he knew full well that lingering paranoia in the Nixon camp about Rocky possibly snatching the nomination from their man at the last minute in a draft precluded such an offer.

It was not until the early hours of Thursday morning, closing day of the convention, that the final decision was made on a vice-presidential nominee. After consulting with thirty Republican leaders, Dad among them, the clear consensus was Thruston Morton, the distinguished Senator from Kentucky. Following the meeting, to these insiders' amazement, Nixon announced what he reported was his and the group's nearly unanimous choice: United Nations Ambassador Henry Cabot Lodge. According to my father, no one, including Nixon, had even mentioned Lodge. In fact, prior to the convention, the vice president had met with Morton and all but told him that he was his first choice. It was another example of how distant Nixon could be from his colleagues, and how frustrating Dad found him to work with.

That ended fleeting speculation in some Washington and Western New York newspapers on my father as an excellent choice for the number two spot, which had drawn a touching and enthusiastic, if delusional, hometown response. At the Spring

Ball of the Republican Club of Lockport held in my father's honor in May of that year, a thousand partygoers stomped and cheered and roared their approval as a congratulatory telegram from Dick Nixon was read and an eighty-foot banner unfurled, emblazoned with huge crimson letters: "Miller for Vice President." When quiet returned to the armory, the "favorite son," impeccable in his dark tuxedo and starched white shirt, eyes twinkling with amusement, quipped: "If I were anywhere else I'd say I'm speechless. However, you know me better than that." It was indeed a portent of things to come, but a purely accidental one.

Dad's main participation in the convention was a rousing speech, punctuated by the applause and cheering after almost every paragraph that he was so adept at eliciting, pleading with the delegates for their help in electing a Republican House of Representatives in November. He outlined, in as soldierly a fashion as he could, exactly how they would do it and why it was not as difficult a task as it may seem: "We have to hold on to every congressional seat we now have and add at least sixty-seven more," the determined chairman blithely but earnestly urged.

It was apparent from their enthusiasm that the party faithful wanted to believe this fantastic game plan, despite the odds. Much to the disappointment of the folks back home who were bursting with pride that a local boy was speaking so prominently on national television, all but the closing sentences of his speech were cut off the air when the networks switched to coverage of President Eisenhower's motorcade leaving his hotel for convention hall.

Not to be outshone by the rising star of her husband, Mother also played a role at the 1960 convention. One of her activities points up the striking difference in how women were regarded in political life and by the media then as compared to now. A highlight of the convention, designed to "get the women's vote," was a fashion show. Not just a regular fashion show, but the "fashion story" of our First Ladies, from Mary Todd Lincoln through Mamie Eisenhower, which would re-create and trace history through fashion. Of course, it included only Republican First Ladies, an editing decision that some might consider questionable. And the very idea of appealing to women voters through fashion rather than a substantive discussion of issues would no doubt elicit gales of laughter, if not outrage, in today's world of liberated feminism.

Nevertheless, the event created great anticipation and excitement in Chicago in July 1960. Mother was among the twelve "comely" wives of dignitaries chosen to participate in the tribute to 100 years of "Great Ladies of America" pageant. It was presented at a luncheon during the convention, subsequently aired on NBC television, and pictured in magazines and newspapers nationwide. All modeled gowns were replicas of the originals worn by the selected First Ladies and displayed in the Smithsonian Institution. It took thirty seamstresses in New York City three weeks to sew them. Despite being roused at 4:30 a.m. for preparations and rehearsal on the big day, Mom managed to control her stage fright, master her pivots, and avoid tripping over her flowing hem to metamorphose into an elegant Lou Hoover, wife of Herbert Hoover. She wore her "classic gown of lustrous ice-blue satin" with "statuesque beauty."[3]

Once the hoopla of the convention was over and work on the hustings began, there were a number of issues my father felt compelled to speak out on as NRCC Chairman. But there were two in particular during the 1960 presidential campaign that really stirred his ire: "reverse religious bigotry" and the alleged "missile gap," as they came to be labeled.

Stepping in, in his fearless fashion, where many others at the time dared not tread, so sensitive was the subject, he tackled head-on a development he deeply disliked:

> *This news conference has been called to condemn as vigorously as I can the things which are being done to inflame religious feeling in the Presidential campaign. I speak as a Catholic and out of a sense of outrage. I charge that those running the Kennedy campaign are deliberately keeping the religious issue alive and inflamed—apparently in the hope that this will produce more votes for Senator Kennedy from among our fellow Catholics.*

It is difficult, thankfully, to remember today how alive and well was anti-Catholic sentiment in some quarters of this country in 1960. When John Kennedy ran for president, he was the first Catholic to have to contend with the issue since Democrat Al Smith of New York was badly defeated in his quest for the presidency in 1928, in part because he was Catholic.

In September of the '60 campaign, the young Massachusetts
Senator was forced into a confrontation about his religion before
a meeting of Protestant ministers in Houston, Texas. By all accounts, he acquitted himself well before this adversarial audience. He reaffirmed his belief in the separation of church and
state, attempting to quiet once and for all fears that if elected
he might put his religious beliefs before his constitutional duties, and he dispelled the ludicrous notion that the Pope or the
Catholic bishops might help him govern. But certain elements of
the Democratic Party would not let the issue die—or so Dad and
many others charged.

As the campaign wore on, evidence surfaced of what they
called "bigotry in reverse"—a calculated, well-financed propaganda campaign exploiting the religious issue, in order to imply
that any vote *against* Kennedy was a vote *for* bigotry. This despite
the fact that his Republican opponent, Richard Nixon, admittedly not always a paragon of clean campaigning, had in this
case at least tried to keep religion out of the contest. He had not
mentioned it himself and he forbade any discussion of it by those
working on his behalf.

While Kennedy professed ignorance of any such exploitive
effort, groups known to be his staunch supporters, such as the
United Auto Workers Union in Detroit headed by Walter Reuther,
were distributing an incendiary leaflet nationwide. It carried on
its cover a cartoon picture of the Statue of Liberty and a Ku Klux
Klansman, with the line: "Which do you choose? Liberty or bigotry?" The ad, insinuating that a vote for Kennedy was a vote for
liberty and a vote for Nixon would be a vote for bigotry, had been
roundly denounced by the Michigan Fair Practices Commission.
Set up by a Democratic governor and comprised of a Catholic
priest, a Jewish Rabbi, and a Protestant bishop, the group had
stated: "Since the leaflet raises the religious issue with a reverse
twist and lowers the whole election debate, it is unfair, and we
condemn it without hesitation."

In addition, the Democratic National Committee, at the insistence of the nominee's brother and campaign manager, Robert
Kennedy, was buying expensive television time to repeatedly re-
run the film of John Kennedy's appearance before the Protestant
ministers. These continuing subtle, and not so subtle, mechanisms for perpetuating the religion factor after it was seemingly

settled, Chairman Miller alleged, were an effort "not to create understanding among non-Catholics but to inflame resentment among Catholics" and win their votes. He was particularly angry because this was not the first time the Kennedy forces had tried to use their candidate's Catholicism as a weapon to secure his electoral success.

In 1956, when the Senator was seeking his party's vice-presidential nod, and again in his fight four years later for the presidential nomination, his supporters had run extensive polls on the Catholic vote, accumulated prodigious statistics, and prepared numerous memoranda. All this was for the purpose of showing party leaders how beneficial Kennedy's religion would be in states and areas with large Catholic populations, particularly the electoral vote-heavy states of the North, and how many Catholic votes they would stand to lose on Election Day if he were not nominated.

My father was himself a tough political strategist who would seek votes for his party almost anywhere he could find them. And yet, using religion to get them seemed appalling and repugnant to him. He would say forthrightly over and over, even when questioned later as the Republican vice-presidential candidate about the role his own Catholicism might play in the 1964 election: "I don't like to inject that question into the discussion. The question of balance on religious grounds has no place in the convention, the campaign, or the election." He also believed deeply that "the intelligence and patriotism of Catholic voters is insulted and damaged by assertions that they are gullible enough to vote for a candidate for high office merely because he is a fellow Catholic."

But perhaps one of the most dishonest ploys of the 1960 presidential campaign, or any campaign for that matter, Dad believed, was candidate Kennedy's assertion that there existed a "missile gap" in our nation's defense. In short, he alleged that president, and former General, Eisenhower had allowed our supply of nuclear weapons to become inferior to Russia's arsenal. The Massachusetts Senator made that manufactured issue one of the cornerstones of his campaign, and he exploited it "even after he had been given classified military information indicating there was no such thing,"[4] Richard Reeves revealed in his 1993 biography of Kennedy. My father called him on the deception time after time.

When the Soviets launched their *Sputnik* satellite in 1957, Americans were shocked and worried that our feared adversary possessed greater delivery capacity for nuclear warheads than did we, that perhaps the delicate balance of mutual deterrence was now slightly tipped, and not in our favor. Kennedy latched onto that fear with such alarmist rhetoric as, "We are facing a gap on which we are gambling with our survival."

Dad, in multiple press releases and speeches, angrily refuted what he considered the Democratic candidate's dangerous charge by listing all the components of our military establishment, which he asserted were more than enough to annihilate the enemy. He added that, considering how precariously both countries were poised on the edge of mutual destruction, "no matter how badly I wanted to be president, I wouldn't run up and down this country stating to the world that we have an inferior military force." Yet Kennedy pressed on, the theme now being "central to the campaign and to his entire political career."[5]

Once elected, President Kennedy became strangely silent on the alleged "missile gap." Then his bright new, albeit unseasoned, Secretary of Defense, Robert McNamara, in a casual, supposedly off-the-record session with newsmen in his office just a month after the inauguration, unwittingly blew the perfidy wide open. His statements hit the papers the next day, to his horror, in the headline: "Kennedy Defense Study Finds No Evidence of a 'Missile Gap.' "

The secretary was forced to explain to his furious president that the truth of the matter was that not only could the United States absorb a full-scale Soviet attack but we would still have enough nuclear capacity left to destroy the entire Soviet Union. By his press conference the following morning, Kennedy had turned 180 degrees from being certain of the "missile gap" during his campaign to a stuttering admission that "it would be premature to reach a judgment as to whether there is a gap or not a gap."[6]

But Chairman Miller's job was not just about issuing press releases and tripping up the Democrats, much as it seemed that he delighted in that detail. Day in and day out, it meant soliciting money, signing checks for the lucky 300 odd GOP candidates whom he decided would receive some amount of financial assistance, and spending hours in conferences with his committee staff to discuss publicity, research, and campaign strategy.

Every Wednesday morning, he met with Vice President Nixon and other top-echelon GOP advisors for a campaign conference. It included Len Hall and Senator Thruston Morton, former and current Republican National Chairmen respectively, and Senator Barry Goldwater, Chairman of the Senate Campaign Committee—all were working together harmoniously for the first time in a while, without bickering over funds or purposes. And his phone never stopped ringing—calls from all parts of the country from Republican candidates and leaders seeking guidance, speakers for rallies, and, typically, money. All this while still tending to his congressional duties and trying to run his own campaign for reelection.

The traveling, speaking, and cheering the troops never ended until Election Day in November. By that time, having paid a visit to about 375 congressional races, Dad had come to know many areas of the country almost down to their street lines and back alleys, made speeches and television appearances from coast to coast, held untold numbers of press conferences, picked at countless "rubber chicken" dinners, and shed nearly ten pounds from his already lean frame. There is no knowing how many cigarettes he had smoked to calm his nerves, for though he always seems so placid on the surface, his nervous energy bubbled just below.

Election Day, November 8, brought a mixed bag for Republicans. Though Nixon lost his bid for the presidency in the closest contest since Grover Cleveland's race in 1884, my father's arduous work building the sinews and muscle of the Party with improved grassroots precinct organization nationwide had paid off. Republicans gained 22 new seats in the House—a far cry from the 67 he had hoped for, but not since the election of 1916 had the party that lost the White House won seats in Congress.

Despite that one bright note, the GOP was left in disarray. There were bitter accusations that the Party's standard-bearer had run a poor campaign in a race that was his to lose, and that he took advice from no one. He had after all been an experienced and well-traveled vice president under an unusually popular president, and he had been ahead of his opponent in the polls by almost two to one after the conventions. Among other things, Dad had urged Nixon to concentrate more on the states with large electoral votes, but instead he spread himself thinly everywhere and ended up losing many of those vital states by razor-thin margins. Lodge proved to be a disappointment to many. In addition to the fact that he drove his staff crazy by insisting on a nap every afternoon, pajamas and all, he was remote and imperious, and conveyed a distinct distaste for politics and campaigning.

My father's own race for reelection in 1960 had understandably been forced to take a back seat to his campaign obligations across the country. When he took the NRCC job, I suspect he knew that would be the case, but he must have hoped that his record and years of service would pull him through. But this time was tougher. Word of his new position and stature in Washington provoked, not surprisingly, opposing reactions from Democrats and Republicans in his home district.

One Niagara County Democrat remarked frankly: "Let's face it, the guy's got it. Maybe this means he'll get a top spot in Washington and we might have a chance to elect a Democrat here. I don't think we could ever beat him." The local Democratic Party had always had trouble finding an opponent for Dad and this year was not much different. They had three men interested, but only on the condition that Bill Miller was not running.

After a primary, they ended up once again with Mariano Lucca, publisher of a Buffalo community paper and indefatigable veteran of two previous elections in which he had been severely trounced by Miller. "It's a habit he can't seem to break," offered the *Niagara Falls Gazette* with unconcealed sarcasm. Yet instead of being gun-shy as you might expect, this feisty little Italian, who prided himself on his eloquence, came out with fists up, charging that my father would now surely neglect his constituents, that he would be so busy with national Republican affairs that he would have little time to tend to the concerns of his district, particularly its chronic unemployment.

Republicans on the other hand, after initial apprehension along those same lines, decided to turn his absence into a political asset. They stressed that Washington's recognition of his talents had brought pride and prestige to the district, which, along with his seniority, had the potential to produce more contracts for its ailing industries. Their theme was that since "the Congressman," as they called him, had been a tireless worker in every election since 1950 for every candidate on the county GOP ticket, getting them out of more than a few tight spots, the least the Party owed him now was to unite and help him out in his own district while he toiled for the GOP nationally.

Niagara County Chairman Ed Brown made sure that happened, warding off an early threat of a primary for Dad, which would have been the first he had ever had. A gala testimonial dinner was held in his honor, with 550 tickets sold and scores more hopeful attendees on the waiting list, with Barry Goldwater in attendance to pay tribute to him, and with telegrams from Nixon and Rockefeller expressing their regrets and affection.

Despite yet another vigorous effort by the AFL-CIO to defeat him, he managed to pull out a sixth decisive victory, but this time by a far smaller margin than ever before—a little over 20,000 votes, compared to 36,000 in 1958. Kennedy's popularity in heavily Catholic Buffalo and the continuous drumbeat of criticism against my father, as well as the fact that he had not been able to launch his congressional campaign until mid-October, had hurt his numbers.

After the dust settled, Bill Miller was widely hailed nationally for the "remarkable" job he had done in reversing the trend and increasing Republican membership in the House after so many losing years. Reelected without contest to his post as NRCC Chairman for another term, he immediately took up his familiar refrain of predicting a GOP takeover of the House of Representatives in 1962. His optimism was based on tabulations that showed Republicans had failed to gain an additional forty seats in the recent election by less than 5 percent of the vote.

But he had an even more important message for his fellow party members at this point: as the minority party, they could not afford the luxury of division and infighting. Nor should they devote themselves to the aspirations of any one leader for the next two years. "Our job now," he urged, "is not to find a presidential candidate for 1964 but to be an effective, cohesive party that can gain governorships and more seats in the Congress in 1962. Otherwise," he asserted without mincing words, "the Republican presidential nomination in 1964 won't be worth a damn ... we'll be turning over rocks to find someone willing to take it."

CHAPTER EIGHT

LEADERSHIP—ANOTHER STEP UP

In February of '61, AP political writer, Jack Bell, was the first to report that Bill Miller was being "boomed" to step up to the post of Republican National Chairman. Senator Thruston Morton was eager to leave the committee, sooner rather than later, to prepare for what he anticipated would be a tough race for reelection in Kentucky the following year. He was reportedly seeking a successor acceptable to former Vice President Nixon, New York's Governor Rockefeller, and Senator Barry Goldwater of Arizona, leaders respectively of the middle, left, and right of the Party and the three most likely contenders for top spot on the ticket three years hence. He wanted someone who had the ability to weld these diametrically opposed GOP factions into a united party front, and to ward off the distinct possibility of the National Committee itself splitting into warring factions.

To growing numbers of Republican leaders both on Capitol Hill and on the National Committee, Miller appeared to fit the bill. He had worked closely with Goldwater, who as Senate Campaign Chairman was his counterpart across the Capitol, had long supported Nixon (though in truth he was now privately somewhat disenchanted with him), and had mended his fences with Rockefeller in two very cordial post-election meetings. His intention had been to include the governor in discussions about the future of the Party and to assure him that his early endorsement of Nixon's nomination in 1960 did not necessarily carry over to 1964, but that he intended to remain neutral on that choice for some time to come. In addition, my father's potential candidacy for the national chairmanship was helped by the fact that he had come to know party leaders from one end of the country to the other and had earned their respect for the work he had done at the NRCC.

There was only one other serious contender for the job—Ray Bliss, chairman of the Ohio Republican State Committee, who had masterfully engineered victory for Nixon in his state in 1960, despite the defection of several other industrial states. Bliss, known primarily to National Committee members and party professionals, was regarded as a top-notch organizer, a "nuts and bolts man" with a canny grasp of precinct politics. But he made no secret of the fact that he disliked, and had little talent for, the speaking chores and public appearances that went with the Party's top job.

The chairmanship of the National Committee was the most powerful job at a party's disposal when it did not control the White House. It was especially so now for Republicans as Nixon had virtually abdicated titular leadership of his party by moving to California and entering state politics. The chairman was entrusted with the primary responsibility of directing party affairs, with the main objective of recapturing the White House. He spoke for the Party as a whole, blurring whatever philosophical or sectional differences might exist among various congressional and other leaders. In the age of television, being inarticulate in public could seriously lessen the effectiveness of even the most skilled technician. So the importance of possessing speaking and public relations skills that would reflect well on the Party and enhance its image could not be overemphasized. These traits were well established as my father's long suit.

While support for him grew as the right man at the right time to revitalize the Party, his own reluctance to be considered for the job grew as well. He felt that for the next two years he might be more valuable in his NRCC post and in helping formulate Republican leadership policy in the House. He also had enormous respect for Bliss' skills as a technician, and he believed those talents might be needed to organize the GOP's effort nationally in the years to come.

With decision time nearing and both Dad and Bliss not certain they were the best choice for the job for differing reasons, the Washington press began predicting: "Mr. Miller's skill in dealing with public issues and presenting them clearly and forcefully has made an impression across the country . . . and added up to a virtual party demand that he allow himself to be drafted." Pressure was mounting to make it known that he would accept the job.

Meanwhile, he had reached an understanding with Bliss that if the Ohioan really wanted the national chairmanship, he himself would be glad to continue as NRCC chief. However, if the Party insisted on him and no other, he stipulated that there must be unanimity on his election. In fact, he was quoted as saying that if any controversy blew up over the job, the committeemen could count him out. He would take the assignment, but he was not plugging for it. Once again, he wished to avert an intra-party battle that would drain energy from the task at hand.

There was some talk on the National Committee at this time, specifically among a small group of midwesterners eager to draft Ray Bliss, about the need for a full-time, salaried chairman instead of a volunteer, part-time chairman who was also a member of Congress. My father did not intend to give up his congressional seat or accept a salary. Nor did he think those options were necessary in order to do the job effectively. The lurking doubts about a part-time chairman were finally resolved for most committee members by the realization that the advantages of having a congressman in the job, with his prominence, visibility, and access to the media, far outweighed any disadvantages, especially when the Party was out of power in the executive branch of government.

Chairman Morton called an RNC meeting for June 2 at the Sheraton Park Hotel in Washington to pick a new chairman. The committee, comprised of a national committeeman and committeewoman from each state and the state chairmen from states that had gone Republican in the last presidential election or had a majority of Republican legislators, was by then leaning heavily in favor of Miller. Some behind-the-scenes maneuvering by his compatriots in the House, who worked the phones to line up additional support for him, as well as the quiet but forceful backing of Governor Rockefeller's forces, put Dad over the top. When it became apparent that Bliss, still "available but not running," was not going to be tapped after all, he somewhat reluctantly dispatched a telegram to Morton asking that his name be withdrawn. My father's unanimous selection, a rarity in RNC history, meant the transfer had been accomplished, as all had hoped, without "bloodletting."

His new position brought marked changes to our household. From now on, he was rarely ever home for long periods, and we missed him terribly. It was already a busy time in our lives, with my high school graduation imminent and preparations for college on the horizon. Mother was expecting my third sibling in

"Diz" Hinch Miller holding her
newborn, William Edward Miller

Little Bill Miller lecturing a friend in his
backyard, the first of many
forceful orations

In sartorial splendor on the front steps
of his boyhood home

Lounging in the dorm at Notre Dame,
ecstatic to be there

First car, and the first in a long line of convertibles

The newlyweds

Hard at work in JAG school in Ann Arbor

On grim duty in Nuremberg—from left, Ed Boedecker, Drexel Sprecher, Dad

Mom and Dad with their first born, Libby

New York Governor Tom Dewey congratulating Dad upon his election
as Niagara County District Attorney in 1948

Dad testifying in early hearings on
his Niagara Power bill

Bill Miller goes to Washington in 1950,
with his green Cadillac convertible that
was stolen in a week, congressional
plates and all

One of countless constituent group
photos on the Capitol steps

With President Dwight Eisenhower

With Vice President Richard Nixon

With Pat Nixon

Mother, as the young president of the 82nd Congress
Club, presenting Mamie Eisenhower with a gift

A family VIP tour of the United
Nations in New York with
Ambassador Henry Cabot Lodge

With congressional leaders,
Congressman Charles Halleck (left) and
Senator Everett Dirksen

As ranking minority member of the House Judiciary committee, hearing testimony
in San Francisco on Japanese-American war claims

Mom as Lou Hoover for the First Ladies
Pageant at the 1960 Republican convention

Voting in 1960, always a photo op

With Ab Hermann, Executive Director at the RNC for Dad and many other national chairmen

Rep. Bob Wilson presenting Dad with a gavel made from the wood of Capitol Hill's famous "Teddy Roosevelt Tree," recently felled, in recognition of "outstanding service" to the NRCC during 18 months as chairman

As Republican National Chairman, working with Bob Wilson, who had replaced him at the Congressional Campaign Committee, and Barry Goldwater, chairman of the Senate Campaign Committee

With Larry Spivak, moderator of *Meet the Press*

In a hotel room on the road during the 1962 campaign, watching President Kennedy address the nation about the Cuban missile crisis

With his friend and governor, Nelson Rockefeller

With Senator Hubert Humphrey, his future opponent in the '64 campaign for whom he had great admiration, and Senator John Tower of Texas

House Minority Leader Charlie Halleck toasting Dad at a testimonial dinner in his honor

On the podium in San Francisco after Dad's acceptance speech

The family's joyous arrival back home in Buffalo after the '64 convention and reunion with little siblings, Billy and Stephie

The crowd greeting us

The ride into Lockport, deluged with well wishers

Crowd passing a microphone to the newly minted VP candidate for a few words

A week of R & R at the Olcott lake cottage —Dad perusing local coverage of his recent triumph

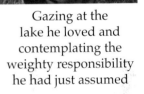

Catching up on the bales of congratulatory mail, son Bill looking on

Gazing at the lake he loved and contemplating the weighty responsibility he had just assumed

Part of the "Cleaver family" portrait – Mary and I "composing" a campaign song for our dad

The official Miller family campaign photo

It's back to work—candidates and wives reunite

Barry and Dad at a private meeting with GOP congressional leaders on Capitol Hill, trying to cement party unity for the campaign ahead

Both families on the podium at the kickoff

Goldwater and Miller in a triumphant handclasp at the Miller campaign kickoff in Lockport, New York

The Republican candidates in Arizona for the Goldwater kickoff, gamely sporting Navajo Indian sombreros

Mother bravely steps out to
campaign alone

Mother and Dad with Father Ted Hesburgh,
President of the University of Notre Dame

Libby, Mother, Dad, and Mary at a
Polish-American event

Campaigning in New York City

Beagle puppy bestowed upon
our family on the campaign trail
—named "B & B" for "Beagles for
Barry and Bill"

The Niagaran and all its inhabitants—crew, press, campaign staff, family, and friends

The "Fab Four"— Dad's trusted campaign aides:
from left, Gib Darrison, Bill Warner, and Bob Smalley

Speaking with a passion

Meeting the press—Jack Casserly, left, Paul
Niven, right

The Goldwater and Miller children: from left, Joanne Goldwater Ross, Richard Holt, husband of Peggy Goldwater, Peggy Jr., Barry Jr., Mike, Libby and Mary Miller

"Barry's Boys" and "Miller's Maids" campaigning

Surprise reception for Libby upon her return to her summer job as a guide at the New York World's Fair after the San Francisco convention

"Vote for my dad!"

Mother and Dad emerging on election night to greet the waiting press, still smiling despite the dismal returns

Home at last—and return to
the practice of law

More time for relaxation and getting
that handicap down

The Millers hosting Barry at
a memorable party in their
Lockport home, October 1967

More time for the
"second family"

Bill Miller as spokesman for a group of former Republican National Chairmen supporting Gerald Ford for the Party's presidential nomination in 1976: from left, Bob Dole, Meade Alcorn, Bill Miller, President Ford, Rogers Morton, Hugh Scott, Len Hall, and Dean Burch

Having some laughs with the Goldwaters and Fords at the gala tenth anniversary celebration of the "Non-Inauguration of the Goldwater/Miller Ticket" in 1975

Making the famous American Express commercial

My father's casket being carried by his oldest and dearest friends into St. John's Church, Lockport, past an honor guard of police officers

Funeral with military honors at Arlington National Cemetery—the flag-draped coffin lifted from the caisson and carried to the gravesite

Mother at the funeral, on the comforting arm of Barry Goldwater. My sister Stephanie on her other arm

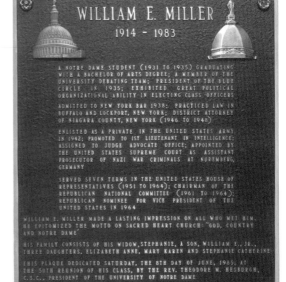

The plaque conceived and dedicated by Bill Miller's Notre Dame Class of '35 to honor their celebrated classmate. It hangs in the Law Building on campus

WILLIAM E. MILLER
1914 - 1983

A NOTRE DAME STUDENT (1931 TO 1935) GRADUATING WITH A BACHELOR OF ARTS DEGREE; A MEMBER OF THE UNIVERSITY DEBATING TEAM; PRESIDENT OF THE BLUE CIRCLE IN 1935; EXHIBITED GREAT POLITICAL ORGANIZATIONAL ABILITY IN ELECTING CLASS OFFICERS

ADMITTED TO NEW YORK BAR 1938; PRACTICED LAW IN BUFFALO AND LOCKPORT, NEW YORK; DISTRICT ATTORNEY OF NIAGARA COUNTY, NEW YORK (1946 TO 1948)

ENLISTED AS A PRIVATE IN THE UNITED STATES ARMY IN 1942; PROMOTED TO 1ST LIEUTENANT IN INTELLIGENCE; ASSIGNED TO JUDGE ADVOCATE OFFICE; APPOINTED BY THE UNITED STATES SUPREME COURT AS ASSISTANT PROSECUTOR OF NAZI WAR CRIMINALS AT NUREMBERG, GERMANY

SERVED SEVEN TERMS IN THE UNITED STATES HOUSE OF REPRESENTATIVES (1951 TO 1964); CHAIRMAN OF THE REPUBLICAN NATIONAL COMMITTEE (1961 TO 1964); REPUBLICAN NOMINEE FOR VICE PRESIDENT OF THE UNITED STATES IN 1964

WILLIAM E. MILLER MADE A LASTING IMPRESSION ON ALL WHO MET HIM. HE EPITOMIZED THE MOTTO ON SACRED HEART CHURCH "GOD, COUNTRY AND NOTRE DAME"

HIS FAMILY CONSISTS OF HIS WIDOW, STEPHANIE, A SON, WILLIAM E., JR., THREE DAUGHTERS, ELIZABETH ANNE, MARY KAREN AND STEPHANIE CATHERINE

THIS PLAQUE DEDICATED SATURDAY, THE 8TH DAY OF JUNE, 1985, AT THE 50TH REUNION OF HIS CLASS, BY THE REV. THEODORE M. HESBURGH, C.S.C., PRESIDENT OF THE UNIVERSITY OF NOTRE DAME

THE CLASS OF 1935

October, which at least kept her near home. Telephones prolifer-
ated. Dad, when in residence, was out earlier in the morning and
in later at night, and there was an air of excitement in the house
whenever one of his now frequently-televised press conferences,
speeches, or appearances on weekly news programs such as *Meet
the Press* or *Issues and Answers* was about to appear on our seven-
teen-inch Zenith. They offered us a chance to actually *see* him for
a half hour. We watched with a mixture of tension and hope.

He did an average of a half-dozen radio or television programs a week and after only a fortnight on the job, he had already
turned down 100 invitations to speak. The National Committee
was being deluged with mail containing generous praise for his
performances, as well as for his selection as chairman—things
like: "Congressman Miller was great on *Meet the Press* Sunday.
Where do I sign up for a Miller for President Club?"[1] By all
reports, the new chairman's forensic style was pleasing to most
party stalwarts. He answered questions fairly, fully, clearly, and
concisely—no excess verbiage. He did not allow his inquisitors
to push him around and when interrupted by them, he could,
without conveying impatience, simply say, "pardon me," and
continue his point.

There were also humorous letters: "I noticed in the press
write-up they described you as 'rotund and energetic.' Must
be the home cooking that did it as we remember when you
could hide behind a number four wood." To which my father
facetiously replied: "I was certainly puzzled to learn that a news
article you read had described me as 'rotund.' I will admit that I
have had a lot on my mind recently and that I assumed a heavy
responsibility when I became chairman, but they don't show up
on the bathroom scale."

Among the fan mail, there were always a few tongue-in-cheek
notes from old Notre Dame pals, designed to help their fellow
alum keep his exalted new stature in perspective: "After reading
some of the press releases concerning one William E. Miller, I am
a little concerned that I might be addressing someone unknown
to me. Bill, you've come a hell of a long way in the practice of the
art and science of politics since the day you got all the Dillon Hall
votes for me when I ran for nomination as president of the junior
class," wrote Tom LaLonde of long ago.

The RNC provided a car and chauffeur, which Dad, not wedded to frills, used only occasionally when he needed time to study. But truth be told, Mary and I loved when the sleek black limo was made available to transport the whole family in unaccustomed luxury to occasional formal events where our father was the guest of honor. An in-town apartment was also offered for the chairman's use after late nights at the committee, but as that seemed to him unnecessary excess, he declined to accept.

What probably surprised us the most with all this new fanfare was the assortment of unexpected gifts that arrived on our doorstep, especially at Christmastime—mostly small items like pickles or fruit, the inevitable fruitcake, and baby gifts for our anticipated new family member. One day, a large original painting of Dad arrived, unannounced—where to hang it?

But the prize-winning gift was the herd of ten black elephants, ranging in height from three to fifteen inches, all carved from Ceylon ebony with ivory tusks and trunks up flung ("for good luck!"). They were sent with a note of congratulations by a local Washington, DC man, as an expression of his "admiration and esteem." To my knowledge, the sender never received any special favors from my father for his generous but unusual offering of his special collection, and the handsome herd still holds a prominent spot in my mother's curio cabinet.

With Dad's increased visibility came more frequent requests for feature stories on "the family," and assorted reporters found their way to what they usually described as our "spacious new Colonial home of red brick with two-story portico supported by white columns" to chat with the women in the household and probe our interests. The articles they produced about the "pretty as a picture" wife and daughters were replete with scintillating descriptions of our family ping-pong matches, our dining habits, the knotty pine kitchen cabinets which Mother never thought she would fill but did, and, of course, our dogs—all details which would no doubt be cut by feature editors today.

Bill Miller, at age 47, was only the second Roman Catholic to be named national chairman in the Republican Party's history, which dated back more than a century—so noted the numerous newspaper articles that chronicled his election. To his chagrin, since he believed religion should be of no relevance to a man's public service, the media saw it as an intentional Republican effort to counterbalance the sitting Democratic president's Catholicism. His religion would also, they surmised, give my father the ability to attack John Kennedy freely without appearing to be a bigot. Though in fact his faith was not a major factor in his recruitment or selection as Republican National Chairman, it was an asset only in that it demonstrated a modicum of the religious tolerance with which the Democrats were now identified. Catholic Democratic national chairmen had long been the rule rather than the exception.

The magnitude of the task Dad had now inherited would prove to be unmatched in tension, drama, complexity, and tough choices by any national chairmanship in recent memory. The only exception might be that of George Bush Sr. during the worst of the Watergate crisis and Richard Nixon's subsequent resignation, when as chairman he struggled vainly to defend a doomed president. Bush, quite understandably, called the job "a political nightmare." Even with my father's apparent qualifications, he would be challenged as never before. There were countless letters that thanked him just for having "the guts" to take it on.

"Loyal opposition comes alive!" was one of many upbeat headlines that greeted his elevation. Roscoe Drummond wrote that Bill Miller "is a veritable breath of fresh air in the nearly motionless atmosphere at national party headquarters." There appeared to be great enthusiasm in the Party and even in the not-easily-impressed media for this "fireball . . . with suave polish"[2] who was willing to challenge "Camelot" and assume the helm of a battered GOP, demoralized as it was after Nixon's narrow loss in 1960. But with a Democrat in the White House, the Democrats in control of Congress by substantial majorities, and Democratic governors outnumbering Republicans by thirty-six to fourteen, the ecstatic headlines belied the reality that Dad had taken on yet another formidable job.

The problems he faced were overwhelming, and they all required immediate and thoughtful attention. Low morale and a poor party image would be near the top of his list. Even lower than morale was the party treasury, now in serious debt. Divisiveness was also one of the prime contenders on the list of priorities, as would be the need for considerable grassroots organizational work. But the problem of the South and how to shape its future within the Republican Party cast a long dark shadow over all else as he took up where Thruston Morton had left off.

The busy new chairman, with his intricate juggling act, spent most mornings in the spacious RNC offices in the Cafritz building on I Street—in meetings, making policy decisions, solving crises, dictating personalized answers to some of the half million letters he would receive a year. Afternoons found him in his congressional office, in Judiciary Committee hearings, or on the House floor. Every Thursday morning he chaired a meeting on the Hill of the joint Senate-House Republican leadership with ten lawmakers. He met regularly with Bob Wilson and Barry Goldwater, chairmen of the Congressional and Senate Campaign Committees, in order to closely coordinate their activities and objectives with his. Communication among those three party organs was crucial and Dad's prior experience with the NRCC facilitated that objective.

While at the National Committee, his energetic, 5 foot 7, 137-pound figure would rarely sit still. He paced his memo-strewn office, rapidly and intensely churning out plans for Republican programs, talking fast and stopping only to take drags on the cigarette usually dangling from his fingers or to flash a bit of humor. Ab Hermann, the committee's crack political director under several national chairmen, sized up his new boss: "I like this guy Miller. I get good vibrations from him." The crusty veteran took to referring to Dad affectionately as "the Skipper."

The first step would be to overhaul the National Committee staff, to get rid of dead wood and beef it up with more experts— he was hired once again to shake things up, and that he would do. Firing people, however, was a tough task for my softhearted father, and he left it to his assistants whenever he could. He immediately drew up an organizational plan, with input from state chairmen around the country, and he sent out periodically a "Chairman's Report," to which one surprised recipient replied: "In all my years on the National Committee I think it is the finest report I have ever received from a chairman, giving us in such detail not only your efforts to date, but outlining what we may expect."

Dad would push ahead with special studies, some already begun, on major national problems, turning to universities for academic brainpower in order to establish authoritative party positions. An expanded research department under Dr.

William Prendergast would become one of the most respected and professional research outfits in the nation's capital. Dr. Paul Bartholomew of Notre Dame was also commissioned to make a thorough, unbiased study of the committee and to recommend changes that would improve its efficiency and effectiveness.

Above all, my father made it known that working for the largest possible Republican victory in 1962 was to be the RNC's immediate and dominant focus. The non-partisan *Congressional Quarterly* took note and reported: "The high command of the Republican Party has formulated a 1962 battle plan which may prove to be the most extensive effort yet undertaken by a party in an off-year election."[3]

That effort included the targeting of about 100 congressional districts, among them ten or twelve seats in the South. Republicans had a history of not working hard enough in off-year elections, and the new chairman would not let that happen again. His theory was that only by winning more governorships, congressional seats, state legislatures, mayors, sheriffs, and county supervisors would the Party have a real shot at Mr. Kennedy in 1964. Toward that effort, he pleaded with presidential aspirants and would-be kingmakers to suppress their personal ambitions until after the '62 elections.

Dad had been deliberately chosen, political columnist David Broder suggested, because he was "an exponent of the 'modern' or 'public relations' approach to political management over a 'traditional' or 'back-room' operator."[4] He was a man with a "jet-age conception of politics, liberally seasoned with good old grass-roots thinking," as The *Manhattan Mercury* of Manhattan, Kansas, put it.[5] Many party leaders agreed privately that the GOP had not found its voice, its presence, or its politics since Kennedy's election, so daunting was it to match the charming young president's luster and the affection with which he was held by his countrymen. Not to mention the difficulty the opposition party always faces in making its arguments heard over what has been called "the giant loudspeaker of the presidency." In the midst of these intimidating hurdles, the job of selling Republicanism to the country, of sprucing up its image and morale, had now fallen squarely in my father's lap.

His would be a multi-pronged response—more direct mailings of political information, more intense recruitment of bright and articulate candidates as he had done at the NRCC, the hiring of knowledgeable specialists to plan strategies for reaching formerly written-off "special constituencies" such as minorities, labor unions, farmers, and various nationalities. There would be a concerted effort, like the one he had also begun in his previous job, to build organizational strength where the Party was weakest—in big cities and the South. No segment of the population or area of the country, according to Chairman Miller, was to be written off. Republicans had done that for far too long.

His revisionist efforts to sharpen and freshen his party's image meant butting heads with some old stalwarts who resisted change and feared a threat to their leadership, in particular, congressional Minority Leaders Everett Dirksen and Charlie Halleck. The consensus was that the duo's weekly televised update on Democratic sins and Republican opposition stands, dubbed by a bemused President Kennedy "The Ev and Charlie Show," was anything but constructive; in fact, it was presenting a tired, dated, and stereotyped image of the Party that was jeopardizing its electoral chances. While Dad respected the leaders and on occasion defended them, he resolved to find a way around them.

Unlike most chairmen before him, my father saw the National Committee as the agent that could "broaden the base of party leadership and keep it from being a closed shop." That meant, he believed, moving younger men into important roles sooner. Many of the newly elected congressmen were expert in various legislative areas, and he wanted their ideas to carry more weight in party councils. And he wanted these new faces out front, speaking for the Party through the media. After pressuring unsuccessfully for their inclusion in the "Ev and Charlie Show," he began searching for alternative ways to remind the country that there were other Republicans around as well.

Dirksen's and Halleck's displeasure with his efforts notwithstanding, he proceeded to lay the groundwork for four ideas that were firsts: a Republican Declaration of Principles, to be hammered out by a cross section of party leaders under the direction of Congressman Melvin Laird; the All-Republican Conference to be held at Eisenhower's farm in Gettysburg, Pennsylvania, on June 30, 1962; the organization of a National Republican Citizens Committee; and the formation of a Governors' Association as an advisory body to the national chairman. Dad and former

President Eisenhower worked closely together on these projects, exerting all the collective persuasive powers they could muster, for they shared the same belief that to win elections, Republicans must become more inclusive and progressive.

The idea of a Declaration of Principles had begun with my father's effort to create a GOP State of the Union message. He had circulated a 4,000-word document among party chieftains, vigorously criticizing the Kennedy administration's record and proposing a series of positive stands to be taken by Republicans in the upcoming session of Congress. It was to be exactly like what is routinely delivered today on national television by the opposition party immediately following a president's State of the Union address. But his document was premature. Their toes having been stepped on in the sensitive area of policy-making, Messrs. Dirksen and Halleck quietly but firmly vetoed the upstart idea.

Yet once Mel Laird finally reached a consensus within his *ad hoc* committee about the contents of the new Declaration of Principles, it was readily adopted by the Republican members of both the House and Senate. By that time, so many members had endorsed the concept that the leadership could not thwart it. The RNC Research Division then faced the unenviable task of fashioning campaign material from that document that would appeal to both conservative and liberal Republicans. It was a ticklish balance to achieve.

The All-Republican Conference was a summit, arranged by the RNC, of leading party members, in and out of office, to pool ideas on how to win control of the House and increase membership in the Senate. Dad warmly welcomed the more than 100 invitees to a free-wheeling and open discussion of any and all issues of concern to the Party and the country. He was anxious to showcase to the media the attractive and diverse leadership the GOP offered, while making it clear that this would not be a policy forming group. This maiden conference was upbeat and went smoothly, and though the original intent was for it to gather every three or four months, budgetary restraints eventually precluded that.

The National Republican Citizens Committee, designed to provide a rich source of volunteers around the country in an assortment of capacities, was an outgrowth of that conclave. It was envisioned that the committee might give the same muscle to the Republicans as COPE, the political education committee of the AFL-CIO, gives to the Democrats.

My father was initially skeptical about this ancillary political organization. It was an appendage to the Party's organizational setup that could be problematic: it could be difficult to control, might be easily taken over by one wing of the Party or another, might minimize the role of the National Committee and interfere with its fund raising sources, and in general might wreak havoc with the semblance of order he was trying to create. He was persuaded to go along with the new organization in deference to President Eisenhower who supported it, but occasionally he felt the need to reign in its over-zealous plans.

The Republican Governors' Association was Dad's baby. It was the culmination of his efforts to bring these important state leaders into closer relationship with the congressional and RNC leadership within the Party. Governor Robert Smylie of Idaho, who would become the group's first chairman in 1963, remembered my father working hard on that project. It had taken a year of careful diplomatic spadework, plagued again by numerous turf sensitivities, to make it happen. There had always been reticence on Capitol Hill to include governors in party affairs. Members of Congress jealously guarded their preeminence in policy making, but Dad regarded the many progressive state chief executives as untapped resources.

The formation of all these new organizations drew the well-publicized ire of Barry Goldwater. In a prickly letter to Chairman Miller and in some public grousing as well, he charged, among other things, that the groups would duplicate the work of the National Committee. In truth, his concern was that too many liberals and moderates were included who might be more favorably disposed toward a Rockefeller nomination than a Goldwater nomination in 1964.

The chairman asked his good friend Barry for a meeting at once. When he explained to him that President Eisenhower strongly backed the idea of the Citizens Committee and that it was vital to have his good will and participation in the mid-term campaigns, Goldwater agreed to back down. In trying to control both the Goldwater and the Dirksen/Halleck rebellions and present a united team to the nation for the upcoming elections, one newspaper columnist asserted, quite perceptively, that my father would need "all the agility of a circus performer who rides several horses around the ring. If one or more of the horses fails to keep a uniform rhythm, the rider's perch can become precarious."[6]

That prediction quickly proved true. Growing dissension in the Party between the Rockefeller and Goldwater forces had spread to the Republican Governors' Association. At its contentious first meeting in Miami, the governors were widely split over a decision on what stand to take on civil rights. Dad flew in for one day to host a Sunday morning breakfast and was given a sizable chunk of the credit for forging a united GOP gubernatorial front on the issue. In urging strong support for civil rights, he moved quietly to divorce that decision from the potentially explosive differences of opinion on whether or not Senator Goldwater represented a defeatist, segregationist policy that could spell disaster for the Republican Party.

The strategy for image reconstruction of the GOP included a large amount of speaking by the chairman himself. He was, after all, elected because he was thought to be a good "front man," hopefully a match for the urbane and eloquent young President Kennedy. In truth, he was the only bona fide spokesperson for the Party as a whole at this point, divided as it was becoming.

In his only head-to-head battle with his Democratic counterpart, John Bailey, a skilled political operator from Connecticut much like Ray Bliss, my father made a quantum leap in meeting the Party's expectations and boosting its morale. The occasion was a live debate with an audience, nationally televised by CBS from the Sky Terrace of the Washington Hotel, a format that played to his strength. Bailey was hardly able to get a word in edgewise as Dad hurled facts and figures at him and adroitly managed to hold the cameras for the majority of the time. When the Democrat complained that he didn't have time to go into something, my father leaned back coolly in his chair and said in a kindly voice, "Take all the time you want, John." Bailey himself was disgusted with the outcome.

Furious at the interviewers—Walter Cronkite, Roger Mudd and Paul Niven—who quizzed him about Cuba (the botched Bay of Pigs invasion being the prime blemish on the administration's record at this point), the Democratic Chairman raged afterwards: "What the hell do I know about Cuba? . . . I'll go on their shows if they want to talk about politics, but I'm no damned foreign-policy expert." The whole episode pointed up the advantage, at least for the Republicans at this juncture, of having a seasoned, well-spoken, and well-versed member of Congress in the national chairmanship rather than a paid political professional. And it was the last time Bailey ever consented to debate his counterpart one-on-one.

"Your father was at his best out in the states turning people on and making them feel they wanted to help him," Elly Petersen, a national committeewoman during Dad's tenure, once told me. "He was charismatic and popular," she said, "and when he visited a state you can be sure he made a hit." He did, in fact, leave as much of the administrative work of the chairmanship as he could to his trusted and highly capable assistants back in Washington, while he hit the road meeting and counseling with far-flung party workers who wanted to get to know the chairman in person.

Jo Good, who organized and ran Republican conventions for thirteen national chairmen, from the 1950s through the 1980s, remembers the final banquet of a National Committee meeting in Minneapolis where her boss was the major speaker and guest of honor. After downing the three bites of dinner that he typically ate and pushing it aside, he picked up a local newspaper and began to read. Jo, alarmed that he might offend his hosts, started to write him a note, when the master of ceremonies introduced him and he got up to speak. "His entire speech, with that large voice coming from that small man, was on what he had seen in that paper, and so tailored was it to his audience that it electrified them," Jo recalled vividly many years later.

The role of vigorous, responsible opposition is integral to the public relations and image-building tasks of a national chairman. My father once explained: "In America, one of the roles of the opposition party is to keep the political spectrum in balance by pointing out truths that otherwise might go unmentioned by the party in power." Two political scientists who made a study of the national committees in the early '60s agreed: "Part of the accepted style of the national chairman is to be continuously, openly, and unremittingly partisan."[7] In short, he sharpens issues, oversimplifies, and moralizes—to invigorate the faithful and attract the sympathies of voters.

Scholarly opinion notwithstanding, however, voicing opposition, even constructively, to a president with high approval ratings and with whom the press was in love was not a prescription for popularity. Yet with few others having the nerve to do it, there was a vacuum Dad knew he had to fill. He believed that the success of our system is predicated on the existence of two strong parties. A cartoon in the *Washington Star* summed up his tricky predicament. It portrayed a feisty, gleeful Chairman Bill Miller, small feet propelled off the ground from the force of smashing an oversized mallet on the head of a staggering, dazed donkey. Republicans liked his style, that tended to energize his party. Democrats most definitely did not.

His criticism, which was sharp, was aimed primarily at Kennedy's domestic programs and at his appointments. He accused the president of succumbing to naming inferior people to critical foreign posts to repay his political debts—not the first or last time that has ever happened, but egregious in this case in my father's opinion. He also questioned whether Kennedy's thirty-six-year old brother Bobby had any experience or qualifications to fill the post of attorney general other than his relation to the president, and whether naming another relative, brother-in-law Sargent Shriver, to head the Peace Corps was appropriate.

Yet where foreign policy decisions were concerned in this grave period of international tensions, the GOP chairman pledged unified Republican support for the president when he moved into action. He did add that, considering the valuable experience Republicans had gained over the past decade in difficult foreign affairs situations, they would like to be "called in on the take-offs and not just on the crash landings."

It was October 22, 1962, a bleak and rainy late fall night. Dad was near the end of a hard-fought campaign to retain his seat in Congress. Still in the white starched shirt and tie he had worn to that night's Rotary dinner, he sat grim-faced and alone in his Niagara Falls motel room, biting the tip of his black-rimmed glasses, a yellow pad on his lap as he watched John Kennedy's ominous televised announcement to the nation that he was quarantining Cuba after a prolonged buildup of Soviet missiles just ninety miles off our shores.

Immediately, the phone rang. "It was a call from Washington. Party leaders wanted the chairman's reaction. It came swiftly—

and it came from the heart. 'We are Americans first, Republicans second,' Mr. Miller dictated."[8] The Republican Party, Dad directed, would close ranks and join the administration in presenting a united front to the world.

He later had one complaint. The president's decision was a good one, but it had been too long in coming. My father and numerous other Republicans, as well as some in the media, had been urging a blockade for weeks. Leaked CIA and State Department intelligence reports, refugee interviews, and intercepted letters from Cubans to their relatives in the states telling of the midnight unloading of ships had all been circulating in the press. When anyone suggested the president was being indecisive, too methodical in analyzing Soviet and Cuban intentions, or lacked the guts to stand up to the Communists, they were, of course, accused of playing politics with a dangerous international situation.

In times of crisis, the role of the opposition in a two-party system is both difficult and delicate, and its responsibilities great. Criticism by the minority can send mixed messages to an adversary, but it can also help shore up an administration's resolve to pursue a tough course if it wavers in mid-crisis. What is the exact moment when it becomes inappropriate to criticize? That is always the tough question.

"It is extremely debatable," Dad once opined, "that America would be strengthened by a veneer of false unity brought about by one party keeping silent, even when it disagrees, for the sake of appearance." He did not consider it necessary, or advisable, to abdicate the obligation of the "loyal opposition" to voice disagreement with an administration's foreign policy plans either before or after they are implemented. Nor did he think they should relinquish their responsibility to offer concrete, specific suggestions for the formulation of future foreign policy.

Senator Robert Taft of Ohio had expressed the same sentiment in 1951: "If you permit appeals to unity to bring an end to criticism, we endanger not only the Constitutional liberties of our country, but even its future existence." And none other than Winston Churchill had spoken similar words, with characteristic eloquence, when he was reproached in 1945 for making a motion to censure the Labor government for its conduct of post-war affairs: "Are we not bound in honor to give our warnings in good time about the future and to record our censure on the present?

Would we not be blameworthy before history if we sat supine and silent while one folly and neglect is piled on top of another and much that we fought for together is lost or frittered away?"

So, true to his philosophy, when Nikita Khrushchev and the Russians built a wall separating East and West Berlin in August 1961, my father bemoaned the fact that our new president had not been able to avert the crisis in a prior Vienna meeting with the Russian leader. And when that failed, he regretted that we and our allies had not stood firm and "kicked down the wall brick by brick as it was being built." When our military commanders in Berlin had requested permission to tear down the wall, "indecision, timidity, and delay in Washington, signaling weakness to our adversaries, had allowed the wall to be built," he and several other critics claimed.

Dad continually protested the "official fog" in which the administration was keeping the Congress and the public with regard to Vietnam, chiding the president for his lack of candor and information. What he feared was exactly what was happening—a vastly expanded "guerilla operation" that was producing significant U.S. involvement and increasing casualties, unbeknownst at that time to the American public, without any sign of immediate or early victory. "The issue is too big to be handled as a one-man show," he alleged.

The intrepid national chairman touched off a furious partisan debate following the Cuban Bay of Pigs fiasco of April '61, when Cuban rebels invaded their homeland to overthrow Fidel Castro and, lacking promised U.S. land and air support, the assault ended in disaster. Although Kennedy accepted blame for the ill-fated invasion, Democrats implied that it was Eisenhower's fault since he had initially conceived the invasion plan.

The former administration had indeed discussed such a plan, conceded my father, but he added: "The tragic mistake in Cuba that President Kennedy made was when he rescinded and revoked the Eisenhower plan to have the Cuban freedom fighters protected by American airpower." Despite his reticence to make partisan attacks on his successor on foreign policy issues, Ike's subsequent assertion that, "speaking as an old soldier," it was axiomatic that "no amphibious operation could succeed unless it had air cover" was vindication for the RNC Chairman's somewhat risky accusation.

Actually, he had some prior indication that Eisenhower might go public with his disapproval. Dad and NRCC Chairman Bob Wilson had been up to visit the former president, at his invitation, shortly after the invasion. Living a quiet, sylvan existence in a small brick cottage on the grounds of Gettysburg College, he was a bit lonely and always eager to reminisce and chat with old colleagues about politics and world affairs. In fact, he seemed to relish involvement even more than when he was in office. When asked his thoughts on the Bay of Pigs, the old general related his disgust with the ineptitude of the whole affair. He made two points: first, if the U.S. decides to invade, then everything should be done to guarantee success; second, there must be an alternative plan if an invasion fails.

Chairman Miller was given to summing up President Kennedy's foreign affairs record concisely: "In the 1960 campaign, Kennedy convinced 51 percent of the American people that American prestige is low [with his "missile gap" charge]; he has now convinced the other 49 percent." Or—"I wonder if all these things haven't made Krushchev think that perhaps we did indeed send a boy to do a man's job and that by a little saber rattling he might accomplish his objectives…" Such remarks, which invariably produced prolonged applause from his partisan audiences, might seem flip, but they contained what my father believed to be the sad truth.

Money, or the lack of it, was the second major problem for Dad to tackle when he came on board as national chairman. The National Committee, in non-presidential election years, had a full-time staff of about ninety and annual expenses of around $750,000. In presidential election years, it expanded to more than 600 people and spent millions of dollars. After November of 1960, the Party was in hock for $1,117,000 and by the time my father came along, there still remained a sizeable deficit. "Only someone with a hole in the head would make this transfer [from the NRCC]," he mused. "I'm leaving a committee with $300,000 in the bank to take over a committee with a $750,000 deficit."

Political money and how to come by it was a far larger problem back in his day than it is today, particularly for the minority party, which by most measures described the Republican Party. Despite Democratic propaganda about the Republicans being the party of the well-to-do, the reality was that by 1962 their financial situation was serious enough to raise questions about the ability of the National Committee to keep its doors open. There was simply no money to pay off the debt and fund all the activities the new chairman hoped would expand the reach and effectiveness of his party. A thousand dollars was a huge gift, "seen as from an angel," recalled Jo Good. Such a paucity of funds is almost impossible to imagine now, when thousands, millions of dollars in soft and hard money deluge political tills routinely.

In short, the GOP was desperate for a fresh source of revenue, to finance the mid-term election races and to replenish impoverished state party organizations. Bill Warner, Dad's top-notch executive director whom he had brought with him from the NRCC, had long pushed the idea of a "sustaining membership" to boost party coffers, and his boss finally made the decision to try it. The National Committee started running full-page newspaper ads, launching television appeals, and buying up mailing lists—all requesting $10 donations. For this, the donor would receive a biweekly newsletter, *Battleline,* and a sustaining membership in the Republican Party.

It was brilliant! Who would have thought such an inconsequential sum could bring in big money? The direct mail idea had long been shelved because the processing of small contributions seemed unprofitable. Also, it was widely held that large amounts could not be raised in small donations. But this conventional wisdom was turned on its ear when the RNC sent out its first test mailing and brought in $700,000; the second mailing brought in over $1,100,000.

What they discovered was that obtaining a large number of contributions of one size, even small ones, allowed the committee to mechanize its processing and thereby hold administrative costs down. So this new revenue stream of modest donations, reducing the Party's dependence on "fat cats" for the first time, proved to be enormously successful, much to my father's immense relief. In fact, it is still the lifeblood of the Party—over 50 percent of its income. The Democrats soon adopted the same system.

Not only did a national chairman have to worry continuously about daily administrative and campaign expenses, but raising funds to foot the bills for a national convention every four years was an additional and major headache. After 1972, millions came from the federal government to help run those massive and costly events, but until then, it was solely the job of the national committees. The chairman had to keep careful watch over every penny spent once convention preparations for 1964 were underway, for if they went over budget, the committee would have to divert vital resources allocated for campaigning to pay off convention expenses.

The gathering cloud of ugly division within his party's ranks was perhaps the most serious of all the pressing problems Dad faced in 1961. It was a contentious time, with conservatives, moderates, and liberals fighting for the very soul of the Party. Unlike so many conservatives, whether Barry Goldwater's minions then or the religious right of today, his political strategy had always been marked by inclusiveness—the "big tent" theory. He believed in emphasizing the GOP's diversity and breadth of appeal, rather than striving for doctrinal purity.

The new chairman remarked tellingly at a press conference immediately following his election, when asked about his party's disunity, that if Senator Eastland, the Democratic Mississippi segregationist, could coexist in the same party with Harlem Democrat Adam Clayton Powell, then Rockefeller and Goldwater ought to be able to do the same. He added that he didn't consider the differences between a Goldwater and a Rockefeller any more irreconcilable than those between John Kennedy and Lyndon Johnson when they were joined together on their national ticket.

Democrats had somehow always been more adept than Republicans at submerging their vast differences, at least in election years. Although my father's "strength in diversity" theory met with considerable skepticism, even puzzlement, from some of his colleagues, he sincerely believed it. And he persisted in espousing it whenever and wherever he spoke around the country. But convincing others of its viability would indeed prove to be a Herculean task.

He had pledged total neutrality in the heated race for the Party's 1964 presidential nomination, and he was scrupulous about keeping that pledge. It was, after all, upon that basis that all factions had originally backed him for the national chairmanship. To those who wrote urging him to support one candidate or another, usually Barry Goldwater, his standard reply was that the National Committee does not make party policy nor select the nominee but only plans the convention. He urged that they make their wishes known to their convention delegates but that, in the end, they support the Party's nominee, even if it was not their choice. "We cannot afford the luxury of being Goldwater Republicans or Rockefeller Republicans or Nixon Republicans," was his constant refrain.

Defeatism, resulting from this divisiveness, was, nevertheless, spreading within party ranks—the feeling that they were doomed to failure because of constant feuding and disarray. This discouragement was being exacerbated, Dad maintained, by the press, "who welcomed the opportunity to feed upon the bones of our party."[9] In preparation for a large GOP gathering in Washington in January 1964, his urgent advance memorandum to the participants begged them, when confronted by political commentators, to "project the image of a party of optimism and not of defeatism . . . If anyone has a preference for an individual for the nomination of president, I urge that you speak affirmatively in his behalf and refrain from downgrading all other opponents."[10]

My father made no commitment as to Nixon's getting a second chance in 1964, except to say that he would have a better shot at it if the former vice president ran for and won the governorship of California in 1962. Nor did he give any hint of preference between Rockefeller and Goldwater, other than to say that he was, of course, strongly supporting Governor Rockefeller in his race for reelection in New York in '62. But as the months wore on, he was increasingly forced to contend with and attempt to constrain the strident conservative voices demanding to be heard.

Build the grassroots of the Party from the precinct level up— that was the gospel according to Bill Miller. Though Republicans in more recent decades have become known for their organized and thorough precinct work, in the early '60s it was far from a model of efficiency or thoroughness. Many who wrote Dad after his election as chairman reported to him that their local organizations had lost their spark and were badly in need of revitalization. So he organized four regional GOP conferences to whip up enthusiasm, to assess party strengths and weaknesses in each area of the country, and to forge a plan of action—in the Northeast, the South, the Midwest, and the West. This exhausting tour of his political domain took him to thirty-three states and meetings with Republican leaders of all fifty states.

The Western meeting in Sun Valley, Idaho, was unceremoniously interrupted for Chairman Miller by the stork. Just as he was hours away from being the main speaker at the closing dinner on September 29, he got word that Mother had gone into George Washington Hospital earlier than expected and was about to deliver their fourth. After quickly arranging a substitute, he boarded a plane for Washington, but the stork won the race and baby Stephanie was born while he was in midair.

Her name was actually an accident of political life. Before the-soon-to-be father left for this latest road trip, he and Mom had not been able to agree on a girl's name—he was pushing for Stephanie; Mother thought that confusing and wanted Catherine. So they decided to put off the decision until after Dad returned home. As fate would have it, during a layover in Chicago on his premature trip, the chairman was deluged by a horde of reporters who pressed him for the name of his newest progeny. Reluctant to say he didn't know, which politicians are notoriously loathe to do, he spontaneously bestowed her with his preference. And so my baby sister's name was etched in print, if not in stone.

Barely had the proud but harried new father donned the obligatory white hospital coat and taken babe in arms to pose for press pictures upon his arrival in Washington, than he was off again on a coast-to-coast speaking tour. Stephie has often attributed her current political liberalism to pique at her itinerant dad for not being present at her birth.

These regional conferences were revealing, and in some ways discouraging for my father. He described the dilemma he faced simply: "I am running a party that doesn't really like politics very much." His researchers told him that 80 percent of the people who stayed home on Election Day in 1960 were Republicans. Of the 50,000 polling places between Maine and Maryland, only 10 percent were manned by loyal workers passing out GOP literature.

With candidates, it was the same story. "What we need is warm bodies," he asserted starkly. While there were any number of people who wanted to run for president, he and the newly political Eisenhower were spending a lot of their time recruiting candidates for assorted lower offices around the country, often in vain. Dad made frequent visits to Gettysburg during his years as national chairman. He did it as a courtesy to the ex president, to keep him apprised of party affairs, but also to gain his valuable insights and ideas. Happily, he and Ike seemed to agree on most issues, particularly on the need to put presidential politics on the back burner and concentrate on the '62 elections.

The regional meetings also reinforced for my father what he had known for some time, that in large urban areas his party was not telling its story by making efficient use of media outlets directed at specific nationality groups. "Why should we lose the Polish vote?" he asked impatiently. "It wasn't our party that sold Poland down the river at Teheran." Republicans had virtually ceded the various demographic groupings of these cities to the Democrats by default, and the heavy Democratic vote in cities habitually overcame Republican majorities in rural areas of a state. Changing just a few of those urban votes could mean the difference between defeat and victory statewide. All in all, Republicans had been "out manned, out-organized, out-spent, and out-worked," summarized Dad, and he was determined it would not happen again. He quipped, his sense of humor always intact despite his travails: "A good precinct worker ought to have more relatives than the votes we've been getting in big city areas."

Even though "taking labor votes from John Kennedy is like trying to take the pennant from the Yanks," as Victor Riesel once rightly pointed out in his syndicated newspaper column,[11] Dad didn't intend to concede those either, at least not without taking a healthy shot at them. His energetic and peripatetic Labor specialist, Robert Gormley, a plumber by trade, was hard at work recruiting second and third echelon union leaders for GOP labor committees.

There was a pressing need for an intensive, year-round national Republican registration drive, for as the chairman reminded party workers around the country, "If we do not get Republicans registered, most of our other efforts will be to no avail."[12] Not a big, one shot drive, but "a quiet, nose-to-the-grindstone, no let-up effort which gets and keeps every Republican registered to vote."[13] The AFL-CIO COPE organization had always done much of that sort of legwork for the Democrats. Now the GOP had to start beating them at their game. So, utilizing suggestions from

Ray Bliss's Big City Report—such as door-to-door canvassing and sending out RNC field representatives to help—my father set that task as a top priority.

There was also evidence to suggest that better Republican manning of polling places in those Democratic boss-controlled cities on Election Day might prevent some of the vote fraud that many believed could have made the difference between defeat and victory for Richard Nixon in 1960. "Next time we're going to get all the votes counted," he half-facetiously, half-seriously intoned. If the GOP could substantially reduce their losses in places like Philadelphia, Detroit, Chicago, St. Louis, New York, and Newark, he firmly believed they could win several of the crucial industrial states.

Of all the challenges Dad faced as national chairman in the early sixties, by far the most troublesome was what to do about the South. As the Democratic Party became more liberal through-out the 1950s and the Republican Party more conservative, south-erners, who for the most part disliked the federal government and passionately guarded the right of their states and localities to make the preponderance of their laws, were beginning to feel more at home in the GOP.

But the desire to preserve their way of life, of which segrega-tion was such an integral part, was so deeply embedded in their concept of states' and individual rights that the two became virtually synonymous. So the excruciating dilemma for my father and the Republican Party at this juncture was this: how do they become a legitimate presence in the states of the old Confederacy without becoming the segregationist party? And how do they increase black support for the GOP, as he was so intent on doing, if that becomes the Party's image?

The Republican Party had been in the minority nationally for decades, in terms of numbers of registered voters. Now the one-party South, from which they had so long been excluded, appeared by the 1960s to be theirs for the taking, and the pros-pect was enticing. Republican voting strength in that area had been rising steadily since 1944 in presidential elections, and Eisenhower and Nixon had made some serious inroads in the southern vote in their elections. Now it was time to get southern-ers on board in all elections for all offices. "The year 1962 will see more Republicans than ever before stand for offices on all levels in the South," promised the ever-optimistic national chairman at the Atlanta regional conference. He was following through on his pledge while at the NRCC that his party would no longer forfeit a third of House seats without a contest.

The crux of the problem in accomplishing this feat was two-fold: to persuade vibrant young people to run for office on the local and state level as Republicans; and to persuade southerners to abandon long-held habit and vote Republican in more than just presidential elections. There were a couple of significant factors working against Dad and the RNC in their effort, dubbed "Operation Dixie," first launched back in 1957 by Chairman Meade Alcorn to organize and fund a Republican Party in the South.

Breaking the stranglehold of Democratic Party patronage was a tough nut to crack. There was a bevy of enthusiastic, ambitious, and articulate young executive types in southern cities who were eager to break the hold of machine politics in their states and build better government through healthy competition. Unable to find any place in the one-party system, they were willing to run with the GOP label, but then often found themselves pressured against that course. One young Atlanta lawyer was ready to enter the race for an important office in Georgia when a large railroad he represented reportedly "advised" him against doing so. Such less than subtle tactics were reminiscent of when vice-presidential candidate Lyndon Johnson made his sweep through his native Southland during the campaign of 1960, reminding southern Democrats which side of their bread the butter was on.

The other force thwarting my father's intentions in the South was, ironically, the growing appeal of his future running mate, Senator Barry Goldwater. The latter's public utterances were increasingly more at odds with Dad's on the subject of the Southern vote, creating a tension for my father between his reticence to rebuke his colleague and his conviction about what was right, about the direction he believed his party must take.

Plain and simple, Bill Miller wanted both the white and the black vote in the South, and he believed there was no reason not to get them. His party stood for fiscal responsibility, a reduction of bureaucracy, and a lessening of governmental expenditures, all things that appeal generally to white southerners. And what's

more, with the exception of President Harry Truman's bold executive order desegregating the armed forces in 1948, the Republican
Party's record on civil rights was far better than that of the
Democrats. It was, after all, powerful segregationist Southern
Democratic committee chairmen who had blocked consideration
of every civil rights bill for the past many decades—which black
voters would understand if only the GOP told its story better.

That was the problem, said Dad—Republicans do not tell their
story well. They are somehow reticent to toot their own horns, so
when the media tells it, the GOP frequently seems to come out
looking soft on civil rights. "Republicans have only themselves to
blame for the bad press we receive," he once observed. "The way
Republicans handle the press is atrocious." RNC chairmen since
Miller, notably Haley Barbour, chairman from 1993 to 1997, have
complained about exactly the same problem—lack of aggressive
marketing of the Republican message, particularly to minorities.
So it would seem that effective marketing has been an elusive
objective for Republicans for some time.

There had been a long-standing lack of communication between black leaders and GOP leadership when my father became
chairman, which he was only partially successful in changing.
Despite his efforts to bring distinguished black men such as Clay
Claiborne, George Lewis, and Grant Reynolds into RNC inner
councils, there were always staff members who somehow managed to shelve those men's initiatives. Unfortunately, such lack of
inclusion gave the impression that Republicans were waiting for
the black vote to come to them, rather than actively pursuing it.

To those who wrote my father complaining about his appointment of Negroes, as they were then called, because any effort to
seek their vote was futile for the GOP, he replied: "I do not feel
that we should concede any vote to the Democratic Party and I
do not believe that our efforts to win the Negro vote is in conflict
with our efforts to win support in southern states. If we are to
remain a national party, win elections, and promote the best interests of America, we must seek the vote of all groups."[14]

But at the same Atlanta meeting where he was laying out
his hopes and vision of a combined black and white vote in the
South, Barry Goldwater was offering a wholly different approach.
It amounted to turning his and the Party's back on the minority
vote, in the South as well as the North. "We ought to forget the

big cities," the Senator announced at a press conference. "We can't out-promise the Democrats, and that's what it takes when you appeal to people as groups." In short, Goldwater, like too many other Republicans, considered the African American vote hopeless and he was willing to concede it. No point in spending time and money going after it. Sadly, and ironically, some forty active black Georgia Republicans were included for the first time in an integrated party dinner at this meeting—at nearly the same time as a group of black Democrats were barred from a testimonial dinner for Democratic Senator Richard Russell of Georgia.

Barry's statements—along with another: "I would like to see our party back up on school integration"—gave southern segregationists a potential presidential candidate who appeared to speak their language. Some party strategists, like Dad, worried that such pronouncements inadvertently gave a segment of the southern population license to vote Republican for the wrong reason.

He regretted in a letter to a colleague that Goldwater was "clouding" the Party's position on civil rights. Though he hated to repudiate a man of whom he was so fond, he was forced to point out in subsequent interviews that the positive Republican stand on civil rights was clearly stated in the 1960 platform. When asked then if the GOP's civil rights policy is essentially Goldwater's policy, he stated bluntly, "No, it is not." The small band of dedicated Georgians who were carrying on a determined effort to create a genuine, broad-based, two-party movement in their state were discouraged by the Arizona senator's words, but they vowed not to quit.[15]

Thus did the GOP effort to become a viable alternative in the South become identified in the minds of many with seeking the racist white vote, despite my father's continual and strenuous efforts to restrain any appeal to racists. Arguably, most scholars today would not attribute the rise of the Republican Party in the South solely to racism, but to the more conservative bent of the Party in economic and constitutional matters as well. While there were undeniably segregationists in its ranks, many of the new breed of southerners who supported Republicans in the 1960s were transplants from the North and young local professionals who were not willing to let the Party retreat into the past.

From 1961 to 1963, the GOP elected from southern states 5 new congressmen, the first Republican governor in Oklahoma's history, the first Republican senator from Texas, 41 members of state legislatures, 6 mayors, 80 city council members, and 100 other candidates to school boards, township committees, etc.—a rather astounding accomplishment considering the starting point. Chairman Miller reminded a reporter in 1963: "We've spent a lot of money down there on the precinct level, and it's beginning to work.... Not one of our candidates in the South ran on the race issue." While possibly not totally accurate, that general truth was pointed out to me when I spoke with the first Republican elected to the South Carolina state legislature in seventy-five years, Charles Boineau.

This pioneer was much heralded in August 1961 when he managed to nab a seat in a special election, against all odds. Despite massive Democratic money and pressure thrown against him, he had upstart Young Republicans working like beavers, pounding the pavement and ringing doorbells on his behalf. Boineau said it was impossible to get many black votes because the Democrats did such a good job of turning them against him as a Republican.

Though his career was brief as the sole GOP member in a body of 170—"It was a little like being a lone bomber pilot over Japan," he told me—he had been elected not only as a bona fide conservative opposed to the "welfare state" he saw in the Democratic Party's legislation, but he had also defeated a third party "states rights" candidate who picked up only a handful of votes. The voters had at last been given a choice between liberalism, conservatism, and sticking with "grandpappy's ghost," as one newspaper put it.[16] Happily for Republican fortunes and Dad's desire to separate them from segregationists, it appeared that the voters had opted not for racism but for the political and economic philosophy that was most in tune with their beliefs.

In 1962, Senator Jacob Javits and other Northern liberal Republicans excoriated some of the Party's leaders (never mentioning my father, however) for allowing segregationists to run on its ticket in the South. They even suggested the GOP limit its efforts there in order to avoid supporting such candidates. My father was angered by this suggestion to, in effect, weed out their candidates, calling it "ridiculous." "It doesn't make sense," he said, "when the Democrats for thirty years have been winning national elections with one-third of their party members strong segregationists.... Certainly there will be individual Republican candidates in the South who are equally as segregationist as their Democratic opponents ... but why should we be murdered on this when the Democrats have ten or twenty times as many elected in their party?"[17]

When Dad was elected national chairman in June of '61 amidst some support for the idea of a full-time paid chairman, he had promised that after six months or so he would reevaluate the combining of his two jobs. If he felt he could not do justice to both, he would resign one or the other. He regarded this as one of the most important decisions of his career.

It would, of course, be difficult to relinquish his seat in Congress in midterm; and stepping down from the chairmanship just as he had undertaken plans and projects to which he was deeply committed was an equally difficult choice. And he still refused to take the job on a full-time, salaried basis—"A paid chairman would be nothing more than a glorified member of the staff at a fancy salary ... he would have to try to please everybody or be threatened with the loss of his job." But there was no doubt about it, his schedule was brutal, visiting thirty-three states in a period of three months. Meantime, he tried not to miss too many votes on the House floor, and to still get back to his district as often as possible to assure his constituents that he was not neglecting them.

A much-needed two-week vacation in the Florida Keys with the family over Christmas gave him time to mull it all over. Our group arrived with a formidable assemblage of baggage—I from college, my father from a road trip, and Mother from Washington with my sister Mary, two toddlers, and two housekeepers in tow. The staff at the luxurious Indies House on Duck Key was solicitous but bemused, and obviously perplexed about whether the same set of parents had spawned this group of siblings of such diverse ages. Mary and I whiled away the glorious days water-skiing and swimming, totally oblivious to the momentous decision with which our poor, weary father was wrestling.

I found a humorous reference to this trip in *Time* magazine some years later that reveals the good-natured relationship Dad shared with his Judiciary colleague and frequent adversary, Manny Celler:

As the Republicans' leading sharpshooter, New York's Congressman William Miller retreated to Florida to meditate the wisdom of surrendering either his chairmanship of the GOP National Committee or his House seat, his fellow New Yorker, Democratic Congressman Emanuel Celler, helpfully counseled him to hang onto the latter. After the recent "Rocky-mandered" reapportionment of New York's congressional districts, gibed Celler, a Republican could not be unseated in Miller's district "by St. Gabriel himself." Responded Miller: "I hope—for once in Celler's life—that he's right."

After subsequently sounding out the sentiments of Western New Yorkers and national committee members on the subject and receiving overwhelming assurances from both that he was giving them excellent service, his mind was nearly made up. A resolution passed by the RNC at its meeting in Oklahoma City in early January offered him additional reassurance: "The Republican National Committee unanimously goes on record publicly to state its individual and collective judgment that Congressman Miller of New York stands today as one of the truly great national chairmen in Republican Party history."

But my father faced more uncertainty in his own congressional race for reelection in 1962 than ever before as a result of the demands on his time nationally. A September primary, his first ever, was the initial hurdle, and while not a very worrisome one, it was necessary for surrogates to conduct his campaign. He wrote an open letter to his constituents explaining why.

He would be detained in Washington until October 13 for one of the longest and balkiest congressional sessions on record, with even the president's own party thwarting his program at every turn. Then no sooner had he gotten back to the district to launch his campaign and try to refit a myriad of cancelled September events into the tight four-week period remaining, when the Cuban missile crisis intervened. After being called to New York City for one of five regional emergency briefings called by Secretary of State Dean Rusk and Defense Secretary Robert McNamara, he suspended his campaign for a week and returned to Washington to consult with other congressional leaders. "The affairs of our nation in these critical times certainly take precedence over political campaigning," were his parting words to his district.

Realizing that time was running out, he decided to tape some of his local campaign television appearances in a Washington studio. He squeezed them into one day, skipping lunch, and racing in between quorum calls on the House floor. "Okay, let's go," he called to his aide. "What's the first subject?" The aide consulted his notes. "How about Medicare?"

A newspaper account of the session went this way: "The television cameras whirred. Mr. Miller launched into a fact-packed presentation of his views on Medicare. This was to be a five-minute TV presentation. He did not consult notes—nor did he use a visual aid device. He halted right at the five-minute mark, right on the button. 'What's next?' Mr. Miller asked. He talked about federal aid to education. His presentation again was flawless. And so it went. He finished eight TV segments in little more than an hour. The TV cameraman looked at him with awe. 'My God,' he said to no one in particular. 'I've never seen anything like this.' "[18]

Niagara and Erie County Democrats, though still facing an uphill battle to defeat a six term incumbent and resigned to recycling an opponent whom Dad had already defeated once, back in 1952, were going all-out to beat him this time. Sensing his vulnerability, national Democrats were positively salivating at the possibility of ousting the outspoken Republican National Chairman from his House seat. Or at least they hoped to pare down his majority and cause what they recognized would be a profound embarrassment to him and his party. With their encouragement and the financial and more-determined-than-ever political support of organized labor, Democratic candidate Dent Lackey hoped this might at last be his year.

A flamboyant, silver-haired, silver-tongued mayor of Niagara Falls, business executive, and Methodist minister, Lackey had, during his race ten years earlier against my father, delivered a fanatic tirade in his Sunday school class about Catholicism. He ended in dramatic style with an insulting mimicry of the Pope. When the incident was reported to Dad, he did not dignify it with a reaction.

So "the congressman" decided to bring in the "big guns" to help him this time, as he had never had to do before. Nelson Rockefeller, now a close personal friend, exuded all the charm, warmth, and simple sincerity that had made him one of most popular politicians of his time as he obligingly appeared at a $6 a plate dinner in Buffalo honoring Bill Miller. Heaven only knows what they ate for $6, but it certainly was not a quid pro quo. For the governor lavishly laid on the praise about the prestige his friend had gained in the nation's capital and the pride he had brought to his district. And he urged that it was now doubly important to return him to Congress in light of the international crises in which we were involved that required his understanding and experience in Washington.

But though many helped, only one man could "carry the ball." My father knew that even though the folks back home understood his national commitments, they wanted to see their candidate. When they don't, "they get to feel that you're getting too big for them," he once explained. So the remaining few weeks in the campaign brought eighteen hour days with six hours sleep a night, filled with breakfast, lunch, and dinner meetings, plant tours, school visits, rallies, and receptions. "It's a mild form of insanity," exclaimed the exhausted candidate.

The results of the '62 mid-term elections were not particularly gratifying to the national chairman, or to Republicans in general. While it had been customary in the twentieth century for the party in power to lose several seats in Congress in a mid-term election, this time the Democrats lost only two seats in the House and gained four in the Senate. Columnist Dave Broder suggested to me that this anomaly could largely be attributed to one factor: during the political hiatus following the Cuban missile crisis, few Republicans, other than Dad, were willing to stick their necks out as partisan spokesmen. As a result, many Democrats who were expected to lose their seats held on to them.

Republicans did, however, win some important governor-ships—George Romney in Michigan, William Scranton in Pennsylvania, John Rhodes in Ohio, and Rockefeller once again in New York. That was an important breakthrough: for the first time, Republican candidates had cracked some of the old Democratic strongholds in northern cities. While Bill Miller and the National Committee could not take total credit, these victories could in some measure be attributed to the vigorous efforts they had undertaken in those cities, where a respectable Republican vote was vital for a GOP candidate to win statewide. "Nine out of ten times a strong organization will carry the candidate," my father always said. "One out of ten times the candidate may carry the organization."

Asked for reaction to the national outcome, Dad, of course, tried to put the best face on results that he conceded were "below his expectations," as well as keep the field of presidential contenders for 1964 wide open. He proclaimed George Romney, the handsome new Republican governor of Michigan, worthy of consideration, and even went so far as to predict that the handily reelected Governor Rockefeller might now be the logical front-runner for the nomination.

His generous words did not extend, however, to Richard Nixon, who had taken himself out of the running for president in '64 in order to run for governor of California in '62 and then lost. I have no doubt that he did not endear himself to the former vice president when he, perhaps too honestly, critiqued Nixon's campaign style, which he found aloof and distant. "If he doesn't wake up and realize he's human, he'll be an elder statesman at a very early age," my father early on told a group of Republican women. "He ran a horrible campaign in 1960 and he's doing the same thing now in his race in California. No one can get within four miles of Nixon in a campaign," he declared with unabashed candor, forgetting momentarily that his informal comments would no doubt be widely disseminated in the media. Which they were.

Dad had occasionally been accused of intentionally stripping the titular leadership of the Republican Party away from Nixon and conferring it on President Eisenhower during these interim years. He always denied the charge, though privately he did believe that the former president, with his immense popularity, did more for the image of the Party than the now twice-defeated former vice president. Though my father and Nixon had been political friends for several years and Nixon often leaned on him for advice with his speeches, particularly after 1960 when he was so sensitive about press criticism, Dad felt that Dick Nixon had had his chance and now it was time to pass the mantle to someone else.

The bottom line in Chairman Miller's assessment of the '62 elections was that President Kennedy's popularity, peaking at about 70 percent, had been a formidable obstacle to overcome, as had a widespread attitude among voters that they should stand behind the president in the ongoing Cuban crisis. In addition, the tremendous sums of money raised by Kennedy affected races in every state. A staff member of the National Committee once remarked at a weekly meeting, in frustration, that the president was, in effect, "the national finance chairman for the Democratic Party."[19]

But above all, my father claimed that the defeatism and pessimism rampant in the Party in 1961 and 1962, which he had tried so desperately to mitigate, had made his fellow Republicans their own worst enemy. They simply took as gospel truth the polls which showed that Kennedy was so popular the GOP did not have a chance. This despite a catchy RNC flyer he had urged his state chairmen to disseminate widely among their workers. It was entitled "Three Strikes is Out," and it listed three prominent polling "flops" in recent history. The intent was to bolster the spirit of the troops whenever they got discouraged about pollsters' dire predictions for their party.

Dad's reelection was by the narrowest margin of his career. He won with 51.5 percent of the vote, a margin of only 5,000 votes. Kennedy's popularity and my father's stinging criticism of him had once again taken its toll, as it had in 1960. His opponent's oft-repeated accusation that his dual roles were making it impossible for him to serve the needs of his district was also persuasive to many.

And then there was the local economy. It had not improved, despite the fact that Dad, on his own and as part of the New York State Steering Committee, had continually endeavored to secure defense contracts for local plants. Bell Aerosystems Company and other local plants had been hard hit by the complete phase-out of frame aircraft after the Korean War. Aircraft companies in California and elsewhere on the West Coast were now winning a disproportionate number of government contracts because they had kept their facilities and labor force abreast of developments in the missile production field. As my father tried to explain, to little avail, "When they [local companies] can produce the best, there will be contracts no matter what the political affiliation of the congressman or the president."

With the mid-term elections now behind him, the RNC Chairman could no longer pretend to put the presidential aspirations of the various contenders in his party on the back burner. But the events of the next year and a half would change the destinies of all the players in this pre-convention drama—of John Kennedy, Barry Goldwater, Nelson Rockefeller, Lyndon Johnson, and not least of all, William Miller—in ways that none of them could have imagined.

CHAPTER NINE

PRELUDE TO A CANDIDACY

The events that led up to the Republican convention of 1964 were some of the most dramatic in political history. The campaign for the Party's presidential nomination would be a particularly bitter and divisive one, leaving one portion of the Grand Old Party ecstatic in victory, the other angry and intransigent in defeat, and most everyone, including my father, emotionally drained from the experience.

Since 1960, the ground had been thoroughly tilled for Arizona Senator Barry Goldwater's 1964 candidacy. It all began officially in December of '61, when F. Clifton White, a conservative New York political activist, called a meeting in Chicago of twenty-three people who were to become the instigators of a draft-Goldwater movement. The impetus for this now historic gathering had been the craggy Arizonan's performance at the 1960 Republican convention. He had eloquently persuaded his fellow conservatives to rally behind the Party's nominee, despite the fact that they had backed him for the nomination that year over Richard Nixon and were angry at being all but ignored by the long dominant, liberal "Eastern" wing of the Party. But he also issued these zealous admirers a call to action: "If we want to take this party back—and I think we can someday—let's go to work." And they did just that.

Though Goldwater never stated unequivocally that he would be a candidate in 1964, he did nothing to discourage supporters' efforts on his behalf over the next two years, and the movement steadily gained momentum despite his ambivalence. It was President John F. Kennedy's assassination in November 1963 that finally forced the Senator's hand and made a decision imperative.

I can remember hearing the surreal news in my college dorm in Boston, and immediately booking a plane for home. I am not certain why I did that. Even though the president had been the subject of my father's sharp partisan rhetoric for three years, I

think I felt like we were all part of the same small world, the political world of the nation's capital, and that world seemed about
to crumble. Somehow I guess I needed to be back there, with my
parents.

Dad had been in St. Louis conducting a Republican National
Committee meeting. Greeted in the Hotel Sheraton Jefferson
lobby upon his arrival by an oversized rocking chair suspended
from the ceiling—a caricature of John Kennedy with his bad
back—he had barked to his aide, Ab Hermann: "Take that damn
thing down." He wasn't big on gimmicks, humorous or otherwise, and he found that one particularly insensitive. The following day, the president was assassinated.

The chairman immediately cancelled the RNC meeting, flew
back to Washington, and called for a thirty-day moratorium on
all partisan political activity. During that time, he declined to
answer political questions, even in his mail. "As Republican
National Chairman, I pledge that our party will stand with the
new administration in this difficult and tragically unexpected
process of transition, with the assurance that our nation and its
interests always come first," was his stock reply. He cancelled a
subsequent committee meeting in mid-December and issued the
order: "All press inquiries to the Republican National Committee
about repercussions in reference to the assassination will be answered by me only." But he decided against postponing a series
of major fundraising dinners scheduled for early the following
year, despite Eisenhower's suggestion, since they were so crucial
for the fortunes of the Party in the upcoming '64 election.

Though he personally grieved at the death of so young a
husband and father, his nagging concern as national chairman
of his party during this period of national mourning was that the
Republican Party was in danger of being "drowned," so prolific
was the praise for the newly sworn President Johnson. Under
cover of the moratorium from political criticism, Johnson was
able to be "all things to all men," as he put it, creating an aura of
invulnerability that threatened to destroy any Republican hopes
of retaking the White House the following November.

In addition, at the conclusion of the moratorium my father
charged that the Democrats had taken every opportunity, unchal-
lenged, to put their opponents in a bad light, blaming them for
obstructing the administration's bills. He reminded all who were

interested that "the top-heavy Democratic majorities in both Houses of the Congress can give them any piece of legislation they want, no matter what Republicans do. If they want a civil rights bill, if they want a foreign aid bill, if they want a bill to paint the Capitol bright green, they've got the votes."[1]

Like much of the world, Goldwater too was in shock from the cruel cutting down of our national leader. He liked Kennedy, in fact considered him a friend. He looked forward to running against him and, for a variety of reasons, not least of which was the president's falling approval ratings and a Congress in disarray, he felt he could beat him. He didn't like nor trust Lyndon Johnson, wasn't sure he could beat him, and didn't relish a run against him. On the other hand, he recognized that the movement for his own candidacy had gone beyond the point of no return, and that he could not now in good conscience abandon all those who had worked so mightily for it. So on January 3, 1964, the grandson of an immigrant Jewish dry goods salesman, would-be savior of scorned conservatives, formally announced his candidacy.

Meanwhile, New York Governor Nelson Rockefeller, newly elected to a second term in 1962 and disappointed about his unsuccessful attempt to win the Party's presidential nomination two years earlier, had himself been running full speed ahead to secure the prize in 1964. Until the spring of '63, his chances seemed promising—indeed, many considered him the front runner for the nomination. But his hopes were dashed again, though he refused to accept it at the time, by the announcement in May of that year of his marriage to a much younger, long-time family friend, Margareta "Happy" Murphy, only a year and a half after a divorce from his wife of thirty-one years.

The public was outraged about Happy, who, in order to marry Rockefeller, had consented to relinquish custody of her children to her ex-husband. Even today, when Americans appears to be somewhat less judgmental about the details of their leaders' personal lives than they were forty years ago, this situation might well still evoke disapproval. The well-publicized pictures of those four small children whose mother had ostensibly left them to marry someone rich and famous tugged at the public's heartstrings.

Still, despite polls that subsequently reflected a precipitous drop in Rockefeller's support among Republicans, he remained in the race, spending so much money that it discouraged other possible anti-Goldwater candidates from competing with him in a long and expensive primary campaign. It wasn't until his narrow loss to Goldwater in the California primary on June 2, 1964, just a little over a month before the opening gavel of the convention, that the New York governor knew the battle was over, at least for him.

The fact that the Arizona Senator had done poorly in several earlier primaries had for a while given his opponents a ray of hope. When he lost the prestigious New Hampshire contest to Henry Cabot Lodge, even my father thought it was over for Barry. When asked by newsman Sander Vanocur, in a casual conversation after being interviewed on *The Today Show*, about who he really thought was going to win the nomination, he commented: "I don't think Lodge is going to get it but I'll tell you one thing—Goldwater is finished." Vanocur said that was the only mistake he ever heard Dad make in political analysis.

The reality was that most states selected their delegates in conventions, and since Barry's "troops" had captured the party organizations that controlled those conventions, they had already accumulated a daunting sum of delegates for their candidate. The California delegation now essentially locked up the nomination for Goldwater. I remember my father's continual frustration that Rockefeller's personal life kept thwarting the promising political career of someone whom, truth be told, he considered perhaps the strongest candidate for his party.

The final chapter of this pre-convention intrigue was a bizarre one. There had been others in the Party waiting in the wings to thwart Goldwater if and when Rockefeller faltered, but all had been reluctant to officially enter the race—Governor George Romney of Michigan, Governor William Scranton of Pennsylvania, Ambassador Henry Cabot Lodge, and, last but not least, former Vice President Richard Nixon, who was ready and willing to pick up the pieces if all the others failed to capture the nomination. They all felt the urgency of doing something, anything, to prevent what they regarded as the strong-willed Arizonan's "extremism" from dealing a mortal blow to the Republican Party. Nelson Rockefeller, even in defeat, doggedly continued to publicly lead this disgruntled but disorganized anti-Goldwater group within the GOP.

But the "group" had two ultimately insurmountable problems. First, they failed to reckon with the wide and durable base of loyalty and support that Goldwater had built among the party faithful since 1960. His speeches and other efforts had raised prodigious amounts of money and forged personal friendships in precincts and counties around the country during his four years as Republican Senate Campaign Chairman.

Second, in a major miscalculation, they hoped (indeed seemed to assume) that former President Eisenhower would endorse their stop-Goldwater efforts. They assumed this despite the fact that the Gettysburg elder statesman had said all along that he would not take sides among contenders for the nomination, and in the general election would support and campaign for the Party's nominee.

It was no secret that although the general liked Barry personally, he was more than a little unsettled by some of the senator's opinions and apprehensive about his apparent tendency to shoot from the hip. Yet as each of the would-be alternative candidates trekked to the farm for a "chat," the only report they could make to the waiting press when they emerged was that they were "encouraged" by their talks. This was, of course, an attempt to give the impression of an endorsement that in fact was not forthcoming. Eisenhower simply did not consider it appropriate for him to insert himself blatantly into the race for his party's nomination.

So at the Republican Governors' Conference in early June of '64, from whence they had hoped to launch an alternative last-minute candidate, the anti-Goldwaterites were still in disarray. Just over a week later, on June 12, a mere month before the convention was to convene in San Francisco, they finally shoved a reluctant Bill Scranton into what would prove to be a futile and bitterly divisive eleventh-hour effort to deprive Goldwater of the nomination. This Scranton move, which had come after much vacillation and several false starts, was also to have a significant impact on Goldwater's ultimate choice of a vice-presidential running mate.

Ed McCabe, former Eisenhower White House aide and longtime friend of my father, recalls well the morning the chairman received Scranton's call informing him that he would officially launch his campaign that day. Ed's law office was located at 17th and I Streets, a block from the Republican National Committee headquarters, and he had gone down to People's Drugstore on the corner for a cup of coffee. Shortly, Dad appeared and took the counter stool next to Ed. After the usual pleasantries, he wearily pushed his Homburg back slightly off his forehead and with a smile, at once amused and perplexed, told his confidante about the interesting phone call he had just received: Scranton had been thinking more about the nomination, had discussed it with his wife Mary, and had decided to go for it.

My father had been talking to all the potential presidential candidates on a regular basis—Rockefeller, Scranton, Romney, and Lodge. He had told them that if they ever decided to enter the race officially, he wanted to be the first to know—as party chairman, he didn't want any surprises. In fact, he had announced at a press conference in October 1963: "…each candidate, as soon as he announces himself, can appoint a liaison man to occupy a desk at Republican National Headquarters to make suggestions and keep the candidate informed on what we are doing."[2] But now the primaries were over and everyone knew Goldwater had delegates to spare. Dad concluded that Rockefeller, who would still do anything to derail his nemesis, had been the one to push Scranton belatedly into the fray.

That was only partially true. Scranton claimed it was Barry Goldwater's vote against the '64 Civil Rights Bill in June that propelled him into the race. He said he didn't care if he was ever president, that he knew Goldwater was not a racist and did not vote "nay" to win Southern support, but he feared that vote would nevertheless forever cast the Republican Party as the white supremacy party. After Eisenhower expressed the same concern to him privately, and after Rockefeller threw the towel in following his loss in the California primary, the first-term Pennsylvania governor decided he had no choice.[3]

My father had worked so hard for so long to keep the Party together. He had a personal friendship with Rockefeller (he and Happy occasionally invited my parents to their Foxhall Road home for dinner), admired for the most part the job he was doing as governor of his state, but thought he had now become a spoiler and was behaving badly. He liked Bill Scranton but frankly felt that he and George Romney, although bright and promising new faces in the Party, were a bit green for this run at the nomination. Lodge, in his opinion, was pompous and stiff. He hadn't cared initially who ran—it all made for a more vital party—but more than anything else, he had wanted to keep this convention reasonably orderly. A last-minute, logistically hopeless candidacy was not what he had anticipated.

In his capacity as official peacemaker and unifier of the Party, he had expressed continually in his public utterances nothing but total confidence that, in the end, all warring factions would bury their hatchets and rally to the support of the nominee. In *Washington Conversation* with CBS reporter Paul Niven and in so many other television appearances he had made during the past months, he had celebrated what he called the "healthy diversity" and competition within his party. He always maintained that the differences among the candidates were not substantial and that there was much they believed in common. His constant plea to his colleagues was: "In building up your preference, do not tear down other Republicans." Now he knew his pleas had fallen on deaf ears.

I was only peripherally aware of the complex political machinations of 1963/64 with which Dad was contending as national chairman, for I was happily ensconced in my junior year at Newton College in Boston. But I do recall Mother's long distance reports that despite his outward optimism, he was privately growing increasingly more vexed at the bitterness and intransigence that were etching worrisome lines of division within party ranks. I, however, remained naively confident that he would ultimately be capable of mending the fractured party back together.

Running concurrently with this turbulent Republican intraparty struggle for dominance was the titanic battle throughout 1963 and '64 to extract, at long last, a strong and meaningful civil rights bill from Congress. Major legislation rarely occurs unless there are social pressures encouraging action, and those social pressures were now mounting and becoming impossible to ignore.

Civil rights protesters were growing ever more vocal and better mobilized, staging sit-ins, boycotts, freedom rides, and peaceful demonstrations and marches, which often ended in rioting when whites responded angrily. All of it, of course, was covered in depth and in living color by the nation's news media. Vivid pictures were beamed nightly into homes across America—of whites beating African Americans, of Police Chief Bull Connor's dogs snarling at protesters, of fire hoses being turned against marchers, of officers using electric cattle prods for crowd control, of a defiant Governor George Wallace, of civil rights worker Medger Evers, murdered in front of his home in full view of his wife and children.

As the violence spread to northern cities like New York, Philadelphia, Chicago, and Newark and ceased to be only a southern problem, an urgency swelled in the nation's capital to respond. This escalating cycle of violence was forging a gradual consensus among middle class Americans everywhere that the problems of black citizens required more than slow-moving court action, which frequently frustrated the intent of previous civil rights laws. Their problems required legislative attention in the Congress.

That meant the issues would inevitably once again be mired in the same complex politics that had inhibited progress for so many years. And sure enough, there was politics aplenty among all parties involved. Despite a sturdy civil rights plank in the 1960 Democratic platform, candidate Kennedy largely avoided the issue during the presidential campaign. He was reluctant to antagonize southern Democrats (as well as, in truth, the people of his own hometown of Boston), whose support he desperately needed to defeat his Republican opponent. His congressional civil rights record in the 1950s had been ambivalent and lukewarm at best, marked by the complicated and sometimes contradictory views about civil rights that plagued most of the nation at that time.

After his election in November 1960, the new president, preoccupied with solving the Cuban, Vietnam, Laos, and Berlin crises and in proving his mettle to a constantly blustering Soviet Premier Krushchev, continued to stay aloof from the civil rights problem. Seemingly oblivious to the severity of black unrest, he failed to produce any new proposals for the next two years. There were, again, political reasons: he needed the South for reelection in 1964, and he needed southern support in Congress for his foreign and domestic programs. Kennedy feared, rightfully, that a bitter and protracted fight for a civil rights bill could torpedo all the above.

Civil rights leaders, however, were disappointed and growing impatient with the apparent lack of passion in a man from whom they had expected so much, and their demands continued unabated. With the administration reluctant to take the lead, forty House Republicans, including my father, finally introduced a fairly comprehensive civil rights bill in January 1963. It would establish a Federal Commission to guarantee equal employment opportunities, curtail the use of literacy tests for voting by creating a presumption of literacy after six grades of school, provide financial assistance to schools seeking to desegregate, make the Civil Rights Commission permanent and expand its power to investigate voting rights abuses, and increase the legal authority of the Attorney General to institute civil suits on behalf of citizens who were the object of discrimination. In an overwhelmingly Democrat-controlled Congress, the bill went nowhere.

Not to be one-upped, Kennedy sent down a package in February that was a weaker version of the Republican proposals and fell far short of the promises in the Democratic platform— "timid and almost reluctant proposals," as Dad and other GOP Judiciary Committee members described them on the House floor. The Republicans were holding the president's dragging feet to the fire, as he and his brother Bobby were still trying to figure out how they could avoid a potentially bruising battle. There were many who were now blaming the administration's delay in delivering on their promises for the fury in the streets. Black author James Baldwin's dire prediction of "the fire next time" appeared to be coming true.

When Kennedy finally did act in June 1963 to propose his own comprehensive civil rights bill, it was, much as it had been for Eisenhower in 1956, because the climate of opinion and the political situation had forced him to act. At first, he had intended to go for the least he could do to please civil rights advocates and not fatally alienate his fellow Democrats of the southern bloc. But ultimately he reportedly decided to champion a stronger bill because it was the "right" thing to do. He proceeded to commit all the moral and persuasive powers of his office to its passage.

A fragile political coalition would indeed be needed to pass the controversial legislation. Title II, which had also been previously proposed by House and Senate Republicans, would be the sticking point—it barred discrimination in a wide range of public accommodations, even those privately owned. Considered by southerners an unprecedented and unconstitutional intrusion by the federal government into private lives and state affairs, that provision was anathema to them. It soon became apparent that no amount of persuasion would win southern support for this legislation.

To substitute for the loss of southern votes, the administration knew it needed to capture the votes of most Republicans for passage, particularly in the Senate where bipartisan support for cloture was the only hope of ending the southern filibuster which was sure to ensue. Cloture is the parliamentary device used in the U.S. Senate to stop debate and call a vote, and it requires the "yeas" of two-thirds or 67 of the 100 members for imposition. While moderates and liberals of both parties were on board to support a broad civil rights bill this year, there were some conservative Republicans, mostly from the rural Midwest where black populations were small and racial difficulties negligible, who were hesitant to give the federal government broad new powers.

While the president liked to give the impression that success of civil rights legislation in this year hinged solely on whether Republicans would go along, my father liked to point out several historical facts that rendered that concern unwarranted: of 49 significant civil rights related roll call votes in House and Senate between 1933 and 1960, 81 percent of the total Republican votes cast were in favor, compared with only a 42 percent favorable Democratic votes. Since 1940, Republican senators had repeatedly voted for cloture in far higher numbers than had Democrats, in numerous unsuccessful attempts to shut down debate and bring open accommodation, anti-lynching, and poll tax legislation to the floor for a vote.

With the two previous civil rights acts of 1957 and 1960, it was primarily the Democrats who fought to kill strengthening amendments and Republicans who fought to include them. In short, Republicans, so long in the minority, were fed up with their own proposals and consistent support for civil rights being ignored and unappreciated, and if the president wanted bipartisan support this time, then he was going to have to give them some of the credit for his success.

The initial focus of activity on what was to become the Civil Rights Act of 1964 took place in the House of Representatives. The administration's bill was referred to the House Judiciary Committee and then directly to subcommittee No.5, chaired by avid civil rights supporter Manny Celler. The ranking Republican, Bill McCulloch, along with my father, joined their plucky colleague in maneuvering the legislation through the committee process.

Tumultuous hearings stretched from June of '63 into the fall, again with impassioned witnesses for and against, and after weighing all the evidence they had collected, the subcommittee actually rewrote the Kennedy Justice Department's original draft to strengthen it. Celler expanded the definition of "public accommodations" to include private schools, law firms, and medical associations and gave the Justice Department sweeping new powers to defend black citizens against abuse of their rights.

When the subcommittee approved this sweeping version on October 1 with little trouble—even southern Democratic members voted in favor, believing that such a radical measure was doomed to ultimate defeat on the floor of both the House and Senate—the victory was widely hailed by civil rights proponents. The Kennedy brothers, however, were outraged. They believed that if the bill were not moderated, there would be no bill at all. But they also knew they risked the wrath of black leaders for any effort to weaken the rewritten proposal.

Once it went to the full Judiciary Committee, the White House stepped up the pressure for compromise. At Attorney General Robert Kennedy's urgent plea, Celler agreed to undo what he had done and return to the original administration formula, with some added language from old Republican proposals. At this point, a majority of Republicans on the committee refused to go along with the diluted measure, asserting their support for a stronger bill. Then Celler himself appeared on television denouncing the changes he had just agreed to and disassociating himself from them. And so began a mini-drama worthy of *Masterpiece Theatre.*

West Virginia Republican Arch Moore, with Dad's support, made a motion to report the tough Celler bill out to the House floor. Part of the reason for that move was canny politics—to put the burden on the Democrats to prove that they indeed wanted strong civil rights legislation. His motion threw the Judiciary Committee into chaos—its chairman had lost control, especially of the balky Southern Democrats whom he could not cajole into doing either his or the president's bidding. To avert the wrath of the Kennedys, Celler's only choice now was to call for adjournment.

The full Judiciary Committee did not meet again for several weeks, since to do so would have necessitated a vote on Congressman Moore's motion. In the interim, the administration lobbied intensely, day and night, among committee members for a moderated bill that would be more likely to pass both House and Senate. The resulting compromise, with which civil rights organizations were not entirely pleased, received Judiciary's endorsement on October 29, 1963, with a vote of 23 to 11. There had been 70 days of public hearings, 275 witnesses, and 5,792 pages of published testimony. Prior to that vote, the stronger bill that Celler, Moore, McCulloch, and my father had originally championed had gone down to a narrow defeat, 19 to15.

In an interesting twist, Celler and Dad had in the end voted against their bill and in favor of the compromise. Though personally they both preferred the former, Manny knew he ought not anger the president any further, and my father had become convinced that bipartisan support for the administration's bill was the only way they would get a bill at all this year. Though weaker than they had hoped, with fewer enforcement mechanisms, the resulting legislation that finally reported to the House floor from Judiciary would, he felt, at least accomplish more in civil rights protection than the Kennedy administration's original request of the past June.

The reason the president actually now had what he considered an acceptable bill was that Senator Dirksen and Congressman Halleck, Republican leaders of the Senate and House, as well as my father, had met with him at his request in the White House to pledge their support in helping him get equitable and moderate compromise legislation to the House floor. That meeting, along with Georgia Democratic Senator Dick Russell's angry reaction to it—"Russell blasts GOP Chiefs for Civil Rights OK"—was reported in media headlines nationwide. The venerable dean of the southern bloc, with undisguised sarcasm, accused his colleagues from the other side of the aisle of "donning the leather shirt and tasseled moccasins of the New Frontier."

This publicity produced a veritable deluge of "disappointed," irate letters in Dad's congressional and National Committee offices, scolding him for his "asinine stand," for his alleged "treachery," and for taking his party "in the wrong direction." Sad to say, almost without exception, those virulent anti-black letters were from southerners who said the only candidate they could support was Barry Goldwater. My father's varied replies were prompt, to the point, and unequivocal:

> Personally, I feel that Senator Russell was very much out of order in leveling such an attack as he did on our leadership relative to Civil Rights.

> The question is whether blind partisanship on this very serious human rights question would be good for the country at this time. On the other hand, I grant you it was a great temptation to let the Kennedys stew in the juice of their own making. However, there are times when we must endeavor to reach above strict partisanship on behalf of the greatest nation the world has ever known.

> Very frankly, it would be most disastrous for the Republican Party to take any other position than that of being in favor of human liberties and freedoms, the principles upon which we were founded one hundred years ago.[4]

One man offered a most interesting explanation for what he called my father's "capitulation": "After all, if John F. Kennedy's personal confessor agrees with William E. Miller's personal confessor that the time has come for Mr. Miller to get into line, how likely would he be to resist?" The author even included a "cc" to the Pope on that one. To another writer's incredible but most serious proposal of "deportation" to solve our civil rights problems, supposedly derived from President Lincoln, Dad gave a far more patient response than I could have managed: "The Negro has become an integral part of our citizenry—the same as other nationality groups—and is a full-fledged American citizen. How would it be possible at this date to single out the Negro for deportation?"[5]

There were writers with more rational concerns, such as a past president of the American Bar Association and specialist in constitutional law who believed all Americans, black and white, would lose precious constitutional rights with the pending civil rights bill. And there were others who disapproved of intolerance and racial inequality but were certain the "cure" would be worse than the problem. To one such correspondent, Dad still wrote empathetically but with obvious anguish:

> *Bill, if I had all the answers to this situation I would change my name to Solomon! However, I do believe that the Negroes of this country are entitled to full citizenship the same as any other nationality group. The Negro is asked to fight for our country in time of war, he is asked to serve his term in the armed services, he is called upon to meet the requirements of citizenship the same as any other group—so how can we honestly deny him the full rights of citizenship when we generously give them to all other nationalities making up such a large part of our population?*
>
> *It's a difficult problem and will remain one for many years to come, in my opinion, but the great unrest on the part of the Negro throughout the world must be faced and that forthrightly. I fully appreciate the complications which this transitional period in our civil rights progress is bringing to all our citizens, but I think with patience and a common sense approach we can solve these problems.*

The most discouraging correspondence of all must have been those letters from some of the new Republican "leaders" in the South, those who had volunteered to help build a struggling party. Unfortunately, along with many fine, open-minded citizens came some segregationists who mourned the loss of the status quo that civil rights progress portended. They were all part of one package, difficult to separate. The latter had no shortage of unsolicited and unappealing advice for Chairman Miller on how the Party ought to be handling the civil rights issue, mainly by supporting Dick Russell, Strom Thurmond et al and disavowing support of civil rights.

While part of him would have liked to turn them all away, political pragmatism dictated against it. The solution, in his mind, would be to make absolutely clear where he and the Republican Party stood on civil rights, that it was the inclusive party of

Lincoln and had no intention of betraying its heritage. "I am well aware of your thinking and the thinking in your state and the South," he would write these new party members, but he went on to firmly and diplomatically explain why the bipartisan efforts of Republican leaders to get civil rights legislation passed "is the best approach for our party."

One rare moment of encouragement for my father in these emotion-charged times came with a letter jointly signed by representatives from the National Council of Churches, the Synagogue Council of America, and the National Catholic Welfare Conference: "We wish to state strongly our warm appreciation for your patriotic and far-sighted decision to put this moral issue above all considerations of partisan differences. You have rendered a real service to the country ... Your courageous action has obtained the necessary political support for the adoption of a strong civil rights bill." Dad thanked the religious leaders for their thoughtfulness but added, somewhat sadly, that their positive letter did not "reflect the attitude of the hundreds of other letters coming to our headquarters."

The next roadblock for the would-be Civil Rights Act was the House Rules Committee, still chaired by Virginia Congressman Howard Smith. Not surprisingly, he promised to hold it hostage indefinitely. Then on November 22, as his bill languished in Rules, the president's life was snuffed out.

Grieving civil rights advocates were unsure if his successor, whose record until he engineered passage of the mild Civil Rights Act of 1957 had been entirely opposed to civil rights, would continue Kennedy's crusade. Would the new president, erstwhile "Master of the Senate,"[6] use his prestige and mastery of parliamentary procedure to placate his fellow southerners and thwart civil rights progress, or would he use it to advance the cause?

Lyndon Johnson, addressing the Congress and the nation for the first time as president on November 27, 1963, called for passage of the pending civil rights bill as a monument to the fallen John Kennedy. Thus under pressure, the balky Rules Committee cleared it for floor consideration, but not until January 30, 1964. After nine days of debate and the rejection of nearly 100 weakening amendments, the measure passed by a lopsided 290-130 vote. A bipartisan coalition of Republicans and northern Democrats had been the key to the bill's success.

There was to be an even more tumultuous journey through the Senate: copious amounts of political maneuvering, eighty-three days of contentious debate, and the almost miraculous imposition of cloture, which for the first time defeated the once impregnable southern segregationist forces whose filibusters had stifled every civil rights bill of the century. Finally, there emerged a bipartisan substitute bill skillfully crafted by Republican Leader Everett Dirksen and Majority Leader Mike Mansfield. It was only slightly weaker than the House-passed bill but enough so to garner the "swing" votes of conservative rural Republicans. The result: on June 19, 1964, a 73-27 victory for the most important piece of civil rights legislation in the nation's history. Only six Republican senators voted "nay," among them Barry Goldwater of Arizona—with unfortunate consequences both for him personally and for the party he was to lead. It was barely a month away from the opening of the Republican convention in San Francisco.

Throughout this battle, my father remained committed to the strongest possible legislation that would at long last address black grievances in a meaningful way. He wanted not only to end the agitation and bloodshed that was poisoning the streets of America, but also to give African American citizens the rights and protections that they had for too long been unlawfully denied. Yet he was mindful, as he always had been, of the dangers of government overreaching. In his questioning of witnesses before committee, he tried to ascertain how much federal intrusion was necessary to eliminate civil rights abuses, and then he endeavored to ensure that legislation included only that much and no more. Interestingly, the right to a jury trial in cases arising from the final bill, the most contentious issue in 1956 for which he had passionately but futilely fought, was included in this legislation without even a whimper of opposition.

The public accommodations section of the new law, or Title II, which assured that black citizens could no longer be excluded from restaurants, hotels, and other public facilities, even if privately owned, was unpalatable to many conservatives. Even some moderates suspected it might prove to be unconstitutional. Barry Goldwater, though he was in favor of all the other ten titles in the Civil Rights Act of 1964, could not bring himself to accept the legality of that one provision. Dad himself had some similar concerns about Title II, being the champion of free private enterprise that he was, but in the end he knew it was absolutely imperative that the Congress finish the work they had begun and failed to complete in 1957 and 1960. And he knew it was the right thing to do. Columnist Charles Krauthammer once wrote, "Decency is what 'compassionate conservatism' is about."

The delicate balancing act required of my father in the weeks leading up to the opening of the twenty-eighth Republican convention in San Francisco on July 13 tested his most practiced diplomatic skills. Although Goldwater appeared to have more than sufficient votes to become the Party's standard-bearer on the first ballot, Romney, Scranton, Rockefeller, and several "favorite sons" were also to be placed in nomination. Rockefeller was bitter and complaining about his "mistreatment"; Scranton was still hoping for a last minute miracle; Romney was patiently waiting in the wings; and Nixon, though he had taken himself out of the running, would gladly have come to the rescue in the event of a balloting deadlock. To make matters even more tense, the venerable party elder statesman in Gettysburg was hovering somewhere in the background vowing not to interfere on behalf of an "eastern establishment" candidate like Scranton, though some anti-Goldwater people were still desperately hoping he might.

A political convention is a monumental job of organization, and most of the details had already been nailed down by June, when Scranton announced his belated candidacy. Both he and Goldwater were booked at the Mark Hopkins Hotel on Nob Hill in San Francisco, but now, with Scranton's new position, that would mean two warring camps occupying the same space, putting the hotel in a constant state of siege.

On the way to San Francisco in mid-June, Dad attempted to sort out the logistical nightmare this new development had created for the convention. It not only necessitated a last minute search for new hotel rooms and office space for Scranton's contingent in an already packed city, but also the reapportioning of floor passes and guest tickets to the *Cow Palace* to accommodate his supporters. The blame for any perceived slights in such a contentious situation falls naturally in the lap of the national chairman, and Chairman Bill Miller had his share of complaints with which to contend.

For example, embittered Rockefeller supporters in the New York delegation accused him of denying them equal access to the convention floor. When the beleaguered chairman explained that the allocation of tickets and credentials was based on a long-standing and rigid formula that reflected past Republican performance at the polls in each state, the furor subsided. As a matter of fact, my father had specifically instructed Jo Good, in charge of convention arrangements, to make certain that no favoritism was shown to anyone.

Despite all precautions, there were several incidents of vindictiveness and spoilers' tactics used by some uncontrollable Goldwaterites, unbeknownst to their leader, which constantly threatened to subvert Dad's efforts to expand the following of the Republican Party. Only a week after the National Committee had published an elaborate brochure detailing the posts of responsibility within the committee held by African Americans, some perverse Goldwater delegates from Tennessee and Georgia succeeded in maneuvering several prominent black men out of their delegations. Worst of all, the black Georgians who were ousted had played a major role in the emergence of that state's GOP.

A more pleasant and eminently more soluble problem laid on my father's shoulders at convention time was an urgent call from President Eisenhower. According to his recounting of the call to Press Secretary Bob Smalley, the conversation went like this:

Ike: *Bill, I understand that rooms are very hard to get for the convention in San Francisco, but do you suppose you have someone there who could arrange a place for me to stay for a couple of days? I would like to see some of it, and I've made this arrangement with ABC...*

Dad: *General, we've set aside the Presidential Suite at the St. Francis for you, and there's also a block of rooms available to you for any family or friends you may want to accommodate.*

Ike: *Oh, you have? Well, that's very nice. Now, I hate to ask for another favor, but do you suppose you could help me get a few convention tickets? I'd like to be able to give some to Freeman Gosden and some other friends...*

Dad proceeded to explain to Eisenhower that as a former president he would have a very large block of the best seats in the house. The general was warmly grateful. "I've never been to a convention before," he said innocently and with some excitement, "except to accept the nomination." Smalley remembers my father recounting this story with more warmth than humor. I'm sure he was wishing that all his dilemmas were that easy to solve.

The most pressing priority for the RNC and its chairman was to use this once-every-four-years opportunity to broaden the Party's appeal and give it a more engaging image. So in an effort to put their best faces forward and at the same time placate all elements of the Party, a wide variety of participants were awarded important roles at the convention.

Though Dad himself was being pushed for the "keynoter" job by many delegates who saw him as the most neutral and eloquent figure the Party had to offer for a national television audience of some seventy million, that would have broken precedent. Not only does the national chairman never keynote his convention, but doing so would give the appearance of one man having too many fingers in the pie, so to speak. Despite all the feelers he was receiving, his usual response was: "Frankly, I would hope there will be another solution. It has always been my aim to broaden the base of the Party and bring in newer and younger faces."

His choice for the post was the attractive, liberal Governor Mark Hatfield of Oregon, a Rockefeller man. After pressuring House Minority Leader Charles Halleck to surrender his traditional privilege of serving as permanent chairman of the convention, he appointed the popular, moderate, and more telegenic Senator Thruston Morton of Kentucky to the job. The naming of conservative Congressman Melvin Laird, future defense secretary under President Nixon, to chair the Platform Committee rounded out the top trio.

With barely concealed frustration over constant charges of favoritism, my father told *New York Times* reporter Warren Weaver Jr. during this period that he was keenly aware of and yet somewhat fatalistic about the perils of appearing even slightly partisan. "There's no way I can avoid charges of partisanship unless I go into hibernation," he lamented. "If I say I think Goldwater is ahead at this time, they say I'm pro-Goldwater. If I say Goldwater doesn't have the nomination locked up yet, they say I'm anti-Goldwater." Though he always appeared calm on the surface and totally in control in public, usually smiling, rarely short-tempered, invariably able to see the humor in even the worst of situations, the clue to his inner tension would always be the number of cigarettes clustered in his ashtrays. And they were plentiful.

At the same time all this was transpiring in my dad's life in early summer of '64, I donned my crisp blue and white guide uniform daily in Flushing Meadow, Long Island, at the New York State Pavilion of the World's Fair. The rest of the family blissfully whiled away lazy days on Lake Ontario, all of us oblivious to both his increasing headaches and the gathering momentum for his own nomination to the second spot on the national ticket.

As for the 1964 vice-presidential candidacy, speculation began, as such speculation begins every four years, well before the opening gavel fell for the convention. In years such as '64, as well as some more recent ones, when state primaries have made the presidential nominee all but a foregone conclusion by convention time, the VP nomination is all there is to speculate about, the only suspenseful event left.

The earliest and most prescient mention of my father for second spot on the national slate in 1964 came on June 2, 1963, more than a year in advance of the convention. It came from *Buffalo Courier-Express* Washington correspondent Lucian Warren, who had covered him for most of his years in Congress. Warren figured that as Nelson Rockefeller's recent remarriage appeared to demolish the heretofore front-runner's prospects for the nomination, it thereby increased Bill Miller's prospects of being the vice-presidential choice on a ticket headed by either Senator Barry Goldwater of Arizona or Governor George Romney of Michigan.

The reasons were obvious, he stated: as a Catholic, Miller might help to recapture some of the Catholics who were staunch Republicans but voted for Kennedy in 1960; as a New Yorker, he would geographically balance Goldwater or Romney. But "Miller's biggest asset on a Republican national ticket," declared the newsman, "is the gifted way, in the eyes of Republicans, that he presents national issues. He is considered the most articulate spokesman of Republican policy today." Coming out of the blue as it did, this article surprised and delighted our family, to say the least, but I don't recall that we dwelled on it for very long.

We thought it exciting that Dad was even mentioned for such an honor but never contemplated that it might become reality.

There were a few other early-out-of-the-gate predictions of his destiny to be the VP candidate in 1964, mostly from the proud Niagara Falls, Buffalo, and Lockport newspapers in his district. But there was also a *Los Angeles Herald Examiner* columnist named George Todt who appeared to make it his mission to win the nomination for Bill Miller. In no less than seven wildly enthusiastic columns, he touted him, among other things, as "a gifted speaker, blessed with sturdy character, good American common sense and an ability to go quickly to the heart of the problem." But my personal favorite was this one: "Miller is really one whale of a guy—mentally and personality-wise he is hard to beat anywhere … and Bill is blessed with a strikingly beautiful and vivacious wife, Stephanie, and two gorgeous daughters, Elizabeth, 20, and Mary, 17. They will become tremendous campaign assets to him and the embattled GOP in the days ahead!" So why didn't we hire this guy as our family's private PR man?

Strange as it may seem, all this early editorial praise for and boosting of my father, wonderful as it was, just didn't affect our lives very much at this point. I was immersed in my life at Newton College, Mary in her high school activities at Stone Ridge in Washington, Mother in rearing two toddlers, and Dad rarely brought politics home. In short, life went on, and while we were not blasé, a certain amount of publicity just went with the territory of being a congressional family and with his job as national chairman. After nearly fourteen years, we had become accustomed to the vagaries of an unpredictable media. In the same way that our parents had consoled us in tearful discussions of an occasional unkind article on our father, so we had learned not to put much credence in glamorous but speculative suggestions about his political future.

Adding fuel to our growing amazement, however, was the constant stream of letters arriving at the National Committee pleading for him to "consider" the second spot on the ticket. There are boxes crammed with them now residing among his papers in a lonely, carefully climate-controlled section of the Rare Book and Manuscript Archives at Cornell University Library. That might be surprising considering the puzzlement with which his eventual nomination was received in some quarters of the country. Many spoke of hearing his speeches or of seeing him on a television program and how impressed they were—he seemed to them "so honest, confident, reassuring, and sincere." Others said he was "the only man in the Republican Party capable of smoothing feathers, calming the boys down, etc."[7]

Dad's replies reminded his ardent proponents that the nomination was not his to "consider" but would be the choice of the presidential nominee, and that in the meantime it was imperative that he and the National Committee remain impeccably neutral about such matters. With his sincere humility, he added that there were many other outstanding Republican leaders in the country who would be more deserving of this recognition: "The whole idea is far fetched and I am very surprised to note the publicity emanating from it," he remarked in one of his letters.

Among all this fan mail, I unearthed a surprising correspondence from a group of law students at Washington and Lee University in Lexington, Virginia, dated spring of 1964—which caught my eye since I have lived for some thirty years now a mere hour from that historic institution. The enthusiastic students were, in all seriousness, inaugurating a regional DRAFT BILL MILLER FOR PRESIDENT drive, which they intended to organize nationally by June 1st.

This was the fantastic scenario they envisioned: "We believe that the national convention will go past the 5th or 6th ballot, and therefore believe that Bill Miller will have a reasonable chance to capture the presidential nomination. We feel that if Bill Miller is nominated, he would have the best chance of beating Johnson, because he can unify the Republican Party." Unfortunately, their project was nipped in the bud when, upon visiting my father in Washington, the aspiring lawyers were told the same thing everyone else approaching him about higher office was told: he was deeply flattered but it was impossible for him to extend them any support.

While there was sporadic mention of him as a logical choice for vice-presidential nominee from 1963 through the early months of 1964, speculation began in earnest in June of '64, after the California primary had assured Goldwater's nomination. Associated Press reporter Walter Mears wrote on June 10 that the senator was considering four eastern GOP leaders for a possible running mate: Pennsylvania Governor William Scranton, Senator

Thruston Morton of Kentucky, Representative William E. Miller of New York, and Governor James Rhodes of Ohio. Congressmen Gerald Ford and Melvin Laird also appeared on other lists. Mears added that Goldwater was at this point hinting that Scranton in particular might want to consider the second spot, since not only would that augment Goldwater's delegate strength but, should they lose, it would position the governor to capture the presidential nomination in 1968.

I remember perusing the *New York Times* while sitting at the breakfast table in the family home of a college friend, Pam McKenna, who had generously offered me room and board for the summer, before setting off for my job at the World's Fair that muggy summer morning. There was Dad's picture above the AP article. We all exclaimed and bubbled about the "what ifs," and it was the first time I seriously entertained the thought that the speculation could indeed become reality. When I emerged from the gridlock of the Long Island Expressway an hour later and arrived at the Fair, I discovered that the news had by now created a considerable furor among my fellow guides—all of which somewhat distracted me from the already marginal French and Russian responses I was supposed to be rendering to the queries of our international visitors.

About this time, a group of California congressmen adopted a resolution proposing fellow Representative Miller for the VP nomination. And a poll in the June 18 issue of *Roll Call*, the weekly newspaper for congressmen and Capitol Hill employees, indicated that he was preferred two to one over Mr. Scranton by the Republican senators and representatives answering the questionnaire.

My father was complimented by all this but still did not take it seriously, at least publicly. He couldn't, for to do so might compromise his assiduously maintained neutrality with regard to the presidential stakes. He chose his words carefully when asked about the race, reminding his listeners that although Goldwater had nearly enough votes to clinch the nomination, he had been in politics long enough to know that until the roll is called and the votes counted, anything can happen in a national convention.

Then on July 3, Walter Trohan, *Chicago Tribune* Washington Bureau Chief, asserted that, with ten days to go until the convention, "Representative William E. Miller, the hard-fighting and fiercely competitive chairman of the Republican National Committee, may well be the GOP vice-presidential nominee." He went on to explain that Scranton, once considered the most unifying choice for the spot, had so alienated and insulted Goldwater since he had launched his belated stop-Goldwater effort on June 12 that Barry would be hard-pressed to offer it to him. Trohan further noted, "Miller's diplomacy, by contrast, is evidenced by the fact that he has earned and kept the friendship and respect of such Republicans as Dwight Eisenhower, Thomas Dewey, Nelson Rockefeller, Scranton, Nixon, and Goldwater. He also has earned the respect of Democrats as a worthy foe."

The *Los Angeles Times* reported also on July 3, quite authoritatively: "Representative William E. Miller of New York, Republican National Chairman, is Senator Barry Goldwater's first choice as his running mate." Apparently at this point, several unnamed Goldwater aides were speaking off the record to the press about the number two spot, placing my father first ("99 percent in"), Gerald Ford still "in contention," and Bill Scranton unlikely "unless the convention forces him down our throat."

Miller and Goldwater, for their parts, were, at least publicly, remaining above the fray. Goldwater said he was superstitious about picking a running mate before he was officially chosen and simply refused to discuss it with his aides or the media. Dad, still mired in last minute administrative details of the convention, was aware of but continued to ignore the constant prognostication.

His response to constant queries about a possible vice-presidential nod varied from "no interest," to "Yes, I would be available as a vice-presidential candidate with Goldwater or any other Republican nominee … I am a team player and have served the Republican Party as national chairman for three years and would continue to serve it in any capacity asked of me," to "If Senator Goldwater were nominated for president and asked my advice, I would urge him to try to persuade Governor William Scranton to accept the vice-presidential nomination." On July 8, it was reported that my father had turned down offers to open a campaign headquarters in San Francisco in his behalf because he felt it might compromise his neutrality.

There is no doubt that in inverse proportion as the fortunes of Governor Scranton fell, Bill Miller's rose. Many Republicans, including Chairman Miller, had hoped that in the end the

Pennsylvania governor could still be united on a ticket with the Arizona Senator. But as Scranton's attacks on Goldwater throughout June and early July became more strident and personal, hopes for that prospect dimmed and the Miller bandwagon gained momentum.

Letters, phone calls, and telegrams began pouring into Goldwater's office, ten to one urging him to consider Bill Miller. Governor Tim Babcock of Montana issued a statement in support of Dad, and the Utah and Nebraska delegations, along with several Southern delegations, passed resolutions endorsing him. There were even some members of the New York delegation, old friends of my father, who, though nominally committed to Rockefeller's hopeless nomination, were eager to be free to announce publicly for Miller for the second spot. The opinions of his congressional colleagues apparently weighed heavily with Goldwater—those are the people who know you best, Barry always believed.

By Monday, July 13, opening day of the tensely awaited convention, "Miller for Vice President" buttons and posters had begun to appear in the Cow Palace and at key traffic intersections throughout San Francisco, and Miller pamphlets were being shoved into the hands of passersby on street corners and delivered to delegates' hotel rooms. With still no outward encouragement from either Goldwater or Miller, twenty congressmen called a news conference to announce a "grass-roots demand from delegates across the country" that Mr. Miller be nominated for vice president.

This consensus that appeared to be gathering about the vice-presidential nominee, it turned out, had been independently created, encouraged, and funded by the zealous efforts of Congressman John Pillion, Dad's long-time friend and congressional colleague from a Western New York district adjacent to his. He was helped by assorted governors and Republican enthusiasts from all parts of the country. They obtained the moral and financial support of some thirty Republican congressmen, all of whom agreed to reach into their pockets for $100 to help cover some of the costs. The magnitude of the campaign that this committed band of admirers ran for my father during convention week, without either his encouragement or discouragement, was quite unprecedented in its organization and vigor.

In fact, Pillion had his hands full trying to keep the impatient Miller supporters waiting for the strategic moment to go public with their drive, for he did not want it to suffer from premature exposure or to interfere with the first order of business, which was the nomination of Goldwater. There was also the slight irony that Dad was still suggesting publicly that Scranton should be considered a possibility for the ticket. Nevertheless, there were soon at least three hotel suites in the convention city—in the Sir Francis Drake and St. Francis hotels—where the main item of business was the Miller nomination. Young Goldwater backers from New York and Arizona were "lining up to help," and assorted Miller paraphernalia was being prodigiously produced and distributed.

Then came the final blow to any remaining chance Governor Scranton might have had for vice-presidential consideration. On the Sunday eve of the convention, a derogatory and insulting letter, allegedly from the governor, was delivered to Goldwater's fifteenth floor Mark Hopkins Hotel suite and simultaneously released to the press. It challenged Barry to a public debate, accused him of being a "minority candidate," "irresponsible," "a radical extremist," and worse.

Though it later turned out the missive, which promptly found its way into the hands of every delegate and alternate in San Francisco, had not been composed, read, or signed by Scranton but rather by an over-zealous member of his staff, it predictably succeeded in further offending Barry and infuriating his supporters. And it clinched the choice of my father, at least in inside circles, to complete the Republican ticket.

NBC reporter Chuck Quinn, who would later be assigned to cover Dad's campaign, regaled me with a humorous behind-the-scenes story that happened about this time. He and fellow NBC reporter, Robert McCormack, both in San Francisco to cover the convention, were sitting in a bar one night—"you learned a lot in bars," he said. They were trying to figure out who would be Barry's running mate, when in wandered Ab Hermann, Chairman Miller's right-hand man at the National Committee. "I'll tell you who I think it's going to be," said Ab conspiratorially in his veteran inside-politico crusty voice. "I think it's going to be Bill Miller." He didn't mention that he himself had been doing some considerable undercover work to make that happen.

Chuck laughed a reporter's all-knowing and derisive laugh. "Cut it out! Who ever heard of him, and he's a Catholic for crying out loud and the great unwashed have never heard of him!" Ab reeled off the litany of why he thought Barry was going to pick my father: balance, religion, well known to Republicans around the country, established credentials in Congress, good politician—and then he left. Quinn still maintained, "it ain't going to happen," but his cohort insisted, "Ab knows a lot of stuff, so maybe we ought to check it out." Chuck offered that he knew Miller and they would just go to his hotel and ask him.

When Dad, always accessible to the media, greeted the pair in his suite, Chuck blurted, "Let me get right to the point. We're here because we had a pretty good tip today that you might be Barry's running mate." My father, with his customary chortle and half grin, replied: "Well, I'll tell you what I know. If it's not going to be Bill Scranton, it's going to be me." The two raced back to NBC to report their scoop, whereupon they were greeted again with laughter and disbelief. When Chuck assured the producers that "if Miller says this is what is, this is what is, because he doesn't lie," they went with the story and gleefully beat the other networks by hours.

In reality, though a Goldwater/Scranton ticket could possibly have promoted a semblance of unity among the disparate wings of the Party, it is questionable whether it was ever wise or even feasible, with or without the fatal letter. The two had served together in the same National Reserve squadron on Capitol Hill during Scranton's one term in Congress, and though Barry liked the Pennsylvanian, he did not consider him a strong leader.

Furthermore, the senator was not preeminently a political being, sometimes to the chagrin of his staff and followers, and it was more important to him that he run with someone with whom he was personally comfortable than to do the "politically correct" thing. He felt that he and his supporters had won a long and bruising struggle to gain control of the Party and return it to where they thought it belonged, and he was not feeling disposed to share the fruits of their labor with the vanquished. And Scranton had hurt him deeply.

There was also the hypothetical question of whether or not the Pennsylvania governor would even accept a nod for second place from a man with whom his abortive and last-ditch campaign had disagreed so fundamentally, even for the considerable boost it might bring to his own future political career. He had vehemently disavowed any interest in the vice-presidential nomination—but then there had been many before him who had done the same and in the end had bowed to the wishes of their party, either out of loyalty or self-interest. As the old saying goes: "The vice-presidential nomination is like the last cookie on the plate but someone always takes it."

The union of Lyndon Johnson and Jack Kennedy on the same ticket in 1960 after a vitriolic primary campaign is often used as the quintessential example. Or Ronald Reagan and George Bush joining forces in 1980 after hurling scathing remarks at each other throughout their presidential primaries. Or Bob Dole and Jack Kemp, adversaries in the 1992 primaries, uniting four years later in campaign harmony. Dad knew better than anyone that anything could happen in the final days of politicking—a convention draft, a sudden change of heart by Goldwater or Scranton, possibly a last minute intervention by Ike in an effort to unite the Party behind a less contentious candidate than Goldwater. Hence his continuing reticence to believe in the certainty of his own selection until he received the invitation from Barry himself—which would come only the day before his name would be officially placed in nomination.

Warren Weaver of the *New York Times* made an interesting observation in his September 6, 1964 column, pointing out that my father's nomination for the vice-presidency "blazed a new, if narrow, trail through the wilderness of national politics, establishing a hitherto unexplored route for party advancement." What Weaver meant was two things: William Miller, at that point, was the first national chairman of either major party to be selected for the vice-presidential nomination; and few nominees had ever come from the House of Representatives. VP candidates had overwhelmingly come from the ranks of senators and governors.

Weaver both raised and answered yet another question about how Dad made what he called "the remarkable leap from the national chairmanship to the vice-presidential nomination." He wrote: "Since his selection last month, his critics in both parties have freely intimated that there was a deal: Mr. Miller helped win the nomination for Senator Goldwater in return for second place on the ticket." But the journalist went on to dispel that notion:

"The best evidence runs against this conspiratorial theory. Those closest to Senator Goldwater—including Miller himself—were convinced until shortly before the national convention that Governor Scranton would emerge as the vice-presidential candidate." Though Weaver was later assigned to cover the Miller campaign for a short time, neither he nor the *New York Times* were ever mistaken for Goldwater/Miller supporters, so his assertions would seem to put to rest any suspicions that Dad had been partial to Goldwater during pre-convention days.

There were actually some solid reasons in favor of my father's selection for the ticket in 1964. As an assistant prosecutor at Nuremberg, a seven-term congressman and member of the Judiciary Committee who had dealt with Japanese American war claims, civil rights, anti-trust legislation, and a long list of other crucial matters, and as a well-traveled national chairman, he could claim a fairly extensive knowledge and grasp of the pressing domestic and foreign issues of the day, and the issues people cared about. With regard to Bill Scranton's potential candidacy on the other hand, Congresswoman and Ambassador Clare Boothe Luce once remarked to the *LA Times*: "The international crisis is too grave to trust to the hands of a one-term congressman, a freshman governor with very limited experience in either domestic or foreign affairs."

A *New York Herald Tribune* reporter summed up after the convention why he saw the erstwhile RNC Chairman as a sensible choice: "Mr. Miller quite possibly has been the hardest working Republican National Chairman in history. He traveled constantly, streamlined his organization, expanded fund-raising activities, mounted a special drive for votes from big cities minority groups, increased his staff, held more regional conferences, and injected more oomph into party doings..."[8]

The primary traditional reasons for selecting someone to fill the second spot on a national ticket had always been ideological and geographic balance. In these years, religious balance had also become at least an unspoken consideration. While Dad would seem to fit the bill on all counts, closer examination reveals that there were actually flaws in that assumption, as were there flaws in the assumption that any or all of these factors could produce a monolithic vote on Election Day.

With regard to the issue of ideological balance, powerful forces were tugging Barry Goldwater in opposing directions simultaneously: should he pick a soul mate of exactly the same philosophy; or someone of another hue who would appeal to a different faction of the Party? Where my father fell in all this was somewhere in the middle. Though less an intense ideologue than a realistic, pragmatic politician, he had sometimes been labeled a conservative, sometimes a moderate. Many expressed dismay when he accepted the nomination in 1964 because they thought of him as considerably more moderate than Goldwater. Others voiced relief that his presence on the ticket would moderate the senator's more radical image. Clifton White, the man who had originated and led the Goldwater movement, once remarked, "I never considered Bill to be one of our team."

Dad's voting record, described by *Congressional Quarterly* as domestically conservative but internationalist in foreign affairs, diverged with Goldwater's on some issues and coincided with it on others. The two men shared a belief in at least two things: first, the continuing threat of Communism and the need to maintain unrelenting force against it; and secondly, the need to give citizens a chance to vote against what they felt was the headlong rush to socialism embodied in the Democratic program. But of major significance that year, and a strong factor in Bill Miller's favor, was that he had voted *for* the 1964 Civil Rights Act, which Barry had voted *against*, and this portended to be an explosive campaign issue.

John McMullan of the *Miami Herald* noted that "Miller's blend of strong conservatism and mild moderation might make the Goldwater brand of Republicanism just a little easier to swallow in some of the less conservative areas." Those words neatly summed up my father's appeal: In lieu of recruiting a liberal to balance the ticket, which the delegates didn't want anyway, they saw him as an acceptable compromise—conservative enough to please the right wing of the Party but hopefully moderate enough to be acceptable to the rest. That, together with the fact that he had been friendly and fair to all factions during his national chairmanship, inspired the belief that perhaps he could build bridges across ideological gaps and bring at least a modicum of unity to a party that had been badly split by the hard-hitting and strident tone of the pre-convention campaigns and the convention itself.

He was perhaps no more and no less than the best that could be hoped for in the circumstances.

Did he bring geographical balance to the ticket in 1964? Only on the surface—Goldwater was from the West, he from the Northeast. But the hope that he might "deliver" the state with the largest electoral vote to the Goldwater column in November was a highly unrealistic one. In fact, in seven of the nine elections held from 1928 to 1960, the winner carried the opponent's home state, indicating that a candidate's state probably matters less than issues and character when voters cast their ballots.

Additionally, Dad's career had been built in Washington, largely independent of the New York State political machine. The fact that he had had the political courage several times throughout the years to openly defy the powers-that-be in the state to stand for what he believed had also not endeared him to some party leaders there. From opposing two of the state's most powerful men, Tom Dewey and Robert Moses, over the Niagara Power Project in the 1950s to endorsing Richard Nixon for the 1960 Republican presidential nomination when his own governor was still in the running, he was known as a bit of a maverick. And the conservative western part of the state that he represented was more akin to Kansas than it was to Manhattan, which left him out of the liberal "club" of New York politicians from downstate who ruled the party organization.

The idea that my father's Catholicism would balance an Episcopalian of some Jewish heritage and reap great hordes of voters for the ticket was also a somewhat dubious proposition. Dean Burch, one of Goldwater's closest confidantes, remarked, "I'll wager the Senator never even considered the fact of Miller's religion. At least he never once mentioned this." Nevertheless, others insisted on assigning it great importance in Dad's resume. At the least, they felt it would force Johnson to pick a Catholic, like Bobby Kennedy (whom he personally disliked), for his running mate, or risk alienating and losing the crucial Democratic Catholic vote in big cities.

Bill Miller was, according to one Catholic newspaper, the first "practicing Catholic" ever nominated by the Republican Party for either spot on a national ticket. Still, it is highly questionable whether voters ever consider the religion of a vice-presidential candidate when they enter the voting booth—or whether they consider a vice presidential candidate at all for that matter. Today, religion is certainly a dead issue, but in 1964 it was thought by some that perhaps my father could recoup a portion of the large Catholic Republican vote that had defected to John Kennedy in 1960. It was optimistically pointed out that while Kennedy had been a Harvard Catholic, Miller was a Notre Dame Catholic, and if you count "subway alumni" (those who did not attend but revere the University), that could translate into millions of votes.

Unaccounted for, however, was the fact that Dad had no intention of making his religion an issue in the campaign. Nor could he, for he had bitterly criticized Kennedy and the Democrats for doing just that in 1960 with his "bigotry-in-reverse" charge. That had been a fairly clear statement on how he felt about injecting religion into political campaigns. "I do hope that before my term as chairman is complete," he once remarked, with just a hint of despair in his voice, "we can lay to rest, once and for all, the issue of religion in a national campaign."

Actually, the practice of balancing a ticket for strictly ideological, geographic, or religious reasons was by 1964, I believe, becoming slightly suspect. Far more serious considerations lurked in the minds of delegates to that convention. The memory of President Kennedy's tragic death in Dallas barely eight months earlier was still a raw one, so the question had to be asked with regard to potential vice-presidential nominees: "Could this person assume the presidency in case of emergency?"

The question of whether or not my father could have done that will, of course, always be hypothetical, and a matter of opinion. When asked if he thought he could be president, he liked to quote Jack Kennedy's response when the same question was posed to him as a young, relatively inexperienced junior senator aspiring to the presidency: "I looked around at all the others running for the job and said, 'If they, why not me?' " Few would remember that before Franklin Roosevelt's 1932 nomination, respected columnist Walter Lippmann wrote that FDR had no qualifications at all to be president, and many in the future president's own party and much of the press agreed.

What are the requirements for being president or vice president of the United States? The Constitution stipulates that a candidate for president must be a U.S. citizen, at least thirty-five years of age, and fourteen years a national resident, but it is silent on the qualifications for a vice president. Is moral character an important requirement? Is foreign affairs experience crucial? What about loyalty, demeanor, speaking ability, or "the vision thing" that George Bush Sr. used to lament he himself did not possess? We as a nation have always been ambivalent and divided about the answers to those questions.

Bill Miller, arguably, had sufficient qualifications "on paper," by virtue of his background and experiences, to recommend him for the job in 1964, despite the fact that he might not have been as widely known to a bipartisan public-at-large as he was to the Republican Party faithful around the country. But all that being said, it is my belief that the fundamental and overriding reason Barry Goldwater picked Dad to run with him was that he knew him to be a man of principle who was not afraid to speak his mind. He was also an energetic campaigner who possessed a highly sophisticated political instinct, a skilled debater who always did his homework, who understood people and knew the issues, a man who never quit. In short, the only kind of candidate Barry thought had the skills and the guts to wage a tough campaign against the master politician, Lyndon Johnson.

Senator Goldwater told me that what he valued the most about my father was his honesty—"That's a hell of an important test when you're talking about someone in politics," he would say. He believed there was no greater compliment you could pay a politician. Of all the presidents in his lifetime, he admired Harry Truman the most –because he was honest, never changed his mind for politics. That's the way he saw Dad: "Bill would never tell you what you wanted to hear, but only what he believed to be the truth."

There was no need to "interview" him for the job, to meticulously scour his background in search of flaws or peccadilloes that might embarrass or sink the ticket. The two men had come to know each other well while doing the tedious political work of getting Republicans elected to Congress, as chairmen of the House and Senate Campaign Committees. After working together for several years, they had developed a mutual respect. Faced with a bitterly divided party and so many who had betrayed and abandoned him, Barry found in my father a man he just liked and admired, but, above all, trusted—a man he considered "his friend."

Goldwater was in many ways a loner. Although he was surrounded by legions of devoted and capable people and had consulted with all the appropriate party leaders along the way, in the end, he often just wanted to make the final decision by himself. For the embattled Senator, all the solicited and unsolicited advice notwithstanding, choosing his friend Bill just *felt* like the right and certainly the most comfortable thing to do.

To be honest, he did not have many choices—vice-presidential running mates can be difficult to recruit even in the most harmonious of times. There were others who might have taken, even coveted the job—Gerald Ford, Mel Laird, Thruston Morton, Governor James Rhodes of Ohio—but no one seemed to fit the bill as well as Bill Miller did at that moment, in Goldwater's mind and heart.

In his uniquely straightforward manner, he told his aides, just before placing "the call" to my father: "I've made up my mind. There's no point in calling a lot of people together to discuss it when I've made up my mind." And so it was that Dad replied when his friend called him with his brief and simple request: "I think you can do a hell of a lot better, but if you want me with you, then I'll go." Both were men of few words.

Regarding the springboard that had propelled my father to this juncture, political columnist David Broder once wrote that the job of national chairman is "among the least understood in American politics." He suggested that because there are no precise duties and powers listed anywhere, it has over the years taken on different configurations depending upon its occupant. It has been "an empty title, or the focus of great intraparty power struggles, or the seat of unrivaled power and influence. The chairmanship is what each chairman is able to make it."[9]

The national committeemen and women of Dad's tenure appeared to approve of what he had made of the job. At his last meeting with them as a group just prior to the opening of the convention (his term would officially end at the close of the convention), their moving commendation of him brought prolonged applause and a standing ovation. Yet the judgment of his service that he treasured perhaps most was from a man he deeply respected, Dwight David Eisenhower:

> *Dear Bill,*
> *...I think you have done a splendid job in the months you have been serving as Chairman of the Republican National Committee. You have brought to the leadership of the Party the enthusiasm and vitality about which I have talked so much (and sometimes, seemingly, in vain)....*

My father had been in the unenviable position from 1961 to 1964 of having to control inexorable forces in the Party that could not be controlled. He gave it his best shot. Probably no national chairman could have solved the plight of the ineffectual coalition attempting to halt the momentum that Goldwater's troops had so thoroughly built toward his victory. They had the votes, and there simply turned out to be no alternative candidate well enough known and organized, with the guts, the commitment, the political stamina, or the decisiveness to tackle the job.

In reality, there can be no definitive judgment on his record as Republican National Chairman. It would be easy to say that because some of what he had toiled for in those three years appeared to be swept away in the 1964 landslide election loss—of which he was a part as Goldwater's partner on the national ticket—he had toiled in vain. But the lasting foundation he laid for a strong financial base of small contributors, of building the party machinery from the ground level up in urban and rural precincts nationwide, and of making the GOP a permanent presence on the local level in the South—all that was not swept away. His successors built on his initiatives.

What the Republican Party has not perpetuated, regrettably, is Dad's spirit of inclusiveness. He spoke from deep in his heart once when he laid out, for a non-partisan audience of political scientists, his most fervent aspirations for the Party he so loved:

> *If I accomplish nothing else during my period of service as chairman of the Republican National Committee, I want to remove a whole series of Chinese walls that have cut off my party from large segments of the American public. Labor Union members constitute one of these groups; Negroes another; those at the lowest economic levels, still another. It is simply intolerable that*

the Republican Party should be cut off by any kind of barrier from these millions of Americans.[10]

He often bemoaned the fact that "we have too many people in our party who want it all their own way or they won't play at all. There is no monolithic solution to every problem." Diversity is a strength, not a weakness he insisted. The echoes of his complaint reverberate loudly forty years later among soul-searching Republicans, as the conservatives controlling the GOP in recent years have made it more and more difficult for moderates to make their voices heard. The defection of Vermont Senator James Jeffords from the Party in 2001 because he reportedly felt the GOP had become increasingly uncomfortable for moderates launched a wave of critical re-examination of the Republican position.

I have no idea whether or not my father would have agreed with Jim Jeffords on any public issues, but he would have agreed with him on one thing: the need for the Republican Party to become more inclusive. He was on record prodigiously about that. Former President Gerald Ford endorsed that same "big tent" theory and, when I interviewed him for this book, he praised the untiring efforts Dad had made in his day to promote it. Ford remarked that the near elimination of the centrist GOP tradition and a starkly ideological party with zero tolerance for "heresy" is not what Chairman Bill Miller had in mind when he attempted to "grow" a party that had inhabited the minority wilderness for three decades.

For better or for worse, there is no doubt that Nelson Rockefeller, Jacob Javits, Mark Hatfield, George Romney—all those unabashed moderate-to-liberal Republicans of the mid-twentieth century—have become distant memories of a forgotten chapter in the evolution of the Grand Old Party. Whether or not one considers the absence of their descendants a loss depends, of course, upon personal perspective, and upon the value one places on ideological purity vs. diversity in political parties.

At the very beginning of his last campaign for reelection to his seat in Congress in 1962, Dad had very firmly vowed that he would not run again. The narrowness of his victory no doubt confirmed that decision—he'd be darned if, after all those years of hard work and dedication, his career would end in defeat. Though he claimed his political prospects played no role in his decision, nothing after that election changed his mind, and he was finally set to retire from political life in 1964. "I owe it to my family to quit," he would admit. "My kids are growing up and I'd like to spend some time with them. I have two daughters, 20 and 17, and two others we didn't plan on, 6 and 3. Since I went to Congress fourteen years ago, I haven't seen as much of the older ones as I'd like to. It's time I started acting like a father."

Alas, not a man of independent means, his second family was producing financial responsibilities that were difficult to meet on a congressional salary of $22,500. Even adjusted for inflation, that was hardly comparable to the $150,000 plus considerable perks that a congressman earns today. In recognizing the toll political life takes on a family and in renouncing the lure of continued fame and power to leave it behind, my father was somewhat ahead of his time. While you hear of it occasionally today, there were not many in his years who left Congress voluntarily. He knew he had to do it before the price he paid was too great.

But now, rather than stepping back into private life as he had long planned, Dad and our whole family were, quite unexpectedly and with some trepidation, launching a brand new adventure, fraught with uncertainty and an ending that we could not know. It would either be retirement from public life four months later and somewhat more prominently than expected, or four more years in Washington and possibilities that we dared not even imagine.

There have been numerous denigrating and oft-quoted remarks made about the office of vice president over the decades. John Adams called it "the most insignificant office that ever the invention of man contrived or imagination conceived," and John Garner, FDR's first vice president, indelicately appraised it as no better than "a bucket of warm spit." Yet these witty descriptions belie the reality that by mid- twentieth century, the vice-presidency had, in fact, acquired considerable prestige and some power, thanks in part to the meaningful responsibilities Dwight Eisenhower had given his vice president, Richard Nixon. It had also become a definite stepping stone to the presidency, either by tragedy (as Harry Truman, Lyndon Johnson, and Gerald Ford discovered) or by virtue of their experience that qualified them for the job, as was the case with Nixon and George H. W. Bush.

In the twenty-seven elections held between 1856, when a newborn Republican Party nominated its first candidates, and 1964, there had been a total of only fifty-four vice-presidential nominees for the two major political parties. That fact caused Ed McCabe, former campaign aide to my father and a prominent Washington attorney, to remind me that people honored with the nomination "form a very small and special club." And there we were, as of July 16, 1964, about to join that club.

I found an amusing letter among Dad's papers one day, one of the avalanche he received upon his nomination from long lost friends and acquaintances in far flung corners of the country. It was penned by an old Lockport pal, then living in Michigan:

> *You have probably forgotten but in 1949, when I accidentally bumped into you at a golf tournament in Spring Lake, New Jersey, I said to you, "Bill, someday you are going to be president." I remembered you threw back your head and laughed and laughed. I am writing now to say that perhaps I wasn't so far wrong after all.*[11]

I can just picture my father. He often threw back his head when he laughed—it was so spontaneous and hearty, and he loved a good laugh. He never took himself too seriously so his friend's prediction must have seemed quite hilarious. After all, he was at that time the mere district attorney of Niagara County. Could the friend have been right about his future? Possibly, but it still seemed like a long shot, to say the very least, from where we stood.

Barry Goldwater said to me years later, "If I'd had any sense, I'd have gone home," after hearing all the polls predicting Johnson would win by 80 percent. I'm sure, deep in his heart, Dad felt the same. But both he and Barry felt the job had to be done, that a message had to be sent to the country they loved, which they believed passionately was moving in the wrong direction. And destiny had picked them to do it.

CHAPTER TEN

THE 1964 CAMPAIGN

The question I have most often been asked over these forty years since my father and our family played our part in the ill-fated campaign of '64 is: "Did you ever really believe you could win?" My answer always is—yes. Even though intellectually we knew it was all but impossible, in some small part of our hearts and minds where the harsh light of reality does not penetrate, we did, at least for a time, believe we could win. In that rarified world that is political campaigning, you inhabit a "zone," wherein everything seems possible and there is eternal hope that all the negatives will be proved wrong, that all the pollsters and prognosticators will in the end have to run in embarrassment from their erroneous surveys and cruel predictions of your certain demise. If it happened for Harry Truman in 1948, it could happen for us. American politics has always been full of surprises.

Surrounded continually, day in and day out, for the better part of three months by wildly enthusiastic and optimistic, if delusional, throngs of believers, you cannot help but believe. Maybe, just maybe, those others don't know what they're talking about. They don't see all the passion and the cheering, the almost mass hysteria for the ticket that we see—all the stalwarts who turn out for airport rallies, barbecues, and whistle stop train tours, even in the pouring rain, in Dubuque, Fresno, and Utica; the legions of tireless and deeply dedicated "troops" who paste stamps, man phones, and trudge the streets with Goldwater/Miller literature in remote places like LaPorte, Beloit, and Hobbs. The support is there, you tell yourself, but it is silent, just not being reached by Mr. Gallup. And in truth, there was some justifiable skepticism about polls in those days, for they were not as sophisticated as they are today. One of Dad's favorite lines was: "This election is not going to be decided by the pollsters and the columnists but by the people."

Even he, who was anything but a misty-eyed political dreamer, seemed to harbor within himself, in the beginning, a small glimmer of hope for victory, or at least for a close election. Only long after the outcome did he admit that deep down he felt from the outset that any Republican, liberal or conservative, was doomed that year. He always doubted that the American people could accept three presidents in three years, despite the fact that there was little love for Lyndon Johnson. He never told Barry or anyone else that, and he maintained a soldierly optimism to the bitter end. And he worked himself to exhaustion to prove even his own instincts wrong.

The only hints of the VP candidate's underlying pessimism surfaced in the final weeks of the campaign, when denying the lopsided polls seemed foolish. Sitting next to his longtime secretary, Naomi Glass, on the plane one day, he asked her what she was going to do "after this was over." When she replied that she "hoped to be working for the vice president," he smiled a little wistfully and countered, "Well what are you *really* going to do?"

Once, Paul Niven, a corpulent and boisterous CBS reporter and favorite card playing buddy of Dad's, lumbered down the aisle of the campaign plane waving a newspaper and mischievously exclaimed: "Hey Bill, I see where gamblers in Las Vegas are giving thirteen to five odds against you and Barry. Would you like to get some of that action?" My father's droll response, laced with a bit of the profanity he was prone to use among men: "I might be a gambler you son-of-a-bitch (he and the reporters covering him played low-stakes card games on the plane between stops), but I'm no idiot." That flash of candor would have made a great story, a headliner. But the reporters standing round never printed it—in those days they didn't do that. What was said on the plane, stayed on the plane. There was great respect for that sense of privacy.

Though the campaign was not set to open officially until Labor Day, the hoopla began immediately upon the close of the convention, which now entered history as a stunning triumph for the Goldwater forces, but one marked with ominous undertones of serious party discord. We stayed on in San Francisco until the following Monday—Dad had some loose ends to tie up and, being now in greater demand than ever, numerous television appearances to make. Mother, Mary, and I at last set out upon the sightseeing and shopping we were unable to do in the crush of pre-convention and convention days, though usually with a photographer or two in tow and some curious onlookers to remind us that our privacy and anonymity were, at least temporarily, suspended. We sandwiched our forays in between the television and newspaper interviews we too were scheduled to do—interest was already high in the young adult Goldwater and Miller progeny.

Our arrival back in Lockport and Olcott for a week of rest was beyond anything we ever anticipated. After the carping from disgruntled Republicans and critical reporters that had already begun for the vice presidential nominee, it was heartwarming to be welcomed back into the arms of hometown friends and supporters. Their love and admiration was so unconditional and their joy in the success of their "local boy" was unmitigated. And what a tumultuous, uproarious, triumphant welcome it was.

The unforgettable evening of July 20 began with every Republican leader on the Niagara Frontier and 1,500 ardent fans whooping it up at Buffalo Airport as our plane from San Francisco landed. The other passengers deplaned but our family stayed on board for a private and ecstatic reunion with little Stephanie and Billy, who fortunately still recognized us and proceeded to smother us all with hugs and kisses.

A deluge of flowers greeted our emergence from the plane—red roses for Mom, pink for Mary and me, and a corsage of baby yellow roses for Stephie, who seemed totally terrified by the encirclement of reporters and photographers. Buffalo Mayor Chester Kowal delighted the raucous crowd by welcoming us with a clever variation on the most controversial line from Barry Goldwater's convention acceptance speech—"Extremism in defense of liberty is no vice": "When I say we are proud of Bill, I don't mean we are *moderately* proud. I mean we are *extremely* proud!"

At a press conference inside the terminal, my father took another stab (there would be many yet to come) at quenching the firestorm of protest that his running mate's line, seemingly in defense of "extremism," had ignited. "Barry should have used the word 'patriotism' instead of 'extremism,' " he explained. "Patriotism in defense of liberty is no vice." At other times, he would interpret Barry's use of "extremism" to mean simply "a passionate commitment to achieve a desirable end." At least it should not, he stressed, be taken to imply that Goldwater backed extremist groups. But nothing he could say would make the issue go away, for "extremism" was indeed a deadly word in the political lexicon of the day. And finally, the newly minted VP candidate, destined to be the workhorse of the ticket, stressed what he would repeat over and over in the months to come—the urgent need for Republicans across the land to strive for solidarity in order to defeat the Democrats in November.

The largest, loudest, and most joyous greeting of our triumphal return was yet to come. As we all piled into a green Cadillac convertible at the airport, a motorcade of more than 100 cars and three busloads of Lockportians fell in behind us, with newsmen from all the media and sheriff's deputies, lights flashing and sirens in full operation, racing ahead. The group followed us for the twenty-mile ride north into Lockport, Route 78 lined the entire way with waving, cheering crowds holding an assortment of homemade signs—"Good Luck Bill," "We Love You Bill!" Just before we reached the Big Bridge over the Erie Canal, at that time reportedly the widest bridge in the world, we were joined by an array of local bands and drum corps that played us into the city with "Happy Days are Here Again."

It was a veritable mob scene on the bridge that muggy July night, with 3,500 people, so many of them familiar faces—old friends, schoolmates, followers of Dad's career since he had launched his first political campaign in 1947 for Niagara County district attorney almost right in this very spot—all screaming, stomping, and jostling to get near enough to see us. We were happily engulfed. In all the tumult, Lockport Mayor Rollin Grant was hard pressed to deliver his planned welcome back for a native son—"The excitement and pride here must be just as great as the day the canal opened!" he shouted. With effort, we waved and handclasped our way, signing autographs as we inched along. The crowd passed a microphone cable over their heads to my father, perched on the back of the car, and he made a short speech—"It's great to be from Lockport," he began in a choked voice.

Then it was off to Olcott for, little did we know, a final celebration with about fifty friends and neighbors who had assembled for a champagne party. First, there was the obligatory posing for photographers on the front lawn of our small, salmon-colored cottage, across which stretched a mammoth "Congratulations and Welcome Home" banner. It was by now after 10 p.m. and my little siblings were keeping their eyes open by sheer force of will, yet they were not about to give in easily to housekeeper Luella's efforts to ready them for bed. Billy started on a round of hand-shaking of his own, greeting one and all, some of them twice, with his tiny hand stuck out and a cheery, "Hi!"—a portent of the politician he too was to become briefly later in his life. And so ended the longest and surely the most emotional and memorable day, after the nomination itself, in our family's history.

It turned out that the week's so-called "relaxation" was done under the watchful eye of frequently scheduled contingents of newspaper, magazine, and television reporters. I recall Mary and I being somewhat distressed since the situation required our hair and attire be considerably more presentable than they would normally be for lazy summer days at the lake. Omnipresent cameras recorded Dad sunning himself on his reclining lawn chair as he reviewed some of his avalanche of mail, or talking on the phone with a steady stream of colleagues, staff, and well wishers, which is how, in fact, he spent most of his week.

They photographed our morning swims, afternoon water skiing, family croquet and badmitton matches, visits with local friends who were enlisted to help us answer the incessantly ringing telephones, and Mary and me, "accomplished musicians," sitting at the old upright piano allegedly "composing a campaign song for our father." A sort of Cleaver-like family portrait was thus amusingly constructed, which is exactly what the curious public longed to see.

It was during the few quiet moments of that week that Dad began to reflect on the daunting responsibility of being a candidate for vice president. I remember him leaning on that wire fence separating our backyard from the steep bluff that fell to the lake, cigarette in hand, sometimes for a half hour, just gazing out at the water. What was he thinking? Was he looking forward to what lay ahead, or remembering the carefree days of his boyhood that he had spent here, or just listening to the gentle lapping of water over smooth pebbles, the water that he feared going into but loved being near? I was hesitant to disturb him, so I never knew. "All the people and all that money invested in a crusade. You feel that you're not a single individual anymore. You're not in control of your own destiny," he would tell reporter Jimmy Breslin a short time later.[1] He knew he was perhaps launching the first losing battle of his career. Despite his best efforts, there would be much that was beyond his control.

Our week of family togetherness ended all too quickly and was to be one of the few times we would all be in the same place at the same time for the next several months. After being sent off to New York City to have formal campaign portraits done, my parents returned to Washington. Dad had the remainder of the congressional session to attend, as well as meetings with his running mate and campaign staff to begin planning strategy, fund raising, and fence-mending. Mom set about combing the attic of our Bethesda home for all the boyhood pictures of the candidate she could muster to supply an insatiable media. I returned to my guide post in the New York State Pavilion at the World's Fair in Flushing Meadow, New York.

And what a return it was, almost but not quite rivaling our Lockport homecoming! Greeting me at the gate, to my utter surprise and some embarrassment, was a sea of cheering blue and white uniformed guides all holding placards reminiscent of the recent convention, only this time emblazoned with *my* name instead of my father's—"The New York State Guides are all for Libby Miller," "We Love Libby," "Welcome Back Libby Miller!" The group showered me with confetti, handed me a massive bouquet of red roses, and escorted me to a waiting Greyhound VIP cart, which led our rollicking, curious parade through the fairgrounds to our pavilion. The open-mouthed gawking of the crowds as the fair policemen parted them to make way for our entourage betrayed the fact that they had no idea who on earth was Libby Miller.

Thereafter, my daily work routine was so interrupted by photographers asking me to pose with unsuspecting visitors or to stand on the gigantic floor map of New York State pointing at Lockport that I decided, a bit sadly, I had to leave my first real job behind. But not before Dad paid us a visit on his first informal campaign foray into New York City, creating quite a furor and still more "photo ops" for his daughter. These frequent disturbances were beginning to hinder my already marginal ability to render translations of the pavilion's displays in French and Russian, one of my primary responsibilities. So I reluctantly turned my badge in and left new friends behind, the only relief being that I would no longer have to don that long-sleeved white blouse, white gloves, white beret, stockings, and high heels daily in ninety degree heat.

Invitations had also begun pouring in for me to appear at various Republican functions. At first, I hadn't imagined I would be actively involved in campaigning. But after being chosen co-chairman of the national Youth for Goldwater-Miller—Barry Goldwater Jr. being the other co-chairman—it became apparent that I could be traveling extensively. The idea of that was somewhat frightening. I wasn't exactly a novice at politics—I had occasionally joined the picnic circuit with my father during his congressional campaigns in western New York—but I had never personally done any amount of public speaking, and this was now a national stage. Still, the chance to see so much of the country and make a contribution to something I knew was important began to feel exciting.

I got my feet wet at a small gathering in a Queens backyard, decorated with posters, crepe-paper bunting wrapped around a clothes line, balloons floating in the metal-sided circular pool. "We didn't think we had a ghost of a chance to get her, but we decided to try," confessed my enthusiastic host Anthony Malito to a visiting reporter. "We knew she had been working at the World's Fair and thought she might like to meet some Queens people."

So I dutifully posed for photographs, circulated, pumped hands, answered questions, and attempted to eat my hotdog and potato salad. Or that is I held my plate but barely ate. With so many guests lined up to chat, I was always leery of getting caught with a mouthful of food. Meanwhile, Lynda Bird Johnson, who was fast becoming my "opposite," hobnobbed nearby at New York Mayor Robert Wagner's official residence, Gracie Mansion, and on the palatial Long Island estate of Henry Ford II—both of us "in quest of votes for their fathers," as the *New York Times* reported. Let the campaign begin!

After an August of accompanying my parents to assorted events, the campaign did begin in earnest in early September, after the Democrats had picked their ticket at their August convention. Though Lyndon Johnson would obviously be the presidential nominee, there was some suspense as to who would be Bill Miller's opposite, and that decision would somewhat affect Republican campaign strategy. Would Johnson be forced to take the Catholic Bobby Kennedy, whom he intensely disliked and mistrusted? Senator Hubert Humphrey of Minnesota finally won the prize.

All campaigns have an official beginning—usually in a certain place from which the candidate believes he or she will draw the inspiration to win. Or at least it used to be that way. Today campaign launchings are often made from places that are less sentimental and more designed to be telegenic, thanks to the advice of political consultants. For both Barry and my father, it was never considered that their inaugural campaign event would take place anywhere but in their beloved home areas, where their roots ran deep. The kickoff in Prescott, Arizona was set for September 3 and the shindig in Lockport for two days later—the Millers and Goldwaters would shuttle en masse to both affairs.

My sister Mary and I received a delectable invitation from the handsome Goldwater boys to fly out early to Phoenix and join them for a few days of sightseeing before all the excitement began. We were thrilled. The press was already trying to pair us up, noting that neither Barry, 26, nor Mike, 24, was engaged or had a steady girlfriend and were therefore quite eligible for me, age 20, and Mary, age 17. "I think we've been waiting for the Miller girls," Mike once quipped mischievously in answer to the repeated questioning.

Upon our arrival, the boys, in the chauvinistic manner common to those days, suggested that we girls cook up a steak dinner that evening. They were quickly informed that all my sister and I knew how to prepare were frozen TV meals. After a relaxing day at the sprawling Goldwater home nestled atop a hill overlooking Phoenix, we were taken the following day on a whirlwind 800 mile aerial tour of the remote and magnificent mountains and deserts of northern Arizona and southern Utah, with Barry Jr. piloting his twin-engine plane and Mike as guide. Back then, Mary and I were happily quite fearless.

We swooped over the Grand Canyon, making occasional stops at dams and mining ghost towns, then alighted for lunch at a trading post crouched in the shadow of one of the towering red sandstone "skyscrapers" that jutted out from the desert expanse of Monument Valley. Awed by this impressive, rugged landscape that I had seen only in movies, I was quoted by one newspaper as remarking insightfully: "It certainly doesn't look much like New York."

It was a fairytale day. We were regaled by local Navajos with stories of Senator Goldwater's regular visits to the post at Christmastime to play Santa Claus to their youngsters, thereby earning the nickname "Mr. Christmas." I made a friend for life of a Navajo mother when I cradled her irresistible baby in my arms. And spotting two young Indians herding sheep across the hot valley floor, Mary and I promptly took off our Goldwater-Miller campaign buttons and attached them to their horses' manes, eliciting wide but puzzled grins and the clicking of a camera lens. A photographer had accompanied us, or followed us—I can't remember which—and we were, quite obviously, already getting the hang of the "photo op."

When our band of four returned to Phoenix at dusk, Mary and I weary and clutching a colorful Navajo rug as a remembrance of our grand odyssey, we at last understood the Goldwater family's deep bonding with their land. Still more exciting events were planned for us before we reunited with our parents at the Prescott kickoff. There, on the steps of the county courthouse, before thousands of string ties, cowboy hats, plaid shirts, and leather faces, my father introduced his friend and running mate, his thunderous words bouncing through the town square:[2]

> Up from the great Southwest has risen this giant of a man, seasoned in the nation's service, straight-talking, a man who has steadfastly refused to sell America short—an honest leader, not a dealer—a man of peace who has the courage to stand eye to eye with those who would make war..."

Lockport did it up big for their native son, with the largest political event ever to be held there. It was an old-time rally that drew more than 15,000 revelers from far and wide, three times the Prescott turnout for the Goldwaters, as they themselves marveled. They came to see the "giant of the desert" and the local boy who had made good. It was Saturday, September 5 and the *Union Sun and Journal* hit the stands with an enormous headline in purple ink: WELCOME BARRY AND BILL! This would be "a day destined to live long in the memory of Lockport and the Niagara Frontier," the paper predicted.

It was a first—the first time a local boy had kicked off his vice-presidential campaign here; the first time a presidential candidate would come to help him do it. An army of workers had for a week been readying the Farm and Home Center on the outskirts of town. Instead of cattle or produce, today there would be carnival rides for children, balloons galore, refreshment booths decked out in red, white and blue bunting, mammoth billboards with larger-than-life mugshots of the candidates, a flag-draped speakers' platform for our families and all the visiting dignitaries, over 100 telephones for the press corps, and security, lots of it.

Unusually rigid security precautions would greet my father and Goldwater and our families upon our arrival this day. Only a few weeks ago, we had driven to an Orleans County Republican picnic with just one police officer as escort. But today there would be more than 100 law enforcement officers on hand. When the late President Kennedy had come to town during his campaign in 1960 and when GOP vice-presidential candidate Henry Cabot Lodge visited the same year, there had been only normal security precautions. But "times have changed," observed Sheriff James Murphy grimly. "The tragedy of President Kennedy's assassination has made us all more aware of what might happen and we want to be in a position to prevent a recurrence of that tragedy." Coupled with that factor, added the sheriff, was the possibility of demonstrations owing to "the somewhat controversial nature of Senator Goldwater's political philosophy," as he diplomatically put it.

Dad himself was beginning to worry a bit about the security situation, and he had told newsmen that he hoped Congress would amend the law to provide Secret Service protection for the candidates of both parties in a presidential election. The idea occurred to him as he was flying to Washington from Olcott with another local congressman. The stewardess had asked him whether, in view of the recent race riots and other demonstrations, he wasn't afraid to be traveling without any police protection. He admitted that "emotions were running high on a lot of issues" and that Senator Goldwater had already received a number of threatening letters. Congress did eventually change the law as he had hoped but not until 1968, after Robert Kennedy's assassination.

"Bill Miller Day" in Lockport was sunny and hot, and quite windy—I remember, because my perfectly arranged hairdo, to my chagrin, escaped its heavy spray net and blew every which way, as copious photos of the day attest. Our plane from Washington touched down at Niagara Falls Municipal Airport at 1 p.m., Goldwater's fifteen minutes later. The arrival of the motorcade bearing both families to the fairgrounds, after traveling a highly secret route, was met with pandemonium. I can still recall the mixture of pride and keen anticipation for the impending challenge that was written on my father's face as he mounted the speakers' platform.

As I greeted and hugged all the Goldwaters and sat in my appointed chair next to Mother, the entire scene was still tinged for me, and I am sure for him, with a slight air of unreality. Here he was, a small town boy, launching his campaign for the vice-presidency of the United States, a mile from the inauspicious frame house where he started life fifty years ago, just down the road from the modest farms and enticing peach orchards where he had romped as a boy. Fearlessly, his hand chopping the air, this diminutive, self-assured, self-made man launched into a blistering attack on his opponent—"Hubert Horatio Humphrey," as he loved to call him—that had the crowd cheering and laughing all at the same time.

Clip Smith, a renowned radio talk show host in the Buffalo area but back then a rookie radio reporter at WUSJ in Lockport, wrote a vignette of the day, from the vantage point of his own tough assignment:

My boss wanted me to get Miller, the hometown hero, for an exclusive interview, but the candidate was constantly pressing the flesh, making the rounds of the fairgrounds surrounded by security guards plus a horde of major network journalists, all of the big names. I knew I had to do something fast. As Barry and Bill were leaving the grounds, I used my 6-4, 250 pound frame to batter through the mob and shouted, "Bill, don't you have a few words for your hometown station?" Miller smiled and said, "I'd like to but we're running out of time." I shot back, "It seems to me like you're running out on the people who gave you your start." He gave me a long hard look and sheepishly replied, "You know, you're right." Then he proceeded to dismiss the network guys, walked me over to a nearby hotdog stand and gave me a twenty-minute exclusive session that covered everything from life on South Street to his summer home in Olcott and many memories and mentions of just plain folks who had propelled him to the top. He shared a hotdog with me, shook my hand, and as he walked away, he added, "You know, a lotta people think I'm a big time politician but I'm just a janitor's kid who got lucky, and that's why I'll never forget where I came from." And then with that wry smile, he added, "And when you hit the big time in radio and TV, don't you ever forget that either." I never did, and I never will forget the time Bill spent with me because he wanted to, not because he had to.

College classes had now started again for me—should I return to Boston or should I remain on the campaign trail? It was senior year, with a thesis to write and comprehensive exams to prepare for in my Russian major, but after impassioned pleas to my parents that the campaign would be an experience I should not miss, an education in itself, we chose the latter.

I would use my dorm room as home base, where I would return periodically to remind the nuns that I was still enrolled and to shuffle my somewhat meager wardrobe so as to match clothes with climate and not be seen too often in the same outfit. Despite my efforts, Mother once called from the campaign trail to remark that she had seen me photographed four times in one week in the same dress. But from the beginning of September on, I was on the road almost non-stop, toting books along to study en route, which I recall rarely happened.

What I did spend my spare time doing between stops was answering by hand all my own mail, which to my utter amazement contained an extraordinary number of marriage proposals and requests for dates from college boys all over the country who had apparently seen me either on television or at a campaign event. There were even bouquets of roses that occasionally arrived, signed only, "A Friend." It was all flattering, but how to decline the invitations without losing the sender's enthusiasm and support for the ticket was a delicate dilemma. I surely did not want to be responsible for losing any votes.

The Republican National Committee proceeded to install a private phone in my room, an important looking white one, which made me instantly and unquestionably the most popular girl in the dorm. The single hall phone, tied up almost continuously with lovelorn dorm mates chatting with boyfriends, would make it impossible to reach me expeditiously. My poor long-suffering roommate, Sheila Sullivan, became an ad hoc secretary when I was away. Weekly schedules were dispatched special delivery, only to be continually updated and expanded as invitations rolled in for the candidates' offspring. They were crammed with assorted rallies, luncheons, receptions, dinners, press conferences, and parades, and punctuated every few weeks by a reunion with Dad's campaign for events that required a family appearance.

Barry Jr., Mike, Mary, and I stumped up and down and across the country from coast to coast and even brazenly into the heart of Johnson land, Austin and Dallas. We were once just fifteen miles from the president's ranch, attending one of the four massive "Go-Goldwater Jamborees" sponsored by the Young Americans for Goldwater/Miller. Sometimes there were TV celebrities in attendance for the festivities but always there were rollicking bands, a cheering gamut of red, white, and blue clad "Goldwater Girls" with their golden skirts and broad-brimmed cowboy hats, "Barry Burgers," polish potato salad allegedly made from my mother's recipe, and a bubbly soft drink aptly named "Gold-Water," billed as "just right for the conservative taste." Since it is well documented that Hillary Clinton, former First Lady and Democratic Senator from New York, was herself a Goldwater Girl, it is more than likely that our paths crossed at one of those gala jamborees. I suspect, however, she prefers not to be reminded of that long-ago chapter in her life.

These jamborees were the Republican counterpart to the LBJ barbecues at which presidential daughters, Lynda Bird and Luci Baines Johnson, presided. Born into politics, those girls were real pros at it, but our quartet had one thing going for it that they did not. To our continuing amusement, the appearance of Barry Jr., whose rugged jutting jaw and handsome, finely chiseled profile strongly resembled his father's, invariably precipitated a deluge of hysterical girls grabbing at his clothes as if he were a rock star. It would routinely take a posse of local policemen to extricate him from the mob and move us through a crowd.

"Children Power—New Dimension in Election Year," headlined the *Washington Post*. "These young people are a new dimension in politics that has to be reckoned with," a prominent politician was quoted as saying. "I'm impressed with their political know-how and I don't see how they could help but win votes."[3] "Barry's Boys and Miller's Maids" was a catchy appellation we garnered along the way.

Family members had long been involved in the campaigns of candidates, or at least put on display as a kind of window into the candidate's character. But it was this election that first brought out "the children" in full force, mainly because we were all of ideal campaigning age. "In a culture obsessed with the inside story, a candidate's wife and children are the ultimate insiders."[4] Mary and I were veritably forced into comparison and competition with the Johnson girls, who were our exact ages, and as I reportedly told the press in Providence, Rhode Island, "We weren't about to concede to them." In the end, it is impossible to measure the cumulative contribution of any offspring to a parent's aura. But I always joked that the electoral results in '64 would attest that despite our frenetically peripatetic three months on the road, Lynda Bird and Luci won the vote wooing contest hands down.

I grew to like campaigning, once my confidence level increased. I was seeing the country, meeting a rich assortment of people, being an important part of something that mattered so much to so many. It was heady and uplifting and discouraging all at the same time. Those three and a half months forced me to dig down deep and find strengths and abilities I did not know I had, to do things I never imagined I could do.

A national political campaign, I was discovering, is a crash course in people skills and public speaking—what a Dale Carnegie course might accomplish in a year. I learned quickly how to conjure up something to say to almost everyone in almost every situation and to use little tricks to instantaneously recall names from my overloaded memory bank. Ever since, I have rarely been at a loss for words, as my husband can attest. An article in the Springfield, Massachusetts newspaper rightly noted after my visit there, "Gone is the little girl who, admittedly, 'used to run to daddy practically in tears' every time she read an article attacking her controversial father...." The only part of campaigning that I never quite mastered was how to ride in an open car and arrive camera-ready for a platform appearance.

It all seems a blur now as I try to recall the dizzying details of those days. A few events still lurk in my memory—visiting Lehigh University where the hall had to be emptied for a bomb

scare before I could deliver my speech, joining Barry Jr. before
a phalanx of photographers to present a "74th birthday" cake to
President Eisenhower at his Gettysburg farm, nervously making
a *Today Show* appearance, being paired with countless "escorts"
whose names I have sadly long forgotten. It is humbling to receive a letter like the one I received only a few years ago from one
such fellow: "In some small measure, I thank you for having been
a small, but a nice part of a vignette in my life."

Yet the event which would be most significant to me personally, though I did not know it at the time, was my very first foray
without my father at my side. It was a baptism by fire at the
Biltmore Hotel in New York City, in a ballroom that seemed to me
immense and filled with thousands of expectant faces as I entered
alone. There I met a blinding battery of television lights, cameras,
and microphones, all thrust in my face for a meaty sound bite,
and all there just for *me*, as I all too quickly realized. I was more
terrified than I have ever been.

I made my speech, did the requisite interviews, and happily
all went well for my first solo gig. But unbeknownst to me, my
future husband, whom I was not to meet until two years later,
was in attendance, dragged there by an enthusiastic Republican
girlfriend. Immersed in medical school and fairly uninterested
in politics at the time, he, as I later learned, looked me over and
proceeded to retire to the adjacent bar, never to even hear my
pearls of political wisdom.

Mary and I "kept our smiles big and our politics simple," as
so many newspaper articles correctly pointed out at the time. We
mostly discussed anecdotes about our experiences on the campaign trail and what our dad was really like. We left it to Barry
Jr. and Mike to hurl the one-liners and verbal zingers that poked
fun at the Democratic nominees and elicited gales of laughter and
cheers of approval from the partisan crowds.

After being lightheartedly cautioned by my father not to say
anything that might make embarrassing headlines, I attempted
to keep my speeches non-specific on issues, but philosophical,
warning young people that they were inheriting a future with a
worrisome trend toward more and more government control. I
was passionate about that. But then came the inevitable question
and answer session, when I would be pelted with queries about
the intricacies of Goldwater conservatism, about the negative

charges against Dad, and about the specifics of my social life (non-existent at the time). As the weeks passed, I got smoother at handling it all, and when I didn't know the answer to a question, I didn't mind admitting I didn't know.

Even though I was going to miss being old enough to vote by two months, I usually urged my audiences to "roll up your sleeves and do the work that needs to be done" to change the trend, i.e. to elect Goldwater/Miller. And I blithely predicted that "the tide has turned in our favor." I am horrified when I now recall forty years later those self-written or sometimes extemporaneous speeches, for I had no other guidance or instructions from GOP campaign headquarters about exactly what I should or should not say other than a packet of materials sent for my use. Left to my own inexperienced resources, I shudder when I think what faux pas I might have made from which the powers above somehow saved me.

Before plunging fully into the campaign, my father was part of a last attempt at pulling together his unraveling party, which by now would have been nothing short of a miracle. At the request of some Goldwater aides, Governor Bill Scranton agreed to host a "summit conference" of key Republican leaders, including Eisenhower, Nixon, Rockefeller, and Romney, and the town of Hershey, Pennsylvania was the chosen site. The hope was to have a productive roundtable discussion, followed by glowing press releases, after which all would disperse amicably to their respective home states agreeing to campaign for the ticket.

That objective, not surprisingly, proved to be elusive, despite Scranton's best efforts. The meeting was a noble idea and it went better than anticipated, but some found Goldwater aloof and inaccessible and generally non-conciliatory, particularly about his recent civil rights vote. Governor Romney got upset and left early, claiming that he could not get reelected on what the Goldwater Republican Party stood for. This despite Dad's assurance: "As chairman of the Congressional Campaign Committee in 1960 and as national chairman for three years, from 1961 on, I tried to build up the two-party system in the South, and I think that we have done this. I may say to you, however, it was never done nor was one dollar ever spent on a program designed to create Republican strength in the South based on the racist issue, or appealing for votes on the basis of the racist issue."[5]

In the end, though no one else was publicly negative, nearly all the participants, with few exceptions, went home and distanced themselves from the ticket. This lack of visible support from party leaders around the country would doom the ticket from the very beginning. And as the weeks wore on, Barry and Bill were too busy campaigning to work intensively on party unity.

The convention bunting had barely been removed from the Cow Palace in San Francisco when the ugliness began. "It is inevitable that a talented tosser of barbs receives a few in return, but the columnists always associated with the liberal cause descended on Mr. Miller with vengeance," noted one writer in the *Buffalo Evening News*.[6] Columnist Drew Pearson, never a fan of my father's, or of any Republican for that matter, appeared to launch, with his poisonous pen, a personal crusade to destroy his credibility and respect. One of his columns brought my sister Mary to tears, but Dad had hugged her to his shoulder and explained, "It's all right honey, it's just part of the game."

Yet even he, a political pro, was dismayed at the virulence and persistence. Pearson was well known to be a liberal Democrat, cozy with Jack Kennedy and now with Lyndon Johnson, entertained regularly by them. But his eye-catching accusations, even when denied, had the power to leave lurking a suspicion that where there is smoke, there is fire. My father spent some time in the beginning attempting to fight the charges and clear his name, but then decided it was a waste of valuable time to be on the defensive, not addressing substantive issues. He even sought the advice of David Lawrence, a sympathetic columnist at *U.S. News & World Report*, about whether there was any way he could strike back through friendlier columns. No, Lawrence told him, columnists don't want to get involved in battles with each other. Let it roll off, he counseled. The damage is minor.[7]

But it didn't feel that way. There were suggestions that there was something shady about the work Congressman Miller had done in Congress for nearly fourteen years on behalf of industries in his district that were the mainstay of its economy, such as Wurlitzer Jukebox and the Lockport Felt Company. "Lobbying" and "conflict of interest," Pearson called it. Dad pointed out that he would have been derelict in his duty had he not fought legislation that might endanger jobs in those industries, and that he did nothing different than every member of Congress does for his or her district. The muckraking columnist further charged that my father owned 27,000 shares of stock in the Felt Company, when he actually owned none at all. When company President Ray Lee called Pearson to "set him straight," the columnist said he didn't need to be set straight and hung up.

All the old untrue news stories were dragged out again, the ones Dad had refuted time and again in years past: that he was being paid off by Niagara Mohawk Power Company to advocate for private power development at Niagara Falls in the 1950s, even though his district and the entire state were overwhelmingly in favor of it; that as district attorney in 1948 he had vowed to "smash the unions" at a Bell Aircraft plant strike, when he had said no such thing but used his office only to restore order and quell the violence that had resulted in injuries and intimidation; that he had abandoned his support of an early civil rights bill to make a deal on killing a public power bill, when his objections to that civil rights bill were strictly constitutional ones.

And there were the inevitable new "stories." Miller had allegedly bought and sold several houses that were "under a covenant prohibiting their sale to persons of the Negro race." Having no knowledge of any such covenants, he had his title researched and discovered that apparently such covenants did once exist throughout the Bethesda/Chevy Chase area where we lived but were actually nullified in 1948 by a Supreme Court ruling, a full ten years before my father purchased the property. Anyway, that was far different, he pointed out, than when Lyndon Johnson had a racial covenant *inserted* in 1945 in the title to a property he had purchased in 1938 *without* such a restriction.

Dad was accused of profiting, as a conflict of interest, from a law firm he had set up in Buffalo in 1961 in anticipation of retiring from Congress in a few years, to ensure that he would have a livelihood to return to that would support his "second" family. This despite the fact that his partners attested that "Miller is inactive in the law firm and did not participate in its affairs or revenue."

These were only a few of the deluge of stories questioning my father's integrity. The final blow was undoubtedly the one questioning whether he had ever truly been an assistant prosecutor at Nuremberg, suggesting that that item in his biographical sketch might be "wishful thinking." Democratic Senator Tom Dodd, himself a senior advisor at the trials, once made an offhand remark to the press that he had "never heard of Bill Miller." Dodd was referring to the fact that he had never seen him actually prosecuting Nazi war criminals in the courtroom, which he never claimed he did. His job as a young assistant prosecutor was to prepare the indictments and trial briefs for the more prestigious and experienced courtroom lawyers.

Though he was loathe to answer what he called this "sleazy smear," he did point out that he and Goldwater had a combined eight years of service in the military during World War II, compared to seven months service by Lyndon Johnson and no military service by Hubert Humphrey. To say that Dad was deeply hurt by these stories, his tough political skin notwithstanding, would be an understatement, not to mention that the rest of us were devastated.

As all these stories, erroneous at their foundation, were endlessly recycled, the lack of initiative on the part of news people was stunning. Rarely, if ever, did they reinvestigate the charges to determine their merit and accuracy; rarely was another side sought or presented, nor was my father's response ever requested. And yet his reputation for integrity and his long record free of personal scandal were clear and well earned. As one fellow congressman vehemently asserted when questioned on the topic, "If he knew something was against the rules, Bill wouldn't have done it—he was too smart and too honest."

If there was anything Bill Miller was, it was honest—that was told to me over and over again by every former colleague with whom I spoke, Republican and Democrat, over many years of interviewing for this book. It wasn't something he flaunted; it was just a given in his life, the essence of what he was, something he did not think much about. "Overly honest," some said, even to the extent of hurting himself financially. What I guess they meant was that there were ways to enrich yourself in Washington, if you were willing to find the loopholes or stretch the rules just a little bit. Indeed, there were many who left the capital a good deal wealthier than they had come. But "Bill Miller never had his hand in the till," his colleagues vouched with assurance.

That fact was borne out by the release of his financial statement, required of the four candidates for national office, which proved that he had become anything but wealthy during his fourteen years in Congress. His net worth was $260,730—by far the lowest of the four candidates. That included a surprise inheritance of $40,000 from his wise and frugal Aunt Margaret, who had long ago helped fund his Notre Dame education with money from investments no one knew she had. "I'll tell you one thing," Dad quipped about his assets, "it'll get me the poor man's vote."

As reporters picked over every number in his comparatively meager portfolio, little was said or written about the long concealed $14,000,000 it was reported that Lyndon Johnson had somehow accrued while on the public payroll for thirty plus years. As my father pointed out, it was "a massive personal fortune made during his years in Congress in an industry wholly controlled by the federal government (the Federal Communications Commission)." He was referring to the highly profitable Texas radio stations owned in Lady Bird Johnson's name, which held a monopoly in the market.

It turned out that much of the "dirt" dredged up on Dad emanated indirectly from the White House, from what was called the "Miller Operation." Originated by presidential aide Bill Moyers, later a respected public television personality, and discreetly delegated to a Bill Haddad in New York City, the operation was financed independently of the White House and the Democratic National Committee and encompassed a paid and volunteer staff of six, including newsmen, businessmen, a Wall Street analyst, and a psychiatrist.[8]

Johnson was known to be pretty thin-skinned when it came to criticism, and my feisty father's unrelenting barrage of it was "driving him nuts," as Barry Goldwater once aptly put it. As a result, there appeared to be a desperate determination to make the Republican vice presidential candidate out to be something of a crook. To aid in that endeavor, the president ordered, in no uncertain terms, his various aides and operatives, both inside and outside the White House, to have FBI and Internal Revenue confidential files leaked to selected favored columnists such as Drew Pearson and Theodore White.[9] He did so against the advice of his Attorney General, Nicholas Katzenbach, who repeatedly told him that Bill Miller had done nothing illegal.[10] It was all part of the political game, but when you got to this level, the game was played hard. It was not for the fainthearted.

So Dad soldiered on, betraying on the surface no discouragement. No matter what he felt—and as a deeply sensitive man I knew the hurt from the assault on his honesty and integrity was profound—I never remember hearing him complain, and we, the family, took our signal from him, as difficult as it often was. Actually, there was little time to remain angry or offended for long, for the schedule kept moving inexorably on. Our constant preoccupation was where we were going next, what we would wear, and what we would say to the groups we met.

Warren Weaver of the *New York Times* once told me that from his long experience of covering national campaigns, they were much tougher forty years ago than they are today. Political handlers today figure out how their candidate can do and say things that will be certain to make the evening news, without having to travel to every dusty outpost in the country.

In the 1964 campaign, while Senator Goldwater hit all the major cities, the vice-presidential candidate was assigned to the "grassroots," to fill in the gaps, to slog through every small to medium size town in the U.S., or so it seemed. Between them, they crisscrossed the country multiple times. And where the candidates did not go, we "children" did. My father joked in the end that there weren't many towns in Indiana that he *didn't* visit. As *Life* magazine put it, the campaign plan for Bill Miller was to "show off his handsome family and skewer Democrats with all the zeal of a small-town district attorney prosecuting his first big case."[11]

To equip him for this arduous journey, he was assigned a sleek blue and white turboprop Electra jet, chartered from Eastern Airlines and promptly painted with its sentimental new name, *The Niagaran*, in honor of his congressional district. It was outfitted with a special communications setup that had never before been attempted, a system that permitted two telephone calls to be made simultaneously while the plane was in flight. There were desks and typewriters, and at every stop local phones were installed immediately by a staff member on loan from New York Telephone so that reporters could call in their stories. A Western Union man was on board to file copy that wasn't phoned, as well as a Railway Express representative to ship film to the networks. As soon as wheels went up, mimeograph machines began churning out schedules and copies of the candidate's speeches for reporters. Work was done at all hours in this traveling office with its large assemblage of staff and press.

The Niagaran "became a strange, warm, unreal, floating home to these gypsies of politics and the press."[12] They kept a tight and unusually smooth-running schedule, sticking amazingly close to those mimeographed time sheets, considering the full and complicated days contained therein. They often visited up to five states in a day, with seven or eight speeches delivered either at airport rallies or events in town. A typical day began with baggage call at 7:00 a.m. and wheels up at 8:00, and ended at 10:30 or 11:00 p.m., when all were thankfully allowed to retire to the local hotel for a few hours sleep.

Actually, "Small-town USA" was fun, if exhausting. The people were friendly and open, genuinely happy to see us, and so eager to please. "There was innocence to places in Iowa that was gone from elsewhere, and rugged strength to Montana, and a gentleness and grace in the South," chronicled Dad's press secretary Bob Smalley.[13] Candidate Miller's coming was a major event for most of these communities—some had never seen a candidate for national office. In Cedar City, Utah, they made it a holiday, with bands and bunting and schools closed. Wherever he went, he made time to confer in his hotel room with local politicians, many of whom were first name friends from his days as national chairman. He knew they were the nuts and bolts of victory and they were always flattered that he took time for them.

Local press coverage of his visit was usually awed and enthusiastic, but the national press people traveling with my father had a hard time getting much attention for the stories they filed. Several of those reporters told me later that his talents could have been better utilized. They thought he had the political depth and savvy of the ticket and that he understood and articulated the issues better than his running mate. But the scheduling was done back at the National Committee, which had now been commandeered by avid Goldwater men.

A new speechwriter came on board *The Niagaran* a few weeks into the campaign. Young Buddy Lewis, conservative son of famed conservative radio personality Fulton Lewis Jr., was to present his boss with his maiden effort in Chautauqua, New York. A special typewriter was flown in for his use.

He was brimming with pride as Dad approached the lectern, "the speech" in hand, looked out over the crowd and, responding to a thunderous welcome, announced emotionally: "I see so many familiar faces here tonight that I'm going to put aside my prepared speech and just speak from the heart." Whereupon he folded up the fruit of Buddy's labor, slid it into his breast pocket, and proceeded to make "what was probably the best speech of his career," recalls the crestfallen speechwriter. And this after Lewis had already given a copy of his prepared speech to the wire services—"I'd already filed on the basis of that text," intoned an ashen UPI man with feigned equanimity. "Smalley, you'd better throw away your mimeograph machine," growled another crusty newsman.[14]

That's the way it was for my father—he had speechwriters, but mostly he ad-libbed. The words, the thoughts, the direction of his speeches were mainly his own. Even the writers admitted that they could not top their boss's ability to organize a presentation well and make it interesting, to establish a rapport with an audience, to rivet their attention, and inject them with his enthusiasm.

Often standing on an upturned wooden crate to be seen over the array of media microphones, he loved to stir a crowd to participate in his speeches, to carry them along with him, changing the pace from high to low and then building it up again to a smashing climax. Slicing away at Lyndon Johnson, he would often pose questions, to which his audience, rising from their seats, would roar back the obvious answers. One of his favorite lines was: "I have now been here since early morning. As a matter of fact, I have been in your state longer than Bobby Kennedy has been in mine!"—referring to the Massachusetts native's carpetbagger status in New York State as a candidate for the United States Senate that year. Wrote Warren Weaver in the *New York Times:* "Observers consider Mr. Miller one of the most skilled speechmakers on the campaign circuit in many years."[15]

Dad had a team of advance people who arrived in the towns he was to visit two weeks ahead of him to nail down the nitty-gritty details that make a candidate look good—making sure the hall was set, the crowds assured, the protesters suppressed. They sat in local bars and read local papers to glean the topics of concern in that area, and they put it all on three-by-five-inch cards, including in very large letters the name of the town, just to make sure the candidate didn't say he was "happy to be in Versailles" when he was in Kearney. But though their work was helpful, they too admitted that my father had an uncanny ability to sense the mood and pulse of an audience on his own, no matter where he was.

He and his staff did eventually develop what was affectionately referred to by the press assigned to follow him as "The Speech." This oration was in a constant state of evolution—dropping paragraphs, inserting new ones, fixing and localizing with references to people and facts remembered from previous travels as national chairman and to issues of importance in particular areas. Yet there were parts of it that remained the same throughout the ten weeks of the campaign. And just about every newsperson on the plane could have delivered those segments, Dad's inflections included, after about a week of hearing them multiple times a day. One night, Chuck Von Fremd of CBS went a step further, yelling "Give 'em hell, Bill!" at all the applause points. "There is no doubt he helped whip the crowd into one of the best we ever had. And no doubt that CBS would have fired him had they known."[16]

To relieve the tedium and make their job a little easier, the staff then developed a unique system to alert the media about when a "news item" would be contained in "The Speech." It would be the only part my father would read verbatim, and just prior to it he would wipe his brow with his handkerchief as a signal. That would rouse the reporters from their somnolence to turn on their tape recorders and cameras and start recording. They could then pack up and send their stories to their respective bureaus.

The "news item" that would most often be contained in his talks was a defense or explanation of what his running mate had said the day before—"All Barry Goldwater ever said was . . ." became his most familiar line. It was not a job that was explicitly given to him. He just knew it was what he was supposed to do, or had to do—to fix the damage, plug the "leakage," "clean up the mess," as his aides put it. Unfortunately, the corrections never got as much play in the media as the original statements—they rarely do. And too many misstatements and clarifications eventually create an impression of incompetence. A fellow congressman once described Dad as a conservative, but one "more inclined to weigh his words [than Barry Goldwater]." There was probably a bit of truth to that.

Part of the problem was that Goldwater's pronouncements—such as the need to reform the Social Security system or the need to wage a war to win in Vietnam, for example—were at the time outrageous and unacceptable to both the media and the public. They were falling on ears that were unaccustomed to hearing bold and challenging suggestions, not exactly designed to win votes. And this from a major party presidential candidate who appeared to care less about getting elected than about getting his message out and speaking the truth as he saw it. Added to that was the fact that the Senator sometimes did not express himself as clearly as he might, and sometimes the excerpts, or "soundbites," the press chose to use from his speeches created erroneous impressions by their incompleteness.

Refuting or trying to counteract the television images of an elderly couple tearing up their Social Security cards or a mushroom cloud of strontium 90 obliterating a beautiful little girl picking daisies in a field—two of the more egregious examples of Democratic ads designed to paint Goldwater as uncaring and unstable—was a losing battle. The Republican National Committee vigorously protested the misrepresentation involved in those commercials, but the Federal Communications Commission was less than cooperative, according to my father, in handling the protests. Today, candidates would be hard-pressed indeed to broadcast such ads and then appear on screen saying they "approved the message."

The bottom line was that for the first time in his life, Bill Miller was not in charge, as he had been in his own races. When he wanted to discuss important issues in the campaign, he found himself continually on the defensive, explaining with increasing annoyance to disgruntled groups or persistent newsmen what Barry had meant to say or how the press had misquoted him. To use a sports analogy such as men are prone to insert in discourse, he was a guy accustomed to playing quarterback who was put in at defensive end—it wasn't his preference, but, as a team player, he would do what was needed.

Playing defense while trying to stay on the offensive addressing issues was a frustrating job and the most daunting challenge he faced throughout this campaign. Senator Robert Dole told me he faced the same problem when he ran with Gerald Ford in 1976 against Jimmy Carter: "Media people always say they want substantive discussions, but then all they do is run polls and magnify the candidates' mistakes," was his assessment. That hit the proverbial nail on the head.

The hard part was that often my father was not sure himself exactly what Barry had meant to say. Communication between the two planes was infrequent and it was difficult to get through to the senator in person when he was on the road. Busy with his own schedule, he never actually heard his running mate's speeches. All he knew was what he read in the papers and heard on the news. Or what his press entourage informed him of when they reboarded the plane each day. Their gleeful and slightly mischievous greeting would be: "Bill, have you heard what Barry said *today*?" And with his familiar wry smile of amusement, half-feigned disgust, and resignation, Dad would ask, "*Now* what has he said?"

Not easily angered, he would wonder what on earth was going on in the Goldwater camp. He was of the opinion that his old friend was listening to too many people, many of whom were unseasoned political novices, and that the strong-willed Arizonan too often spoke impulsively or in fatigue. The Miller staff consisted of so many savvy political strategists who had come from the National Committee, whose advice and wisdom could have been invaluable to the overall effort. But Barry's people, chiefly the imperious new RNC Executive Director John Grenier, chose not to utilize this wealth of veteran talent—much to the senator's regret, as he told me in later years.

Even Goldwater would later admit that his team, superbly organized in the run-up to the nomination, floundered once they took charge of the Republican National Committee. There were too many rash and unceremonious firings of competent staffers just because they had not been with the senator from the very beginning. Like Research Director Bill Prendergast, widely considered one of the most respected and knowledgeable political researchers in Washington, who was told he had one day to clear his desk and leave.

Though the odds were, admittedly, strongly against the ticket, my father never believed in his gut that "the game" was being played to win, and as a keen competitor, that bothered him. Conservative leadership, he feared, was acting like winning the nomination was validation enough and winning the election, though glorious, would be gravy. There are historians of the '64 campaign, Theodore White among them, [17] who have since corroborated this personal assessment.

I remember a particular explanation Dad tried to make of one of Barry's more controversial statements, and it ended in a hilarious mess that became legendary in our campaign lore. When the senator suggested that the Supreme NATO Commander ought to have discretionary power to authorize, without reaching the president for permission, the use of tactical nuclear weapons in the field in the event that our men were fired upon with such weapons, the furor that ensued was nothing less than seismic. The issue was causing havoc among voters. Goldwater was portrayed as a lunatic who might blow up the world, who was unfit to have his finger on "the button," and far worse. His loyal running mate, of course, came to the rescue.

Without the time to gather a great deal of information on the subject in the urgency of the moment, my father started out explaining that the president would naturally have sole control of THE bomb—"All Barry was talking about were small tactical nuclear weapons that a GI could carry onto the field of battle on his back." Luckily, Paul Niven, a CBS reporter assigned to our plane, who despite his best efforts to remain detached had by now become a close friend and admirer of Dad's, decided most kindly not to use that less-than-accurate explanation in his report that night. And beyond that, since he possessed some basic knowledge of weaponry himself, he proceeded to give his candidate-pupil a crash course on the nature of tactical nuclear weapons.

"It's impossible for one man to carry one of these things himself. They weigh almost 300 pounds!" he told my father. So the next night, in St. Louis, Dad, duly informed, got up to give his speech, took out his handkerchief to wipe his brow at the "newsy" part about tactical nuclear weapons, and Niven gave the signal for his crew to start filming: "What Barry is talking about are weapons that *two* GIs could carry on their shoulders onto a field of battle," he exclaimed confidently.

"No, no," Paul patiently explained afterwards, deciding once again not to use the planned soundbite. "You don't understand. If they carried this thing onto the field, it's so heavy they'd never be able to use it—the recoil on it would send them as far in one direction as the missile would go in the other." The would-be vice president professed to finally understand and promised he would get it right the next night. He would say that a few soldiers could mount the tactical nuclear weapon on a *jeep* and drive it onto the field of battle. Niven gave that version a thumbs up.

So now on the third night of this saga, in a huge arena in San Francisco packed with 3,000 people, Paul was ready to film my father's explication of the tactical nuclear weapons fiasco for the CBS news. Out came the white handkerchief at the critical moment, but alas, "tactical" unhappily came out sounding very much like "testicle." Whereupon Paul Niven, all 300 pounds of him, fell off his collapsible wooden chair in hysterics, emitted a loud "shit," and ordered his crew to turn off the cameras. Dad, usually so precise in his speech, was chagrined at his alleged slip and never again tried that story.

Though the line between the reality and the perception of what a candidate is saying and how much the media creates that perception is difficult to find, it has been generally agreed among conservatives that a predominantly liberal media was severely biased against the Republican ticket in the '64 campaign. The odd thing is that my father never fully believed that. And neither did Goldwater. Chuck Quinn of NBC News, who covered our campaign but spent a few days on Barry's plane, once asked the Senator if he thought the press had been unfair to him, considering the terrible beating he had been taking. He said no, not really—he probably deserved it. He knew there were many things he had to say that would not come across well in the media, but he did not blame the reporters. If anything, both candidates blamed the people back in New York and Washington who put the news together—the "Huntley-Brinkleys" and other commentators and columnists who, they felt, often distorted the work of their traveling correspondents.

Dad, for example, had a most discouraging encounter with Time Inc. Chief Henry Luce when he was invited to a luncheon with the company's senior editorial and corporate executives in their elegant dining room atop the Time-Life Building, where ironically I was to begin my career in journalism a year later. Luce dominated the conversation, allowing his brighter and friendlier subordinates barely a question. Though my father reportedly "handled himself with consummate skill," he was disgusted. "What the hell did we go through that for? They didn't want our views. Luce has already made up his mind and he's going to be for Johnson," he fumed to his aide. And as the weeks wore on, the staff never did feel that *Time* was interested in objectivity or even accuracy.[18]

There were, very definitely, some egregious examples of what appeared to be biased field reporting. Like when *New York Times* reporter Warren Weaver insisted at the university in Provo, Utah that there were only 6,000 in attendance for a Miller appearance, even after the university president informed him that their auditorium, obviously completely full, held 14,000. Dad always cheered his listeners by telling them that, despite the polls and the media, he was getting tumultuous, foot-stomping welcomes wherever he went, crowds that often waited patiently at virtually every hour of the day and night in extreme heat, rain, and bitter cold—all of which the media rarely reported:

> *We have had them even when the press has ignored them in order to concentrate its attention on hecklers. We have had them in the thousands when the press has reported them in the hundreds, and when they have been in the hundreds, the press so frequently and conveniently has failed to mention that they have been sellout breakfasts, luncheons or dinners, limited in size only by the size of the hall where they were held. They have failed to mention that in many cases even a turnout of a few hundred has represented a substantial part of the population of small communities.*

Yet, for the most part, my father held a personal regard for the traveling press. Proof was his absolute trust of them. Chuck Quinn claims he was the most candid and honest politician he ever covered—"everyone in the press corps on the plane loved him for that," said Chuck. "He did not always tell everything he knew—no politician should—but he never misled us," added Paul Niven. They appreciated and respected that particular quality because they are so often lied to by politicians. Quinn noted parenthetically that Nixon, Johnson, and Clinton, as well as numerous other Presidents, Senators, and Press Secretaries, were examples of those who were not always honest with the press. Unlike most campaign planes, where the candidate's compartment is strictly off limits to the media, there was never a problem getting access to Dad—reporters had the run of the plane.

He said pretty much exactly what he thought, a rarity for a politician, and he didn't need his press secretary at his side to filter what he said, for he had an innate sense of the boundaries. If he had not trusted reporters, he would never have been so open. In fact, there were so many outrageous and totally honest things said on *The Niagaran* that would have made headline stories, such as the candidate occasionally admitting the hopelessness of their cause—but they were never reported. Without ever stipulating what was on and off the record, the press just knew what was not for publication. And it never occurred to my father or his staff that it would be otherwise. The thing was that he understood their needs and how the game was to be played, just as he had when at the NRCC and the RNC. Hal Bruno, once of *Newsweek* and then *ABC-TV News*, told me that those were the people who were most successful in politics—to be engaged in constant warfare with the press was self-defeating.

Quinn remarked that, in his experience, such openness was particularly unusual for a Republican. Republican candidates were typically more reticent and less fun to cover than Democrats, or so he claimed. Bill Miller was the only exception to that observation that he could remember. Reporters had a ball with him, and he truly enjoyed their companionship. He was a real man's man, nothing pompous or stiff about him. They would play low stakes card games together between stops on the plane, Dad, the consummate competitor, usually cleaning out all the newsmen's spare change. If it was bridge, Mom would sometimes be his partner, he amazingly patient, considering how much he hated to lose, if her level of play did not rise to that of their opponents. Chuck Von Fremd of CBS once kidded him, "You know, Bill, if you weren't running for VP, you'd make one heck of a riverboat gambler."

The incredible thing, reporters always marveled, was how he could arrive for an airport stop, lay down his cards, put his jacket back on, "shoot" his dazzling white cuffs, straighten his tie, run a comb through his glistening black hair, greet his hosts, make a rip-roaring speech, get back on the plane, pick up his cards, and remember exactly what had been played before he left. Without a moment's hesitation, he would make his bid—"Four hearts!"

As is well documented, everything changed after Watergate— the openness that was possible in my father's time became a thing of the past. The media's trust in the honesty of political figures sunk to an all-time low, and politicians came to see the media as adversaries ready to ambush them at any moment. Never again could a Jack Kennedy—considering that reporters on his 1960 campaign bus joked that his campaign slogan should be "Let's shack with Jack"—trust that these reporters would turn their backs on flagrant sexual dalliances and other indiscretions. There was a new determination in the "fourth estate" to expose the hypocrisy of those in public life who tried to appear to be something they were not.

All things considered, the kinship that developed among the staff, the media, and the candidate on *The Niagaran* during those hectic and pressure-filled months on the road was considered extraordinary. Indeed it resulted in a phenomenon that was unique in the annals of political campaigns, as far as anyone could remember—regular reunions of the entire group, faithfully, for the next twenty years, until their leader passed away. They traveled from hundreds of miles to be there, many without plentiful financial resources. The band of media folks assigned to Dad even used to joke that if the ticket had been reversed, they might have voted Republican for the first time in their lives.

Still, the story that may say the most about his relationship with the press is the one about the reporter who allegedly griped when assigned to cover the GOP's No. 2 man that he did not want to cover "that miserable little man." When the newsman left the campaign a week before the election, he wept, and when he died suddenly, quite young, a year and a half after the campaign, his widow asked my father to be an honorary pallbearer.

Word had it that the Eastern Airlines pilots who came with our plane, though highly competent and fine men, thought the world ended at St. Louis, for they had never flown to some of the remote places they were now asked to go. They seemed often unaware of important logistical details, such as what runways could not accommodate the weight of our plane, or when some of these small airports extinguished their lights at night.

When we arrived in Kearney, Nebraska after dark, for example, we had to circle the airport until the state police arrived to put lanterns on the runway. As we approached the Medford, Oregon airfield, their control tower radioed *The Niagaran*: "You're not *really* going to try to land at *this* airport are you?" Out of Albuquerque, the tower quietly informed the pilot it didn't look like he would clear the Sandia Mountains. Such events were hardly reassuring to those already-phobic passengers like John Barnett of Railway Express, who habitually lowered his window shades upon takeoff and landing.

The campaign visit to Laramie, Wyoming proved to be the most hapless and hysterical of all, another legendary tale told and retold numerous times in the years to come. There was only one small hotel in the town and with seventy people in my father's entourage, the advance team knew they had to secure every last room available—seventy-three rooms and a suite for the candidate and his wife to be exact. Since there turned out to be no such thing as a suite, the hotel staff, trying their best to be accommodating, took one room and quickly built a partition across the middle. The new "wall" was makeshift and unpainted, and the resulting "suite" had an unusual configuration and only one double bed.

Dad retired to his "suite" to shower and change before a dinner meeting—Mother had already dressed and gone downstairs. He went into the bedroom, pulled the door shut, and found the handle in his hand. He was now unable to open the door to get back into the other "room" where he realized he had left his clothes, and where the telephone was located as well.

Thankfully able to see the humor in his ridiculous situation, "The distinguished candidate for Vice President of the United States," as he was usually introduced, wrapped a sheet around his bare self, leaned out the window, and yelled to whomever could hear: "Hi, I'm Bill Miller. Could you please send somebody up here to let me out of my room?" He used to say jokingly thereafter, "That's the last time that town will ever get a candidate for major office."

My father's closest helpmate in all of this, most always by his side, was my mother. Although he loved being with people, "pressing the flesh" and making small talk in large crowds for long periods of time was not his favorite part of politicking. It was Mom who would lag behind, shaking more and more hands and squeezing her partner's elbow to tell him he needed to do the same, like it or not. When groups of young supporters pushed forward seeking autographs, as the campaign motorcade waited impatiently and the advance team struggled to keep the candidate on schedule, it would be Mother who would insist that they take an extra few minutes to sign their names to slips of paper and campaign literature.

She was described as "glamorous," "gorgeous," "dazzling, refined, and elegant," "an attractive brunette with sparkling eyes," "a living doll," "a radiant mother of four," "a standout in the current crop of good-looking political wives," "slender and attractive as one of her own daughters"—an endless list of flowery descriptions, all of which would now be taboo. Such extravagant praise, as well as the meticulous detailing of exactly what candidates' wives were wearing from their head to their toes, routine many years ago, would doubtless be considered sexist today.

But in reality, Mother was beautiful, with her poise, charm, and grace, with her radiant smile as she waved her white-gloved hand and carried her sheaves of roses. She was a frequently acknowledged asset to her husband and to the ticket, winning hearts and, we hoped, votes wherever she went. I can never remember her being without a warm and appropriate word for all the thousands of people she met, no matter how much her feet ached.

In fact, her capable handling of her new "job" now seems quite extraordinary when I realize that she was only forty-one years old. She at first looked upon the prospect of campaigning non-stop for nearly three months with some trepidation. Not only did she not want to leave her two little ones, Billy and Stephanie, but she is at her core a shy and private person. And she most certainly did not want to answer political questions.

Mom, in the beginning, was of the Peggy Goldwater school of politics—be seen and not heard. The most she would say is "a few noncontroversial, harmless words when called upon to do so," as she herself described it. A Republican official usually preceded her to lay down strict ground rules which barred all questions on anything other than "home, children, recipes, and allied fireside topics."[19] Only once did a gaggle of Washington newspaper women succeed in literally backing her against a wall and jabbing her with political questions until she reluctantly and laughingly made her first political comments.

But as luck, or lack of luck, would have it, it turned out that this campaign of 1964 would be the first time in history that "both political parties are laying out separate schedules of appearances for the wives and children of their presidential and vice presidential candidates." [20] After warming up for a month or so, Mother finally mustered the courage to leave her background role at Dad's side and go off on her own for a multi-day swing through the East, Midwest, and South, accompanied only by her trusted aide and press secretary, Jana Hruska. He bid her a pithy farewell: "Good-bye dear, just be yourself and don't ruin us." So off she went, and my father professed to be pleased with the headlines that rolled in, such as "Stephanie Miller Stumps Jersey in Charming Solo."

Eventually, Mom came to speak somewhat eloquently on the importance of the women's vote, and to develop a quiet but steely political savvy in the way she occasionally critiqued the press for their inaccuracies and dodged questions she was loathe to answer. As when she was asked about her husband's sharp tongue—"He has a very colorful way of talking.... He has a wonderful command of the English language. I just don't know what people mean when they accuse him of sharp talk." At a luncheon for 1,000 honoring her in Pennsylvania where she spoke for a full fifteen minutes, telling of how her first public talks lasted for three quarters of a minute and worked up to five minutes, her bravery earned her a standing ovation. By the time she got to Chicago for "Peg and Steph Day," Mother had become a real pro and was even enjoying the hustings and the thrill of seeing the country.

It was decided by the powers-that-be in the campaign hierarchy that Mom should spend considerable time visiting Polish and Ukrainian communities in cities like Detroit, Buffalo, Chicago, and Philadelphia. She would polka at weddings, attend Pulaski Day parades and Captive Nations rallies, and speak on every Polish radio program that aired. The rationale was that Republicans ought to be able to reclaim those heavily Democratic ethnic votes, seeing as the Eastern European nations fell behind the Iron Curtain after Yalta, on the watch of a Democratic president, Franklin Delano Roosevelt. Dad always said his wife's Slavic heritage would come in handy, though "it is doubtful whether Barry Goldwater knew of Mrs. Miller's ethnic background when he decided that Bill Miller ... would add most to his presidential ticket."[21]

The problem was that not only did Mother not speak fluent Polish, but what few words she did remember from hearing her parents speak as a child were rusty, to be kind. So for her new assignment, she took her energetic Polish-speaking mother along, my grandmother Mary Wagner, formerly Mary Nowak, who I am not sure had ever been out of Buffalo. Grandma composed a brief speech in Polish, telling the story of her parents' emigration, which after some coaching her daughter actually became quite adept at delivering. Confirming that, a woman who heard her in Chicago and a week later in Pittsburgh rushed up to her excitedly and exclaimed, "My, you've improved so!"

"Stephania's" (Polish version of Stephanie) newly mastered Polish words invariably precipitated a great outpouring of emotion wherever she went, with a deluge of fans converging upon the podium, tears in their eyes, to express their gratitude for a visit from "one of their own." As they all gushed rapidly in their native tongue to the bewildered "First Lady of Polonia," as they had christened her, under the misimpression that she too spoke it fluently, Mom could only look beseechingly to Grandma for help. Despite those disconcerting finales, the duo usually left with a generous gift of Polish sausage.

And the results of all her hard work? According to Theodore H. White in *The Making of the President—1964*, "In Polish working-class wards in the Midwest (Indiana, Illinois, North Dakota, Ohio), Goldwater managed to shave the Democratic percentages of 1960—but whether this was an echo of backlash or an ethnic identification with William Miller's handsome Polish American wife, one cannot say."[22] We prefer to think it was the latter.

Though Barry himself seemed to be "taking aim at an awful lot of issues with a shotgun," as one concerned Republican operative put it, perhaps spreading himself too thin, Dad really had three specific topics he most wanted to bring before the public. They were: the need for a restoration of integrity in the highest councils of government, the need for a firm foreign policy based on strength, and the need for fiscal responsibility and restraint in the management of public funds, i.e. cutting back on the overwhelming bigness of government and restoring to private citizens more control over their lives.

The subject of moral leadership in government was always at the top of his list. He tried and tried, to little avail, to bring to the media's attention the improprieties that had surrounded Lyndon Johnson's career since his earliest days in Washington, all of which were later detailed in three monumental volumes by Robert Caro.[23] Almost legendary were the ruthlessness, manipulation, and tendency to play fast and loose with the rules that had enabled Johnson to become so extraordinarily wealthy and powerful in public life, yet he was far too feared to be exposed during his lifetime. Not only that, but his closest aide and confidant, indeed the "son" he never had, Bobby Baker, managed to increase his net worth from zero to millions during his career as secretary to the majority in the Senate under Johnson's aegis. When Baker was eventually convicted of theft and fraud and served time in jail, his old mentor disavowed any relationship with him.

There was, however, one place my father would not go on the morality issue. A sensational story broke in mid-October, only weeks away from Election Day, that threatened to derail the president's headlong rush to victory, or so he and his staff feared. Another of his closest aides and a longtime personal friend, Walter Jenkins, had been hospitalized for nervous exhaustion following his arrest at a Washington, D.C. YMCA on "morals charges." Though the administration made strenuous efforts to suppress the news stories, details finally emerged and they had to do with Jenkins, a married man, propositioning another man in the men's room. There were immediate allegations that such behavior might make him susceptible to Russian blackmail.

Dad was in San Bernardino, California at the time the story broke and his research director, Dave Krogseng, received a call from the Goldwater people in Washington: "Miller has got to take the lead in going after this Jenkins issue," they urged. Dave took the request to his boss, who immediately responded, "No, we're not going to do this. We're not going to play politics with a personal tragedy." How ironic, thought Dave. Here is this man, whom some in the media liked to portray as ruthlessly hard-hitting, showing the utmost compassion, just when he could seize a golden opportunity to perhaps turn his losing campaign around. Only when it later leaked that Jenkins had two previous arrests on similar charges and either the FBI had failed to inform the president or the White House had concealed the information did the case become part of my father's "lack of morals in government" charges, because of obvious security concerns.

Amazingly, and to the distress of many, both at the time and in retrospect, neither member of the Republican ticket made as much of an issue of Vietnam during the campaign of '64 as they might have. That was partially because of President Johnson's emergency action on August 4 ordering retaliatory air attacks on North Vietnamese PT boats that had allegedly attacked our destroyers, unprovoked, in the Gulf of Tonkin. It was another of those moments of international tension, like the Cuban missile crisis faced by President Kennedy, that tends to silence the opposition and rally the nation. "It has certainly removed Vietnam as a political issue in the presidential campaign as of now," announced the Republican VP candidate.

First of all, neither Goldwater nor my father wanted his patriotism questioned; and secondly, when Barry did suggest that we should bomb the supply routes in Vietnam, he was accused of being "trigger-happy" and apt to lead us into full-fledged war. Only decades later, when the Johnson White House tapes were released, was it learned that there never was conclusive proof of North Vietnamese attacks on our ships at sea. Apparently, Johnson and his Defense Secretary Robert McNamara used the alleged "incident" to provoke Congress into giving them open-ended authority to wage military action in Vietnam. The resulting Gulf of Tonkin Resolution is considered the official beginning of the Vietnam War.

As candidate Miller repeatedly pointed out in his campaign speeches, we were *already* virtually at war, "though they don't call it a war." This despite the fact that President Kennedy had increased our troops from 300 to over 22,000 and President Johnson had upped them yet again to 200,000, and the administration had, to date, awarded over a thousand medals and purple hearts for valor in combat. Yet somehow, as former Congressman and Defense Secretary Mel Laird recalled to me, "Barry let Johnson get away with saying that if you vote for Goldwater, you're voting for war, when he himself had already started to escalate the war." Laird feels that the judgment not to attack Johnson for that hypocrisy was a poor one. He is probably right, though it is always easy to second-guess campaigns from the perspective of decades later.

Dad usually circumvented the whole issue by suggesting that we might not be at war in Vietnam at all if we had stood up to the Communists in the Bay of Pigs, in Berlin, and in Laos. "Only Barry Goldwater and the Republicans understand Communism and understand that only the strong will be free," he would exclaim with great emotion. Becoming more emboldened and emotional on the subject as the weeks wore on, his harshest assertion would be: "This is a war the Democrats don't know how to end and they don't know how to win. American boys are once again (as in Korea) being committed to battle under instructions to do enough to die but not enough to win." The administration does not have a plan, he accused. They wait until we are on the brink of war to act: "When we are afraid to recognize communism as the enemy and are afraid to say or do anything which we fear might upset the rulers of the Communist world, then we are planting the seeds of future surrender." And that was as much as he would say about the war that supposedly was not a war.

What Barry was actually proposing in Vietnam was exactly what General Eisenhower had suggested several years earlier—that air power, not ground troops, was the only way to win a war in Southeast Asia. Using ground forces would only produce an endless war of attrition, both men warned, and we would be the losers. Ten years, 58,000 American and over a million Vietnamese deaths later, there were many who said, and still say today, that perhaps they should have listened to Goldwater/Miller in 1964.

The issue of big government was, of course, a staple in my father's speeches. His favorite comments on the subject, which our reporter friends loved to parrot verbatim, were: "government has one hand in everyone's business and the other in everyone's pocket," "no government can give you anything it hasn't first taken away from you," and "any government that gets so big it can give you everything you want has also gotten so big it can take away from you everything you have got." Needless to say, those lines faithfully elicited howls of approval from his listeners.

And speaking of big government programs, Social Security, one of the biggest, became a lightning rod when Goldwater's pronouncements on it were understood to mean that he would make the system totally voluntary. His running mate tried to clarify the situation by saying that all they wanted was for the system to be fiscally sound, which it portended not to be in the near future. They also suggested that some portion of it should be voluntary—a suggestion which is today considered quite reasonable.

There were other issues that popped up now and then in the campaign that were not on Dad's original agenda, but deal with them he did. Most notably at the time, there was the brouhaha over the John Birch Society, a group that is now a footnote of history long faded from memory. It was a fanatical group, on the outermost fringes of conservatism, who were known to be a bit paranoid about the Communist menace. With Goldwater sharing their concern about the need to remain vigilant about communism, the "Birchers" were naturally drawn to his candidacy. And the media, with help from the Democrats, proceeded to pummel the Republican ticket for that support, yet another issue to put them on the defensive.

While the Society's founder, Robert Welch, was given to making slightly wacky and highly controversial statements, the most famous of which was his questioning of the patriotism and commitment to fighting communism of the much-beloved war hero Dwight Eisenhower, their membership was for the most part comprised of upstanding, patriotic, concerned citizens. Though strong in California, the John Birch Society was small in number nationally and had no participation or power in the councils of the GOP.

What's more, the group was hardly any more conservative than the Americans for Democratic Action (ADA) or the leadership of big city labor unions were liberal, as my father repeatedly pointed out. And these latter groups were integral cogs in the Democratic machine from one end of the country to the other, and had members in high places in the administrations of both Presidents Kennedy and Johnson. Johnson's running mate, Hubert Humphrey, was, as a matter of fact, the vice chairman of the ADA—which position he finally resigned as a result of his opponent's persistent badgering.

Nevertheless, the media seemed to take a certain delight in portraying zealous conservatives such as the "Birchers" as dangerous "kooks." Though it would probably be safe to say that most people back in the early '60s considered them more of an annoyance than a danger, journalists continually backed Dad and Barry into a corner about whether or not they accepted John

Birch support. Yet they never pressed Democratic vice-presidential candidate Hubert Humphrey on his life-long ADA membership, as Bill Miller liked to remind his audiences. While he and
Goldwater had no love for the "Birchers," they preferred not to
publicly either embrace or alienate them, for they knew it was a
"damned if you do and damned if you don't" situation.

If they sought the group's support, they would unquestionably be excoriated by the press and the Democrats—who were
enjoying the pickle in which their opponents found themselves—
for courting the votes of "extremists." If they repudiated John
Birch support, they might offend, and lose, thousands of their
hardest working "grass roots" workers, especially in the electoral
vote-rich state of California. It was a little like what Bob Dole once
told me, with his droll humor: "I used to stay up at night thinking
of someone I didn't want to vote for me, and I couldn't think of
anyone." During weeks of grilling by reporters, my father went
from saying he "didn't know much about the organization," to
he "wouldn't invite their support," to "there would be no members of the John Birch Society in a Goldwater administration."
Predictably, the latter statement, uttered in frustration, upset a
great many conservatives.

One of his themes in his speeches on the road was the need to
restore law and order to the streets of our cities so that Americans
felt safe again. He was referring to the violent and senseless demonstrations that had inflamed these cities throughout the torrid
summer of 1964, even after the first comprehensive Civil Rights
Bill had been passed by Congress and signed into law in June.

"They were not race riots ... they were an anarchy, a revolt
led by wild youth against authority, against discipline...," wrote
Theodore White.[24] Even Roy Wilkins, then executive director
of the NAACP, agreed: "The teenage Negro hoodlums in New
York City are undercutting and wrecking the gains made by the
hundreds of Negroes and white youngsters who went to jail for
human rights."[25] Yet, because of his running mate's vote against
the recent Civil Rights Bill, any remarks Dad made about the riots
were invariably construed, again by the media, as implied racism, as an appeal to the "white backlash" vote. And they elicited
the question over and over again—"Do you disavow the support
of the Ku Klux Klan?"

No matter how many times he vehemently disavowed and disdained the support of the Klan, the issue would not go away. "They are supposed to be anti-color, anti-religious, anti-Catholic, and anti-Jewish. Senator Goldwater is half Jewish and Protestant and I am wholly Catholic. We are certainly not accepting the support or endorsement of organizations like the KKK," declared my father. I am not sure how much clearer his position could have been.

To be very honest, his reaction to all of this was disgust, and deep personal hurt. For many years in Congress, he had supported and worked for equal rights for black people, had been outraged by what he had learned in committee of their mistreatment, and had sincerely tried to right those wrongs. But he also believed passionately that we must be a nation of laws, albeit with freedom to protest within those laws. Though he understood that the source of black fury was despair, he insisted that it must be redirected back into normal American political channels.

He was quoted over and over again as saying he hopes "the Republican Party does not gain any votes because of the so-called 'white backlash.' " He insisted that Goldwater, too, was a firm believer in equal rights for everyone, that he had worked hard for that back in his home state of Arizona, and that he had voted for every other civil rights bill before the Senate with the exception of the most recent one. And Dad asserted doggedly that although his running mate had strong doubts about the constitutionality of some key provisions of the '64 bill, he would indeed enforce it as the law of the land. All this rhetoric was to no avail, for the Goldwater/Miller ticket was stamped indelibly in the minds of many with the image of bigotry.

The weeks flew by and the vice presidential entourage trudged on, with some highs but more lows, some snafus and some successes, always many laughs, and with ever-increasing weariness. The candidate was hanged in effigy in St. Cloud, Minnesota, the hecklers were becoming more annoying, and Mother's hairdryer and makeup kit were occasionally lost by the baggage men, a major crisis in those days when wall hairdryers were not a fixture in every hotel. A speech my father was handed to deliver in Portland, Oregon, which time pressures precluded him from reviewing, accused Lyndon Johnson of lying in several of his charges against Barry Goldwater. "Don't ever call him a liar again in anything we write or say," he scolded his press secretary afterwards. "I don't like to do that."

The National Committee was scheduling Dad to the hilt, so much so that it was becoming physically impossible to get him and his staff back to Washington for the weekly Sunday morning meetings that had originally been planned with Goldwater and his staff—an unfortunate development for the efficiency of the campaign effort. A heavy cold plagued him for weeks, until finally a hotel doctor in Evanston, Illinois diagnosed a touch of flu and left him with some pills that were large enough to choke a horse, as my father with his signature good humor noted. "I think we got a goddam vet," he muttered as he looked disbelievingly at two of them lying in the palm of his hand."[26]

A memo from his exasperated campaign chief Bill Warner to the RNC schedulers exhorted them to please "take a look and see whether or not we are killing this man." There were too many late nights and early mornings, times when the candidate was not in his best humor, and little time to think, rest, or refresh, Warner complained. Press Secretary Smalley remembers that all too often he had to stand outside his boss' shower door to converse over the noise of the beating water. "If this plane ever goes down, I'm going to say, Smalley, you didn't give us time to file...," groused one harassed newsman.[27] And the advance work was getting sloppy. One week the team wasn't sure whether *The Niagaran* was going to Marietta, Georgia or Marietta, Ohio, so they sent background research on both.

There were the buses and the motorcade that never appeared in Kearney, Nebraska, for the simple reason that the plane was due to land fifty miles away in Grand Island, where a full fairgrounds awaited Bill Miller's arrival. The local congressman, fortunately a good friend of his, was immediately conscripted to help roust out the unsuspecting townspeople for a proper greeting in Kearney, even in the driving rain. To top it all off, the local hotel was not up to the standards that our slightly sardonic press corps had come to expect—small table fans to combat the sweltering heat and trains running by their windows every half hour—and so they dubbed it derisively "the Kearney Hilton."

In Sioux City, Iowa, an adorable but unhousebroken red-bowed Beagle puppy, a "Beagles for Barry and Bill" sign hanging from its neck, was shoved into the candidate's hands and aptly named by the press, "B & B." It was, quite obviously, a publicity stunt, meant to capitalize on the furor Lyndon Johnson had caused around the world when photographers caught him picking up his beagle by the ears until he howled. The gift was intended for my little brother and sister, which was a cute thought. But imagine thinking we could transport the poor little thing all the way back to Washington, with several stops in between, without the necessities for ensuring that he did not make a total mess of the plane. In fact, one night no one remembered to remove him from the plane to the hotel and *The Niagaran* the next morning was not a happy sight at wheels up.

A great furor arose during a visit to New Orleans. Somehow the scheduling office at the National Committee in Washington, now run not entirely efficiently, had inadvertently booked my father and his group into what apparently was the only remaining segregated hotel in the city. When the staff discovered this fact, they took it upon themselves to hide their black members in their rooms so as not to cause an "incident." And when Dad learned of the situation the next day, he was "spitting tacks," as an aide put it. "It is just inconceivable that this could happen in this day and age," he fumed. If that wasn't bad enough, some local people had arranged for candidate Miller to be photographed with one of the strongest segregationists left in the South—a rare but inexcusable lapse in advance work. No one picked up the grievous mistake until it was too late.

The VP nominee kept vigorously punching away at the Democratic ticket in his usual pugnacious style, but it was difficult to really get at them. The president just stayed presidential and both Johnson and Humphrey declined to debate, though my father had encouraged face to face encounters. A bill had passed the House and Senate and gone to conference that would suspend the provisions of the Federal Communications Act to make possible such debates, but Johnson made it known he wanted the measure killed and Humphrey voted to kill. Dad relished the chance to meet his opposite, for though the Senator from Minnesota was a bright and competent man, Bill Miller's crisp debating skills were widely acknowledged to be superior. But such a meeting was never to be.

One of the lowest moments of an increasingly discouraging campaign came when our hometown newspaper, the *Lockport Union Sun and Journal,* endorsed the Democratic ticket. The small paper, the only one in town, had long been owned by the Corson family and Peter Corson and my father were personal friends and golfing buddies. So it was somewhat of an uncomfortable situation for Pete when he was forced to give his friend advance notice of the paper's decision.

Editor Peter Barrecchi had already written an editorial endorsing the Republican ticket, when at the last moment a heated battle within the Corson family, with the Johnson contingent winning out, cancelled his piece. The disagreement had not been about preferring Johnson, but about not being able to support Barry Goldwater. The final editorial stated that though the paper proudly supported Mr. Miller, it was with great sadness that they could not support the entire ticket: "Just a heartbeat away from the president, we would prefer to have a man of the caliber and ability of Representative Miller.... We wish we could vote for him for vice president without supporting his running mate."[28] Though Dad professed to understand their dilemma, it was small consolation in light of the profound embarrassment caused him when the media trumpeted news of the Johnson endorsement nationwide.

A Saturday whistle-stop train tour through New York State—from Buffalo to Westchester County, a ten-stop, fifteen-hour day in all—was our last hurrah as a campaign family. My father was a fighter to the end, his voice as resonant and vigorous in Westchester as it had been in Buffalo, but by now I could tell that even his ever-buoyant optimism was fading. When a friend on the train insisted they were still going to get the 265 electoral votes they needed for victory, he just shook his head, smiled, and said, "I wish you were right, but all I'm regretting is that it's going to be as lopsided as it is."

The weather was wintry now and there were football games to compete with, but still my parents emerged, shivering, onto the train's platform at each stop, Mary and I huddled at their side, to assure somewhat sparse but hopeful and still wildly enthusiastic crowds that they were "headed for victory." It was a Herculean effort, but we would not disappoint those who had turned out and waited in the frigid temperatures, sometimes for more than an hour, just to get a glimpse of us and an autograph or two.

The final week that would bring a merciful end to the campaign would take Mom and Dad to twenty states throughout the South, Midwest, and Far West. I continued to blanket events in Massachusetts—"It seems as if Libby has Massachusetts pretty well covered," remarked Mom facetiously—and ended my campaigning days at a huge and energetic rally in Madison Square Garden, New York with Barry Goldwater Jr.

There were so many people who still wanted so much of us, so many events yet to attend and places to be where the votes were "crucial" we were told, and it was so excruciating to say no. We wanted to do it all, but time was running out and tough choices had to be made by the schedulers, fact separated from emotion in all the impassioned entreaties. Did they make the right choices? We could not know.

It had been impossible to imagine the end. "It was impossible to think of football and Halloween and all the normal pursuits of all the normal people who weren't obsessed with this incredible thing which spun and turned and twisted us through the life of America," wrote Bob Smalley rightly and most poetically."[29] But then the bustle of motorcades, receptions, press conferences, speeches, and tightly scheduled air hops was over, as suddenly as it had begun over three months ago.

The end was hard, inevitable, but hard. By that time, we knew in our minds that victory was all but impossible. But in our hearts—well, there had been all sorts of uplifting and encouraging letters in the end, with words like "it's turning the corner Bill, we can feel it," and "the tide is turning in our favor and victory seems closer each day." Charles Percy, running for governor of Illinois, wrote that he was "encouraged with the apparent upswing which began a few days ago." And always, there was the conspiratorial mention among believers of "the undercurrent" that no one was gauging. "I marveled at the candidate, always fresh, always neat, always able to do without the scotch or the martini, always crackling with humor," Smalley wrote. " 'Given one break, I think we could still win this thing,' he said to me. 'Don't you think?' "[30]

Oddly enough, one of our last stops, in Bartlesville, Oklahoma, had brought out perhaps one of the most delirious crowds we had yet seen. But I had not seen the worst of the increasingly bitter campaign. I had not been in North Philadelphia, where Dad spoke on a makeshift platform and "the Democrats had a sound truck driving around the perimeter of his crowd, trying somewhat effectively to drown him out. The crowd and the community were hostile at best, and it was the only time he pleaded with his audience, 'Please, America, listen to us. Listen to what Barry Goldwater and I are trying to say. Our way of life for you and your children is at stake...' "[31]

So I still hoped against hope that it might be close, or even an upset. In my youthful naiveté, I could not imagine that when voters went into the privacy of their voting booths they would not recognize that even though Lyndon Johnson had promised everything to everyone, he could never deliver.

On the other hand, he was a known quantity, the incumbent of only a year who many felt was entitled to an opportunity to prove his mettle, the sympathetic figure who had comforted a nation just a year earlier in its deepest sorrow, our second president in three years. Would the country countenance a third president in three years? My father, and Barry himself, had doubted it from the beginning. And Johnson had certainly succeeded, no question about it, in making of Barry Goldwater a frightening fringe figure who was mentally unstable and incompetent to govern.

The Niagaran whisked the whole Miller entourage back to the Buffalo airport the day before the election, where a cheering crowd of 300 greeted us as we disembarked. In a caravan of two dozen vehicles we made our way to the spacious home of our generous friend Ray Lee, in Lockport, back where it had all begun and where other longtime friends awaited.

Ray's home and yard had by now been transformed into a giant election headquarters. Auxiliary power generators had been brought in and a temporary transmitter set up to boost power for the television networks to beam interviews nationwide. Immense trucks with cranes clogged the street in front, slightly impeding the constant flow of cars that drove by to have a look. Hundreds of curious well-wishers, held back by police and sheriff's deputies, gawked at the spectacle from the perimeter, periodically shouting, "We want Bill!" A mammoth searchlight bathed it all. For a small town, it was a surreal circus.

The media, about 150 strong, were ensconced in the Lee's basement and a heated pine-paneled garage. Both had been elaborately appointed for their convenience and comfort, wired with the maze of cables necessary for thirty telephones and several Western Union telegraph and wire service teletype machines, all of which workmen had been installing for a full week. Drinks and food were abundantly provided for all who had made the "journey" with us.

Mother and Dad made the obligatory well-photographed visit to their polling station in Olcott the next day, to cast the most important ballot of their lives. As they entered the crowded hall, television cameras flicked on and flashbulbs from newspaper reporters' cameras bathed them in a glaring light. They were smiling cheerfully and confidently to the end, betraying no signs of weariness as they were badgered with the usual question: "Do you think you're going to win?" My father, honest man that he was and with his sense of humor still intact, replied presciently, "If Lyndon Johnson has his way, I'll be back here very shortly." And then he and his bride, votes cast, hit the golf course for some much needed relaxation.

Later, as the polls closed and the dire returns began rolling in, they both wandered down intermittently to the media's lair at the Lee's house to make sure the reporters had what they needed, and to lighten their own mood with the jocularity they could expect from their journalist friends. As Dad pulled a long sheet off the AP wire machine and perused it, one of them yelled, "You reading more and enjoying it less Bill?" The soon-to-be-defeated candidate broke into that old amused half-grin and chuckled, "Who's the guy with the sense of humor?"

It became obvious even before sunset on Election Day that the ticket was losing, and losing badly. My father wanted to concede sooner rather than later—he wasn't one for indecisively dragging things out. As the hours ticked by and he heard nothing from Barry on the upstairs bedroom phone dedicated solely to contact between the two men, he grew impatient. He lay stretched out on the bed watching the uniformly bleak television reports, with only Press Secretary Bob Smalley at his side, and finally he half rose and blurted: "Christ, I wish he would get it over with."

So finally, unwilling to continue the charade of hope, he told Bob: "Well, we can't wait any longer, get Barry on the phone." They reached the Senator's home in Arizona, only to discover that he had retired to bed at 11 p.m., without making the usual concession speech. After a brief discussion, it was decided that Dad would take the heat that night and be the first one to face the media. Barry did not actually formally concede until the next morning.

It was teeth-chatteringly cold at 1 a.m. when this man who had tried so hard for so long to be heard, now with an unmistakably haggard face and no coat or hat, stepped outside the front door of the Lee house to meet the equally exhausted but expectant press, promptly assembled—microphones, cameras, blinding lights jutting out of the night and dangling above our heads, pens and pads, all at the ready. It was a sober group, business-like and doing their job, but obviously feeling some measure of the pain and let-down that they understood the man they had followed for three arduous months was feeling at that moment. The man they had not wanted to like but had grown, most of them, to love and respect. And for all their usual crustiness, there was a gentleness to their questioning.

Mother stood at Dad's side, as always, struggling to maintain the requisite emotional control; Mary and I pressed in on his other side with those unmerciful, dangling bulbs lighting our tears for all the world to see. He would make no formal statement until his running mate had made his, but he all but conceded that defeat was certain. No, he did not think theirs was a futile effort; no, he was not bitter—the American people had spoken and he could accept that; no, he had no plans to continue in political life. "I did the best I know how and I have no regrets."

Then we edged our way out to the waiting crowd, many of whom had stood in the damp and chilly night for hours to shake the hometown boy's hand. As my father greeted most of them by name, a middle-aged woman with tears streaming down her face grasped his hand, saying over and over, "Next time Bill, next time." Finally, lights were extinguished, whirring cameras went silent, pads slid into pockets. Some embraces and handshakes, some heartfelt expressions of sympathy from his media pals, then the stampede to the garage to file stories. And a brief odyssey was over, as well as a long career.

At that point in time, the Republican loss in the election of 1964 ranked as one of the worst landslides in our history—only six states won, after, for Dad's part, traveling 80,000 miles and

visiting forty-three states. Only Alf Landon's loss to Franklin
Roosevelt in 1936 was worse—two states and 1.5% of the popular
vote. The landslide record has since been broken by George
McGovern and Walter Mondale—the Democratic presidential
candidates who lost to the Republicans in 1972 and 1984, both
garnering only one state. That was some consolation, but not
much—Bill Miller only lived to see the first of those debacles.

He and Goldwater had lost by a whopping 16,000,000 votes
to Lyndon Johnson and Hubert Humphrey—and yet they had
won 27,000,000 votes. That was nothing to sneeze at, as journalists
were prone to do at the time. Theirs was a "movement" more
than a candidacy, University of Virginia political analyst Larry
Sabato once explained in a speech, and "movements don't win
elections." A "movement" is comprised of people who feel passionately about something or someone, who feel they are not
being heard and want to send a message, who desperately want
to effect change. But there typically are not enough of them to
win, according to Sabato's theory. Yet this "movement," as history records, did go on to win in 1980, albeit with Ronald Reagan,
and some would argue that Reagan might not have won then had
it not been for the ground previously tilled by the Goldwater/
Miller ticket.

Sabato was right that probably almost every one of that
minority of 27,000,000 votes cast for the Goldwater/Miller ticket
in 1964 was a passionate one. And though there were plainly not
enough of them to win that year, those votes were, many of them,
from people who had never before been involved in politics, who
stayed involved, and who changed, for better or for worse, the
alignment and the center of power in the Republican Party for
decades to come. As Bill Brock, an enthusiastic thirty-three-year-
old neophyte congressman back in '64, wrote me years later:
"People came out of the woodwork to help ... out of a love for
both men and a respect for their integrity and their willingness to
state tough, but honest responses to questions on complex issues.
Neither ever ducked or wavered, and those of us in their cause
would have done anything for them."[32]

There were the usual postmortems after the dust of the campaign had settled, for my father could not know then what legacy
his and his running mate's toils would leave. He wondered if he
could have done more to heal and unify the Party—he had said

early on, "Since I have not been a supporter for any particular individual or faction, I think I can unify the Party and I predict this will be my role in the campaign."

But all who wrote him afterwards said no—the damage had been done in the bitter primaries prior to the convention, and with Senator Goldwater's vote against the 1964 Civil Rights Bill. As Gerald Ford reminded me, "Barry was the focal point of the ticket and no vice-presidential candidate could have made a difference." With the exception of Dick Nixon, Chuck Percy, Bill Scranton, and President Eisenhower, who campaigned for the ticket until he fell ill in mid-October, all the other powerhouses in the GOP stayed as far away from Goldwater as they could, fearing he would bring them down with him. This despite the fact that Dad himself campaigned enthusiastically for any and all Republican candidates wherever he traveled throughout the country.

Add to the above a booming economy, which traditionally re-elects incumbents, and Vietnam not yet the issue it would become only months after the election, there was just not enough reason for people to want a change, opined former Congressman Jack Kemp. Wrote Richard Nixon to my father after the election:

> *Having been a candidate for vice president on two occasions, I know how difficult that assignment is. You are always put in the position of defending your running mate and do not have the advantage of being able to change the strategy and tactics when you believe the situation demands it. You handled a most difficult assignment with great skill, loyalty, and courage. And the Miller family added luster and glamour to our cause wherever they appeared.*

Colorado Senator Peter Dominick added: "Bless you both for your courage, your dignity, and your faith in the American people." But that had not been enough to overcome the forces pulling against them.

American politics, arguably, is a game played between the two 35-yard lines, at least at the presidential level—anything beyond that is out of bounds. It must be played mainly in the middle of the field because the American people are frightened by and will reject anything they perceive to be extreme. Whether through his own fault or the fault of the media, Barry Goldwater got painted with the extremist label, and that sealed his and my father's fate. Image makers and handlers did not reign supreme then as they do today, nor was Barry a very malleable person. Reagan, on the other hand, scrambled to the middle after he had the nomination locked up, and he routinely quoted only two presidents: Franklin Roosevelt and Harry Truman.

"Public service and private misery are inseparably linked together," Thomas Jefferson once quite perceptively remarked to James Monroe. Lucian Warren, who had covered my father for the *Buffalo Courier Express* from the beginning of his career, echoed pretty much the same sentiment when he wrote: "Every man who gets to the top or near the top in public life has to take his lumps, for the game of politics in America is a fierce one, a kind of verbal jungle warfare. Bill Miller was no exception and the punishment inflicted upon him has been heavy, much of it unfair or distorted."

Still, despite the pain of those cruel distortions, the disappointment in the enormity of the loss, and the exhaustion, Dad, Mother, Mary, and I all agreed that the ride had been fun, that the experience had been worth it, that we had been lucky to have had it. We had seen more of this land than most people see in a lifetime, had made countless new friends, and had been warmed by their sincerity and their immense capacity to care about their country and its future. We felt humbled and indebted, and always would, for all they had done on our behalf. We were grateful for the chance to work our hearts out for something in which we believed, deeply, and for the richness that experience had brought to each of our lives. It had changed all of us in ways that we would only understand as the years passed and the campaign of '64 came to feel like it had been another life. Mostly, we were aware that the tumult and the shouting and the treasure trove of bittersweet memories of those three months, indelibly etched upon our psyches, would stay with us forever.

CHAPTER ELEVEN

SMALL TOWN BOY GOES HOME

The Niagaran departed Buffalo for Washington the day after the election for the last time—the last time we would drive straight onto a runway to board our waiting plane, the last time screaming sirens would escort us there, the last time flashbulbs would meet us. The camaraderie and joviality that had always marked this group of fellow travelers as unusual and forged them into a "family" resumed on board, almost as if it had not been rudely interrupted by the event that would end their daily rendezvous with each other.

The defeated vice-presidential candidate was almost jubilant, his pent-up battle tension at last released. One of the press' frequent antics over the past many weeks had been to write a speech for him to deliver over the plane's speaker at the end of a long day, parodying his official orations and noting the foibles and faux pas of various staff members. Several of the reporters had tried this exercise on previous candidates they had covered, Richard Nixon among them, with considerably less success—they discovered that a sense of self importance tended to inhibit a sense of humor.

Dad, by contrast, had always been a good sport about the ritual, never reticent about being the butt of humor. And in his final "speech," he even got in a few cracks of his own. "I sometimes think how nice it would be if Bob Gray (of AP) were running for public office and I could report estimates of *his* crowds," he intoned, half facetiously and half seriously about the reporter who had made note of the small empty portion of a nearly filled auditorium on a campaign stop. As his intimate, "you-had-to-be-there" audience howled with laughter, that familiar impish grin spread triumphantly across his smooth, oval face.

Now it was back to real life, the "fleeting narcotic euphoria," as I once heard political campaigning described, having quickly subsided with the stark realization that a mountainous backlog of work awaited me at college, the last days of the 88th Congress awaited the "lame duck" congressman, and Mother had to return to tending her toddlers. A political campaign suspends life in a way, and coming down off the "high" of a campaign, with its endless blur of faces, outstretched hands, and political cheers, is disorienting—one day you're there and the next day you're not. There is nothing gradual or gentle about the transition back to the routine of ordinary life, and the adjustments were difficult for all of us, each in a different way.

Most of the plans had already been made for my parents' return to Lockport—a law practice set up, a house bought the previous January. The vice-presidential campaign had been but an unexpected detour from their long-held intention to return to private life. But now there were friends and associates who were urging my father to reconsider his future.

It was a terrible "waste of talent" for him to leave public life now, they claimed, after all the expertise, experience, and prestige he had accrued. But the reality that his admirers failed to grasp is that since he had relinquished his congressional seat (Lyndon Johnson had run for the Senate and the vice-presidency simultaneously in 1960, but by 1964 that was no longer allowed), running again for Congress in two years would put him back on the lowest rung of seniority if he were elected. And in those days, seniority was everything. After a fourteen-year climb to the position of second ranking Republican on the Judiciary Committee, where he could wield considerable influence on important legislation, starting over had no appeal whatsoever to Dad at this point in his life.

There were others who reminded the erstwhile legislator that he could earn considerably more money in a law or lobbying firm in Washington, D.C. than he could in Buffalo, New York. That was indeed a serious consideration for him at age fifty with a "second family" to educate and little to show financially for his years in Congress. Ironically, the Millers had arrived in Washington with a 6 and a 3 year old and left fourteen years later with a 6 and a 3 year old. The fact was that a great many former congressmen did and still do stay on in the nation's capital after defeat or retirement, choosing to hover near the limelight and the center of power, too inured with it to leave it behind. They don't often "go back to Pocatello," as the saying goes.

But my father was too proud for that. "I could never see myself holding my hat in my hand, going to some freshman congressman begging for something," he declared emphatically. "It never appealed to me." The idea of lobbying after a campaign for the second highest office in the land just wasn't compatible with his sense of what was appropriate.

He also wasn't sure how easy it would be for him to build a lucrative law practice in Washington. The climate of the recent campaign had been bitter and ugly, and it was unclear how welcome the soundly vanquished Republican vice-presidential candidate would be in a city now controlled by a Democratic administration. Politics is often a game played for a price, and perhaps the absence of more gainful retirement breadwinning opportunities was the price Dad paid. In any case, he didn't feel he had the financial resources to wait and see what might come along. He needed an income immediately, and his Buffalo law firm was waiting.

Bill Miller had been somewhat of an anomaly in politics, having never planned a long career there nor plotted each step along his rise to the top. While not without ambition, his innate modesty undoubtedly made it relatively easy in the end to leave all the trappings of political life and power behind. Added to that was my parents' real desire to spend the rest of their days with their hometown friends who were without the pretensions of Washington political types. They had never really caught "Potomac fever."

The most significant contribution of my father's political career was yet to unfold and, amazingly, it is known to only a handful of people. It could be said that at the eleventh hour, it was he who saved the Party he had loved and served for so long from breaking asunder. Party unity was the very thing he had worked his heart out for as national chairman and as a vice-presidential candidate, and it had eluded him. Keeping the Republican Party with all its factions united and strong enough "to fight another day," as he would so often put it, had always been his primary goal, for he believed passionately that a strong two-party system was the best and most stable form of democracy.

So his first post-election order of business, after getting his family resettled, was to join with his former running mate and Republican National Chairman Dean Burch, away from the judgmental glare of the media, to analyze and reassess the election returns and to prepare for what was threatening to become a titanic battle for future control of the GOP. Rumblings of outrage were already emanating from all corners of the country about the disastrous defeat the conservative wing had wrought for the Party, its congressional and gubernatorial ranks having been seriously thinned as candidates, both new and incumbent, fell with the top of the ticket. The outrage was likely to soon become a groundswell for change. How would it be handled by those who had led the Party into this dire situation, and particularly by the man who was now its "titular" head, Barry Goldwater? Some hard decisions had to be made about that. Rest was also needed at this point for the haggard threesome, so Jamaica was the chosen site for their meeting.

What was playing out in this bitter post-election fall and winter was, of course, a replay of the pre-convention struggle between conservatives and liberals. Only this time the battle focused not on a presidential candidate but on the National Committee and its chairmanship, as the Party's only ongoing leadership mechanisms. They were now controlled by the conservatives and Burch was Goldwater's handpicked successor to my father. Could or should Burch stay on to lead a clearly dispirited and contentious party, or should the whole committee be purged as moderates and liberals were demanding? The air was rife with speculation that conservatives might break away to form a third party if they were ousted from control of the Republican Party, so long and hard had they fought to secure their position.

There was, in fact, enough blame to go around for everyone in this mess: liberals blamed conservatives for leading the Grand Old Party to inevitable disaster; conservatives blamed liberals for deserting the ticket and thereby causing defeat. Meanwhile, Dean Burch had no intention of stepping down, nor did his mentor, Senator Goldwater, intend for him to do so. Both dug their heels in on that. Even Dad at this point was suggesting that Burch should be kept on for at least a year: "In the meantime, if he shows bias against the liberal wing of our party or demonstrates in other ways that he is not a good chairman, that would be the time to let him go. But he should be given a chance to prove that he will work out well as a political technician during this interim period."

Ironically, the man leading the drive against Dean Burch was Governor Robert Smylie of Idaho—the very man my father had pushed for chair of the new Republican Governors' Conference that he had launched during his tenure as national chairman in an effort to broaden the base of party leadership. But now old alliances were falling away in an atmosphere of vengeance, and the two men found themselves working at odds with each other.

It would all come down to the votes of the 125 national committeemen and women, who were scheduled to meet January 22-23 in Chicago. Both sides began lobbying them heavily. Smylie's forces had the problem of finding an acceptable alternative to Dean Burch should they succeed in forcing him out. Ray Bliss, the successful Ohio state chairman who had been briefly considered when Bill Miller won the RNC chairmanship three years earlier, began to emerge as a neutral possibility. Publicly, Bliss made it known that he wanted no part of the job over the opposition of the Goldwater forces, but Dad knew otherwise. He was certain that the Ohioan hungered for it.

The decision in Jamaica was to divide up the membership of the National Committee three ways and to contact them all by phone. The trio's argument in favor of keeping Burch would be that he was in fact a most competent, articulate, and politically astute leader, and not intensely ideological, all of which was true and would have no doubt been appreciated in a less strident time. As the day grew near for the Chicago meeting, it appeared that Dean might survive, but by only a slim margin.

And then something happened that changed the course of events. My father's campaign press secretary, Bob Smalley, got a tip-off when Dean Burch said to him one night in a chance meeting: "What's the matter with Miller?" When asked what he meant, Dean reported that Dad was beginning to hold back on the telephone calls, seemingly reluctant to proceed.

Bob wrote an eyewitness account of what subsequently occurred and I use his account verbatim, with his permission, for it would serve no purpose to paraphrase it:

On Friday, the 8th of January, I had a call to come to Senator Goldwater's apartment in Washington at nine o'clock the next morning. It was raining when I arrived in the parking lot, where I met Bill Miller leaving his car, and he seemed his old jaunty self, full of disrespectful wisecracks as we made our way in.

Burch was there, in addition to the senator, and so was Goldwater's longtime political aide, Tony Smith. Five of us. Burch quickly told Tony and me what had happened to bring us together. On Thursday night at a meeting in the same room, attended only by the three principals in the drama—Goldwater, Miller, and Burch—the Republican Party had been saved from suicide.

Miller had launched a fervent conversation with his old friend and running mate about the future of the Party and the country. He pleaded two key points:

1. Burch could win his first test, perhaps even a second, but as long as the leadership battle was on he would have to spend full time plotting his own survival against the next assault.

2. In the meantime, the Party's business of recovering to fight another day would come to a halt, contributions would dry up, and the staff would be paralyzed pending the outcome.

Goldwater, no less a fervent Republican partisan than Miller, agreed, saying he was amenable to any reasonable move to spare the Party from further destruction, so long as those who had stayed with it, and with him, were not punished for doing so. But as a presidential loser and head of the Party, he also was deeply concerned with what kind of Republican Party survived. In the face of Johnson's tremendous new majorities in the House and Senate, which would give him virtually everything he wanted, "including one helluva lot you and I don't believe in," Goldwater said he felt the Republican Party had to offer a distinct contrast if its survival was to have practical political value.

Miller agreed, precisely. "But Barry," he said, "this party isn't going to live to fight for what we believe in—it's not going to be able to do anything in 1966, let alone '68—if it concentrates for six months or a year on an internal fight over who's going to control it. Warming to his subject, he went on: "I've got small kids, so does Dean, and you've got grandchildren. We all care about what kind of country we leave them. That's why what's at stake here is bigger than who's chairman of the Republican National Committee."

"The Republican Party is the last hope we've got in this country to stop what you and I don't like. It's the only party there is with any kind of chance to bring about what we believe in, what we want to give to our kids. It's the only thing we have to keep a two-party system alive. We can destroy it fighting over the carcass, or we can give it a chance. For

our kids. You are the only man now, Barry," Bill Miller pleaded, "who can save the Party from suicide." Barry Goldwater agreed to accept Ray Bliss as successor to Dean Burch.

The decision having been made, the task at hand that Saturday morning, just eight days before the scheduled National Committee meeting, was to work out the mechanics of a transfer of power from Burch to Bliss. In this, Miller, with his consummate political skill, was completely in command. First, he said, Bliss could not take over before April. There must be no appearance of a rout, retreat, or surrender; instead, there must be time for an orderly transfer, time for Dean to complete work he had begun, and to resuscitate himself personally. Second, the four principals—Goldwater, Burch, Blis,s and Miller—should get out of Washington with its Inauguration atmosphere to make their announcement of the change elsewhere. Goldwater's mountainside house outside Phoenix was agreed upon as the place, and the following Tuesday as the day.

Next, Miller called Bliss and told him bluntly he would be the next chairman of the Republican National Committee, and would become so with the full concurrence of both the senator and Dean Burch. He told Bliss to make travel arrangements to arrive in Phoenix next Monday evening, and to keep his plans absolutely secret. He could travel with one person, no more, who knew the destination and the reason for the trip. Goldwater would go home over the weekend, and Miller, Burch, and I would travel together from Washington Monday afternoon. Bill then gave me the phone and had me dictate to Bliss a short statement I had just drafted which was to be released out of Columbus after he left, only if there was inquiry, to cover his tracks without revealing his whereabouts.

Our travel plans were made in the same secrecy, and on Monday we were driven to Baltimore and directly onto the field to board a TWA flight for Phoenix. Bliss and an aide were on hand as we arrived in the splendid living room of the Goldwater home. The statements I had prepared were read and edited, then dittoed in the Goldwater kitchen. Early the next morning, the senator's secretary started calling the press, the wires, and the networks to inform them that we were holding a press conference at 11 o'clock. You could hear jaws dropping at the other end of the phone when we invited them to the Senator's home to meet with Goldwater, Miller, Burch, and Bliss. They came by the score. Under the bright Arizona sun, Senator Goldwater officially announced that Dean Burch would retire as chairman in the interest of party unity, and that

Ray Bliss had generously agreed to succeed him. The others then read their statements and took questions.

The story burst into the lead on all three major networks and in the media all over the country. Most Republicans, on both sides of the fight, with the exception of some arch conservatives, reacted with relief. The Party had been spared an internecine death and now would fight another day. Throughout both political parties there was a widespread sense that the two-party system also had survived; the dangers of either fragmentation or single-party domination had been avoided.

On the trip back from Phoenix, Bill Miller and I parted in Chicago for different airplanes. He looked me in the eye, laughed, didn't say anything, then turned and disappeared quickly into the crowd.

My father never spoke of this historic contribution to his party to anyone as far as I know. I can never remember him touting his own accomplishments, and this was no exception. But according to the *Los Angeles Times*, "Some Republican insiders attributed the sudden change of heart on the part of Burch and Goldwater to the influence of William E. Miller...." [1]

The truth was that as a compassionate human being, he had wished to avoid personal humiliation for Dean Burch, as well as an embarrassing repudiation in Chicago of his former running mate. But above all else, Dad held a lifelong aversion to splinter parties, which began with learning firsthand about the weaknesses they had brought to Europe, and especially Germany, both before and after the war.

The American two-party system was almost sacred to him, for he believed that, unlike the parliamentary system that our forefathers had shunned, it precluded special interest minority parties from acting as kingmakers. And he knew well that third parties, even those that raise important issues, eventually become irrelevant spoilers because of our winner-take-all system. Thanks to his efforts, and the acquiescence of Goldwater and Burch to his plea, the Republican Party did regain strength by remaining a coalition, albeit an uneasy one, and thereby went on to recoup many of its congressional losses in 1966 and win the presidency in 1968.

Once settled in his Buffalo law practice and his newly renovated home in Lockport on gracious, tree-lined Willow Street, my father relished the newfound peace in his life and the second chance at fatherhood—being "the oldest guy at little league baseball games," as he loved to say. Yet in some ways it was not easy to come home. "Having gone through a national campaign is one thing I don't think you ever get over," he once remarked. "You are changed forever. For ten solid weeks you're up in the morning for breakfast in Alabama and lunch in Los Angeles." And despite a certain relief, a part of him missed that challenge, and the feeling that he could contribute where he had so much talent and knowledge.

He had burned out relatively young, for though his congressional career was short by the standards of those who remain in Congress for thirty plus years, it was intense, with the final four years keeping him in the spotlight and on the road for two and three weeks at a time, covering all fifty states. That was a grind for a man who had a congressional seat and a family to tend to as well. His life had been a meteoric rise from one success to another, making an impact at each stage, but the unremitting pressures of each successive job that he internalized so completely took a physical and emotional toll.

In addition, I am certain there lurked some regrets in his mind, not because he hadn't done the best job he could but because he felt within himself that he would have made a good vice president, even a good president. The jobs did not intimidate him. He had loved politics—the combat, the debate, the issues, the strategizing, putting it all together. And he had an understated but very real pride in being a politician.

Dad had been fortunate to serve in Congress at a time when there was a collegiality that no longer exists, when you respected your adversaries and had good friends on both sides of the aisle, when there was no bitterness over differences of opinion and philosophy. It was before show business and politics had become fused, before the political "industry" with its incessant polls and all-knowing consultants had taken over. He missed it all in a way, even though I suspect he sensed even then that it was beginning to change. Wrapped up as I was in my own life at the time, I realize now that I was largely uncomprehending of what Dad was feeling during those difficult early years of readjustment to private life. Never one to share his disappointments or his concerns, he neither complained nor blamed, and his innate cheerfulness cloaked his inner sadness for all but my mother.

Despite his determination to leave the public spotlight, he was, predictably, besieged with requests to speak—to assorted Republican meetings and fundraising dinners, at campaign functions for candidates around the country, and to his most favorite crowd, the colleges. "It's tremendously important to reach the young people," he would always say, and he relished every opportunity to meet and talk with them about politics and to inspire them to serve. His only stipulation was that he would limit his engagements on the lecture circuit to two a month.

And so the once embattled congressman and vice-presidential candidate settled into a comparatively uneventful routine of daily trips from Lockport to work in Buffalo, bank board meetings, golf outings, little league baseball and football games, and much relished card games with his buddies at the Tuscarora Club at the end of a day. There were occasional visits to Washington on law business where he would usually reunite with his old running mate for a game of golf. Once invited to join famed bridge champion Charles Goren for dinner and a night of bridge, he gladly accepted but added: "If I can't make it, Charlie, I'll send my check by messenger." Wherever he roamed, he was always tickled by the stares he attracted, of recognition or near recognition—the quizzical look of those who knew he looked familiar but were uncertain "if they had seen me on *Gunsmoke* or if I was their neighborhood mailman," as he liked to describe the occurrences with his inimitable self-deprecating humor.

Interspersed with my father's regular routine were the hilarious reunions of *The Niagaran* crew, faithfully, once a year. The tenth anniversary gathering of all the political advisors, staff, reporters (some as illustrious as Roger Mudd and Ray Scherer), and even the airline pilots and stewardesses—all the political gypsies who had formed a curious sort of camaraderie during those shared days on the road that had taken them temporarily away from their usual relationships—was chronicled by Warren Weaver of the *New York Times*, himself a bona fide member of the group.

His article was headlined: "After 10 Years, a Forgotten Politician Looks Back on a Forgotten Campaign":

Political campaigns, which bring a mixed bag of strangers close together for a short but intense period, sometimes produce

an annual reunion or two in succeeding years. But, as far as
anyone could tell, a 10th anniversary celebration by as large a
group of former camp followers was unprecedented. The Miller
campaign was different. It was small, with most Republican
attention focused on the outspoken Barry Goldwater. It was
informal, the last time that Vice-Presidential candidates oper-
ated outside the tight security blanket of the Secret Service. It
was highly personal, with reporters playing bridge with the
candidate....[2]

My father, basking in the genuine fondness of his erstwhile
followers, his jet black hair, at sixty, only imperceptibly streaked
with gray, his slight physique still trim and jaunty and sporting
natty attire, reminisced about fond and crazy memories, like
the night the plane landed at Kearney, Nebraska, in a modified
cornfield, instead of Grand Island where a large and expectant
crowd awaited.

One of the few forays he made into the national political arena
in these years was during the race for the Republican presidential
nomination in 1968. He consented to be a delegate to the Party's
convention in Miami that summer, solidly committed to his
governor, Nelson Rockefeller, whose nomination he seconded.
He then traveled the country speaking on his behalf. In an appearance on the Merv Griffin Show, he even defended Rocky's
controversial state sales tax since it funded the state's excellent
educational facilities—a bit of an aberration, since Bill Miller
was generally not known for supporting tax increases, but also
another indication of his flexibility. Meanwhile, Richard Nixon
had achieved one of the more miraculous comebacks in political
memory and he too sought the nomination and a second chance
at the presidency.

Once again, Rockefeller's late and reluctant entry into the race
proved to be his undoing, but he remained grateful to Dad for his
support: "If ever a man had a secret, or not so secret, weapon,
I did—in you. I truly think that you won more friends for me
than any effort of my own. You are a magnificent campaigner,
a real politician in the best sense of the word, and a wonderful
friend."[3] Always to be counted upon for a humorous take on
serious matters, my father was reported as telling a television
commentator, when the victorious Nixon chose the relatively un-

known Maryland Governor Spiro Agnew as his vice-presidential running mate: "That's the funniest thing that's happened since they nominated me."

He was often asked how he, a moderate conservative, could support a liberal like Nelson Rockefeller, for not only had he supported Rocky in 1968, but he had worked for him in his previous gubernatorial race of 1966. I can remember his frequent visits to New York City back then to attend campaign strategy sessions as I worked at my first post-college job at Time Inc. The most memorable of his visits was on the night of the famous blackout. After feeling my way down thirty floors of the Time/Life building near Rockefeller Center, I arrived breathless for our previously arranged "date" at Toots Shor—not even the unnerving blackness of empty Manhattan streets could keep me from a special evening with my father, *and* a free meal I should admit—and his friend Toots managed to cook for us and for a few other brave patrons a sumptuous meal by candlelight.

Dad's response to the queries about his seeming political inconsistency revealed much about his own philosophy of politics, which was more about right and wrong than about right and left, and was driven more by his sharp problem-solving mind and keen understanding of issues than by pure ideology. It was the same response he would give when asked in 1974 if he approved of President Gerald Ford's choice of Rockefeller to be his vice president, in the wake of Nixon's resignation over Watergate. And it explained why he and Rockefeller, despite their apparent philosophical differences, had bonded politically and shared a warm friendship over the years.

Despite Senator Goldwater's vigorous opposition to the Rockefeller nomination on the grounds that the New York governor's liberal image would be unpopular with Republicans, my father begged to differ with his friend and former colleague: "Myself, I've never been wedded to the title conservative. In fourteen years in Congress, I found myself in odd company on odd days on odd issues. To be governor of a state like New York, you have to be realistic—and that's just what Rockefeller is. He's not a boy scout. He's a practical man—a problem-solver—who looks at things as they are." And he proceeded to list all the Governor's qualifications, both domestic and international, for his prospective new job.

When accusations are leveled against politicians for "flip-flopping" on issues, I recall Dad's openness to new considerations and how, though he held a core philosophy of government that guided him, his stands on some individual issues evolved over time. Is such adaptability thoughtful and intelligent growth or spineless and unprincipled vacillation, and should it be an asset or a detriment to a political career?

The answers to those questions are ultimately decided by the voters, a conglomerate of disparate people free to make their own judgments. But unfortunately, many of them are not aware that a vote against a particular bill does not always mean a legislator is against the main purpose of that bill. It may just be that he or she is against all the extras, the "pork," that gets tacked on, or against a certain section that they feel subverts the original intent. Such was the case with my father's last minute opposition to the ill-fated 1956 Civil Rights Bill when he was unsuccessful in obtaining a trial by jury amendment. Though an ardent supporter of civil rights, he was determined that new laws should be constitutionally sound and fair.

All in all, there is no doubt that Bill Miller's brand of "compassionate conservatism," before there was such a term, and his disdain for political labels differed markedly from the rigidity of some in the right wing of today's Republican Party. Many of them might be dismayed to learn that he even once said in an interview: "I'm not one who believes that my party has all the answers to all our problems."

Despite the passage of years and his insistence that he was just "a country lawyer," the press, remembering Dad's political savvy and candid insights, continued to seek him out for an occasional interview. It might be on the length of political campaigns—"They are too arduous, too expensive, and too boring for the people.... In view of the fast air travel now available and the wide exposure given by television, four weeks is sufficient for a campaign." Today's prospective presidential nominees might wholeheartedly agree with him on that, as their nine or ten month campaigns struggle for exposure while dreading overexposure.

Or it might be on young people—"The more we can get young people of character and integrity into politics, the better political parties we will have." Regardless of the personal hardships he intimately knew to be involved in public service, he always passionately preached the importance of political involvement and education, especially to youth: "The extent to which the decisions of government reflect your aspirations, your hopes, your ideals will depend exactly on the extent to which you participate in the election processes of America."

In 1970, my father took on one last public service job when he was named by Governor Rockefeller to chair the Niagara Frontier Transportation Authority. For the next four years he used his keen knowledge of the legislative and bureaucratic processes to oversee and make improvements in the marine terminal at the Port of Buffalo and at the Buffalo and Niagara Falls International Airports, while pushing for a regional airport for the area and launching plans for a rapid transit system in Buffalo.

When a national furor erupted in 1971 over the leak to a *New York Times* reporter of a secret Pentagon study of decision-making on the Vietnam War, including Lyndon Johnson's plans to escalate the war while advocating a peace posture on the campaign trail in 1964, it threw the one-time Republican VP candidate's seven-year-old campaign back on the front pages with a vengeance—and reporters back on his doorstep. In an exhaustive interview with the *Buffalo Evening News* about the expose that had come to be called "The Pentagon Papers," he revealed that he had actually been apprised midway through the campaign of the Johnson escalation plans by Goldwater, who himself had been briefed on the plans by friends in the Johnson administration who felt they were doing a patriotic duty.[4]

So why did the GOP team keep this bombshell under wraps? "We had no documentation to prove our assertions ... and I don't think anything we would have said would have changed their plans," said Dad. In fact, he rather doubted that he or Barry would have been believed, so successfully had the Democrats painted their opponents as warmongers who were likely to precipitate a nuclear holocaust in the Far East. In a rare venting of pique with the press, he blamed them for distorting Goldwater's Vietnam position and losing him millions of votes. But in discussing the war with *The News* reporter, feet propped up on an open drawer of his office desk, he spoke most strongly about President Johnson's decisions, and his hypocrisy.

"Johnson had these plans (to escalate) during the campaign when he was telling people in Indiana at a political rally that he was going to let Asian boys fight Asian wars and no American boys were going there," he asserted with just a hint of bitterness in his still resonant voice. And what's more, he added, Johnson did it in the wrong way. "He escalated it by constant bombings, 90 percent of which I think were a waste of money ... and they never did anything to the Port of Haiphong or cut off the Ho Chi Minh Trail or the sanctuaries in Cambodia and Laos." We never showed the North Vietnamese and the Russians that we meant business, that we intended to win the war, claimed my father. And he predicted that at some point he and Goldwater, if the South Vietnamese continued to lack the will to defend themselves, would have decided that "it was the wrong war in the wrong place at the wrong time and we would have brought everybody home."

Summing up in retrospect the 1964 campaign, he mused, with obvious sorrow, that "it was a campaign marked by distortion, hypocrisy, and downright dishonesty. If the people of the country don't have full respect for the intellectual integrity and honesty of public officials and those who wage campaigns for public office, then you threaten the fabric that keeps the country together. I think therefore the campaign was probably rather tragic in its results. I think history will probably show that."

At the end of the interview, Dad added that he did not condone stealing classified government documents and that whoever was responsible ought to be prosecuted. This despite the fact that the belated uncovering of "The Pentagon Papers" had, in a way, vindicated the Goldwater/Miller team on the issue they were loathe to exploit in the fall of 1964 and that was arguably the nemesis of their campaign—the war in Vietnam and how, or whether, to conduct it.[5]

And then came the Watergate break-in, and the former Republican national chairman was coaxed out yet again from political hibernation to offer his insights on what on earth the Nixon operatives had in mind when they went blundering into the Democratic National Committee offices in Washington's Watergate Hotel complex in the wee hours of the morning on June 17, 1972. He ascribed the clumsy burglary to a combination of ideological zeal and extreme paranoia over the upcoming election, in which it appeared Nixon would be pitted against the lion of the liberal left, George McGovern.

Despite the fact that most of the world knew that McGovern would be one of the most unelectable candidates in American history, Nixon's recent electoral track record had not been impressive. As my father bluntly pointed out, "He had started out as the favorite in 1960 and lost narrowly to Kennedy. He was defeated for governor of California in 1962 and started out as a heavy favorite against Humphrey in 1968 and nearly lost"—hence the ill-fated effort of the administration's "dirty tricks" squad to ferret out any disagreeable plans the opposition might have this time around to hasten their leader's demise.

In a television appearance on the topic, he made the unorthodox proposal that a special prosecutor for the Watergate case be chosen by the Democratic majority in Congress. Only in that way, he offered, could the poisonous air be completely cleared, since almost everyone even remotely associated with the Nixon administration was tainted. He also suggested early on that if the president was shown to have been involved in any way, he should be impeached. Strong words about a former colleague and friend, but strong also had been the affront to the principles of fair play and honesty in politics that were so sacred to Dad.

He reportedly "exhibited a professional's disdain for the thick-fingered Watergate antics, repeatedly drawing a distinction between such 'young, arrogant, and inexperienced' Watergate figures as former White House counsel John Dean [who had by then resigned] and such time-toughened organizational stalwarts as former GOP National Chairmen Ray Bliss and Senator Bob Dole. He even refused to describe such figures as Dean as 'politicians.' "[6] The real politicians, he emphasized, would not have gotten ensnared in anything as ludicrous as Watergate. The break-in, he seemed to be saying, aside from its criminality, was an intolerable affront to political professionalism and judgment.

Congressman Miller, on the other hand, as this Buffalo reporter noted, had been throughout his career "an adaptable professional who seldom, if ever, went on an ideological binge at the expense of his party organization." He called my father "a textbook example of adaptability," in tune with his conservative running mate in 1964 but three years later able to endorse the liberal Nelson Rockefeller for the Republican presidential nomination, because he believed him more electable than the twice-defeated Nixon. "Despite his toughness and bite," Ray

Herman concluded, "one can't envision Bill Miller breaking into a building for some dreamy ideal."[7]

There seemed to be no end of topics in these tumultuous days of the early '70s on which his opinions were sought. Events were moving quickly—Nixon's direct involvement in the Watergate affair was becoming clearer, his impeachment appeared imminent, his Vice President Spiro Agnew was forced to resign over income tax evasion and revelations of accepting bribes and kickbacks, and House Minority Leader Gerald Ford was chosen to replace him. And then in August of 1974, the unimaginable happened—Richard Nixon resigned the presidency, elevating Ford to the highest office in the land.

Jibes on Ford's intelligence began at once, with constant repetition by the media of Lyndon Johnson's offhand remark that the former Republican congressional leader "had played too many football games without a helmet." But one journalist who was hesitant to put the "dummy" tag on anyone who had worked his way through Yale Law School knew where he could go for the real scoop on the new president. My father had arrived in Congress two years after Jerry Ford and they were not only colleagues but good friends, as were Mom and Betty Ford.

"He's the real All-American boy and honest as can be," Dad told Bob Curran of the *Buffalo Evening News*. "When I was Republican National Chairman in '62 and was invited to come out and help in his campaign, he was so worried about the circumstances. He didn't want any part of private plane offers. So I came by commercial plane. The National Committee picked up my tab and he paid his own fare. That made an impression on me," remembered my father, "as some of the other people asking for help didn't concern themselves with such matters. I would be very surprised to hear that he has any assets other than those that are in the congressional pension and retirement system. Or that he has made one dollar on the outside since he arrived in Washington in 1949."[8]

So much for Ford's honesty. Still, Curran wanted an answer to the big question: What about the LBJ knock on his intelligence? "That was made after Ford fought Johnson's defense budget. Ford is a fiscal conservative," explained Dad. "I'd never call him one of the most brilliant men I met in Washington. He might not get the answers right away, as some others do, but he always gets the answers in the end. When he got up in the House to explain an appropriations bill, all the answers were there. And in those days he was working with a small staff. Now he'll have an enormous staff. Right now he is exactly what the American people need," concluded my father. And for good measure he added, "I know that talk about Jerry being a 'square' is going to make some people think he's a stuffed shirt. Well, he's got a good sense of humor and is fine company."[9]

In 1974, the event occurred that definitively robbed Bill Miller of his heretofore purposefully cultivated obscurity—the thing he should have done *before* he ran for vice president, as he so often joked afterwards, for it ironically left him more famous and recognizable than he had been as a national candidate ten years earlier. He received a call one day in his Buffalo law office from Daisy Sinclair of Oglivy & Mather advertising agency in New York. She had been given what she considered the highly embarrassing job of recruiting a former vice-presidential nominee to do a breakout new television ad for American Express. Remember that this was well before former Senator and presidential candidate Bob Dole had what some viewed as the astonishing temerity to make a TV ad for Viagra. In those days, it was unheard of for politicians to make commercials for anything but themselves.

So Daisy was praying that she would get a secretary on the phone when none other than Dad himself answered her call. Her tentative voice nervously rising an octave and fully expecting "no" for an answer, she proceeded to explain her request and her hope that she was not insulting him by asking. To her overwhelming relief, my father, who at first thought it might be a friend pulling his leg, just laughed and laughed and exclaimed, "I was wondering when you guys would get around to me!"

A few years earlier, Oglivy and Mather had started a "real people" ad campaign for American Express that was fairly successful but that they eventually felt lacked the "prestige" that was vital to the marketing of the upscale card. In an effort to bump it up a notch, they came up with a new idea. As Executive Creative Director William Taylor explained it: "Get someone half-famous, someone whose face was well-known but whose name wasn't, and make a game out of it. Get this person to admit the whole world didn't know who he was and that, despite his extraordinary success, he often needed the American Express card to get recognition. It would be fun and involving, and the product—our card—was hero."

But the theory about exactly what type of personalities should be used to make these ads would evolve. The first place they looked was among the dozens of television and movie actors who are seen often but whose names aren't usually remembered. Then the client, American Express, asked a sensible question: Do we want a campaign that locks us into obscure Hollywood character actors? The answer was no. So the creative people began expanding the concept. What about a person whose *name* was famous but whose face wasn't, or someone whose accomplishments were well-known but not the name, or whose voice was known but not the face? So they tried an astronaut who had walked on the moon, Miss America 1974, and Mel Blanc, the voice of Bugs Bunny.

"The campaign was rolling but still ahead was the turning point," explained Bill Taylor. "Our campaign survived, thanks to a copywriter named Pieter Verbeck who walked into my office one day and said: 'Why don't you try to get William Miller?' He had been very much in the public eye for a short, intense period and then faded into oblivion, the perfect example of whatever-happened-to," Taylor continued with animation revived by the memory of their "coup." "The William Miller spot quickly became our star commercial and I think it still ranks as one of the most memorable of the series." A subsequent ad with another politician, retired Senator Sam Ervin who had recently chaired the tumultuous Watergate investigation committee but called himself "a little ol' country lawyer from North Carolina," ranked up there close to the Miller ad in popularity.

While my father thought making the commercial might be fun, he did first take the precaution of calling Barry Goldwater and offering to forget the whole thing if his erstwhile running mate thought it in poor taste. "Barry told me, 'Christ, tell 'em *I'm* available,'" he reported. So with that blessing, off he went on a new adventure.

The thirty-second spot required a one-day shoot in New York City on a specially designed and built stage that was a facsimile of an upscale restaurant, for which the "star" would be paid $15,000 for the year his commercial aired. Dad arrived the day before his shoot, settled into the hotel room Oglivy and Mather had secured for him, and got briefed on the following day's schedule. His visitor from the ad agency gave him stern instructions to wash his hair in the morning—despite his protest that he always does it at night so it is less unruly—and then she took a look at the outfit he planned to wear. With ill-concealed horror at his conservative narrow tie and unfashionable shirt, she whisked him off to Saks Fifth Avenue to purchase replacements. "As long as they were paying me, I didn't mind wearing their clothes," he later remarked with amusement.

"Do you know me? I ran for vice president of the United States in 1964, so I shouldn't have trouble charging a meal, should I? Well, I do. That's why I carry an American Express card. I use it at restaurants, stores, airlines, and hotels all over the world. In Tokyo and Paris ... and in upstate New York. Why with this, they treat me as if I'd won. The American Express card ... don't leave home without it"..., said the man with the tantalizingly familiar face. Then if you hadn't yet figured out who he was, the camera zoomed in on a computer clacking out his name on the Amex credit card he was holding.

With newly washed hair popping up at odd angles as he had predicted, my father was a bit nervous as his maiden day in the advertising world began. This was a form of communication he was not entirely accustomed to, and he was amazed at the number of takes it took to hit the thirty seconds of dialogue on the nose—an entire day's worth, to be exact. Even for a man of concise words, such precision was not easy. "Thank God for his sense of humor and willingness to laugh at himself," recalls the director Mark Ross, who periodically patted his subject's hair down and calmed him so that his mischievous, cocked smile appeared naturally on cue.

The Miller spot ran throughout 1975 and created so much buzz that Amex decided to extend its run into the following year. They brought it back yet again in the election year of 1980 and in a 1995 network retrospective on the top fifty ads of the century. The whole star-studded "Do you know me?" campaign ran until 1979 with about eighty ads in all and was one of the most effective campaigns ever, causing applications for the American Express card to skyrocket.

For Dad's part, he complained that the commercial was so successful that he lost both his obscurity and his television contract predicated on that obscurity—"I'm now known by everyone, so American Express canceled my contract. In fact, I think I'd advise anybody to make a commercial first, then run for vice president," he would say, only half in jest. He became so well-known nationally that much of his mail began to arrive with the simple address of "Lockport" or "Olcott." Indeed, his rebirth of fame as the quintessential anonymity-plus-outstanding credentials subject led to a series of speeches, interviews, and TV appearances that he quite enjoyed.

One of the most memorable was his speech before the prestigious Washington Press Club in 1976, at a 1,000 person banquet populated by legislators, assorted presidential contenders, and the high and mighty of the capital's press world—a tough and critical audience. His was reportedly "a dinner-stopping speech that roused a lethargic audience to a standing ovation," according to the *Washington Star*,[10] as he pointed out that people running for vice president don't always end up the same way.

"I lost by sixteen million votes and wasn't invited out for six years. Sargent Shriver lost by twenty million [when paired with George McGovern in 1972] and now he's running for president. Nelson Rockefeller got no votes but the job," my father declared amidst uproarious laughter, "and Spiro Agnew won by twenty million votes [in 1972] but now I can practice law and he can't. But he's making money and I'm not." And then he told the august group with mock seriousness: "I couldn't have reached this distinguished plateau of obscurity but for the full cooperation of the press." As one reporter summed up the evening: "Bill Miller told the truth and the truth can be very funny, not to mention ironic."

In January 1975, a gala Washington social event interrupted my parents' usual low-key schedule. It was "The Tenth Anniversary of the Non-Inauguration of the Goldwater/Miller Ticket," as the event was formally billed on the engraved invitations. President Gerald Ford and First Lady Betty were among the nearly 300 guests—mostly old staffers and supporters who journeyed from all parts of the country, sporting their old campaign buttons, "a select band of survivors" as they were aptly called.

The group assembled at the Mayflower Hotel to drink and dine and to engage in some reunion hugging and bussing, some nostalgic remembering, and some good old-fashioned roasting. By this time, the hard edge of their conservative grief had abated and aversion to the late Lyndon Johnson mellowed, though one erstwhile warrior was overheard to remark, "Lyndon Johnson was a rotten man." The jokes and conversations were occasionally peppered with feisty one-liners like "we fought a good fight," "we told you so," and "we were right" though "it wasn't our year," but mostly, joviality reigned.

My father, expansive at this auspicious celebration of his "non-inauguration," was hyperbolic in his praise of his former running mate: "He was right then and he's right now," he said, "and tonight, ten years later, I'm more proud than ever that I was on his ticket." In return, Goldwater admitted: "It took great courage to accept the Republican vice-presidential nomination in '64, to live one heartbeat away from political oblivion." And Barry went on to praise his partner and declare that he would most assuredly choose him again.

Now you might say that much ado was being made about little at this event, considering that these people had lost their fight in such a landslide, but it just proved the truth of something folk singer Pete Seeger once said at a concert in my heyday of the sixties, something to the effect of things don't always turn out the way you want, but you always meet some great people along the way. Barry said it his way: "God bless the day we met, and God bless all the days we shall meet." Amen.

Election year 1976 was now in full swing and with the GOP trying to pull itself out of its post-Watergate slump, former California governor Ronald Reagan was gunning for Gerald Ford's job. It was then that the president sought Dad's help and advice, as he had many times before. What Ford asked is that he and the eleven other living former Republican National Chairmen publicly endorse him. All fell in line, with the one exception of George Bush, who was at the time Director of the CIA and could not therefore involve himself in partisan politics.

At a White House breakfast with Ford and a subsequent press conference on the lawn, my father served as spokesman for the group, an impressive and hopefully persuasive roster of political heavyweights that included Bob Dole, Rogers Morton, Dean Burch, Mead Alcorn, Len Hall, Hugh Scott, and Herb Brownell. Actually, Bill Miller himself had almost not made the event. Having inadvertently left his identification back at his hotel, the White House guards were about to unceremoniously turn him away at the gate when the presidential staff intervened, proving that his anonymity was still well intact.

"Because of the president's performance in office in the last nineteen months, we support President Ford for our party's nomination," declared the nearly dismissed leader of this political assemblage. "On his record, we believe he deserves that nomination." It was admittedly a bit ironic that the man who had once stumped the nation as the vice- presidential running mate of "Mr. Conservative," Barry Goldwater, would now stump for someone other than the current "Mr. Conservative," Ronald Reagan. But Dad had served in Congress with Ford, considered him a friend, and, above all, felt there was no reason for a change when a Republican incumbent president was doing a good job. Though he and the others worked successfully to secure the necessary convention delegates for Ford, in the end, the president would attribute his loss to Jimmy Carter in the November election to the Reagan challenge.

Four years later, when Jerry Ford decided to try once again for the White House, my father did not support his effort. By this time, Reagan had worked for three years to gain the nomination and had built up a loyal and enthusiastic following, much as Goldwater had in 1964, and any attempt to deny him the nomination might split the Party wide open. That had always been Dad's chief concern—his party's tendency to self-destruct.

Though he worried somewhat about the erstwhile movie star and former California governor's national electability, he believed that Ford had forfeited his right to the nomination by failing to act as the titular leader of the GOP during the previous four years. "Instead, he was out playing golf with Jackie Gleason and Bob Hope and making speeches at $5,000 and $10,000 a crack. He's certainly done little for the Republican Party since leaving office," my father ruefully and perhaps a bit too candidly noted.[11] At this point, he was unsure of what kind of president Reagan would make, but he allowed that although "he may not be the very best brain that could be found in the country, he has a good track record as governor of California and an ability to surround himself with excellent people."[12]

He also offered, whenever he was interviewed, that his friend George Bush would be the best running mate for Reagan, considering that "his broad experience as Director of the CIA, GOP

National Chairman, Ambassador to the United Nations, and head of the mission to China would give the ticket an experience that both Kemp and Reagan lack." He liked Bush and had made one of the first speeches on his behalf when he ran unsuccessfully for the U.S. Senate from Texas in 1964. In fact, he had been invited to join Bush's National Steering Committee early on when the Texan was considering a run for the nomination in 1980. Jack Kemp, the charismatic Buffalo Bills quarterback who had led his team to two AFL championships and whom Dad, an ardent Bills fan all his life, had befriended and mentored at the start of his congressional career in 1971, was also being touted for the second spot. But in my father's opinion, the New York congressman was at this point just too young for the nomination, despite his considerable oratorical skill and campaigning ability.

Asked often about the points of comparison between the eventual Reagan-Bush campaign and the 1964 Goldwater-Miller effort, Dad believed that there were few. "It's a totally different situation. We were running against an incumbent president but the memory of Jack Kennedy was strong. The economy was relatively good, Johnson said he would not escalate the Vietnam War, and there was no really good reason to throw out anyone from the White House. Now we have an incumbent president," he continued, "who started out in a fairly good situation and we end up with a double-digit inflation, double-digit unemployment, and double-digit interest rates." He added that he took great satisfaction in seeing many of the ideas he and Goldwater espoused in 1964 become popular with Ronald Reagan.

The years passed and my father's proclaimed life of country lawyering would continue to be punctuated periodically by noteworthy events such as testimonial dinners in his honor, a hole-in-one on the 160-yard, par three 16th hole of the Augusta National golf course, even an occasional round of golf with Billy Casper. Barry Goldwater continued to be a dear friend to our family, traveling to Lynchburg, Virginia, at my invitation, to speak at Randolph-Macon Woman's College and to be my guest on my half-hour television interview program on our local ABC affiliate station. He visited Lockport for an "intimate" dinner party of 400 in his honor under a yellow and white tent in the torch-lit backyard of my parents' home, an event the town did not soon forget. And at a testimonial dinner for Dad, he made the slightly facetious but magnanimous statement: "The longer history extends, the more the people of this country realize the mistake they made in 1964 when Bill Miller did not become the vice president—and I won't say anything else about the rest of the ticket."

It was two weeks after my youngest sister Stephanie's May graduation from the University of Southern California with a major in drama, the heir apparent to our trial lawyer/politician father's penchant for performance. Mom and Dad came to Lynchburg for a visit with me and my family. As usual, the household was hectic, with their then 11, 13, and 15-year-old grandchildren coming and going. There was little time to sit for quiet conversation.

But one late afternoon, I found myself out on our deck with my father, just the two of us. He had seemed a bit tired and subdued and I asked if he was feeling well. It was then that he explained to me that he was scheduled for an arteriogram upon his return home. Not one to frequent doctors offices except for his regular checkups, he had gone recently only at Mother's insistence when he confessed to her that he had experienced a few episodes of momentary blindness—an indicator of possible carotid artery disease.

He made light of the imminent diagnostic procedure—it was "routine," he said, and I wanted to believe him. He always had a way of making things seem "all right" even when they weren't. But as I peered into his strangely red and watering eyes, there seemed a perceptible sadness to them that unsettled me, almost as if he had a private intuition that perhaps all was not well, though he was trying his stoic and matter-of-fact best to hide it. He had already had one medical mishap three years earlier when his right hand was left partially numb as an unfortunate aftermath of a prostate operation, which to his great disappointment had ended his golfing days. In retrospect, I think he harbored a real fear, even a certain resignation that something might go awry again.

And it did. Dad entered Millard Fillmore Hospital in Buffalo on June 5 for his "routine" operation, and he never came home again. Two and a half weeks later, on June 24, he died of complications from the arteriogram, his team of doctors strangely non-communicative and vague throughout about what was going on. The procedure had apparently knocked off patches of plaque that traveled throughout his arterial system and gradually shut it down.

We were in shock. It didn't seem possible—this man who looked so youthful and fit at sixty-nine, to all appearances in good health, his black hair only slightly tinged with gray, still so witty and sharp during his recent visit, who had danced the night away with my mother at a wedding reception only the day before he entered the hospital, was now gone.

His friends and all who knew him were equally shocked, for they had no inkling that he had any serious health problems. They came from miles around to pay their respects at Joe Kennedy's Funeral Parlor on Walnut Street, next door to the Tuscarora Club where the man they loved or admired or knew only by reputation had spent so many retirement afternoons playing cards.

As Mother and I and my siblings, husband, and children stood greeting for hours, in pained disbelief and crushing sorrow, with the open casket nearby containing that man we had known and loved, so alive only two weeks ago and now inert, visitors related startling stories of quiet kindnesses and favors, large and small, that he had done for them about which we in the family knew nothing at all. I had always considered my father a kind and thoughtful man, but those stories and the hundreds of letters that followed told us that we had never fully understood the depth of his concern and compassion for others. "If he had a weakness," wrote a former campaign aide, "it would be that below his tough, strong exterior, he had a heart full of kindness and respect for those around him."[13]

The funeral service at St. John's Catholic Church in Lockport was deeply moving, with the magnificent music Dad's old high school friend, Don Conlin, had managed to lovingly pull together in a matter of three days with instrumentation and forty-five choir singers from an array of Catholic and Protestant churches. It was even more so for the presence of the old warrior from Arizona who had traveled there, with crippled hips and bad heart, to eulogize his political partner of twenty years ago.

There he sat, head bowed in grief for his friend five years his junior who had died too soon. Barry shuffled to the podium amidst the whirring and flashing of television and newspaper cameras and, with quavering voice, delivered his tribute to "one of the greatest men I have ever known":

> *...Man was born to serve.... And if they serve well, the dust that trails them as they walk down the path of life settles on all people, and makes all people better. Now the question comes: Did he serve well?*

> *Yes, he served well. He served with love and devotion to his wonderful family. He served with love and devotion to his country.... Because of these things, and because of the way he was, and to me is, he made everyone of us better, and he made this country a better place to live.*

> *So I can say with no prejudice, with a heart filled with fondness and love, that the dust that will follow Bill, will follow his trail that he made through his life, will settle on us and remind us of our responsibilities to our God, our family, and our country...*

And then he left the podium in tears.

"Being at your Dad's funeral was not the easiest thing that I have ever gone through," Barry would write me shortly afterwards. "Thinking about him and talking about it was almost impossible because it was a friendship between us that people just don't understand. When I said he's the kind of man I want to be with, I think that covers it all." Then referring to his deteriorating hips with his trademark irreverent humor, he wrote: "They got me back in the hospital, but I'll tell you, every time I go, there is so damn little left to whittle on that I think they've given up. At least, I hope so. The operations are not fun, but they remind one that there were some pleasant things in younger life that must be paid for later."

That afternoon, we all flew to Washington for my father's interment in Arlington National Cemetery. Why was he to be buried there when Lockport was so dear to his heart, I asked my mother. "Because he was proud of his achievements as a self-made man who had started with so little," she told me, "and he felt it would leave a proud legacy for his children as well." Our pride in him—that had always been so important to Dad, in some ways the motivating force in his life, perhaps because he had not been proud of his father and that had been hard.

Oddly enough, he had asked his mortician friend, Joe Kennedy, only weeks before his passing to inquire if he would be eligible for burial in Arlington, being uncertain if one had to be currently on active duty at the time of death. It turned out he was eligible because of his service in the U.S. Army from 1942 to 1946, in conjunction with his fourteen years of service to the country as a United States congressman. His startling inquiry caused Mother to wonder at the time if her spouse did indeed have a premonition that his end was near, but then she decided that they had just gotten to the age when you discuss such things.

The burial, with full military honors, was majestic, a true patriot's farewell—the flag-draped casket transferred at the gates of the cemetery from a hearse to a caisson drawn by six shimmering black horses ridden by ramrod stiff Army men in dress blues, a three-volley rifle salute, then the solemn procession past the endless rows of erect white veterans' stones to the gravesite. An Army escort and military band with its muffled drums fell in behind the gun carriage, followed by the motorcade of our family and friends.

A brief ceremony concluded with an Army officer carefully and crisply folding the casket flag in a triangular shape and handing it tenderly to the grieving widow, and an Army bugler sounding a mournful "Taps" over the hushed, sun-dappled Virginia countryside as our group walked silently back to the waiting limousines. Senator Goldwater limped over to Mother, bent down to kiss her, then turned toward the casket and covered his heart with his hand to pay last respects to his friend. I remember seeing Senator Bob Dole wipe a tear from his cheek.

The site where Dad was laid to rest is a fitting one, on a peaceful hillside near Senator Ken Keating, his fellow New Yorker and longtime colleague in the Congress with whom he sometimes sparred but often agreed, and always remained fast friends. I can almost picture them still good-naturedly debating legislative issues up there. It sits just below the wide-columned Lee Mansion and John Kennedy's celebrated gravesite with its eternal flame. His handsome gray granite stone overlooks a panoramic view of the Potomac and the white marble city where he came of age, where he tried to make a difference, and where this man once widely heralded as one of the best political minds and most effective orators of his day is now all but forgotten. Such is the ironic and fleeting nature of political fame and power, but I am certain he himself, with his characteristic humility and humor, is still making jokes about his own "obscurity."

Time stops up there on that hillside when you visit—"The living come with grassy tread, to read the gravestones on the hill," wrote Robert Frost[14]—and forces reflection on the countless lives arrayed before you, on the stories sealed forever beneath those stones. Of my father's, I think of "the road not taken" (Frost again), of other directions he could have gone in his career but didn't that would have made his life and ours very different than they were—if he had never gone to Congress, if he had only stayed one or two terms as he had originally intended. If he had not been offered and accepted the vice-presidential nomination but remained in Congress instead, there were many who predicted he might have been a natural choice for Minority Leader of the House, and perhaps Speaker someday. As partisan as his years as national chairman had required him to be, he was, by most reports, liked and respected across party lines for his astute legal mind, conciliatory nature, and ability to persuade and compromise. But he went where he was called, and went willingly, to serve his country, as did all the others who were now his companions in this peaceful place.

The message of Dad's life as he lived it was that politics need not be a dirty word, and the many letters received after his death confirm that he inspired many who knew or encountered him to believe that. But his old friend Barry sensed even then that times were changing and that my father's credo might not last. "We are not going to see many Bill Millers around in the future because the whole system of our government, our way of life ... in this country has changed. I hope I am wrong in this because our country and the world could use more of him," mourned the aging senator on the Senate floor the day after the funeral.[15]

When Ron Reagan Jr. made note in a eulogy at his father's funeral in June 2004 that his father never "wore his religion on his sleeve," it struck such a familiar note with me. Bill Miller's devotion to his Catholic faith was deeply rooted, though he rarely discussed it. Yet he did not wear it on his sleeve, as do many in politics today. He simply lived it. He disliked, even feared, the idea of his or anyone else's religion being injected into political discourse. Religion was not a part of either his or

Senator Goldwater's conservatism. Though his religious beliefs infused his life and his actions, they did not necessarily dictate his stands on political issues. Nor did he use them as a measure by which to pass judgment on others for their motives or stands which differed from his. His tendency was to believe the best of most people.

Bill Miller's passing was noted in newspapers and television newscasts nationwide. President and Mrs. Reagan wrote Mother a note she especially cherished, which Senator Goldwater read and hand delivered to her at the funeral Mass:

Dear Stephanie,

Nancy and I were deeply saddened to learn of Bill's death. During the 1964 campaign, Bill Miller gained the respect and gratitude of all Americans for his capable articulation of the principles of our party. All of us who have come after him are his beneficiaries, and we will remember his contribution for a long time to come..."

George Christopher, who had been mayor of San Francisco when my father had chosen his city for the convention site in 1964, wrote: "Those of us who have participated in what often-times is a cold, hard, and calculating political process must have an abiding respect for men like Bill Miller.... I recall the smile, the friendly handshake, and the trust that Bill Miller inspired. He was a man you could call 'friend' and not worry about being disillusioned."

Dad was eulogized on the House and Senate floors by numerous former colleagues, Republican and Democrat. Among them, Senator Daniel Moynihan noted that besides being "a tough-minded and principled spokesman for conservatism and commonsense in public affairs, Bill Miller understood, as well, the meaning of generosity of spirit when ministering to the private needs of family, friends, and those who are less fortunate." Jack Kemp recalled that "the Goldwater-Miller ticket was one that ran with dignity and lost with honor, and indeed carried conservative ideas and patriotic principles to a level that helped advance this cause to victory in 1980.... The American people owe him a great debt of gratitude, and we will miss his humor, his wisdom, his warmth, and his devotion to our country tremendously."[16] And Jack inserted Edgar Guest's poem "Courage" in *The Congressional Record*, as "a fitting tribute to Bill":

> *Courage was never designed for show*
> *It isn't a thing that can come and go;*
> *It's written in victory or defeat*
> *And every trial a man may meet.*
> *It's part of his hours, his days and his years,*
> *Back of his smiles and behind his tears.*
> *Courage is more than a daring deed;*
> *It's the breath of life and a strong man's creed.*

But of all the accolades, my father might have loved most a Letter-to-the-Editor that appeared in the Lockport *Union Sun and Journal* a few weeks after his funeral. It was written by a colorful local African American woman named Cat Williams who lived near the Tuscarora Club, and whom he used to greet faithfully on his way to and from his card games. She was also near the funeral parlor where he lay in repose and she witnessed the mixed crowds of dignitaries and ordinary folk coming and going for two days to pay their respects. Cat captured him in a simple yet eloquent way:

> *While Mr. Miller has been cited for his popularity and states-manship among his colleagues and other "greats," there's a missing link I'd like to forge—how he treated the masses and the "man in the street."… it's the masses that make or break you. Mr. Miller knew how to treat those from all walks of life. Never was he too good to say "hi," or give a light beep of his horn.*
>
> *If I was to pick out his most endearing quality, I'd opt for his sense of humor. The ability to laugh at oneself is half the battle won…*
>
> *Mr. Miller himself started the "obscurity" jokes, although he never went into obscurity…. The "Bill who?" jokes caught on because everyone knew who Bill Miller was…. How could you help but be drawn to a man who made losing an election bid by a million votes sound like an honor? Yes, instead of being bitter—as President Nixon was when he lost ("They won't have old Nixon to kick around anymore…")—Mr. Miller took it in stride and showed his greatness…*

In 1964 I ran into a lot of hostility for backing the Goldwater-Millerticket. Why would a black woman with any sense back a team which wasn't for the poor? Because I was afraid of just what's happening today.

I was brought up to believe that someone who handed you every-thing wasn't always your friend. Goldwater-Miller didn't hate blacks or the poor. But, they wanted to put everyone off the dole who was employable before we broke the whole country. In 1964 jobs were going begging.

With his "Great Society," Lyndon Johnson was the best friend (president) that the blacks ever had—also, our worst enemy. I know there were whites on welfare too, but Johnson trained generations of us to look no further—even when we were intel-ligent and able-bodied.... We refused to view the long-range harm which we are reaping today. Sen. Goldwater and Mr. Miller didn't lose that election. We did...

If only they had won...

Perhaps journalist Tom Brokaw has described my father and others of his generation better than anyone—I can person-ally attest that he captured the essence of First Lieutenant and Congressman Bill Miller. Brokaw, in his book, *The Greatest Generation*, wrote of a generation marked by personal responsibil-ity and self-sacrificing, who were honest and honorable people. They never spoke of their experiences and families didn't ask. Faith was big in their lives, their patriotism unabashed. So many returnees entered politics, for they considered it a public service, a way to continue to serve the country they loved, not a way to position themselves for a lucrative job afterwards:

...they stood fast against the totalitarianism of their former allies, the Russians. They were rocked by the social and politi-cal upheaval of the sixties.... They weren't perfect. They made mistakes. They allowed McCarthyism and racism to go unchal-lenged for too long ... they were part of historic challenges and achievements of a magnitude the world had never before witnessed.... Although they were transformed by their experi-ences and quietly proud of what they had done, their stories did

not come easily. They didn't volunteer them ... they love their country and they're not afraid to say just that.[17]

Dad had many proud moments in his lifetime of sixty-nine years, but if he had lived to see the moving memorial that his beloved Notre Dame Class of '35 conceived to commemorate his life, it very possibly would have been his proudest moment of all. His love for the school and the pride he felt in being part of its hallowed traditions was deep and permeating, all the more so because he had once been such an unlikely prospect for the privilege of attending at all. Dedicated by Father Ted Hesburgh at the 50th Class Reunion in 1985, two years after his death, the handsome bronze plaque is affixed to the wall in the south entrance of the Law School. One corner features a relief of Notre Dame's Golden Dome, the other a relief of the United States Capitol dome.

The plaque goes on to list the major achievements of my father's life after his years on campus—securing the coveted Moot Court prize from Albany Law School; his rise from a private in the U.S. Army during World War II to selection as an assistant prosecutor for the Nuremberg War Crimes Trials in 1945; outstanding trial lawyer and District Attorney of Niagara County, New York; influential member of the United States Congress for fourteen years; fearless leader of the Republican Party as its National Chairman during three tumultuous years; and his selection as the vice-presidential nominee of the Republican Party in 1964, the only Notre Dame alum ever nominated for such high office. But if that doesn't tell the full story of his legacy, the final words, etched in gold, do: "William E. Miller made a lasting impression on all who met him. He epitomized the motto on Sacred Heart Church: 'God, Country and Notre Dame.' "

ENDNOTES

CHAPTER 1: The Nomination

[1] Jimmy Breslin, *Buffalo Evening News,* August 20, 1964, Section I, p. 20.
[2] Jack Meddoff and Jerry Allen, *Buffalo Evening News,* September 10, 1964.

CHAPTER 2: Small Town Boy

[1] Leslie H. Southwick, *Presidential Also-Rans and Running Mates, 1788-1980* (London: McFarland & Co. Inc. Publishers, 1984), p. 614.
[2] Professor Thomas Stritch, *My Notre Dame: Memories and reflections of sixty years* (Notre Dame: University of Notre Dame Press, 1991), p. 13.
[3] Ibid, p. 14.
[4] *The Scholastic,* November 30, 1934, p. 6.

CHAPTER 3: The Road to Nuremberg

[1] Leslie H. Southwick, *Presidential Also-Rans and Running Mates* (London: McFarland & Co. Inc. Publishers, 1984), p. 614.
[2] Duval A. Edwards, *Spy Catchers of the U.S. Army in the War with Japan* (Gig Harbor, WA: Red Apple Publishing, 1994).
[3] Ian Sayer and Douglas Botting, *America's Secret Army: The Untold Story of the Counter Intelligence Corps* (New York: Franklin & Watts, 1989).
[4] Joseph E. Persico, *Nuremberg: Infamy on Trial* (New York: Penguin Books USA Inc., 1994), p. 11.
[5] Ibid, p. 8.
[6] Tom Brokaw, *The Greatest Generation* (New York: Random House, Inc., 1998).
[7] Lorenz Eitner, *The Criminal State and Its Servants: Reminiscences of the Nuremberg War Crimes Trials (The Minnesota Review,* Volume III, Number 2, Winter 1963), pp. 162-163.
[8] Ibid.
[9] Courtesy of Dartmouth College Library, Hanover, New Hampshire, Rauner Collection, *Frank Wallis Papers,* pp. 84-88.
[10] Robert G. Storey, *Documentation Division Office Instructions, Number 1,* from the National Archives.
[11] Telford Taylor, *The Anatomy of the Nuremberg Trials* (New York: Alfred A. Knopf, Inc., 1992), p. 79.
[12] Courtesy of Dartmouth College Library, *Frank Wallis papers,* p. 70.
[13] Ibid, pp. 116-117.
[14] Ibid, p. 125.
[15] Ibid, p. 132.
[16] Ibid, p. 139.

[17] *Life* magazine, Dec. 10, 1945, Vol. 19, No. 24, p. 27.
[18] Joseph Persico, *Nuremberg: Infamy on Trial*, p. 443.
[19] Ibid, p. 443.

CHAPTER 4: Congress—Fierce Fight over the Niagara

[1] Joseph E. Persico, *Nuremberg: Infamy on Trial* (New York: Penguin Books USA Inc., 1994), p. 437.
[2] *Buffalo Evening News*, June 12, 1950, p. 1.
[3] *The Wall Street Journal*, December 9, 1971, p. 1.
[4] Robert A. Caro, *Master of the Senate*, Vol. 3.
[5] Lucian Warren, *Buffalo Courier-Express*, April 22, 1954.
[6] *Ibid*, July 19, 1956.
[7] Robert A. Caro, *The Power Broker, Robert Moses and the Fall of New York* (New York: Vintage Books, Random House, 1975).
[8] Miller papers, Carl A. Kroch Library of Cornell University, Rare Book and Manuscript Collection.

CHAPTER 5: Congress—A Role in the First Civil Rights Debate

[1] Joel Connelly, *Seattle Post-Intelligencer*, May 22, 2002.
[2] Robert A. Caro, *The Years of Lyndon Johnson: Master of the Senate* (New York: Alfred A. Knopf, 2002).
[3] *The Congressional Record*, July 19, 1956, p. 13563.
[4] Ibid, p. 893.
[5] Ibid, p. 1033.
[6] Robert A. Caro, p. 1034.

CHAPTER 6: Congress—The Tumultuous Fifties Roll On

[1] 352 U.S. 445 (1957).

CHAPTER 7: First Leadership Role

[1] Michael Tomasky, *The Good Soldier (New York Magazine:* December 17, 2001), p. 28.
[2] *One Hundred Year History of the National Republican Congressional Campaign Committee*, published 1966 by the NRCC.
[3] Peg Zwecker, *Chicago Life, Chicago Daily News*, July 23, 1960, p. 9.
[4] Richard Reeves, *President Kennedy: Profile of Power* (New York: Simon & Schuster Inc., 1993), p. 37.
[5] Ibid, pp. 58-59.
[6] Ibid, p. 59.

CHAPTER 8: Leadership—Another Step Up

[1] Miller Congressional and RNC Papers, Kroch Library of Cornell University, Rare Book and Manuscript Collections; Ithaca, New York.

[2] *The Manhattan Mercury,* Manhattan, Kansas, June 12, 1961.

[3] *Congressional Quarterly,* Washington, D.C., August 15, 1961.

[4] David Broder, *Strategists for '62 and '64 (The New York Times Magazine:* October 15, 1961, Section 6), p. 27.

[5] *The Manhattan Mercury,* June 12, 1961.

[6] Lucian C. Warren, *Buffalo Courier-Express,* July 8, 1962.

[7] Ibid, p. 70.

[8] Herb Crispell, *Buffalo Evening News,* July 18, 1964.

[9] Republican National Committee Memorandum from Chairman Miller to Republican Leaders, December 31, 1963.

[10] Ibid.

[11] Victor Riesel, *Buffalo Courier Express,* March 27, 1963.

[12] Miller Papers, letter to Republican Party State Chairmen, September 1, 1961.

[13] Ibid.

[14] Miller Papers, RNC letters.

[15] Ralph McGill, *New York Herald Tribune,* November 26, 1961.

[16] *The New York Daily News,* August 10, 1961.

[17] David Broder, "Miller Hits GOP Liberals on Southern Tactics Demand," the *Evening Star,* November 27, 1962.

[18] Herb Crispell, *Buffalo Evening News,* July 18, 1964.

[19] Miller Papers, Minutes of RNC Staff Meeting, June 4, 1962.

CHAPTER 9: Prelude to a Candidacy

[1] RNC Press Release: Republican National Chairman, William E. Miller, signals end of Moratorium, December 23, 1963.

[2] Transcribed from tape of press conference by courtesy of RNC staff. See also *Congressional Quarterly,* November 1, 1963, p. 1884.

[3] Telephone interview with William Scranton, 1996.

[4] Miller Congressional and RNC Papers, Kroch Rare Book and Manuscript Library of Cornell University, Ithaca, New York.

[5] Ibid.

[6] The name given Lyndon Johnson by his biographer, Robert A. Caro.

[7] Miller Papers.

[8] John G. Rogers, *New York Herald Tribune,* July 17, 1964, p. 6.

[9] David Broder, *Strategists for '62 and '64 (The New York Times Magazine:* October 15, 1961, Section 6), p. 26.

[10] Speech before the American Political Science Association, St. Louis, Missouri.

[11] Miller Papers .

CHAPTER 10: The 1964 Campaign

[1] Jimmy Breslin, Special to the *Buffalo Evening News,* August 20, 1964, Section I, p. 20.

[2] Ambassador Robert M. Smalley, Press Secretary to William E. Miller in 1964, from his upcoming memoir.

[3] Marie Smith, The *Washington Post,* October 25, 1964, p. F3.

[4] Shaila K. Dewan, the *New York Times,* September 5, 2004, p. 1.

[5] Transcript of the Hershey meeting.

[6] Jack Meddoff and Jerry Allen, *Buffalo Evening News,* September 11, 1964.

[7] Robert M. Smalley.

[8] Johnson Library Papers, General PL6-3.

[9] Michael Beschloss, *Reaching for Glory: Lyndon Johnson's Secret White House Tapes, 1964-65* (New York: Simon & Schuster, 2001), pp. 33, 44, 82.

[10] Michael Beschloss, p. 82.

[11] Chris Welles, *Life* magazine, August 7, 1964, p. 36.

[12] Robert M. Smalley.

[13] Ibid.

[14] Ibid.

[15] Warren Weaver Jr., *The New York Times,* October 4, 1964.

[16] Robert M. Smalley.

[17] Theodore H. White, *The Making of the President 1964* (New York: Atheneum Publishers, 1965), pp. 343-344.

[18] Robert M. Smalley.

[19] Dorothy McCardle, *The Washington Post,* October 13, 1964, p. C1.

[20] Isabelle Shelton, *The Sunday Star,* September 27, 1964, p. E-3.

[21] Ruth Montgomery, *San Antonio Light,* August 3, 1964.

[22] Theodore H. White, p. 384.

[23] Robert Caro, *The Years of Lyndon Johnson: The Path to Power, Means of Ascent, Master of the Senate.*

[24] Theodore H. White, p. 231.

[25] Ibid, p. 230.

[26] Robert M. Smalley.

[27] Ibid.

[28] *Union Sun and Journal,* October 27, 1964.

[29] Robert M. Smalley.

[30] Ibid.

[31] Ibid.

[32] Letter from Congressman Bill Brock, April 15, 1996.

CHAPTER 11: Small Town Boy Goes Home

[1] Robert J. Donovan, *The Los Angeles Times,* January 11, 1965.

[2] Warren Weaver Jr., *The New York Times,* June 3, 1974, p. 23.

[3] Personal letters, William E. Miller papers, Cornell University Kroch Library.

[4] Lee Coppola, *Buffalo Evening News,* June 26, 1971, p. B-3.

[5] Ibid.

[6] Ray Herman, *Buffalo Courier Express,* May 13, 1973, p. 22.

[7] Ibid.

[8] Bob Curran, *Buffalo Evening News,* August 16, 1974.

[9] Ibid.

[10] Judy Flander, *The Washington Star,* January 29, 1976, p. C2.

[11] Paul Budenhagen, *The Lockport Union Sun and Journal.*

[12] Anne Sherwood, *The Buffalo Evening News,* August 30, 1980, p. B1.

[13] Letter from Bob Phillipson, 1964 campaign aide.

[14] Robert Frost, "In a Disused Graveyard."

[15] *The Congressional Record,* June 29, 1983, No. 93, p. S9405.

[16] *The Congressional Record,* 98th Congress, First Session, Tuesday, June 28, 1983, Vol. 129, No. 92.

[17] Tom Brokaw, *The Greatest Generation* (New York: Random House, 1998), pp. xx-xxi.